Caroline Taggart was born in London of Scottish parents, spent most of her childhood in New Zealand and went to university in Sheffield. Confused for some time, she now thinks of herself as a Londoner, but continues to change allegiance whenever it suits her, particularly during the rugby season.

Having worked in publishing for eleven years, she gave up a perfectly respectable job to become a freelance editor in 1989. Since then she has worked bizarre hours, gone out to lunch a lot and indulged her lifelong dislike of getting up in the morning. She has edited or contributed to books on subjects ranging from Rupert Bear to the workings of the House of Commons, and co-written an illustrated guide to dogs. This is the first book with her name on the cover.

She lives in Pimlico, London.

The Essential Handbook for Mature Students

Caroline Taggart

Foreword by Philippa Gregory

Kyle Cathie Limited

First published 1994 in Great Britain by
Kyle Cathie Limited
7/8 Hatherley Street, London SW1P 2QT

ISBN 1 85626 095 X

Caroline Taggart is hereby identified as the author of this
work in accordance with Section 77 of the Copyright,
Designs and Patents Act 1988.

A Cataloguing in Publication record for this title is
available from the British Library.

Typeset by York House Typographic Ltd., London
Printed by Cox & Wyman Ltd., Reading

In loving memory of my father, who would have been pleased to see me doing something mature at last

Contents

Acknowledgements

My thanks are due first of all to Philippa Gregory and Paul Carter, whose idea the book was and who pointed me in many of the right directions. Thanks again to Philippa for generously finding the time to contribute a foreword and a chapter, and to Kyle for giving me the opportunity to write the rest.

The book could not have been written without the help of the universities' and colleges' Admissions Officers, Registrars, Mature Students' Advisers and External Relations Officers who took the trouble to fill in a questionnaire and send me details about their institutions. I am grateful to them all, and to the members of staff at other organisations mentioned in the book for providing further information.

Special thanks to Jackie Mair of the Higher Education Quality Council for her kindness and enthusiasm, for two very jolly mornings spent playing with the ECCTIS database and for a number of useful contacts. Thanks also to Dr Philip Jones of HEQC, Chris West of ECCTIS, Mike Abramson of the University of Central Lancashire, John Bird of the University of the West of England, Alan Parton of the University of Coventry for information, encouragement and copies of published and unpublished papers.

Extra special thanks to David Green for allowing his brains to be picked so blatantly, and to Heather Magrill for putting up with it for two hours before asking if we could talk about something else please.

Finally, thanks to my mother for her helpful comments on Chapter 7, to my sister Ann for letting me use her computer at such length when she was dying to get on with her own book, to Mike for tireless, ungrudging moral support, and to all the friends who have put up with the monomania of my conversation over the last months.

Foreword by Philippa Gregory

This is a book designed to help the mature student in the difficult decision to attend a university or college, and to help in the choice of *which* university or college. The idea for it came when my husband had just started his degree course as a forty-year-old student at a College of Art, and my older sister was thinking of leaving her job to return to study. It seemed like everyone in the world was going back to college – confronting the same anxieties and experiencing similar joys.

I had taught mature students at polytechnic, at university, on access courses and for the Open University, and I was very aware of the enormous commitment that older students bring to their education. Teaching such people is sometimes an unnerving experience: at a lecture on Dickens' *Hard Times* I suddenly realised that I was explaining the rigour of industrial work to a lecture hall of ex-steel workers. Every one of them knew more than I did and indeed they all knew more than Dickens about the lives of workers in heavy industry. Like many teachers of mature students I learned from them, as they were apparently being taught by me.

I started my own BA degree at the University of Sussex aged twenty-one, after a three-year apprenticeship on a newspaper. I earned my place by the simple method of walking in unannounced to the Dean's office, and asking him if I might enrol. Rather taken aback, he put his sandwiches away, conducted a lightning interview, and gave me a place. This technique is not recommended – more usual methods of application are listed inside this book. But I never regretted leaving a promising career and an increasing salary. Attending the university was a life-changing decision for me. I read like an addict, I was knocked out by the intellectual challenges, I made a couple of lasting friendships, and I fell completely and utterly in love with historical theory and the process of historical research.

That passion led me to work for my Ph.D. at the University of Edinburgh where the division between mature students and students of the usual age was totally blurred by the tendency of some graduates to linger on and on over their theses, ageing visibly every year. On completing my dissertation I started to teach and to write, and my working life now is devoted to research and writing, and I cannot imagine more interesting and rewarding work.

It's not always such a smooth ride nor such a happy ending; but my decision to leave my job and get the university education which I lost in a momentary absence of mind at eighteen was the most important and most fruitful decision in my life. So I must declare myself an education evangelist. I genuinely believe that the way to a happier life is through learning and understanding, and I feel enormous regret when I meet people who missed out on their education in their youth, and dare not take the plunge in later years. This book is written for you to say – think about it! It might be the most wonderful step you ever take.

It will not be unfailingly wonderful. Even at twenty-one I sensed a difference between me and the eighteen-year-old school leavers which many mature students feel. The mature student has learned a powerful work discipline and is often impatient of the more leisurely pace of college or university life. The mature student is often doing a double-shift, still a full-time home-maker or worker while studying for a degree, and this is physically arduous as well as taxing emotionally and intellectually. Sometimes mature students are suspicious of what they see as over-intellectualising, and fanciful theories; sometimes they are simply scared rigid. Younger students may seem emotionally immature but have been in training for the past six years and can be lightning sharp and quick-witted. When a class of mixed ages settles down and learns to respect each other there is a powerful combination of skills which enhances every seminar or tutorial. By the start of the second year it is hard to tell the difference between the work of the nineteen-year-old and the work of a fifty-year-old.

Fifty-year-old? Sixty-year-old? Ninety? The upper age limit should extend for ever. Increasingly people are realising that education and learning is a life-long process, too precious to be the exclusive domain of the young. Institutions which are open to mature students seldom have an upper age limit, and some of the brightest students are drawing a pension rather than a grant. If you are 60+ you still have a right to an education, and you can still gain a place. You will be judged on your ability to complete the course, on your intellectual ability and your commitment, and sometimes the older and wiser the better.

University or college education is far more accessible to the mature student than it used to be, partly because there are proportionally more mature applicants than ever before, but also because many institutions have come to admire and respect their mature students for their application, commitment and enthusiasm. If it has cost you dear to get your place, then you will work for it when you are there.

And it *will* cost you. Inside this book you will find detailed information about grants and loans which are available, but nothing can adjust the gap between a good salary and a student's grant. To gain a degree as a mature student requires enormous adaptation for you and your family.

It's a difficult decision with a lot in the balance. This book should help you to see some of the disadvantages and some of the pitfalls. But I hope it will also inspire you, who are teetering on the brink, to spread your wing and fly.

Introduction

For anyone who wants to, there has never been a better time to enter Higher Education. In 1969 there were 60,000 university students in the UK; in 1991, before the creation of 33 'new' universities from what used to be called polytechnics, there were 370,000. In the academic year 1993/4 there are about a million students in England alone taking courses in government-funded institutions of Higher Education, not to mention all those in Scotland, Wales, Northern Ireland and privately funded colleges.

Government bodies and the individual universities and colleges are committed to widening access to Higher Education, providing flexibility of approach and greater opportunities for anybody who is likely to benefit from a degree course. Demographic changes – the fact that we are living longer but producing fewer children – mean that there are more vacancies for educated, specialised people in the workplace than there are young graduates to fill them. The world needs older graduates too. University funding also depends to a certain extent on 'bums on seats' – they need to attract students on to their courses.

So Higher Education is no longer the exclusive privilege of the wealthy or of eighteen-year-olds coming straight from school – it is available to you.

If you are over twenty-one at the time you start a course, you are in a privileged position. You don't have to have A levels or other conventional qualifications, and there are all sorts of mechanisms for giving credit to your life experience instead. You will be expected to show 'evidence of recent study' – more about that later – but if you are truly committed to studying a certain course, enthusiasm and motivation will carry you a long way.

The organisation of Higher Education has altered radically in the last few years. The Further and Higher Education Act of 1992 abolished the distinction between universities and polytechnics, allowing them all to call themselves universities. The 'old' universities (there were 56 of them in 1991) had long been entitled to award degrees, while polytechnic degrees had been awarded by a central body called the Council for National Academic Awards (CNAA). This was now abolished and the 'new' universities were given powers to award their own degrees. Universities also award or validate degrees offered by government-funded or private colleges.

The applications procedure changed too. The two 'clearing houses' which administered applications – the University Central Council on Admissions (UCCA) and the Polytechnics Central Admissions System (PCAS) – were replaced by a joint Universities and Colleges Admissions Service (UCAS), which is in operation for the first time for 1994 admissions.

A number of independent colleges have no longer found it practical to operate on their own and have merged with or become constituent colleges of local universities, retaining varying degrees of autonomy and identity.

In the midst of all this, the government stated its desire that 'the distinctive emphasis on vocational studies developed mainly by polytechnics and colleges is maintained and extended'.

There are those who see the abolition of the distinction between universities and polytechnics as a major step towards equality of opportunity; there are others who think calling two different types of institution by the same name whilst trying to maintain the distinctive character of one of them is daft. It is not the role of this book to enter into that debate, but a few points arising from it may be worth considering, because they have a bearing on how you choose which university or college to attend.

The old universities, particularly the genuinely old ones such as Oxford, Cambridge and the ancient universities of Scotland, have traditionally set stringent academic standards. They have admitted only candidates of the highest calibre, producing learned graduates who may, or may not, have had any experience of the outside world.

The former polytechnics did – and still do – offer practical, vocational courses. They tended to be less rigid in their structure, allowing unusual combinations of subjects or permitting students to study part-time. If you went to a poly, you were more likely to have the chance to do work experience. But academic prejudice was such it was felt you didn't get such a 'good degree' at the end of it.

Despite all the changes, some of this prejudice remains, and it works both ways. 'Establishment' employers like certain sectors of the Civil Service may still prefer graduates from Oxbridge or the other older universities. Younger industries may feel that a graduate of a new university is likely to have a more practical approach and be more use on the job from day one.

In the meantime the old barriers are gradually coming down. Liverpool and Newcastle, both founded in the 19th century, are among those taking steps to make their courses more flexible and therefore more appealing to mature students; while research being undertaken by new universities such as Plymouth and Thames Valley has in certain fields reached levels of national excellence.

There are arguments for and against the new flexibility of approach. It is wonderful to be able to study any subject you like in combination with any other subject you like, but this could make the department's timetabling a nightmare. A more rigid structure is more efficient from the administrative point of view, and that efficiency might give the teaching staff more time for research. It is in students' interest for the staff to do research, as it means that courses are absolutely up-to-the-minute and take into account any recent advances in knowledge. Excellence in research also brings financial rewards, so you are likely to find better facilities in a research-oriented department.

What all this boils down to is that there is enormous freedom of choice, but that you have to make a lot of decisions for yourself. There is a vast amount of information available to help you make those decisions, but you have to sift through it and work out what is best for you. The good news is that you can, if you really want to, do almost anything you like – it is up to you to grasp the opportunity.

In compiling the entries for this book, I have included universities old and new, Colleges and Institutes of Higher Education and some which are principally Colleges of

Further Education but which also offer degree courses. Colleges which only offer 'top up' degrees (one year courses taken after completion of an HND) have in the main been excluded, as have those which provide the first year or two of teaching on a franchise basis, with students transferring to the associated university to complete the course.

I have included independent specialist colleges which award degrees, usually in Agriculture, the Performing Arts or Theology. I have also given separate entries to a number of colleges which are officially part of a university but retain a separate identity by virtue of their distance from the rest of the institution, such as Charlotte Mason College in the University of Lancaster, or because of the specialist nature of their teaching, such as the Birmingham Conservatoire in the University of Central England.

This approach, and the fluctuations within Higher Education, is bound to produce anomalies, for which I can only apologise. I would be happy to receive details from any institution which has been unfairly overlooked so it can be included in future editions.

1

How Does Higher Education Work?

For the purposes of this book, a degree means a first degree – a course normally lasting a minimum of three years that entitles you to put the words Bachelor of Whatever after your name. In England, Wales and Northern Ireland most courses automatically lead to Honours degrees in three years, and you are only awarded an Ordinary or Pass degree if you fail to achieve the standard required. The common exceptions to this are Medicine, Dentistry and Veterinary Science, which do not usually award Honours though they may give distinctions to students of exceptional merit.

Honours are divided into first class, upper or lower second (2.1 or 2.2) and third class – a first or a 2.1 is what is sweepingly referred to as a 'good degree' and you will usually have to achieve this level to be accepted on to a post-graduate course. Only extremely bright people and swots get firsts. If you get a 2.1 you've done very well and a 2.2 is fine – both suggest that you have worked hard but that you realise there is more to university life than books.

In Scotland, the system is slightly different and most first degrees take four years. At the end of three years you earn an Ordinary degree and the fourth year, if you take it, is devoted to specialist studies leading to Honours, classified as above. There is no disgrace in achieving an Ordinary degree – it simply reflects the fact that you have chosen a particular course of study, possibly following the Combined Studies route which is only now becoming popular in England but has a long-established tradition in Scotland. At the old Scottish universities the first degree in Arts is commonly an MA rather than a BA – though this is not true of the newer universities like Strathclyde or Heriot-Watt, nor is it the case with Science subjects.

Studying some subjects requires more than three years, even if there are no optional extras. Dentistry, Medicine and Veterinary Science commonly take five years and Architecture six; and may then require a further year's work experience before you are entitled to practise.

Education degrees, either BEd or BA/BSc with Qualified Teacher Status (QTS), are usually available in two modes: a four-year course starting, as it were, from scratch, or a two-year course aimed at mature students who have some post-A level qualifications or experience – this would normally mean an HND or equivalent, plus some relevant work experience. Although there are exceptions, it is generally the case that if you want to teach at nursery or primary level you take an Education degree, in which teaching practice plays an integral part from the start; if you intend to teach at secondary level you take a degree in your chosen subject and then do a year's Postgraduate Certificate of Education (PGCE). PGCEs and the institutions that offer them fall outside the scope of this book.

PROFESSIONAL ACCREDITATION

Education degrees are not the only ones that equip you to get on with the job once you reach the outside world. Many courses lead to professional recognition or State Registration (and exemption from another tier of exams). Common examples are Nursing and the paramedical fields – Osteopathy, Physiotherapy, Radiography, etc; also Accountancy, Engineering, Law and Surveying. To practise in any of these professions you need to reach a standard set down by a professional body – the Royal Institute of Chartered Surveyors, the Chartered Association of Certified Accountants or whoever – and your degree will be accepted as evidence that you have reached the required standard. You will still have to go through the formalities of registering and pay the registration fee, but you will have done the work.

Degree courses leading to this sort of qualification cannot offer the sort of flexibility that is available in some other subjects: there are certain core subjects that simply have to be covered.

The section 'Degrees Available' within each entry in Chapter 5 does not specify that such courses include professional recognition, but it is safe to assume that they do.

MODES OF STUDY

The previous section describes the general pattern of full-time degree courses studied exclusively at the university or college concerned. But flexibility is the buzzword of the 1990s and there are now a number of other possibilities worth considering before deciding what to do.

Part-time Study

Not everyone can give up all other commitments and devote themselves to full-time study. Universities and colleges increasingly recognise this fact and provide opportunities for mature students to take four, five or six years to complete a course that would take three years full-time. The modular scheme (see page 10) is particularly well suited to this mode of study – you simply take fewer units at a time and build up the required number of credits more slowly.

With this system you have considerable control over the number of hours you put in – if the normal full-time load is three units and that requires attendance for fifteen hours a week, you can choose to take only one unit and attend for five hours (though don't forget to set aside additional time for private study – see page 476). Under these circumstances you would normally be taking classes during the day, alongside students taking the same course full-time. Ask the Admissions Office or the department which runs the course you are interested in for details.

In addition some institutions have purpose-designed part-time courses, which may permit attendance at classes in the evening or on Saturdays. This sort of course would normally be the responsibility of the Continuing Education Unit, to whom you should address enquiries.

If they run enough part-time courses to justify it, universities and colleges will publish a part-time prospectus. Ask the Registry, the Admissions Office or the Continuing Education Unit for a copy. For part-time study you apply direct to the university or college, not through UCAS or ADAR, so the normal deadlines do not necessarily apply.

Franchised Courses

One consideration that is more of a problem for mature people than younger students is location. Most eighteen-year-olds are dying to leave home, whereas family commitments may mean you *have* to study at your local institution.

With this in mind, a number of universities have introduced a scheme that is variously known as franchising, an Associate College scheme or a Linked College scheme. It has also been described as 'taking the product to the customer'.

Under these schemes, you are able to do the first year (and sometimes more) of your studies at a college that is not the 'parent' university. Depending on the nature of the arrangement between the institutions, the course may be designed and developed at a university but taught elsewhere, or two colleges may jointly prepare a course and seek funding for it.

In either case, what is important to you is that an established university validates the course, giving a guarantee that it reaches a certain standard, and that it is on offer somewhere convenient. Another variation on this theme is the 2 + 2 scheme pioneered by the University of Salford, whereby students study for two years at a local college and then transfer to Salford to complete the course.

Franchised colleges also teach foundation years (or Year 0) in courses offered by the university: these are frequently referred to as 'extended' courses and are particularly common in Engineering, Science and Technology, subjects for which background knowledge (normally to A level standard in the appropriate subject) is assumed. When you embark on a foundation course, you may already have applied for and been accepted on a full degree programme; alternatively you may only have enrolled for the foundation year. In the latter case, successful completion of the foundation studies will normally guarantee a place on a related degree course at the parent university. (It will also equip you to apply with confidence to a similar course elsewhere should you so wish.)

There are arguments for and against the concept of franchised courses. The strongest argument against is that the franchised institutions will normally be colleges of Further rather than Higher Education, and may not be able to provide the facilities that would be available at the parent university. Certainly the teachers in FE colleges are less likely than their counterparts in HE to be engaged in ground-breaking research.

Nevertheless, you have the security of knowing that the course is validated by the university in question; you have access to the university's library and other facilities, both academic and social, exactly as if you were a student on site; you are likely to be in a smaller class, which gives your teachers more time to deal with any problems you may have; and you have the over-riding advantage, the reason you chose this route in the first place, that you live just down the road. Another benefit is that the vast majority of students following this sort of programme will be 'mature', so you won't be the only thirty- or forty-year-old in a class of school leavers.

Franchising arrangements are spreading throughout the UK: a report published in 1993 estimated that 40 per cent of Higher Education institutions in England had some form of collaborative arrangements, although only about 1 per cent of students took advantage of them. An expansion of some 400 per cent in student numbers was forecast over the next three years.

University prospectuses and Academic Registrars are the best source of information about opportunities of this kind, but the University of Central Lancashire, De Montfort (whose links extend as far north as York from their base in Leicester), Greenwich, the South Bank University and the University of the West of England are among the pioneers of franchised courses.

'Sandwich' Courses

Courses at what used to be called polytechnics have always been designed to prepare graduates for employment; the 'old' universities are increasingly recognising the virtues of this approach. One of the most important ways of achieving this end is to give students work experience as part of the course.

These periods of supervised work placement within the structure of a course are called 'sandwiches'. They used to be the norm only in Engineering and Technology; now they are found in Accountancy, Business Studies, Law, Pure Science, Graphic Design, Hotel Management . . . In some courses they are compulsory, in some optional, but you are always encouraged to take advantage of any such opportunities that may be available.

One of the great attractions of work placements is that you are paid by your employer. In theory you are also still entitled to a grant, but the amount of your salary may affect this. Your LEA will advise you (see Chapter 3). The university or college will still expect to receive tuition fees, normally 50 per cent of what you pay for full-time attendance, but if your LEA pays your fees the rest of the time it will continue to do so.

Sandwiches may be 'thick' or 'thin'. A thick sandwich normally means a full academic year, between the second and third years of study, turning a three-year course into a four-year one. Thin sandwiches may be placements of anything from a few weeks to three or four months, and a course may contain two or more of them at different stages. This has the obvious advantage of providing a broader spectrum, but lacks the in-depth experience of a year in the same place.

The faculties and departments which run sandwich courses have all built up contacts with local industries over the years and will work closely with them to ensure that you get the supervision and the experience you need. Many departments have a work-placement service to help secure suitable employment. Be warned, however, that the final responsibility for finding a job rests with you.

Satisfactory completion of the work placement(s) is an essential part of any sandwich degree. Your supervisor's account of your performance will form part of the overall assessment; you may also be expected to write a report on an aspect of your work.

Study Abroad – for Linguists

The 'year abroad' is still an important part of language study. If you are specialising in a single language (even a joint honours course in say French and Business Studies or German and Politics) you will normally be expected to spend an academic year in a country where that language is spoken. Your choice is not necessarily restricted to the 'home' country – if you are studying Spanish, for example, you may be able to go to Mexico.

You may spend time as a student at a university, following courses aimed at native speakers of the language, or you may take a job as a language assistant in a school, offering conversation classes to students of English. In the latter case, you will be paid (a pittance); in either case you should still be eligible for a grant, but the amount may depend on the country you are living in – consult your LEA for up-to-date information.

If you are taking joint honours in two languages, you will probably have to divide the year in two, spending half the session in each of two countries. Under these circumstances you will probably not have the option of being an assistant, but will have to carry on being a student.

It is difficult to study languages without spending any time abroad, but if other commitments make it impossible for you to go away for a year, you may be allowed to go for a shorter period. Talk to the department's Admissions Tutor and put your case: this sort of thing is usually decided on an individual basis.

Other Study Opportunities Abroad

It is no longer only specialist language students who do a year abroad. Opportunities for students on every sort of course to spend time overseas are increasing all the time. Work placements do not have to be in this country. And there are a number of international schemes which promote opportunities for study abroad.

The most important of these is called ERASMUS – the European Community Action Scheme for the Mobility of University Students. It was founded in 1987 and now involves all the countries of the EC plus the seven members of EFTA – effectively all of Western Europe, including Scandinavia and Iceland. Its purpose is to provide grants that enable students in the participating nations to spend a period of study at a university in another member state (the word university is used here as shorthand for all recognised Higher Education institutions). The grant is designed to cover *extra* expenses – foreign travel, higher cost of living, etc – not normal living expenses: your LEA grant is meant to do that.

Participation in ERASMUS is not just a jaunt – in frontier-free Europe, experience of another country's culture and attitudes, as well as knowledge of the language, is a great advantage in the eyes of many employers.

The period abroad may be anything from three months to a year and is instead of rather than in addition to the time you spend at your own university. In other words, you study an appropriate course while you are in Europe and this counts towards your degree when you get home.

ERASMUS links are between individual departments, so not every department in a university may participate and you do not have a completely free choice as to where you go. You may find yourself studying Chemistry in Lisbon, while a Geography student at the same university goes to Grenoble and a Chemistry student at another university goes to Heidelberg. Nor can you necessarily go just because you want to. You don't apply for a grant on an individual basis. ERASMUS gives funding to participating universities to dole out as they see fit, so you need your department's approval for the trip. The agreement of the university you intend to visit is also needed; they do not get paid for the privilege of entertaining you – your tuition fees still go to your home university.

University prospectuses give some outline of their ERASMUS links and you can read between the lines to see how widespread these are and how enthusiastically the university is promoting the idea. Some of the best opportunities are at Aberdeen, Aberystwyth, Dundee, Exeter, Glasgow, Kent, King's College London, Newcastle, Oxford Brookes and Wolverhampton, but over 200 UK universities participate in ERASMUS and the network continues to spread.

More information is available through individual universities or colleges, or from the UK ERASMUS Students' Grant Council, which is based at the University of Kent, Canterbury CT2 7PD, telephone 0227 762712. Full details of every ERASMUS link are given in *ERASMUS – the UK Guide*, available from ISCO Publications, 12a–18a Princess Way, Camberley GU15 3SP, price £8.80; if you are ordering a single copy add £1.10 for postage and packing.

ERASMUS is only the largest of these international schemes: LINGUA operates in exactly the same way but is aimed at linguists; TEMPUS – the Trans-European Mobility Scheme for University Students – offers similar links with Eastern Europe; COMETT – the European Community Action Programme for Education and Training for Technology – concentrates on technological subjects and provides work placements rather than time at university. Outside Europe the links don't tend to suffer from acronyms, but there are increasing openings for study in the USA, Canada and Japan. Consult the prospectus and ask your department what opportunities may be available to you.

Modular Courses

Once upon a time, when you applied to university or college, you chose a main subject to study and a subsidiary subject that went with it. If you chose English to major in, you would take another Arts subject – History, say, or Biblical Studies – as a subsid. If your main subject was Maths, your subsid might be Chemistry or Physics or, at a pinch, Economics. If you applied for joint honours, you would choose two major subjects, but again they would be in obvious combinations – Psychology and Sociology, French and German and so on. You would study these subjects – and these subjects only – for three or four years, and then over a period of two weeks would sit lots of exams on the work you had done since the beginning.

No longer. Many institutions have now introduced a modular scheme which – subject to the restraints described below – offers a wide choice of subjects that need not all relate to your specialism. If you are taking a single or joint honours degree, certain topics may be compulsory or you may have to complete a specified minimum number of units in the major subjects. Then there will be various options or electives, whether from within the main subject area or not, which you can choose to make up the required number of units. Often you don't have to make a final decision about your main and subsidiary subjects until the end of the first year.

Many universities and colleges now offer Combined Honours programmes in which you design your own programme of study. Providing the timetable can accommodate it and that studies have some academic coherence, you can combine subjects from different Schools or Faculties, so that studying Engineering with Japanese, Law with European Studies or Computing with Philosophy is perfectly possible.

Under the modular system you build up your degree by accumulating credits, by studying modules or units. Most units last for a semester – a teaching period of fourteen to sixteen weeks, of which the last three may be devoted to revision and assessment. You are examined or assessed on each unit separately, either by some form of continuous assessment (see page 482) or by written, oral or practical exams, or both, during or at the end of the semester.

This revolution has not had an equal effect on all disciplines: with one or two exceptions, vocational degrees such as Medicine and Veterinary Science tend to follow the traditional pattern with, understandably, a large proportion of compulsory courses and considerable emphasis on 'final' written and clinical exams.

A typical modular scheme works like this. Each module (or unit) is designated a Level – 1, 2 or 3 – and a number of credits, say 20. To gain an honours degree you need to accumulate 360 credits, of which at least 120 must be at Level 3 and not more than 120 at Level 1. So over three years' full-time study you would take six modules a year, and the levels would correspond roughly to the progress you would make through first-, second- and third-year work in a traditional scheme. Just as for university entry, you need to meet certain basic course requirements, so you would normally be expected to have studied Level 1 of a subject before embarking on Level 2, and so on.

The number of credits assigned to each unit, the number of units you are expected to take and the terminology used to describe them varies from place to place, but the concept is much the same in any institution offering modular degree programmes. As a very rough guide, you can expect to spend 80–100 hours on each unit. Probably less than half of that will be formal teaching; the rest is time you should allocate to private study and work on assignments or projects (see Chapter 7).

In addition to giving you more opportunity to study what you want, this system has two great advantages. Firstly, a modular programme is much easier to follow part-time than a traditional course – instead of doing three modules at a time, you can opt for one or two – and secondly, the credits you build up count for something even if you have to abandon your studies part way through. In the old days you went to university for three years and at the end of it came out with a degree. If for any reason you fell by the wayside, you had nothing. Now many institutions award a Certificate of Higher Education for 120 credits and a Diploma of Higher Education for 240.

If you go back to the same course at a later date, or move to another town and approach a different university or college, you should be given credit for the study you have completed. The concept of Credit Accumulation and Transfer (CATS, see below) is neither universal nor standardised, but it is spreading.

Although many universities and colleges now divide their academic year into two semesters, running from October to February and February to June, as far as attendance is concerned there are still three terms, with holidays falling around Christmas and Easter.

The Credit Accumulation and Transfer Scheme (CATS) and Assessment of Prior Experiential Learning (APEL)

These two associated concepts are further developments of the new flexibility in Higher Education and of the increasingly widespread belief that you should not have to study again something you have already studied satisfactorily, or that you know about from your life experience.

In a university or college that operates a CATS scheme, you can – with the help of the academic staff – design your own programme of study, full- or part-time, taking course units/modules from different subject areas if you wish. As you complete each unit, you gain the number of credits it carries (see under *Modular Degrees*, above). You can, to a certain extent, make the programme up as you go along – you may not have to commit yourself to a particular speciality until you have accumulated half the credits you need for your degree.

This means that if you change your mind – you find the subject you thought you were interested in doesn't suit you after all – you can transfer the credit you have accumulated to another course. If you move from one institution to another, you can take that credit with you. If circumstances change and you want to switch from full- to part-time study or vice versa, you can do so.

In practice, credit transfer from one course to another or from one institution to another has not been exploited to the full; most students in CATS schemes simply take advantage of the flexibility it allows the individual within a single course of study.

It is not only through the degree-course modules that you accumulate credit. Professional qualifications or work-oriented training courses may earn you points that will count towards a degree, exempting you from a certain portion of your formal studies. Previous experience can be harnessed in the same way: if you have worked as a lab technician for a number of years, say, your experience may be assessed as the equivalent of a certain number of credits, and you could find yourself starting a Chemistry degree course in the second year. (It is extremely rare for anybody to be exempted from more than the equivalent of one-year's worth of study, whatever their previous experience or qualifications.) It is not just formal work experience that counts – you can be given credit for voluntary work or for bringing up children.

It is important, however, that whatever you learned from your experience is current, however long ago the experience itself was: you not only have to have *done* something, you need to have benefited from it in terms of knowledge, skills or understanding, to have retained that benefit, and be able to convince an expert that you can transfer that benefit to the course of study you wish to undertake.

If the university or college you are applying to operates a CATS scheme, it will say so in the prospectus and tell you how to apply: in some cases you should still go through the relevant clearing house (UCAS or ADAR), in others you write direct to the university or college.

If you wish to have your work or life experience assessed, contact the Access Unit or Continuing Education Office at the institution which interests you. They will advise on preparing a portfolio of evidence to support your claim. This might include letters from employers or supervisors, a personal record of some community service, an essay or an article that shows you are reasonably literate, a certificate awarded at the end of a previous course, and so on.

Neither CATS nor APEL is organised formally on a nationwide basis in England and Wales. There used to be a CNAA CATS scheme, for which institutions and individuals could register, but this arrangement died with the CNAA. Now, individual institutions operate their own programmes, although some are organised into regional consortia with mutual co-operation. In Scotland, universities and colleges participate in SCOTCAT, the Scottish Credit Accumulation and Transfer scheme.

Up-to-date details of credit transfer opportunities are kept on the ECCTIS database (see page 42) but their most recent 'hard copy' directory was published when the CNAA scheme was still in existence and is therefore out of date.

— 2 —

Preparing Yourself for Higher Education

ENTRY REQUIREMENTS

Almost all the institutions listed in this book have comparable general entry (or matriculation) requirements: in England, Wales and Northern Ireland, these normally mean passes in two subjects at A level and in three different subjects at GCSE level. Two passes at AS level will normally be accepted as the equivalent of one A level. In Scotland the normal requirement is three passes at Scottish Higher level.

A number of other qualifications are almost always acceptable: English, Welsh and Northern Irish universities accept Scottish qualifications and vice versa; the European or International Baccalauréate is generally recognised. Some institutions 'officially' accept BTEC or City and Guilds awards, National Vocational Qualifications or professional qualifications as satisfying the general entrance requirements; others will consider them on an individual basis as part of a mature student's application.

The general entry requirements are the *minimum* required: candidates who are made conditional offers through UCAS will normally be expected to obtain 'good' A level passes – grade C or above – before being given a place. The level of the offer will vary from institution to institution and indeed from department to department within the same institution. If you apply to do Politics at Exeter, you will probably be asked for three Bs, but for Physics you will get in with a B and a C or two Cs; at the Queen's University of Belfast you may be admitted to either course with three Cs. This does not reflect well or badly on the specific course – it is more to do with the number of places available versus the anticipated demand.

These general entry requirements are very frequently waived for mature students, but you should be aware that they exist, for two reasons. One is that if you are sitting A levels in order to prepare yourself for university, however old you are, you may well be asked to achieve these grades too. This is only fair – when comparing like with like, why should an Admissions Tutor accept a lower standard of performance just because a candidate is over twenty-one?

The other reason is that you may run up against bureaucratic problems, particularly if you are applying to a federated university such as London or Wales, where the general requirements are established by the larger body. A department or college may be willing to admit you without formal qualifications, but the administration may insist on O level Maths or English. You should be able to find ways round this, especially if you have the Admissions Tutor on your side. Don't be afraid to persist, and to make suggestions yourself. You could, for example, offer to do a special test to show that you have the basic grounding they require.

In addition to general entry requirements, you may have to satisfy specific departmental requirements, and these are less likely to be waived because they are relevant to your ability to follow the course. It is very common for Education courses to insist on O level English and Maths. You can study some foreign languages *ab initio* – that is, without prior knowledge of them – but most courses in the more popular European languages, especially French, will assume you have reached the equivalent of A-level standard. Many Science or Engineering courses also presuppose a certain knowledge, usually reflected in a relevant A level – Biology, Chemistry, Physics or whatever.

The department may accept an alternative qualification or evidence of relevant experience, but if you don't have the knowledge, you won't be able to follow the course. This is why there are now so many foundation courses in Science, Engineering and Technology on offer (see page 26) – it is worth taking the extra year to prepare yourself properly.

Some universities, colleges or individual departments are completely inflexible about their requirements, not even accepting BTEC HNDs in place of A levels or Scottish Highers. This is most common in Dentistry, Medicine and Veterinary Science. You should probably face the fact that if you do not have excellent grades in conventional exams – and particularly if you are over thirty – you are unlikely to gain a place on a course in any of those subjects.

In theory, many institutions have no upper age limit for mature students. As a general rule, however, places on vocational courses such as Education, Nursing or Physiotherapy are not often allocated to anyone who will have less than fifteen years' working life after graduation. So forty to forty-fiveish is about the top limit here.

Alternative Qualifications

The now almost universal policy of promoting 'wider access' to Higher Education may make it sound as if it is easy to obtain a place on a degree course. It is certainly *easier* than it used to be, as far as those without 'traditional qualifications' are concerned, but this does not mean you can walk into a course without any preparation at all.

Time and again throughout this book and in university and college prospectuses you will come across words like 'commitment' and 'motivation'. Admissions tutors may be favourably disposed towards mature students, but they will require some indication that you are genuinely interested in the subject, that you have the basic intellectual ability to cope with the course and that you are likely to last the distance. 'Evidence of recent study' is the expression most often used: if you left school many years ago, they will want to know what you've been doing to educate yourself in the interim. If you did A levels three years ago and got bad grades, they will need to be convinced that you have changed in some way and are more likely to succeed on their course now than you were then. You can't sit around and do nothing from the age of eighteen and suddenly expect special treatment the moment you turn twenty-one. Admissions Tutors are not stupid.

Universities and colleges want their students to do well. They want to be able to say – to the world at large and perhaps to the people providing the funding for their research in particular – 'Look at all these students of ours who got good degrees. We are obviously supplying a high standard of education and you should continue to give us money/send your children here.' Their livelihood, even their continued existence, ultimately depends on this. So before they take you on, they want to be as certain as they can be that you will be a credit to them.

Come to that, *you* want to do well for your *own* satisfaction. Whatever your ultimate aim in returning to study may be, you want to enjoy the course and get a good degree at the end of it. So you need to do some groundwork. You will be more confident and better equipped to benefit from the course if you do.

The following are some of the most widely recognised ways in which you can prepare yourself for a degree course.

A Levels

If you didn't do them (or Scottish Highers) at school, they are on offer at umpteen Adult Education Colleges throughout the country, taught part-time, through day or evening classes, to anyone over the age of sixteen. There are unlikely to be any entry requirements; you simply register, pay your fee (perhaps £150 for the year) and emerge with an A level at the end of the year. A single A level may well be acceptable to

Admissions Tutors – it provides the 'evidence of recent study' that they are looking for.

But remember the warning given above about grades.

Access Courses

'Access' is a widely and loosely used term denoting all kinds of educational opportunity at almost any level. Recognised Access courses to Higher Education are something more specific, and constitute one of the most important routes into Higher Education for those without traditional qualifications. To avoid confusion, these Access courses are always dignified with an initial capital in official publications and prospectuses.

Access courses are designed for anyone without conventional entry qualifications to an institution of Higher Education who does not feel ready to embark on a Higher Education course without some preparation. They are geared particularly towards mature students who have been away from study for some time, and towards 'those parts of the community which are traditionally under-represented in Higher Education'. This is an expression you will come across frequently, and it's good news for women wanting to return to study after having a family, for those suffering from disabilities, members of ethnic minorities and anyone who felt hard done by at school.

Access courses to Higher Education in England, Wales and Northern Ireland are validated locally by an Authorised Validating Agency (AVA) under the auspices of the Higher Education Quality Council (HEQC). The AVAs are consortia of Higher and Further Education institutions, working together to link local adult education opportunities with the Further and Higher Education bodies. The East Anglian Access Consortium, for example, comprises the University of East Anglia and four colleges of Further and Higher Education in Suffolk and Norfolk, while the Manchester Open College Federation consists of some thirty establishments in Manchester and the surrounding area.

Although the HEQC does not inspect every course, it does examine the validating process employed by each AVA. It also awards a nationally recognised 'kitemark' to any AVA-approved course. In other words, you can be confident that a kitemarked Access course has reached a certain standard which meets universities' general entrance requirements.

In Scotland the Scottish Wider Access Programme (SWAP) is committed to establishing a wide range of Access courses in conjunction with schools and colleges of Further and Higher Education. Three consortia – in the north, south-east and west of Scotland – monitor courses and the SWAP quality assurance is the equivalent of the kitemark in other parts of the UK.

There is one major difference, however. In Scotland, if you complete an Access programme satisfactorily and obtain an appropriate reference from the establishment providing the programme, you are *guaranteed* a place on a Higher Education course. In England, Wales and Northern Ireland, you are merely better qualified to apply and entitled to compete on equal terms with everyone else!

There are some 1200 Access courses in England, Wales and Northern Ireland, 900 of them kitemarked and a substantial number of the rest awaiting validation. They cater for about 30,000 adult students. In addition there are about 200 comparable programmes in Scotland. The vast majority are offered in Further Education Colleges, with about 10 per cent in institutions of Higher Education. Perhaps 20 per cent of all mature students in the UK are 'graduates' of Access courses, and the qualification is recognised – and welcomed – increasingly by universities and colleges.

Access courses typically last a year and involve a minimum of about 500 hours of study, including class work, project work and private study. However, there is no hard and fast pattern. Some courses are officially full-time; others can be followed part-time during the day and/or evening. Depending on what is available in your area, you may be able to take a straightforward course in a single subject, or to choose part of a modular programme which enables you to accumulate credits. Some Access courses are linked to local universities, so that the course is effectively a foundation year for a specific degree. Most aim simply to equip you to go on to Higher Education and broaden the choice of options available.

All this obviously involves a certain amount of commitment. If you are seriously thinking of embarking on a degree course, you will have thought about this already, but it is also worth considering whether you *need* an Access course. If you have one A level and some relevant work experience, for example, the university or college of your choice may recognise that as adequate preparation, and a year spent on an Access course may mean an unnecessary delay in achieving your end. On the other hand, it may provide a necessary boost to your confidence and break you in to the concept of Higher Education gently.

If you know which university or college you want to attend and what you want to study, speak to the course tutor or student adviser *early* i.e. at least a year before the course is due to begin, and ask their advice. Your local Institute of Further Education or whoever is providing the Access courses should also have advisers. Don't be afraid to ask.

Remember that the closing date for application through UCAS is 15 December for courses beginning the following October, and most institutions which welcome direct applications from mature students like to receive them about that time too. So if you talk to somebody in October who advises that an Access course isn't necessary, you still have time to apply by mid-December.

Business and Technology Education Council (BTEC) and Scottish Vocational Education Council (SCOTVEC)

BTEC is an independent body established by the Department of Education and Science to validate courses run by colleges, schools and some universities which lead to the qualification of BTEC Certificates and Diplomas. Any establishment offering courses leading to these awards will have been approved by BTEC, so you can be sure the qualification you are getting is of a recognised standard.

The diplomas are at two levels, National and Higher National. The Higher National Diploma (HND) is generally regarded as equivalent to a pass degree and in many cases may be acceptable not only as a university entrance qualification but as a pathway to an accelerated programme at university – a number of one- or two-year courses leading to honours degrees, particularly in Education, are designed specifically for holders of an HND.

Entry requirements for HND programmes are slightly lower than those for degree courses: you need one A level and a few good GCSEs, or a BTEC National Certificate or Diploma, or equivalent.

BTEC courses are available at over a thousand centres in England, Wales and Northern Ireland – if you do not know of a college nearby where they are taught, ask at your local library. The courses are generally vocational or practical rather than academic, but they are available in a very wide range of subjects from Home Economics to Mechanical and Manufacturing Engineering. Courses normally last two years full-time and are subject to a mandatory grant from your LEA in the same way as degree courses. If you study part-time, you should be able to complete the course in three years, but you will not be eligible for a grant. However, most employers recognise the value of BTEC qualifications and many part-time BTEC students are sponsored by their employers.

If, for whatever reason, you do not study enough modules to be awarded an HNC or HND, you can still be given credit for what you have done in the form of a Certificate of Achievement detailing the modules you have completed.

For further information, contact your local college or the Business and Technology Education Council, Central House, Upper Woburn Place, London WC1H 0HH, telephone 071–413 8400.

BTEC only covers England, Wales and Northern Ireland. The Scottish equivalent is SCOTVEC, the Scottish Vocational Education Council, Hanover House, 24 Douglas St, Glasgow G2 7NQ, telephone 041–248 7900. It offers vocational and practical qualifications built up from units or modules of study, which may be obtained in the classroom or in the workplace. Over 2700 different modules are available in subjects ranging from secretarial and office skills to art and photography.

Accumulating sufficient modules will lead to the awards of National Certificate, Higher National Certificate or

Diploma (HNC or HND) and to Scottish Vocational Qualifications. These awards are on a par with the English/Welsh certificates and diplomas awarded by BTEC, and university and college Admissions Offices will treat them in the same way.

A Record of Education and Training shows your achievements within the SCOTVEC framework, listing separately National Certificate Modules, Higher National Units and Workplace-assessed Units. SCOTVEC keep computerised records of everyone who is registered with them and will update your record whenever you successfully complete a unit. You will be sent an updated record annually, provided that you have successfully completed a unit during the year.

Note: the BTEC Certificate of Achievement and the SCOTVEC RET are not to be confused with the Record of Achievement (ROA) which is now popular as a sort of CV issued to school leavers.

National Vocational Qualifications (NVQs)

NVQs are a recent invention, designed with the specific needs of industry and the workplace in mind. They are about work, about training you – often on the job – to be more competent at what you are already doing and preparing you for the next step up. At the lower levels they are entirely task-oriented, while the higher levels require increasing depth of understanding of principles. NVQs have the backing of the TUC, the CBI and various awarding bodies such as BTEC and City and Guilds.

NVQs may be awarded by one of these bodies, or by a guild or council associated with a particular industry. They are available through over a hundred such bodies, including the British Institute of Innkeeping, the Institute of the Motor Industry and the Pensions Management Institute.

NVQs are organised into units, which students may use as 'building blocks' towards qualifications. They are awarded at five different levels, with Level 3 now widely accepted as the equivalent of A levels, and Levels 4 and 5 increasingly counted as credits towards a Higher Education award. They are extraordinarily flexible: you can prove your competence at work, or you can study at college or at home, or both, and there is no time limit.

A word of caution, however: a report by Professor Alan Smithers of the University of Manchester, commissioned by Channel 4 and published in December 1993, described the NVQ system as 'deeply flawed' and criticised its lack of emphasis on understanding, theory and retained knowledge. In response, the chief executive of the NCVQ welcomed constructive criticism but expressed surprise at factual inaccuracies in the report. It is perhaps fairest to say that the system is in its infancy and there is doubtless scope for improvement.

More information is available through the National Database of Vocational Qualifications – ask your local college, careers office or Training and Enterprise Council (TEC) where the nearest access point is – or direct from the National Council for Vocational Qualifications, 22 Euston Rd, London NW1 2BZ, telephone 071–387 9898.

Scottish Vocational Qualifications, which operate along the same lines, are administered by SCOTVEC (see above).

City and Guilds

City and Guilds has been providing work-related qualifications for well over a hundred years, and now works very closely with the National Council for Vocational Qualifications – many of its certificates are NVQs. Courses are run at thousands of centres – schools, colleges, Institutes of Adult Education, training centres, the workplace – but they have all been approved; wherever a City and Guilds course is offered you know it has reached the required C & G standard.

There are usually no entry requirements and you may not even have to take a course – if you think your experience, knowledge or skills are sufficient, you can (for a small fee) take only the assessment.

City and Guilds awards are at seven different levels, from GCSE to senior management and professional status; Level 3 equates with NVQ Level 3 and will be accepted as an alternative to A levels by those institutions which recognise these qualifications.

For further information, contact your local Adult Education Centre or the City and Guilds of London Institute, 76 Portland Place, London W1N 4AA, telephone 071–278 2468.

Open College Networks

The National Open College Network, which now has fourteen full and eight associate members throughout England and Wales, exists to promote Continuing Education for adults and to provide a nationally recognised system of credit for the learning its students acquire, without putting them through examinations. OCN students are awarded credits for learning at four levels, of which the highest equates to A level. Credit can be built up from Adult Education courses, community-based activities, training courses run by voluntary groups or employers, and so on. OCNs also offer both Access courses and NVQ qualifications as a specific preparation for Higher Education.

For further information, contact the National Open College Network on 051–709 9090.

Open or Distance Learning

You may think of distance learning as having to get up at five in the morning to watch an Open University programme on BBC 2, but the concept has evolved a great deal in recent years. Organisations which offer distance learning send you course materials and, in some cases, a list of books and other materials that you are expected to buy. You are allocated a tutor who sets assignments and marks each one as you complete it. The beauty of distance learning is that you can study at your own pace and at home; the main problem is potential isolation, although summer schools and networks of local students are working to avoid this.

Three major sources of distance learning – the National Extension College, the Open University and the Rapid Results College – have their own entries in this book (see pages 244, 265 and 281). In addition to the degree courses listed there, all provide GCSEs, A levels, vocational courses or foundation courses which some institutions of Higher Education accept as satisfying their general entry requirements.

There is also a new initiative in distance learning of which prospective mature students should be aware: the Open Learning Foundation. This has been established by over twenty universities – mostly 'new' universities in England and Wales – with a view to providing distance learning facilities within existing or developing courses. The principle is roughly the same as in the established distance learning schools – you are provided with course materials and, under the guidance of a tutor, study on your own – and emerge with a degree from the university concerned.

For further information, contact the Open Learning Foundation Group, 24 Angel Gate, City Rd, London EC1V 2ES, telephone 071–833 3757.

Foundation Courses

Foundation courses are not the same as Access courses; they are often taught at the university or college as an integral part of a degree for those who do not have the qualifications or knowledge to embark on the course straight away. Alternatively, they may be offered at a local College of Further Education, but recognised as a suitable preparation for a specified course (though this does not guarantee you a place). In these cases, you will often be awarded a diploma at the end of the course.

Foundation courses are particularly relevant to subjects where background knowledge is assumed, such as Engineering, Science and Technology or Art and Design, and a number of Art and Design courses insist on your taking a foundation course first.

Foundation courses – sometimes called Year Zero – are normally full-time and last a year. If the course is part of a degree programme it is likely to be subject to a mandatory grant; if not you may be entitled to a discretionary award (see page 30). Contact the Admissions Tutor or Course Tutor at the college or university to check.

Associate Student Scheme

This is particularly useful if you are not sure whether you want to undertake a full degree course, or if you have doubts about which subject you wish to study. In some universities and colleges, you are allowed to register for single units of a course, and you will be given credit for these if you decide to embark on the whole degree. You will not be eligible for a grant, but you pay only modest tuition fees for each unit.

Contact the Centre for Continuing Education at the university or college you would like to attend to see if this mode of study is permitted.

STUDENTS WITH SPECIAL NEEDS

Most of the institutions listed in this book have an Equal Opportunities policy and publish a statement to that effect in their prospectus. But although that means that they guarantee to treat a disabled student's application just like any other in academic terms, with the best will in the world some of them will not be able to cope with your physical needs.

Many universities and colleges are modern and purpose-built; many are not. A number have a main building that dates back to the 19th century or beyond, supplemented by newer residences and teaching blocks. Obviously, the more recent the buildings, the more likely they are to have been built with the needs of the disabled in mind. Many Halls of Residence now have some rooms which cater for those in wheelchairs; where facilities exist, you are likely to be allocated suitable accommodation for the duration of your course.

Some institutions which do not have the facilities to cope with students in wheelchairs have made commendable efforts in other directions: Bristol and Durham, for example, both old universities in hilly cities, offer special support to the deaf or hearing-impaired.

The best way to find out if the university or college you would like to attend can accommodate you is to contact them directly. Some will have a Special Needs Adviser; otherwise ask to speak to the Head of Student Services.

For further information and support, contact SKILL, the National Bureau for Students with Disabilities, 336 Brixton Rd, London SW9 7AA, telephone 071–074 0565. This is a voluntary organisation committed to developing opportunities at all levels of adult education, training and the transition to employment for anyone with disabilities or learning difficulties. Many of its members are institutions (and you may find that your proposed university or college already belongs). Alternatively you can become an individual member: the current subscription is £25, reduced to £7 for students and the unwaged.

SKILL publishes a number of books and pamphlets that are probably of more interest to those working with the disabled than to the individual student, but it also offers an information service, open from 2 p.m. to 5 p.m. Monday to Friday, which will advise you on how to apply, finances and other practical matters. SKILL has twelve regional groups which provide a network of support for members.

— 3 —

Money

Nobody expects to be rich as a student, and the depressing truth is that times have rarely been tougher. If you have been earning a decent salary, you are in for a shock. For your own sake make sure that you understand what your financial position is likely to be before you give up your job and commit yourself to full-time education. Budgeting is easier if you live in a Hall of Residence because you know in advance exactly what your living expenses are likely to be; sharing a flat or house with other students is usually cheaper, but there are more 'hidden extras' – like food and the electricity bill. If you are living at home, you (and your family) should be aware that you are about to take a substantial drop in income (see Chapter 8 for more advice on this).

The government froze the level of student grants in 1990, which means that even with the current low rates of inflation their value 'in real terms' will gradually be whittled away. To supplement the lack of grant, a system of student loans was introduced, but these, funnily enough, are index-linked, so the amount you have to pay back increases with inflation.

The good news is that whatever your age, providing you meet certain basic requirements and that you are following an eligible course, if you are entering full-time Higher Education for the first time, your Local Education Authority (LEA) *must* pay you a grant. That is the LEA local to where you normally live, not where you are going to study. Almost all the courses listed in this book attract what is called a mandatory award.[1] The catch is that they are means-tested and will be reduced if your income, or that of your parents or spouse, exceeds a certain limit (see below).

Part-time courses, distance learning and one or two others are eligible for a discretionary award. That means that if the LEA has any money left over after it's paid all its mandatory grants, it might give some of it to you. If so, the amount is also at the LEA's discretion. Do not hold your breath. If you are only eligible for a discretionary grant, start looking round for other sources of funding.

If you are studying Occupational Therapy, Physio-therapy, Radiography, Orthoptics, Dental Hygiene or Dental Therapy (but not Dentistry) in England or Wales, the Department of Health may pay you a grant. Contact the Department of Health, Students Grant Unit, Norcross, Blackpool FY5 3TA for details. The sums involved are exactly the same as if you receive a grant from the LEA, but you can't have both.

The legislation governing all these things is complicated and your LEA is the best source of advice. Look up

---

[1] Strictly speaking, an award covers tuition fees and grant; the grant is the contribution towards your living costs. Most students' fees are paid by the LEA direct to the university or college anyway, so the word grant tends to be used loosely to cover any money you receive from the LEA.

'Education' in the phone book for the address and number of your local authority.[2]

GRANTS

To be eligible for a grant, you must study on an eligible course. A full-time or sandwich first-degree course at a UK university, another publicly funded college or specified private or NHS institution is eligible; so are most foundation courses provided you enrol for the full degree course and the university or college considers the foundation year, albeit optional, as an integral part of the course.

You must also be personally eligible. This means that you must have been 'ordinarily resident' in the British Isles for three years before the start of your course. Temporary employment abroad would not disqualify you, though having been in the UK for the purposes of education when your normal residence is elsewhere, would.

Some students from abroad, notably those from EC countries who have, or whose parents have, migrant worker status, or those from anywhere in the world who have refugee status, may also be eligible for awards: if you think this might apply to you, contact your LEA for more information.

If you have previously embarked on a course of Higher Education for which you received money from public funds of any kind (and that could mean from a government department, not necessarily an LEA) for more than twenty weeks, you may be eligible for a reduced grant, or for no grant at all.

In England, Wales or Northern Ireland you can apply for a grant any time between January of the year your course is

---

[2] The expression LEA is used in England and Wales only. In Northern Ireland the same system applies but awards are made by Education and Library Boards (known as 'the Boards') – again, look in the phone book under 'Education' for your local office. Arrangements in Scotland are slightly different and all applications are dealt with by the Student Awards Branch of the Scottish Office Education Department, Gyleview House, 3 Redheughs Rigg, Edinburgh EH12 9HH.

due to start and the end of the first term; in Scotland between April and the end of the following January. The sooner the better, as if you leave it too late, the decisions may not have been made nor the paperwork completed in time to let you have a cheque at the start of your course. *If you live in England, Wales or Northern Ireland, do not wait until you have an offer of a place, or until you know your exam results.* Students in Scotland may not apply until they have an unconditional offer of a place, which means you do need to wait for your results.

The first part of the application enables the LEA to decide, according to the criteria outlined above, whether you are eligible for a grant. The second part is the grant assessment form, which you must complete with the help of your parents or spouse, giving information about your income and theirs, so that the LEA can decide whether or not to reduce your grant. This is also your opportunity to apply for extra allowances (see below). Finally, there is a college acceptance form. You should send this to your university or college as soon as it offers you an unconditional place, or as soon as you know that your exam results meet its requirements. The college will send the form on to the LEA, which will not pay anybody anything until it has received it.

HOW MUCH DO YOU GET?

In 1993/4, the full basic grant for a student in London living away from their parents' home was £2845 and elsewhere £2265. If you live in your parents' home the rate is much reduced; if you have left your parents' home and are living in your own home, you are still eligible for the full rate. There are some extra allowances payable to those who have to spend more than the usual number of weeks per year at college, for those with extraordinary travel expenses as part of the course, for the disabled – and for mature students.

If at the start of your course you are twenty-six years old and have been earning (or receiving in benefit) at least £12,000 in total in the three years previously, you are entitled to an extra payment of £290 (£280 in Scotland). Don't spend it all at once. This rate increases as you get older, so that by the time you are twenty-nine or more the mature student's payment is £1005 (£980 in Scotland).

In addition, you can claim allowances for dependants – children, non-earning spouses or adult dependants who are not your spouse. The maximum payment here is £1750 a year.

Like the basic grant, these allowances are means-tested, and whose means are tested depends on your status. Your parents may be expected to contribute to your upkeep if you have not yet achieved independent status. To become an independent student, at the start of the academic year for which you are applying for a grant, you must be at least twenty-five, or have been married at least two years, or have been self-supporting for at least three years. If any of these apply, your parents can be as rich as they like and it won't affect your grant. However, if you are married, your husband or wife's income is taken into consideration when assessing a grant. (The advisory booklets all use the words 'husband or wife' – unmarried partners do not seem to have the same obligations.)

The grant assessment form asks for details of income and certain types of regular expenditure. You are allowed a certain amount of income before the grant is reduced – up to £3735 from a scholarship or from your employer; up to £2925 from a pension; up to £1750 in trust income. Student loans and any holiday or part-time work you take on during your course does not affect your grant. Your parents or spouse also have allowances – for payments such as interest, life assurance, domestic help and other dependants. When all this is taken into account, the LEA works out your parents' or spouse's residual income and calculates any contribution they are expected to make. This is on a sliding scale – if your spouse's residual income is less than £11,350, he or she is not expected to make any contribution and you will receive a full award; if it is £45,020 or more he or she will be asked to contribute £5800 and your grant will be reduced to practically nothing. The parameters for parental income are slightly higher, but the principle is the same.

When the amount of your grant is agreed, your LEA will send a cheque at the start of each term, normally direct to the college or university, who will advise you where to go to collect it. Unless you live in Scotland, you do not need to apply again next year – a single application covers the full length of your course, though the LEA will review it each year and make any adjustments it deems necessary. Scottish students do need to re-apply for each year of the course, ideally by 31 May, because in the summer priority is given to new applications that could not be processed until exam results were known. Wherever you live, if your financial circumstances change in a way that is likely to affect your grant, you should let your LEA know at once.

You are still eligible for a grant if the course involves a work placement of any kind, or if you have to study abroad. But the amount you are paid and the country in which you spend time will affect the level of your grant.

LOANS

You qualify for a student loan in the same way as you qualify for a grant – by being an eligible person studying on an eligible course. You must also be under fifty when the course starts. And because loans are paid through banks and building societies, not sent to you by cheque as grants are, you must have an account which can handle direct credits and debits. Student loans are not means-tested – as long as you have not reneged on a previous agreement, you can borrow the maximum amount allowed (see below) whatever your income. The regulations are the same wherever you live or study within the UK.

You can only apply for a loan once a year and until the academic year has started. It is up to you to decide how much to borrow, and provided you don't apply late in the academic year you can opt to have the loan paid in one, two or three instalments.

Student loan eligibility certificates and application forms are available through your university or college, which must authorise the certificate. In order for them to do this, you must produce your birth or adoption certificate, or documentary proof of your date and place of birth if this was outside the UK. You also need to provide evidence that you have the right sort of bank or building society account. Your college then sends the certificate to the Student Loans Company Ltd, 100 Bothwell St, Glasgow G2 7JD. You fill in the application form and send it to the same address.

By this time you must have decided how much you want to borrow. This is up to you, but remember that you can only apply once in an academic year, so in assessing your needs it might be better to err on the side of generosity. For 1993/4 the maximum loan was £940 for students studying in London and £800 elsewhere, except that final-year students were only entitled to £685 or £585 (because their education is deemed to have finished at the end of the summer term and the loan is not meant to cover the following long vacation).

Once your application has been processed you will receive a loan agreement and direct debiting mandate, which you must sign, date and return. The Student Loans Company will then pay your loan (or the first instalment) into your bank or building society account.

You must return the signed loan agreement and direct debit instructions by 31 July, or your application will not be processed and you will have forfeited the right to a loan for that academic year.

Interest is accrued on the loan from the day the money is paid into your account, and added to the principal which must eventually be paid back. Repayments start in the April after the course finishes. If for any reason you leave the course before the scheduled completion date, you must tell the Student Loans Company, as repayments will begin earlier than they had expected.

Loans are normally paid back by direct debit in a series of monthly instalments – usually over five years, but up to seven if you borrowed for five years or more. This arrangement may change, but the Student Loans Company or your college will advise on the system that is in place when you take out your loan.

If problems arise in making your repayments, you can apply to have them deferred for a year at a time. In order to qualify for deferment, your earnings must not exceed 85 per cent of the national average, a figure which the government works out every year. For the year ending 31 July 1994 you qualify for deferment if your income is not more than £1165 gross a month (just under £14,000 a year). Note that this is *your* income – the income of your parents or spouse is not taken into consideration when assessing the possibility of deferment. If your repayments are deferred for a year and you are still in difficulties at the end of that time, you can apply for deferment again.

Any outstanding loan is cancelled on death or, provided you have not defaulted on your repayments, when you reach the age of fifty (sixty if you were over forty when you started your course) or after twenty-five years if that is sooner.

The Student Loans Company has a helpline, 0345 300 900, which you can call for more information.

FEES

If you are eligible for a grant, tuition fees will normally be paid direct by the LEA to the university or college, and you won't have to worry about them. If you are *not* eligible for a grant, you will have to pay them yourself. Fees not only cover tuition but registration, exams, graduation and your subscription to the Students' Union. (For expenses not covered by fees, see under *Extra Expenses*, page 40.)

In almost all universities, tuition fees for UK and EC students are subsidised by the government and the LEA pays only part of the actual cost. For 1993/4, basic fees for the academic year were: £1300 for classroom-based subjects; £2770 for lab- or workshop-based subjects (usually Engineering or Science subjects but Art, Drama, Music, etc may also come under this heading); £4985 for the clinical part of Medicine or Dentistry courses. However, if you are paying your own fees these figures are usually drastically reduced – in 1993/4, a self-financing student was typically paying £750–£800 for the academic year. This reduction may happen automatically or you may have to apply for remission of fees – the Academic Registrar or Admissions Office at the college or university will advise you.

If you are on a sandwich course, you pay a reduced fee – normally 50 per cent of the basic tuition fee – during your 'year out'.

If your studies are being sponsored (by your employer, for example) and the amount of the sponsorship is such that you do not qualify for a grant, the university or college will send your sponsor an invoice at the start of the academic session, but you will need to produce written confirmation of the sponsorship before you are allowed to register.

Some of the colleges listed in this book – and, uniquely, the University of Buckingham – are privately funded and do not receive the government contribution mentioned above. This means that the fees they charge have to cover the full cost of tuition, and that can make a lot of difference to the average student budget. In these circumstances, the LEA makes a contribution to fees – currently just under £700 – which is likely to be several thousand pounds short of the sum you need. See individual entries in Chapter 5 for more details, but be warned that private education is just as expensive for adults as it is for children.

OTHER SOURCES OF INCOME

Some of the money the government isn't paying you in grants goes to the universities and colleges to provide what are known as Access Funds. If you are in financial difficulty and have investigated other possible sources of funding (including taking out a Student Loan), you can apply for a grant or loan from these funds. Individual universities and colleges handle their Access Funds in different ways: ask the Student Services Department or the office from which you collected your grant for advice on the procedure. The money available is limited and is there to alleviate cases of genuine hardship, so you should prepare a pretty convincing argument before you apply.

The other way to keep yourself off the breadline is sponsorship, but you must think about this before you get to university. Your best bet is your employer, if the course you are taking is intended to improve your performance or prospects in your job, and if you are prepared to commit yourself to coming back to work for the same employer for a number of years after you graduate. Make your enquiries –

of your immediate boss, your personnel department or whoever seems most appropriate – *early*: they will need time to think about it, and if they say no you will need time to explore other avenues.

The armed forces and some major companies – the big names in computing or the motor industry, for example – sponsor students. They are likely to be particularly interested in those studying Computing, Engineering, Business or other subjects relevant to their activities, but some may be prepared to consider students in other disciplines. Depending on the nature of the scheme, it may be necessary to commit yourself to doing your sandwich year or other work experience with them, or to work for them for a fixed period after graduation. You may or may not be guaranteed a job afterwards. In any case, you will be paid throughout your course at a level that will make you much richer than most of your fellow students, though your LEA will cut your grant accordingly.

Detailed information on likely sources of sponsorship can be found in *Sponsorship for Students 1994*, available from Careers and Occupational Information Centre, Room E455, Moorfoot, Sheffield S1 4PQ, price £5; or *A Guide to Student Sponsorship*, from Student Sponsorship Information Services, P.O. Box 36, Newton le Willows, Merseyside WA12 0DW, price £7.75. Look for these publications in your local library before sending off a cheque.

Some universities – Warwick and UMIST among them – run their own sponsorship offices. You should contact them for information as soon as you submit your UCAS application, though they will probably not be able to do anything definite until you have firmly accepted an unconditional offer of a place. You should also keep your eyes open for advertisements in the national papers.

If you are taking a vocational course, whether full-time, part-time or through distance learning, and do not receive a full grant, you may be eligible for a Career Development Loan. This can be for any amount from £2000 to £5000, up to a maximum of 80 per cent of your fees and expenses. A CDL is normally only available for one year. If you need help for longer, apply to your local Training and Enterprise Council (TEC – look them up in the phone book or ask at your nearest

Jobcentre). Special conditions apply if you are unemployed or already a full-time student.

More information about CDLs is available from Jobcentres and TECs, from careers advisers or from universities and colleges. You can also get a free explanatory booklet by phoning 0800 585 505.

Many universities and colleges provide scholarships or bursaries of some kind, and give details in their prospectuses. The funding for these normally comes either from the estate of a wealthy benefactor or from industry, and money may only be available to students studying a prescribed subject.

There may also be some restriction on how you spend the money. The Royal and Ancient Golf Club at St Andrews sponsors two bursaries a year for students at the University of Dundee who have a single-figure golf handicap and wish to progress in the golfing world as well as in their studies; the bursary is supposed to cover golfing expenses.

Dundee also offers up to twenty-four bursaries a year for first-year students of Engineering. Music scholarships are not uncommon – Oxford and Cambridge both have Organ Awards, for students of that instrument; Exeter offers both Organ and Choral Scholarships. Swansea has undergraduate entrance scholarships for 'outstanding students in the field of artistic, cultural or sporting activity', while Aberystwyth has some open scholarships and some restricted to Welsh students.

Competition for all bursaries and scholarships is extremely fierce, but if you have a particular talent you may be lucky. The money is going to be paid out to somebody – why shouldn't it be you? Well before your course is due to start, ask the Registry or Admissions Office if there are any awards of this kind for which you might be eligible. You may find you have to apply – and even sit the qualifying exam – by the previous December.

COUNCIL TAX

Everyone over the age of eighteen, including full-time students, is liable for council tax. As a student, you pay it in your place of study, but are exempt if you live in a Hall of Residence or share accommodation exclusively with other students. If, however, you share a house or flat with someone who is not exempt, you may become liable yourself . . . Contact the council tax office at your place of study for guidance.

EXTRA EXPENSES

You may know in advance exactly what your basic living expenses are going to be, and there is a fighting chance that your fees will be paid for you, but your course, whatever the subject, will involve you in other inevitable expenses.

Books are the most obvious thing. Do not imagine you can get away without buying quite a lot of them. No matter how vast the library is, it is not going to stock enough copies of every book to go round all the members of your class, and books that are in great demand are often on a 'short loan' system, which means you may only be permitted to borrow them overnight or over the weekend. Most Students' Union bookshops operate a second-hand service which enables you to pick books up quite cheaply, but you should still budget for a substantial outlay in this department.

For any courses involving lab work you will have to provide your own white coats and if you are doing Archaeology, Biology, Geography or the like you will have to contribute something to the cost of field trips. Art and Photography are other subjects where the expenses may mount up – you will be expected to own your own camera and while the basic materials for course work should be provided, you will almost certainly have to supplement these when you are working on your final-year project. For Architecture you will require drawing equipment, for Horticulture wellington boots and specialist tools. For Music, unless you are studying piano or another keyboard, you are likely to have to supply your own instrument. And, however good the university or college computing facilities are, if you are in the habit of writing essays on a word-processor bring your own.

— 4 —

So, like ~ what's the BEER like here, then?

An Informal Meeting can be mutually revealing

How to Get There: Information and Applications

There are three ways of applying for courses in the institutions listed in this book: through the universities and colleges clearing house UCAS; through the similar organisation which deals with Art and Design courses, ADAR; and direct to the college or university itself. UCAS and ADAR have standard procedures which include more or less fixed timetables; any institution to which you apply direct will have its own rules.

The vital common feature is that they all work a long time in advance. Most courses start in September or October, and for UCAS you should be thinking about applying *a year before you want to start your course*. That is thinking about *applying*, not thinking about what you want to do and where you want to do it.

Family commitments and other constraints may mean there is very little choice about where you study – you have to go to the local university or college. But if you live in or near a big city, there may be a number of local places for you to choose from; and, if you're not restricted to a small area, be sure you pick somewhere you will be happy and which will provide a course that suits your needs.

ECCTIS 2000

One of the most comprehensive sources of information is ECCTIS 2000, a government-owned information service (the initials originally stood for something like the Educational Courses and Credit Transfer Information Service, but now it prefers to be known by its acronym). This is a massive database giving details of nearly 100,000 courses at 700 institutions of Further and Higher Education throughout the UK. It also gives brief descriptions of many of the universities and colleges themselves – a sort of potted prospectus – but, as the universities pay to have these details included, not all of them are represented.

The joy of ECCTIS is that you can look up information from any starting point you want – subject, single, joint or combined honours, type of institution, mode of study (full-time, part-time or sandwich), location, etc. If your urgent need is to study French and Spanish part-time, it will tell you that there are thirteen places in the country where this is offered, and you can then look these up individually. If, however, your priority is to do your studying in Barnstaple, it will tell you what is available (no degrees, sadly, but lots of HND courses at North Devon College).

The database also includes details of credit transfer and CATS schemes (see page 12). ECCTIS publishes two books, *The Students' Guide to Educational Credit Transfer* and *Educational Credit Transfer Directory*, but these are both out of date and it is their current policy to maintain the information on computer rather than in hard copy publications.

ECCTIS provides information about student finances, including insurance services and tax relief; about UCAS application procedures; about degree awarding and validating bodies; about student charters; input from the Law Society, from the English Nursing Board about courses in Nursing, Midwifery and Health Visiting, from SKILL about facilities for the disabled, and so on.

The information is not edited in any way, so ECCTIS has imposed no value judgements. The data is merely presented as it comes from the various sources. But the information is in very user-friendly and digestible form – you don't have to be a computer expert, a financial whizz or an expert in the jargon of Higher Education to make good use of it.

ECCTIS is now available in over 50 per cent of schools in the UK, and in many other educational institutions, libraries and careers centres. You may have to pay a token fee to use it. Over the next ten years fewer and fewer universities will be producing prospectuses on paper; it will become the norm to seek this sort of information through CD-ROM. As such, ECCTIS is ahead of the game and it is worth familiarising yourself with what it has to offer.

ECCTIS is based in the same building as UCAS – Fulton House, Jessop Avenue, Cheltenham GL50 3SH. You can phone them on 0242 528724 to find out where your nearest access point is.

THE PROSPECTUS

Once you have a shortlist of possible universities or colleges, you need to find out more about each one. Every institution listed in this book produces information about itself. As far as the would-be student is concerned, the most important source of information is a glossy annual prospectus which describes the place and its facilities and gives details of each course. You can obtain a copy free simply by ringing up and asking for one, though occasionally you will be asked to send a stamped addressed envelope. You should mention that you are a mature student – many places produce separate guides or leaflets to help you.

Assuming you know roughly which subject you want to study, the prospectus will describe the options available to you within that subject area. It will tell you how long the

course will last, whether you can study it part-time; what
special entry requirements there are, if any; what courses or
units are compulsory; how much freedom of choice you
have in choosing other units; whether the emphasis of the
course is practical or academic.

Given a choice of institutions, contrasting descriptions of
courses between them may concentrate your mind on what
you want to do: if you have a general interest in History, say,
you may find that you can choose to specialise in Medieval,
Modern or International History, or to follow a broader-
based course combining aspects of all three. The same may
be true within a single institution offering a range of courses
in a single subject area.

The prospectus will tell you what the university's general
entrance requirements are and whether or not they may be
waived for mature students. It will tell you how to apply,
whether through UCAS, ADAR or direct. It will also give
you a lot of general information. Is the university on a
campus with everything close together, or does it have
several sites (this is often true of the old polys, and *may* entail
you trekking across town between classes)? Is it in the city
centre or miles outside? What are the bus services or the
parking facilities like? What sort of accommodation does it
offer? What about sports and social facilities? Medical
facilities? Childcare? Wheelchair access? If it was founded
by a branch of the Church (and a lot of 19th-century teacher
training colleges were), will it expect you to be a practising
Christian? And so on.

Only you can decide what is important to you, and the
prospectus should answer a lot of these questions. It should
also provide contact names and telephone numbers for
more specific information, whether about the course or
about student life in general.

OPEN DAYS

So, you have read a few prospectuses, and found a course or
two that appeals to you. The next step is to go and have a
look at the place. Remember that you are going to spend at
least three years there and, particularly if you are moving to

a strange town, it is madness to commit yourself without seeing what it is like.

Some universities and colleges have fixed Open Days or Preview Days, others are happy to show you around any time by appointment. Dates for Open Days vary, but they are usually in June/July or September for institutions in the UCAS system and in the spring term for those in ADAR, which has a later closing date for applications. For UCAS courses, that means you should visit *over a year* before you intend to start your course.

Remember that an Open Day is an opportunity for you to look round and ask questions informally. It is not the same as an interview, which is part of the formal applications procedure. There should be the opportunity to meet staff and students on your prospective course, and look round the Students' Union and other buildings as well as the department. Ask the students (particularly other mature students) how they like the course and the place. Don't be shy – if there's something you want to see that isn't on the official tour, ask.

If the prospectus doesn't mention Open Days, ring up and ask if you can come anyway. If it has dates that are inconvenient, see if they'll show you round at a time that suits you. If they say no, ask yourself why. Have they got something to hide? Or can they just not be bothered with you?

ADVICE ABOUT THE COURSE

Many Admissions Tutors will be happy to have an informal chat, whether over the phone or in person (by appointment). This can be particularly valuable to mature students who want advice before they submit a formal application. You can find out at an early stage whether your qualifications or experience are likely to be acceptable, and you can ask questions that the prospectus may not have answered: how much of your study time will be in formal sessions and how much will you be expected to do on your own, for example. Now that so many courses have a flexible structure, you may need guidance in choosing options, and the

Admissions Tutor will be able to help. If your proposed course includes a sandwich element, you can find out more about the arrangements for work placements. You may also like to know how many other mature students there are in the department – you probably don't want to be the only forty-year-old in a class of fifty school leavers if you can avoid it.

HOW TO APPLY

OK, you've got all the information you want. You know what course you want to do where. It's time to fill in the forms.

Universities and Colleges Admissions Service (UCAS)

UCAS came into being after the demise of UCCA and PCAS and is operating for the first time for 1994 admissions. Most of the universities and colleges listed in this book now handle applications through UCAS. You fill in a single application form and UCAS sends it to all the right people.

UCAS will accept applications from 1 September of the year preceding proposed entry, and the normal deadline is 15 December. For Oxford or Cambridge the closing date is 15 October, both for applications to UCAS and for the forms sent direct to the university (see individual entries on pages 106 and 267). UCAS will process applications received as late as August the following year, but it is up to the individual institutions whether they are able or willing to consider them.

To apply through UCAS, you need their handbook and the application form which is supplied with it. Obtain these direct from UCAS at Fulton House, Jessop Avenue, Cheltenham, GL50 3SH, telephone 0242 227788. The handbook lists, in alphabetical order, all the institutions which are part of the UCAS system – there are nearly 200 of them, ranging from large universities like Birmingham or Glasgow where you can study an enormous range of subjects, to tiny specialist colleges like the Courtauld Institute, which offers courses exclusively in the History of Art, or the Jews' College, where you can only take Jewish Studies. Each institution has a unique code comprising letters and numbers.

Under each institution is a list of courses on offer, grouped alphabetically in faculties or subject areas. Again, each course has a code number. You can apply for a maximum of eight courses (but see note on Medicine and Dentistry, below).

The application form comes complete with a detailed instruction sheet, which explains what is required of you at each stage. Fill in the form very clearly in black – it will be photocopied and reduced, and nobody will view your application favourably if they have to struggle to read it.

Mostly the form is straightforward, asking for the personal details and educational and work background you would expect to provide in a job application. Sometimes your answer must take the form of a coded symbol, but this is explained clearly on the instruction sheet.

Section 3 is where you list the courses you wish to apply for. There are spaces for the code names for institution and course and for other details. Enter up to eight courses (you may apply for more than one course at the same place if you wish) in alphabetical order: you are expressing no preference at this stage. Note that you are not allowed to apply to both Cambridge and Oxford (although you may apply for more than one course at either) unless you are applying for an Organ Scholarship.

If you are applying for Medicine or Dentistry be aware that the Committee of Deans of Medical Schools advises you not to apply for more than five courses in these fields. Their attitude is that if you are unsuccessful in five applications, you are likely to be unsuccessful in eight. You can, however, use up the other three choices by applying for other courses without prejudicing your application to the Medical or Dental Schools.

Section 10 of the application form is particularly important to mature students. It is headed 'Further Information' and is your chance to sell yourself. There are no hard and fast rules about what you write here: you could explain why you want to study the courses you have chosen, detail other activities that demonstrate your interest in the subject, mention uncompleted courses or work experience that may be relevant, show how your career prospects will be enhanced by the course, try and convey your commitment.

Because the space is limited it is a good idea to try out your answer on a photocopy first to reduce the risk of making a mess of the form. Do not attach anything to the form, but you may like to send your CV direct to the universities or colleges so that they have it to hand when they are considering the application.

You then sign the form, fill in your name and address on the postcard which UCAS will send in acknowledgement of your application, stick a stamp on it and pass the form and card to your referee with the application fee (currently £12).

The back page of the form should be completed by your referee. For school leavers this is normally their Head Teacher, but for mature students it might be a current or recent employer, a training officer, careers officer or some such responsible person. The form gives instructions to referees, too: they are asked to give their views on such things as your suitability for the course, academic achievement and prospects, personal qualities and any relevant information which may affect your performance on the course. It is the referee who sends the form off to UCAS.

What Happens Next?

Within a few days, you should receive your postcard. This merely means that your application has arrived safely. Some time later, possibly as much as six weeks if the application was sent close to the 15 December deadline, you will receive an acknowledgement letter giving you an UCAS application number, which you should quote in all future communications with UCAS and with the institutions to which you are applying, and a record of the institutions to which your application has been sent. Check that this is right – if it isn't, tell UCAS immediately.

Over the next few months, the relevant staff on the courses to which you have applied will consider your application and respond to you via UCAS. You may be rejected outright, accepted conditionally or unconditionally, or invited for an interview. Conditional offers are normally dependent on exam or course results, and will specify the grades you are expected to achieve; if this does not apply to you, any offers you receive are likely to be unconditional, but you are more likely to be interviewed. Most universities and colleges interview all mature candidates who look suitable on paper. After the interview you will receive an acceptance or rejection.

Each of your eight choices will consider you independently of the others and in their own good time, so if you applied in December, eight answers should filter through to you by about the end of April. When you receive the last one, you will also be given a date by which you should reply, although if you are waiting to attend an Open Day you can ask for this deadline to be extended.

In the UCAS system you are allowed to accept two conditional offers, one firmly and one as insurance. The firm acceptance should be for the place you really want to go to, the insurance for one you would be happy to go to if you didn't get the required grades for your first choice. You are making a commitment at this point – if you get the required grades, you are obliged to take up the offer you have accepted firmly (unless you give up the idea of Higher Education altogether for this year). You are not allowed to change your mind later and accept your insurance offer.

If you do not get the required grades for either of the offers you have accepted, UCAS runs a clearing service in August and September: lists of courses which still have places available are published and it is up to you to approach the universities and colleges direct and put your case.

Art and Design Admissions Registry (ADAR)

ADAR runs a similar service to UCAS, but concentrates on courses in Arts, Crafts and Design. These may be at specialist colleges, or in the Faculty of Art and Design at a university for which other applications are made through UCAS. Courses are detailed in the ADAR handbook, available for £3 from Arts and Design Admissions Registry, Penn House, 9 Broad St, Hereford HR4 9AP, telephone 0432 266653.

ADAR does not work quite as far in advance as UCAS. Application and registration forms are available from 1 February, on payment of a registration fee (currently £16). The registration form should be completed and returned to ADAR promptly and the application form sent to your first choice of college by 31 March.

The registration form is straightforward and requires the usual personal information, plus details of your educational background, including exams for which results are not yet known, and the courses for which you have applied. You choose three courses, one 'first choice', one 'second choice' and one 'alternative second choice'. Your application will only be forwarded to the 'alternative second choice' if you are not offered an interview at second choice stage.

In theory you can have different courses at the same college as your first and second choices; in practice this may not be a good idea as the same members of staff may receive both sets of applications and may consider you equally unsuitable for both courses! If you do want to organise your application in this way, ring the college first and ask how they will react to it.

Popular courses often fill most or all their places with 'first choice' applicants and the ADAR handbook gives an indication both of the number of places available on each course and of the percentage allocated at first, second and pool stages. Don't waste your time applying as second choice to a course that will have no places left by the time it receives your form.

The course application form requires exactly the same personal and educational details as the registration form, and the same information about courses applied to, but allows you a page and a half to expound about yourself, your experience, your career aspirations and anything else you wish to add in support of your application. It also contains space for a referee's report. If you have left education recently your referee should be your head teacher; otherwise you should ask your current or most recent employer or some other responsible person who knows you and your

work, and can make a valid judgement about your suitability for an Art and Design course. When your referee has
completed their report, they should send the form direct to
your first choice of college, *not to ADAR.*

The timetable then proceeds as follows (these are the
exact dates for 1994, and may vary by a day or two from year
to year).

Some time during April you will hear whether or not your
first choice college wants to interview you. By 9 May the
interview should have happened and you should have
heard whether or not you have been offered a place – this
may be conditional on your forthcoming exam results. If you
have not been offered a place, your application will be
forwarded to your second choice, and you should have a
decision from them by 8 June. At this point lists of remaining
vacancies are forwarded to ADAR and thence to students
who have not yet been accommodated. It is then up to you to
contact colleges direct and try to find yourself a place.

Direct Application

For a number of the smaller and more specialist colleges,
you apply direct. You also apply direct if you wish to study
part-time at a university or college to which you would
apply through UCAS or ADAR for a full-time course, or if
you are a local resident applying to a single institution
within the UCAS system. This involves getting hold of an
application form and filling it in.

There are two important things to remember here: follow
the instructions, so that you give the information that is
required of you; and return the form by the required date.
Even if no official deadline is given (and a number of colleges
will receive applications throughout the year), you should
still apply as early as possible – probably about a year in
advance – or ring the college concerned for advice.

College application forms are not substantially different
from standard job application forms – or, if you prefer, they
are like the UCAS form without the code numbers. You are
asked for your personal details, educational and work
background, and details of relevant qualifications. You will

probably also be asked about awards, grants or sponsorship (i.e. who is going to pay your fees?), and to expand on your reasons for wanting to follow this particular course of study. The application form for the British School of Osteopathy, for example, gives you half an A4 sheet on which to 'write a brief account of the reasons for your interest in Osteopathy and complementary health care'. As with the UCAS form, this is the time to sell yourself and convince whoever is reading the form that you have an intelligent and informed interest in the subject, and a serious commitment to studying it.

If you are applying to a college of music and/or drama, you will usually find that they hold auditions twice a year, in October/November and in the spring. Apply in time to be auditioned the first time round – places on these courses are always much in demand, and if you leave your application until the second phase, you may find that you are too late. Some colleges ask for a registration fee to be sent with the application form, others only require it if you are called for an audition. In either case the sum is likely to be in the region of £25–£35.

Many colleges to which you apply directly ask for a reference to be sent with the application. As with the clearing houses, your referee should be someone who has known you for at least two years in a capacity that qualifies them to express an opinion about your ability to follow the course in question – an employer, former employer, teacher or careers adviser. Give them your completed form and ask them to send it on to the college with the reference.

Alternatively, a college will ask for the name and address of one or more referee, to whom they will apply direct. If they ask for an academic referee and you have not been in formal education for some years, an employer or careers adviser would probably be an acceptable alternative, but ring and check with the college first.

A 'character' reference can come from an employer, teacher or careers adviser, or from any professional person who knows you personally. If you are on good terms with your doctor or vicar, that is ideal, but a friend who is a civil servant or in some other 'respectable' employment will be perfectly acceptable. Remember that it is courteous to ask your referee's permission before giving out their name and address.

Deferred Entry

Within the UCAS system you can, if you wish, apply to a university or college a year in advance i.e. in autumn 1994 for a course starting in autumn 1996. Most institutions will accept applications for deferred entry, and there is usually a paragraph about it in the section on 'How to Apply' in the prospectus. If there isn't, contact the departmental Admissions Tutor for advice.

You will have to have a good reason for wanting to defer the start of your course – going abroad for a year, for example – and if you are made a conditional offer you will have to satisfy its requirements by 31 August of the year *before* your course begins. You cannot apply early to secure a place on a popular course, with the intention of taking A levels or an Access course in the intervening year.

Interviews

An interview for a place at university or college is no different from an interview for a job or anything else. It is a chance for them to see if they want you and, equally importantly, for you to see if you want them. Most universities which take mature applicants at all seriously will invite you for interview – after all, they are judging you at least partly on your enthusiasm, motivation and potential, which are much easier to assess face to face.

An interview may last ten minutes or you may be there all day, talking to various members of staff and to students and having a look round. Don't be afraid to ask questions – this is your big opportunity to find out what the place is really like.

The same general rules apply for all interviews – dress smartly, but not so smartly that you are uncomfortable or you look as if you're going on to a dinner dance afterwards; turn up on time; smile but don't giggle; be friendly but not gushing.

Do some homework beforehand. You will have read the course description in the prospectus, and you may well have talked to someone in the department on an informal basis. Be prepared to answer questions on why you want to study this subject in general and this course in particular. If what you like is the flexibility of the course, don't pretend that you are awestruck by the department's high standard of research, or vice versa. Either reason is valid. If you want to pursue a vocational course – Social Work, say, or Occupational Therapy – it is particularly important that you have some idea of the sort of work you would be doing when you have qualified and convince your interviewer that you have a sensible end in sight.

Don't be intimidated by interviews. Remember they need you more than you need them. You're doing this voluntarily so, if you don't like the place or the people, you don't have to go there, even if they make you an offer. If you've applied through UCAS, chances are you have seven other possibilities up your sleeve.

Portfolios

If you are applying for an Art or Design course you will almost certainly be asked to submit a portfolio of work. In many cases this will be the most important aspect of your application, so you should make a careful selection of your best work, including no more than about twenty-five pieces. If your work is difficult to transport for any reason, you may show photographs instead, but you should label them with details of the dimensions and the media used.

You should present your work in a standard artist's portfolio, measuring about 30 by 40 inches. Wherever possible put the work in flat so that it is easy to look at – like writing legibly in exams, it saves the examiners having to waste time working out what you're trying to say and keeps them favourably disposed towards you.

Individual colleges within the ADAR scheme will advise you on how to submit a portfolio when they invite you for interview. Six universities involved in the UCAS scheme have developed a Central Portfolio Submission Scheme, which means that, even if you are applying to Art courses all over the country, you can put your best work into one portfolio and know that everyone relevant will see it. The universities concerned are Aberystwyth, Edinburgh, Lancaster, Leeds, Newcastle and Reading. Once your UCAS form has been processed (normally by the end of January if you have applied in time for the 15 December deadline), you will be sent details of what to do. Alternatively, ring the Department of Fine Art at the University of Reading, which organises the scheme.

In examining portfolios, Admissions Tutors are looking for evidence of talent, commitment and potential. They want to know that you have a basic ability to draw, but also that you are capable of creative thinking. They will assess your eye for colour, your sensitivity to different media and your willingness to experiment with a variety of techniques.

You should include a sketchbook showing 'work in progress', and finished versions of some of your sketches to show how you progress from a rough idea to a polished piece of work. Your portfolio must also have some relevance to the specific area of study: you are unlikely to be accepted on a fashion design or sculpture course on the basis of a portfolio of landscape paintings.

Auditions

For performance-based courses in Music, Theatre or Dance, admission is likely to be by interview and audition. You may be asked to prepare two or three pieces of your own choice in contrasting styles; alternatively, set audition pieces may be prescribed. Musicians are also likely to be tested on their sight-reading ability. Auditions for Acting courses often require participation in a workshop with other interviewees, as well as performing prepared pieces.

Most prospectuses give an outline of the audition requirements and when you are invited for interview you will be told in more detail what is expected of you. You will probably spend all day at the college. Try not to be too daunted by this – remember that it is also an excellent opportunity for you to look around, ask questions and find out whether the course will suit you.

Entrance Exams

If you do not have formal qualifications and cannot show evidence of recent relevant study, you may be required to take a special entrance exam. This may be a formal test, lasting say two hours 'under exam conditions'; alternatively, you may be given two or three weeks in which to write an essay. Either way, this is an opportunity to demonstrate that you have the basic literacy skills needed to pursue the proposed course of study and have some grasp of the subject.

If you are asked to do such a test, try not to see it as an obstacle designed to deter mature students. In fact, it is insurance against embarking on a course for which you are not prepared. Far better to find out early that you need to start your studies at a lower level, than to go through the hassle of applying for a place and a grant and then find that you are floundering in the first week.

If, despite all that research, you are not happy on your course, do not despair. You may be able to transfer to another course, particularly on a modular programme – the best time to do this is at the end of the first year, but it may be possible at other stages too. If your circumstances change, you may be able to postpone entry to the course, or 'drop out' and start again later. If you transfer to another college, you may be given credit for work you have already done (see CATS, page 12).

If you abandon a course before the end of an academic year, you should inform your LEA – you will probably have to pay back a proportion of your grant. If you then re-apply for a grant you should still be eligible for the amount that would have been payable had you continued the original course. Providing you transfer to another eligible course, you will still be able to take out a student loan as described on page 34.

Which University/College?

The entries in this section can be no more than a guide to each institution: to describe every course and every facility would necessitate a work to rival the *Encyclopedia Britannica*. Every college and university listed below produces a wealth of information for prospective students, and the UCAS and ADAR handbooks list all the available courses at institutions registered with them.

What I have attempted to do is give a feel for each place: the general paragraph (in italics) contains whatever information about the institution or its setting I felt might be of interest; there follows an outline of the courses available, a description of the facilities that might be of particular relevance to mature students and an indication of how receptive the institution is to applicants who do not have standard academic qualifications. It is worth reading the entries for other universities or colleges in the same area as the one that interests you, as these might contain additional information about the city or its environs.

In order to avoid endless repetition, a few points that are common to most institutions are not covered in the individual entries:

ACCOMMODATION

Most universities and colleges of any size own or run some accommodation for students. The most common form is the Hall of Residence, which provides single or double study-bedrooms for anything from about fifty to several hundred students. Some Halls provide meals (normally excluding weekday lunches) with all students taking meals in a communal dining room; others are self-catering, with perhaps six or eight students sharing cooking facilities. Most halls have common rooms and bars and organise social activities.

Halls are considered a good introduction to college living, providing an easy way into a social life for first-year students and relieving them of the responsibility of having to look after themselves in the early stages of their course.

University flats are self-catering; they may be self-contained or grouped around communal kitchens.

Rooms in Hall and university flats are fully furnished, with chairs, a desk, a desk lamp and bookshelves as well as bed and wardrobe. Rent usually includes light, heat and bedding.

Rent varies from place to place: in 1993–4 you could expect to pay about £75 a week for full board in a Hall in London, £50–£65 a week at Leicester, £49 at the University of Dundee. Self-catering is obviously cheaper – between about £25 and £40 a week.

If you are a student at Cambridge, Durham or Oxford you will also be a member of a college, in which you will probably live for two years of a three-year course. Rents vary, but are generally slightly more expensive than Halls of Residence elsewhere.

Despite the almost universal increase in interest in attracting mature students, very few universities and colleges yet provide adequate accommodation for couples or families. Almost every Accommodation Office strongly advises that you have arranged accommodation for your family before you commit them to moving to a strange town. Many places will provide you with free or very cheap accommodation in a Hall of Residence for a few days in the summer holidays while you look around for somewhere more permanent to live.

CRECHES

Most universities, though by no means all specialist colleges, now provide some form of day care for the children of staff and students. The University and/or the Students' Union may subsidise fees or reduce them for those on very limited incomes. Costs vary enormously, from £15 to over £70 a week, with something in the region of £3–£5 for a half-day session being the norm. Some nurseries are registered with local councils, which should guarantee their facilities and staff reach a certain standard; most have qualified and experienced staff. A few are 'unofficial', run by students for the benefit of students. Whatever the arrangements, visit the nursery yourself and make sure you are happy with what is on offer: if not, you may be able to apply for financial assistance with childcare arrangements you make privately.

All university or college nurseries and creches have fewer places available than there are children who need them, so you should make initial enquiries as soon as possible. Don't wait until you have a confirmed offer of a place.

LIBRARIES, COMPUTING AND INFORMATION SERVICES

In addition to providing books and other learning materials, many university and college libraries now have access to all sorts of CD-Rom databases and bibliographic information. If they don't stock a book, they can almost certainly get it for you. The Joint Academic Network, known inevitably as

JANET, links all the universities in the UK and provides access to an enormous wealth of information.

All this can be fairly overpowering at the start of a course, so most universities provide an introduction to the library and its facilities during the 'Freshers' week before the start of the first term. If they don't, ask to be shown around – the librarians are skilled people who are there to help you.

When you register at the start of your course you will be given information about the library, its opening hours and its rules. One of the rules is likely to be that certain books are available on short-term loan only: if they are core texts to which everyone on a certain course will need to refer, you will not be allowed to take them away for more than a couple of days. And, of course, as in any public library, there will be a substantial reference section from which books cannot be borrowed at all.

In addition to the main library (or libraries if the college or university is on more than one site), most faculties or departments will have their own, smaller libraries, specialising in the subjects they teach.

Most courses, even Arts ones, now include an element of computing and if you do not have basic computer skills it is a good idea to acquire them at an early stage. Again, the Computer Services Unit will probably provide introductory courses (though you may have to pay a token fee) in the early part of your first term.

HEALTH CARE

The larger universities and colleges have their own Health Service, employing doctors, nurses and dentists to deal with routine and emergency care of students and staff. If you do not live locally and do not have your own GP within easy reach, you can register with the Student Health Service. If you prefer not to use the Student Health Service, or if your university or college does not run one, register with a local GP. In either case, you can consult your own GP if necessary when you are at home during the holidays, and re-register with him/her at the end of the course.

Many smaller colleges which do not have their own Health Service have nursing staff on site and a doctor on call in case of emergencies.

COUNSELLING AND WELFARE

All universities and colleges want their students to succeed, which means they will do their best to help you tackle any problems that may arise. Wherever you are, there will be a Student Welfare Office, a Counselling Service or something of that sort whose staff are trained to deal with the sort of problems all students face – financial difficulties, emotional or sexual problems, homesickness, exam nerves – in the strictest confidence. Many universities and colleges have a Mature Students Adviser with particular expertise in the problems of older students. You will probably be assigned to a personal tutor, normally a member of staff of the department in which you are studying, who should be the first person you approach with any difficulties, particularly academic ones. Many institutions also have a resident chaplain, and some have centres of worship that cater for all religions.

SPORTS AND SOCIAL FACILITIES

Most universities and colleges of any size have an active Students' Union, to which all students automatically belong, which runs clubs and organises social events of all kinds. Most also have comprehensive sporting facilities – gyms, playing fields, squash courts, swimming pools, etc – and offer the opportunity to learn a new activity or to compete at various levels. Smaller colleges often have an affiliation with the local university which enables students to use the facilities of the larger place; two adjacent colleges (such as Loughborough University and College of Art and Design) may share resources.

Membership of the Students' Union normally brings with it automatic membership of the National Union of Students, but there is no obligation to take part in any political activities unless you wish to (and there is likely to be ample opportunity if you do wish to).

Any club or society within the Students' Union is run by students, so it can only prosper if people participate. If the Union doesn't have a society for an activity that interests you, there is nothing to stop you putting a notice on the notice board and trying to start one.

CAREERS ADVICE

Almost every institution listed here has at least one Careers Officer who is available to give any advice or information you may require at any stage in the course. Degree courses are increasingly vocational in their approach and many, particularly in the fields of Engineering and Business Studies, have strong links with industry. This means that course tutors will also be able to advise you, and you may establish useful contacts as the course progresses.

The background information given in Chapters 1, 2 and 4 will clarify many of the points made in the following entries. A list of abbreviations used for degree titles is given on page 513.

The University of Aberdeen
Aberdeen AB9 1FX

Tel: 0224 273504 **Fax:** 0224 488611
Contact: Admissions Office

Number of Undergraduates: Over 8000
Percentage of Mature Students: About 26%
Male/Female Ratio: 1 : 1
Upper Age Limit for Mature Students: None specified

Learning Facilities: The libraries hold a total of more than a million items, including specialist collections, manuscripts and archives, notably the George Washington Wilson photographic archive of Victorian and Edwardian Scotland. The main library has 700 study places and there are 700 more in the other five libraries. There are comprehensive computing services and well-equipped language labs which include facilities for computer-assisted learning. Relevant courses have excellent technical and clinical facilities.

Creche Facilities: For children aged nought to five. Apply early for a place.

Mature Students Adviser: The Centre for Continuing Education will advise on applications, all students have a personal Academic Adviser and the full range of welfare services is available.

Accommodation: The University has plans to expand its accommodation. At the moment traditional Halls of Residence provide study-bedrooms for 40% of the student body and a place is guaranteed to any first-year student whose home is outside Aberdeen. There are also self-catering flats some of which may be suitable for married students, but no specific provision for couples or families.

Aberdeen University was formed in 1860 from the long-resisted merger of two medieval universities – Kings College, founded in 1495, and Marischal College, 1593. It is bizarre to think that for a period of over 250 years there were two universities in Aberdeen (and others elsewhere in Scotland) and only two in all of England.

Marischal College is a particularly splendid granite building, a fine example of the slightly austere beauty which the local stone imparts to the city. There is nothing austere about the oil boom, however, and Aberdeen has undergone massive expansion in order to deal with its role as the petroleum capital of Europe. It also boasts a striking coastline and easy access to the magnificent scenery of the Cairngorms and the Grampians.

Degrees Available: MA in Arts and Social Science subjects; BD; BTh; BEng or BScEng; LLB with a number of options; BSc in a range of Science subjects; BSc Health Sci; BTechnol; MB, ChB. Some courses are taught at the Scottish Agricultural College, and include such subjects as Agriculture, Animal or Crop Science, Arboriculture and Aquaculture. Petroleum Geology is available as part of a dual honours BSc.
Students of Medicine may take a one-year intercalated BSc between the preclinical and clinical parts of their course.
Courses in the Faculties of Arts, Divinity and Science are modular and there is a part-time programme in these areas and in Engineering and Health Science. Students may also enrol for individual subject study, completing units which count towards a degree course should they choose to take one.
Students without standard qualifications may join a ten-week, full-time residential Access programme taught in the summer

holidays before the start of the course. There is also a foundation year in Engineering.

Assessment: A combination of exams and continuous assessment, the balance varying from course to course.

How to Apply: Through UCAS. Aberdeen welcomes applications from prospective mature students, who may contact the Centre for Continuing Education for guidance about whether their qualifications are likely to be acceptable.

The University of Wales, Aberystwyth
Aberystwyth SY23 2AX

Tel: 0970 622021 (undergraduate admissions)
0970 623111 (other enquiries)
Contact: Admissions Office

Number of Undergraduates: Over 4000
Percentage of Mature Students: About 16%
Male/Female Ratio: About 1 : 1
Upper Age Limit for Mature Students: None

Learning Facilities: Aberystwyth boasts excellent University libraries with stocks totalling over 600,000 volumes, subscriptions to 3000 periodicals and over a thousand study places. In addition, the National Library of Wales, a copyright library with a collection of over four million books, maps and prints, is based at Aberystwyth and students are granted access to it by arrangement. Computing, language laboratory and audio-visual facilities are modern and extensive.

Creche Facilities: For children over the age of 18 months, with reduced fees for student parents.

Mature Students Adviser: Yes, and the University publishes a booklet entitled 'Opportunities for Mature Students', available from the Admissions Officer. Study skills courses for mature students are also offered.

Accommodation: All first-year students are guaranteed a place, usually in catering Halls of Residence. There are self-catering flats suitable for mature students, but no special provisions for couples or families.

Aberystwyth is the oldest of the colleges which make up the University of Wales, and has an established tradition of high academic standards which, despite its comparative remoteness, attract students from all over the world. It is also widely held to be a friendly and happy place to study. The Welsh language is strongly represented both on campus and in the town, and some courses are available through the medium of Welsh.

The pretty little seaside town benefits enormously from the facilities of its University, particularly the Arts Centre which, with its thousand-seater concert hall, 300-seater theatre, cinema screens and gallery spaces, attracts arts lovers from all over Mid and West Wales. For the more energetic, the glories of Snowdonia are on the doorstep.

Degrees Available: BA or BScEcon in a range of Arts and Social Science subjects; BD; LLB; BSc in a wide range of subjects; BEng in Software Engineering only (four years including a year's sandwich). There is a four-year course in Physics, of which the first is basically a foundation year, and a four-year course in Agriculture including a year's work placement on a farm or in an agricultural industry. The University also runs a Year in Employment scheme whereby all students may apply for a year's work placement between their second and third years of study.

Assessment: The emphasis is on exams, but most courses supplement this with continuous assessment, which may include a major project or dissertation.

How to Apply: Through UCAS, but you are invited to write to the Admissions Officer for advice first. A variety of alternative qualifications may be acceptable, and credit may be given for prior learning and/or experience.

The Academy of Live and Recorded Arts (ALRA)

The Royal Victoria Building, Trinity Rd, London SW18 3SX

Tel: 081–870 6475
Contact: Gillian Davison, Administrator

Number of Undergraduates: 150
Percentage of Mature Students: Varies
Male/Female Ratio: Varies
Upper Age Limit for Mature Students: None

Learning Facilities: TV and radio studios, two studio theatres, dance hall and rehearsal rooms.

Creche Facilities: No

Mature Students Adviser: Course tutor
Accommodation: None provided, but the Secretary keeps a list of local accommodation.

Situated in a massive Victorian building in South London, ALRA is an independent theatre school with a wealth of up-to-date facilities. It provides students with modern theatrical training for the theatre and for television, video and cinema. The prospectus stresses the need for hard work, commitment and high standards, but also emphasises the friendly nature of the Academy and the individual attention students receive. ALRA graduates have gone on to success in all aspects of theatre and the performing arts.

Degrees Available: A three-year Actor's Course and Musical Theatre Course, intended to equip potential actors, dancers and singers for professional life. The Actor's Course is accredited by the National Council for Drama Training. An intensive one-year post-graduate course aimed at mature and experienced students, and a course in stage management are also available.

Assessment: Informal assessment throughout, with a formal presentation at the end of each term.

How to Apply: Direct to the Academy, no later than July for entry in October of the same year. Admission is by audition and interview.

Anglia Polytechnic University
East Rd, Cambridge CB1 1PT

Tel: 0223 63271 **Fax:** 0223 352973
Victoria Rd South, Chelmsford CM1 1LL
Tel: 0245 493131 **Fax:** 0245 490835
Sawyers Hall Lane, Brentwood CM15 9BT
Tel: 0277 264504 **Fax:** 0277 211 363
Contact: Admissions Office on each campus

Number of Undergraduates: About 3500
Percentage of Mature Students: About 40%
Male/Female Ratio: 1 : 1
Upper Age Limit for Mature Students: None

Learning Facilities: Libraries on four sites containing over 300,000 items – books, journals, maps and audio-visual material of all kinds. There are comprehensive computing facilities throughout the University and a Media Production department to provide television and video equipment and produce related teaching and learning materials.

Creche Facilities: On all three campuses, for children aged two to five. Contact the Nursery Supervisor as soon as possible to book a place.

Mature Students Adviser: Within Student Services.

Accommodation: There are self-catering Halls at Cambridge and Chelmsford, and some University houses at Brentwood. In addition, the University controls nearly a thousand bed spaces in managed houses. The Accommodation Office will help all students and give priority to first years whose home is not within reasonable commuting distance. No special provision for couples or families.

Anglia is a composite university with three main campuses – at Cambridge, Chelmsford and Brentwood; a smaller campus at Danbury, near Chelmsford, where conferences and management training are held; and a number of regional colleges: see separate entries for Colchester Institute (page 128), City College, Norwich (page 127), Norfolk Institute of Art and Design (page 253) and Writtle College (page 389). The oldest part is the Cambridge campus, founded by John Ruskin in 1858. Major expansion is taking place at Chelmsford and a new 'state of the art' learning centre should be open for the 1994/95 session.

Anglia is particularly active in promoting international links, in Europe and worldwide; many students now have the opportunity to study abroad, and the student community is a cosmopolitan one.

Degrees Available: At Cambridge: BA and BSc in an Interfaculty Scheme allowing a wide choice of subjects and combinations of subjects in Arts, Social Science and Science; also BA in Illustration or Graphic Arts and BSc in Radiography.

At Chelmsford: BA, BSc or BEng in subjects connected with Building, Business, Information and Technology; also in Nursing; LLB.

At Brentwood: BA or BSc in Combined Studies, with a limited number of subjects available; BEd in primary or secondary teaching, the secondary courses for mature applicants with post A-level qualifications or experience.

The first year of a few Science and Arts courses may be taken on a franchise basis at regional colleges: contact the Admissions Office for details.

All degrees are modular and many can be followed part-time.

Assessment: A combination of exams and coursework, including seminars, dissertations and practical work, as appropriate, with each module assessed separately.

How to Apply: Through ADAR for Illustration and Graphic Arts, otherwise through UCAS.

Anglia welcomes applications from those wishing to return to study after a gap and a wide range of alternative qualifications will be considered – Access Courses, professional qualifications, Open University credits, etc. Relevant skills developed in paid or voluntary work or independent study will also be taken into account, and the University operates a CATS scheme (see page 12), so that credit can be given for prior learning.

You are welcome to contact Student Services on your nearest campus to discuss your application before you submit it formally.

Institute of Archaeology
University College London,
31–34 Gordon Square, London WC1H 0PY

Tel: 071–380 7495 **Fax:** 071–383 2572
Contact: Receptionist

Number of Undergraduates: About 300
Percentage of Mature Students: About 40%
Male/Female Ratio: About 1 : 1
Upper Age Limit for Mature Students: None

Learning Facilities: The Institute has one of the finest archaeological libraries in the world, with 31,000 books, 22,000 pamphlets and nearly 2000 periodicals, of which 850 are current subscriptions. During term-time the library is open until 9 p.m. two evenings a week; it is also open on Saturday. There are first-class specialist teaching and research facilities, including over 20 dedicated laboratories.

The Institute was founded in the 1930s through the efforts of the great archaeologist Sir Mortimer Wheeler and his wife. Since 1986 it has been part of University College London, combining its own expertise with that of UCL's – where departments of Egyptology and Classical Archaeology already existed – to produce a unique Centre for Archaeology and Ancient World Studies. The range and depth of courses available in Archaeology are second to no other institution in the UK, and arguably the world.

The Institute occupies a separate site, just across the road from UCL and round the corner from Senate House and the University of London Students' Union.

For more information, see University College London (page 362).

Degrees Available: BA or BSc in Archaeology, full- or part-time. Part-time you would normally complete the degree in six years.

Assessment: The course is made up of units, which are assessed separately. All students produce a major project and complete at least 70 days field work experience.

How to Apply: Through UCAS to University College London. You are welcome to contact the Admissions Tutor at the Institute for an informal discussion before submitting your application.

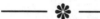

Architectural Association School of Architecture
34–36 Bedford Square, London WC1B 3ES

Tel: 071–636 0974 **Fax:** 071–414 0782
Contact: Sandra Morris, Registrar

Number of Undergraduates: 300
Percentage of Mature Students: 33%
Male/Female Ratio: 3 : 2
Upper Age Limit for Mature Students: None

Learning Facilities: The library has 25,000 books and is open from 10 a.m. to 6.30 p.m. on Tuesdays, Thursdays and Fridays and till 6 p.m. on Mondays and Wednesdays. The School has computer facilities, a photographic darkroom, video studio, etching press and a workshop with welding and casting facilities.

Creche Facilities: No
Mature Students Adviser: Contact the Registrar's Office.
Accommodation: There is no college accommodation, but students are helped to find accommodation at the start of the academic session.

Degrees Available: Exemption from the RIBA Part 1 and 2 examinations (i.e. the equivalent of a first degree and diploma in Architecture). This can take five years, comprising one year's foundation course, two years in the Intermediate School and two in the Diploma School. New students who have obtained satisfactory qualifications elsewhere may join the course at the Intermediate or Diploma stage.

The School runs a one-year full-time foundation course and a one-year day-release Access Course.

Assessment: A design portfolio and other submissions (in, for example, General Studies and Technical Studies) are made at each stage of the course.

How to Apply: Write to the Registrar's Office for an application form. Applications are processed on an individual basis and there is no official deadline. Non-traditional qualifications are accepted at the discretion of the school. Placing is dependent on interview and portfolio assessment.

Askham Bryan College
Askham Bryan, York YO2 3PR

Tel: 0904 702121 **Fax:** 0904 702629
Contact: Registrar

Number of Undergraduates: About 15 out of a total of about 400 full-time students
Percentage of Mature Students: About 25%
Male/Female Ratio: 7 : 3 overall
Upper Age Limit for Mature Students: None specified

Learning Facilities: The library has extensive stocks of books, periodicals and audio-visual materials relevant to the courses. There is comprehensive computing equipment, a forestry training centre, college farms, a horticultural unit and workshops and labs for Engineering and Applied Science.

Creche Facilities: No
Mature Students Adviser: No, but all students have a personal tutor.
Accommodation: The College residence (self-catering) can accommodate 244 students; the Student Support Service Manager will help find rented accommodation in the surrounding villages or in York. No special provision for couples or families.

Askham Bryan is a specialist college, providing education and training at a number of levels for those wishing to work in the land-based industries. In addition to the specialist facilities mentioned above, it has an association with the nearby York Riding School, where students can use the superb facilities and keep their own horses!

The College has an active Students' Union with plenty of social activity; the large student population of York, four miles away, means that there are lots of additional facilities there.

Degrees Available: BA in Business Management; BSc in Land Management and Technology or in Land Resources Management. These are one-year 'top-up' courses for those who have completed a suitable HND (also available at the college).

Assessment: By a combination of written tests and practical assessments. Degrees are modular and each unit is assessed separately during and at end of semester in which it is taught.

How to Apply: Through UCAS.

The College welcomes applications from prospective mature students. Prior learning and/or experience will be taken into account when considering your application, but remember that the degree courses are designed primarily for those who have already completed an HND. You are welcome to contact the Registrations Office to discuss your needs and to arrange an informal visit or interview.

Aston University

Aston Triangle, Birmingham B4 7ET

Tel: 021–359 6313 **Fax:** 021–333 6350
Contact: Registry

Number of Undergraduates: About 3750
Percentage of Mature Students: 13%
Male/Female Ratio: 6 : 5
Upper Age Limit for Mature Students: None

Learning Facilities: The spacious library has 350,000 volumes and 600 reader spaces; it is open 13 hours a day during the week and shorter hours at the weekend. The Information Technology facilities are among the best at any UK university and the Centre for Continuing Education provides tutored video instruction, by which lectures or classes are made available on video for revision purposes or to enable students to catch up on something they have missed.

Creche Facilities: For children from the age of 6 weeks. You are advised to apply well in advance.

Mature Students Adviser: Not as such: services for mature students are integrated into general student services.

Accommodation: Places are available for about two-thirds of all full-time students, and guaranteed for first-years who do not live within easy commuting distance. Most accommodation is in the form of single study-bedrooms organised into self-catering units of between three and twelve people. Studio flats are available for 66 married students (without children).

Aston prides itself on the practical approach of its courses and the marketable qualifications it gives its students: it has an enviable record of graduate employment. About two-thirds of undergraduates spend a 'sandwich' year in industry as part of their course.

The University is on a modern campus near the centre of Birmingham, with easy access to almost anywhere.

Degrees Available: BEng or BSc, either three-year full-time or four-year sandwich courses. There is also a four-year BSc in International Business and Modern Languages with a year spent abroad in France or Germany. The Combined Honours programme in Science allows great flexibility in combinations of subjects.

A four-year 'steps' course in Engineering comprises a foundation year followed by the standard three-year BEng programme.

There is also an Access course in Life and Health Sciences.

All undergraduate degree courses are full-time.

Assessment: A combination of exams, continuous assessment and project work. Where applicable, your performance during your sandwich year will also be assessed.

How to Apply: Through UCAS. Prospective mature students without traditional qualifications will normally be interviewed and assessed on an individual basis: the University will be looking for evidence of recent successful academic study (professional qualifications, Access courses, etc), but suitability for the course and motivation are also important.

Avon and Gloucestershire College of Health
Glenside, Blackberry Hill, Stapleton, Bristol BS16 1DD

Tel: 0272 585655 **Fax:** 0272 758498
Contact: Recruitment Office (0272 650485)

Number of Undergraduates: About 1500
Percentage of Mature Students: 45%

Male/Female Ratio: About 1 : 9
Upper Age Limit for Mature Students: None specified

Learning Facilities: The library provides a wide range of books, periodicals and audio-visual materials. There is a modern computer suite and up-to-date technical and clinical facilities.

Creche Facilities: No
Mature Students Adviser: No, but all students have a personal tutor.
Accommodation: Normally offered to all first-year students whose homes are outside the county of Avon. No special provision for couples or families.

The Glenside Centre, the main teaching centre of the College, is housed in a Victorian building on the River Frome, an attractive setting about four miles out of Bristol. The College has close links with the University of Bristol and the University of the West of England, and students have access to the resources of these larger institutions.

Degrees Available: BSc in Midwifery, Physiotherapy or Radiography.
   Part-time study may be possible – contact the College for details.

Assessment: A combination of exams and continuous assessment, with clinical, practical and casework all taken into consideration.

How to Apply: Through UCAS, but contact the College first to discuss your needs. You should expect to be invited for interview. You will need to show evidence of recent academic study, such as an appropriate BTEC, Open University or Access course with Biological Science studied at an acceptable level. Vocational motivation is also essential.

University of Wales Bangor
Bangor, LL57 2DG

Tel: 0248 351151
Contact: Academic Registrar

Number of Undergraduates: 3720 full-time
Percentage of Mature Students: 32%
Male/Female Ratio: 4 : 3
Upper Age Limit for Mature Students: None

Learning Facilities: Eight libraries with a total of 500,000 books, pamphlets and periodicals and space for 800 readers. The Department of Archives and Manuscripts and the Welsh Library (the latter with much printed material in Welsh) are a rich source of information on all things Welsh. An Information Service Directorate helps students find the information they need for set work or private research. There are comprehensive computing facilities. Bangor pioneered the use of digital language laboratory technology in Britain: the language lab computers are able to record and play back digital sound.

Three farms within easy reach of the University provide facilities for teaching and research in the School of Agricultural and Forest Sciences; there is a field station and a Natural History Museum to supplement teaching in the School of Biological Sciences; and students of Ocean Science and Marine Biology benefit from two research vessels run by the University.

Creche Facilities: Creche run by the Students' Union; day care nursery run by the University with play schemes after school and in the holidays for children up to the age of 11.

Mature Students Adviser: Two – one for Arts and Social Science, one for Science and Engineering. The University produces a cheerful booklet answering questions mature students are likely to ask, and there is a Mature Students' Association.

An induction course on Study Skills is held before the start of the academic year, with other sessions later in the year. Accommodation: 11 Halls of Residence accommodate 2000 students in single rooms. Some offer part-board, more are self-catering. All first-year students who have been offered a place before clearing are allocated University accommodation. There are a few units available for families.

Bangor is one of the six constituent colleges of the University of Wales. Some 10% of its students speak Welsh as their first language, and all signs, official documents, etc, at the College are written in both Welsh and English. The setting on the edges of Snowdonia means that Bangor has great appeal for walkers and climbers.

In addition to the normal welfare provisions, the University runs a support service for students with dyslexia or related learning difficulties.

Degrees Available: BA in Arts and Social Science subjects; BD Theology; BMus; BSc in a wide variety of subjects with the normal Biology, Chemistry and Physics supplemented by Agriculture, Forestry, Ocean Science and related fields; BSc General in Radiography and Diagnostic Imaging; BEng.

Some science and engineering courses are four-year sandwiches with a year's industrial or other appropriate placement; some are four-year franchised courses (see page 4) with the first two years spent at the North East Wales Institute at Wrexham (see separate entry, page 255) or at Llandrillo College. These courses are particularly suitable for those without traditional or relevant qualifications, as the first two years constitute a foundation course.

BA degrees may be obtained through part-time study over seven years, with the study load about a quarter to a third of that of a full-time student.

Assessment: Continuous assessment, exams, project work and practicals. Practicals are particularly important in Biological Sciences.

How to Apply: Through UCAS, but mature students are welcome to contact course tutors first to discuss individual requirements. A wide range of non-traditional qualifications may be accepted. The University welcomes applications from mature students who have the motivation and commitment to study for a degree and who have reached an appropriate standard of general education.

Bangor Normal College
Bangor LL57 2PX

Tel: 0248 370171 **Fax:** 0248 370461
Contact: Mr G.M. Lloyd, Assistant Principal

Number of Undergraduates: 940
Percentage of Mature Students: 27%
Male/Female Ratio: 1 : 2
Upper Age Limit for Mature Students: None

Learning Facilities: The library has over 60,000 volumes. There is one computer work station for every eight students, plus a TV studio, video editing suite, radio studio, photographic and reprographics facilities and laboratories.

Creche Facilities: Available at reasonable rates by arrangement with the University College of North Wales Bangor.
Mature Students Adviser: No

Accommodation: Self-catering accommodation in College hostels; all first-year students who requested it (82% of the total) were accommodated in 1993/94. No special arrangements for couples or families.

Bangor Normal College is on two sites, one in Upper Bangor, close to the University College, and one about a mile away, towards Anglesey. Easy access to Snowdonia makes this a favourite college for walkers and climbers. The prospectus is published in English and Welsh; most courses are conducted in English but the Normal College is very much a Welsh institution with a bilingual atmosphere. This will be particularly stimulating to those with some knowledge of Welsh who wish to extend their knowledge of the language.

Degrees Available: BA in Administration, Communication, Environmental Planning and Management, and Tourism and Leisure Management only; BEd (four years), including a qualification to teach at primary level.
The BA in Communication requires competence in Welsh.
All courses are full-time.

Assessment: In addition to exams in compulsory units, BA courses require a 10,000-word dissertation on a subject of the student's choice in the final year. Satisfactory performance in teaching practice is an integral part of the BEd course.

How to Apply: Through UCAS. GNVQs and BTECs are recognised as alternatives to traditional qualifications. Mature applicants for the BA courses must have O level or equivalent in English or Welsh; for the BEd courses they must have English Language and Maths.

University of Bath
Claverton Down, Bath BA2 7AY

Tel: 0225 826826
Contact: Mrs Gillian Trevett, Senior Assistant Registrar, or the Admissions Tutor for the relevant course

Number of Undergraduates: 3989
Percentage of Mature Students: About 11%
Male/Female Ratio: About 3 : 2
Upper Age Limit for Mature Students: None

Learning Facilities: The library has 300,000 books, subscriptions to 2000 periodicals and seating for 540. In term-time it is open incredible hours – until midnight during the week and from 10 a.m. to 8 p.m. at weekends. There are abundant computer facilities, most of them networked, and the Centre for Educational Resources and Development provides audio-visual aids, a television studio and photographic unit.

Creche Facilities: Day nursery, closed for an hour and a half at lunchtime, for two- to five-year-olds. Places are limited and there is a waiting list.

Mature Students Adviser: No, but all students have a personal tutor and the full range of welfare services is available.

Accommodation: Places for 1540 students in University residences. These are self-catering, but conveniently situated for the University's main refectories. All first-year students are offered accommodation. No special provision for couples or families.

The University of Bath, founded in the 1960s, occupies a compact, purpose-built campus on a hill on the east side of the city. Bath is an ancient and carefully preserved city whose thriving cultural activities include the acclaimed Bath Festival, but it is small and easy to get out of for those who prefer the nearby Mendip Hills or Wye Valley.

Despite its historical setting, the University prides itself on modern facilities and a practical approach to the future employment prospects of its students.

Degrees Available: BA in a choice of Modern Languages (including Italian and Russian for beginners), European Studies and Politics only; BSc in a range of Science and Social Science subjects, Architectural Studies and Quantity Surveying; BEng in a range of subjects.

Some of the Engineering courses include an Education element and lead to Qualified Teacher Status; some are four- or five-year sandwiches; some, also four-year, are available with French or German and involve a year abroad. The titles of three courses in the Department of Electronic and Electrical Engineering include the words 'for the European Market', and these are also four-year courses involving study abroad, as is the BEng in Chemical Engineering and Environmental Management.

A BSc in Physiotherapy is awarded by the University but taught at the Bath School of Physiotherapy.

Although the University runs no Access courses as such, an Access course in Sociology taught at the City of Bath College may be accepted as an entry qualification.

Assessment: Exams and project work. You must also show a reasonable level of competence in practical training and/or laboratory work where relevant.

How to Apply: Through UCAS. Bath welcomes applications from prospective mature students and there are no fixed entry requirements. You should be prepared to demonstrate 'the necessary ability, study skills and appropriate level of knowledge of any subject listed as a course requirement'.

Bath College of Higher Education
Newton Park, Bath BA2 9BN

Tel: 0225 873701
Contact: Mrs F.J. Roseberry, Senior Registrar

Number of Undergraduates: 2102 full-time, 55 part-time
Percentage of Mature Students: 34%
Male/Female Ratio: 1 : 4
Upper Age Limit for Mature Students: 45 for teacher training courses; otherwise none

Learning Facilities: Libraries on two sites hold a total of 145,000 volumes and subscribe to 500 periodicals. Both are open until 8 p.m. several days a week, and Newton Park is also open on Saturday mornings. The College has an extensive collection of audio-visual materials and a specialist book and slide library for art and design courses. General use computing facilities are available, with dedicated facilities in some departments.

Creche Facilities: No
Mature Students Adviser: No, but there are full welfare services available to all students.
Accommodation: 67% of first-year students are allocated College accommodation. There are no special provisions for couples or families.

BCHE is situated on two sites, Art and Design on Sion Hill, within walking distance of the centre of Bath, and the main campus at Newton Park, four miles west of the city. Both sites combine Georgian elegance with modern buildings and equipment. The music section is particularly proud of its facilities, with the Michael Tippett Centre at Newton Park including an auditorium with superb acoustics, sound studio and rehearsal space.

Degrees Available: BA in Ceramics, Fine Art, Graphic Design, Music or Sound and Image; BSc in Food Management, Human Ecology or Social Sciences; BA/BSc with Qualified Teacher Status; BA/BSc Combined; BA Creative Arts.

All courses permit considerable flexibility. The honours courses can be completed over five years with 12 hours' attendance at college and about 22 hours' independent study per week. A modular scheme operates in the BA/BSc with QTS, Combined and Creative Arts degrees. Thus a student for a BA with QTS can take such diverse subjects as Environmental Biology, Creative Studies in English and Textile Design Studies, on a part-time basis if required. The college operates a CATS system for some courses (see page 12) – call Dr Jon Press on the above number for details.

Assessment: By continuous assessment and exams, with about 60% of the overall assessment through course work. Satisfactory performance on teaching practice is essential in QTS courses.

How to Apply: Through ADAR for Art and Design, through UCAS for other full-time courses. For part-time study and for entry to the CATS scheme, contact the College direct.

Mature students without traditional qualifications are considered individually and sympathetically, with no standard entry requirements. They must be able to 'demonstrate the necessary motivation, potential and knowledge to follow the course successfully'. Applications from students on kitemarked Access courses are welcome.

Mature students are particularly advised to apply early – i.e. preferably in October of the year before the course begins. Because they receive individual attention, processing of applications takes time. Admissions staff do not have time to give mature candidates the attention they deserve if new applications are received in June-September for October entry.

Bedford College of Higher Education
37 Lansdowne Rd, Bedford MK40 2BZ

Tel: 0234 351966
Contact: Assistant Academic Registrar

Number of Undergraduates: About 2500
Percentage of Mature Students: About 40%
Male/Female Ratio: About 2 : 3

Upper Age Limit for Mature Students: None specified

Learning Facilities: There is a main library on each site, with large stocks of books, journals and audio-visual materials. A wide range of databases is also available.

Creche Facilities: At Polhill, with facilities for children aged three to five.

Mature Students Adviser: Not specifically, but there is a full-time counsellor to help all students.

Accommodation: There are four Halls of Residence but demand for places is always high and priority is given to young students leaving home for the first time. The Accommodation Office has a comprehensive list of suitable rented accommodation and the College aims to ensure that all its students have a comfortable place to live.

Bedford has a long-established tradition in the field of teacher training, and was one of the first places to train women as teachers of Physical Education. The College is on three main sites, although degree courses are taught at only two of them. Phys Ed, Environmental Studies and the Expressive Arts are taught at Lansdowne, close to the centre of town, with Primary Education, the Humanities and Business Studies at Polhill, a little way out of town to the east.

An attractive and typically English-looking town on the River Ouse, Bedford has large Italian, Polish and Indian populations and the cultural diversity that goes with them. It is about halfway between London and Birmingham, close to the M1 and easy to get to from almost anywhere in England.

Degrees Available: BA or BSc in a limited number of subjects; BEd (four years) specialising in Physical Education at secondary level, or in one of eight subjects (including Physical Education) in a modular scheme at primary level. The BA and BSc courses are also modular and may be followed part-time, in which case they would normally take five years to complete.

The first year of some BSc courses from De Montfort University can also be followed at Bedford in accordance with the linked student scheme (see page 4); students would then transfer to De Montfort's Leicester campus for the rest of the course. Contact the College for details.

Bedford also runs a programme of Access courses.

Assessment: Successful performance in teaching practice is a major part of the BEd degree and all courses include a major final-year project.

How to Apply: Through UCAS. Applications are welcome from students on one of the College's Access courses, or from those with relevant experience, especially of working with children. GCSE or equivalent in English Language and Maths is still required.

For part-time study or to become an Associate Student, contact the Course Director at the above address.

Birkbeck College (University of London)
Malet St, London WC1E 7HX

Tel: 071–580 6622 **Fax:** 071–631 6270
Contact: Registrar's Office for general enquiries; the Secretary or Admissions Tutor of the relevant department for enquiries about individual courses

Number of Undergraduates: About 2200
Percentage of Mature Students: 90%
Male/Female Ratio: 1 : 1
Upper Age Limit for Mature Students: None

Learning Facilities: There are two extensive libraries, computer facilities and a Language Centre. In term-time the main library is open until 10.30 p.m. during the week, the Gresse St library until 9.30 and both are open all day on Saturday. Students are also entitled to use the main University of London library, which is next door.

Creche Facilities: An evening nursery, open from 5.30 to 9 p.m., looks after children from the age of 6 months.
Mature Students Adviser: You will be assigned a personal tutor. Development or renewal of study skills is covered in the early part of all courses.
Accommodation: The College has no accommodation of its own, but full-time students and those undertaking a period of full-time study in a part-time course may apply for a place in a University of London Hall of Residence, or consult the University Accommodation Office, Senate House, Malet St, London WC1E 7HU, telephone 071–636 2818, for advice.

Birkbeck is unique among the institutions of Higher Education described in this book in that all its undergraduate courses are part-time, taught in the evening with the needs of mature students and those with work or domestic commitments in mind.

Degrees Available: BA; BSc; LLB. All courses are taught part-time and you can expect to obtain a degree after four years. Full-time study is possible in the latter stages of some courses.

The College also provides Access courses in Law, Contemporary Studies and Science – these can be completed after a year's part-time study.

Assessment: A combination of exams, dissertations, field work and practical work as appropriate. Most Birkbeck degrees are modular, assessed at the end of each unit.

How to Apply: Direct, on an application form obtainable from the Registry (071–631 6307/6390). You may submit an application from January onwards for courses due to start the following autumn. The prospectus gives closing dates or dates of interviews for each course. If places are still available, a second round of interviews may be held in September, in which case you should apply by the end of August, but the more popular courses will be full by then.

The normal entry requirements may be waived for mature students and credit may be given for previous study.

The University of Birmingham
Edgbaston, Birmingham B15 2TT

Tel: 021–414 3344 **Fax:** 021–414 3907
Contact: Director of Admissions

Number of Undergraduates: 11,453
Percentage of Mature Students: 11%
Male/Female Ratio: About 1 : 1
Upper Age Limit for Mature Students: None

Learning Facilities: The library has two million books. The Computing Service provides extensive computer facilities and short courses. There is also a Modern Languages Unit with language labs. All Science, Technology and Engineering departments have appropriate technical facilities and support.

Creche Facilities: A day nursery is run for pre-school children from the age of three weeks.

Mature Students Adviser: Yes, based in the Student Support and Counselling Service. The University also publishes a leaflet entitled 'Mature Students Guide to the Student Support and Counselling Service', concerned largely with financial matters.

Accommodation: The University guarantees accommodation in Halls or self-catering student villages for first-year students who are single and/or coming alone to Birmingham. A student village about two miles south of the University has facilities for families.

One of the most popular universities in the UK, Birmingham is situated on a single campus about two miles from the city centre. It boasts some of the best sports and social facilities in the country and runs an outdoor pursuits centre at Coniston in the Lake District.

Birmingham, as England's second city, boasts all the facilities one would expect, with three particularly fine concert venues – the new International Conference Centre Arena, the Symphony Hall and the NEC – catering for all musical tastes.

Degrees Available: BA in a wide variety of subjects, including African Studies, East Mediterranean History, and Portuguese, Russian and Modern Greek as well as the more frequently offered modern languages; BMus; BCom in Business Administration with a modern language; BSocSc in Economics, International Studies and Money, Banking and Finance, all with a modern language; LLB; BSc; BEng; BDS; BMedSc in Biomaterials and Medical Science; BNurs; BPhys; MB, ChB.
There are also foundation courses in Engineering and Access courses in Engineering and in Business Studies.

Assessment: A mixture of exams and continuous assessment.

How to Apply: Through UCAS. Although UCAS's closing date is 15 December, mature students are advised to apply early, preferably in September or October of the year before entry. Birmingham recognises a wide range of non-standard qualifications.

Birmingham Conservatoire
Paradise Place, Birmingham B3 5HG

Tel: 021–331 5901/2 **Fax:** 021–331 5906
Contact: Admissions Secretary

Number of Undergraduates: About 300
Percentage of Mature Students: About 1%
Male/Female Ratio: 1 : 1

Upper Age Limit for Mature Students: None specified

Learning Facilities: A specialist library supplies scores and audio-visual material as well as books and journals relevant to the courses. There are modern facilities for teaching and practice, an electronics studio, a recording studio and recital hall. Students also have access to all the facilities of the University of Central England.

Creche Facilities: Available through the University of Central England.

Mature Students Adviser: All students have a personal tutor; other welfare and counselling services are available through the University.

Accommodation: Through the University Accommodation Office.

The Conservatoire – officially the Faculty of Music at the University of Central England – is the largest university music department in the UK and has been teaching music for over a century. It provides all the facilities of the traditional Conservatoire, giving students the opportunity to develop their musical talents in individual and ensemble performance; these facilities are supplemented by the academic and social elements of the university environment.

The Conservatoire occupies a modern building in central Birmingham, and professional concert performances take place in its renowned Adrian Boult Hall.

Degrees Available: BA in Music; BMus (four years); BEd (Mus), run jointly with the Faculty of Education at the University of Central England.

The BMus is essentially for would-be performers and composers; the BA prepares students for a wider range of careers. If appropriate, transfer between the two courses is possible, usually at the end of the first year.

Assessment: Exams, course work, presentations, recitals and a project. The performance aspects of the course are particularly important.

How to Apply: Direct to the Conservatoire for the BA or BMus: obtain an application form from the Admissions Secretary. Auditions are normally held in November and March, and application forms should be returned by end October and end February respectively. You are advised to apply before these deadlines, as auditions are allocated on a first-come first-served basis. Once you accept an appointment for an audition, you will be asked for a non-returnable audition fee, currently £35 per principal study.

Candidates who do not meet the standard entry requirements are welcome to apply, but should contact the Vice-Principal for more information first.

For the BEd, apply through UCAS to the University of Central England.

Bishop Grosseteste College
Lincoln LN1 3DY

Tel: 0522 527347 **Fax:** 0522 530243
Contact: College Registry

Number of Undergraduates: 750
Percentage of Mature Students: 19%
Male/Female Ratio: 1 : 7
Upper Age Limit for Mature Students: None

Learning Facilities: The library has 123,000 volumes, with an on-line link to the University of Hull library. A full range of computer facilities and learning support is available.

Creche Facilities: No
Mature Students Adviser: No
Accommodation: Available in single rooms with full board. 100% of first year students can be accommodated. No special provisions for couples or families.

Bishop Grosseteste College was founded as a Church of England College in 1862, and now welcomes students of any faith or none. Some 99% of its students enter primary teaching. Degrees are validated by the University of Hull.

The spacious campus is near the centre of Lincoln, an attractive city boasting Roman remains, a Norman castle, cobbled streets and the lovely cathedral, home of the famous Lincoln Imp.

Degrees Available: BA or BSc with QTS. These are normally four-year courses leading to qualifications in primary teaching, but part-time study is possible by arrangement.

How to Apply: Through UCAS. GNVQs at Level 3, BTEC awards or an NNEB (Nursery Nursing diploma) may be acceptable as alternative entry qualifications, and credits may be transferred from other courses. GCSE or equivalent in English Language and Maths is required, as is study beyond GCSE level in your specialist subject.

Blackpool and the Fylde College
Ashfield Rd, Bispham, Blackpool FY2 0HB

Tel: 0253 352352 **Fax:** 0253 356127
Contact: Admissions Officer

Number of Undergraduates: About 200 on degree courses, out of a total student body of about 30,000, mostly on part-time Community Education programmes.
Percentage of Mature Students: Varies
Male/Female Ratio: Varies
Upper Age Limit for Mature Students: None

Learning Facilities: Library and Learning Resources Centres on all four campuses.

Creche Facilities: On the Ansdell and Bispham campuses, for children aged two to five.

Accommodation: One Hall of Residence on the Fleetwood campus and plentiful rented accommodation in and around Blackpool. There is also a specially adapted Hall providing facilities for the disabled. Most students are local, but the Accommodation Officer has a list of suitable accommodation and will give any help that is required.

Blackpool and the Fylde College is an associate college of Lancaster University, though only the Design course is offered through Lancaster; other degree courses are in association with the University of Central Lancashire. The College is on several campuses, with Management courses taught at Bispham in the north of Blackpool and Photography and Design at the central Blackpool site in Palatine Rd.

Degrees Available: BA in Design, Photography, Hospitality Management or Hotel, Catering and Institutional Management. There is also a foundation course in Art and Design.

Assessment: A mixture of exams and continuous assessment, with practical creative work particularly important in Design and Photography.

How to Apply: Through ADAR for Design and Photography; otherwise through UCAS to the University of Central Lancashire. You are welcome to contact the Adult Guidance Adviser for an informal discussion before submitting your application. The College tries to interview all suitable candidates before offering them a place.

Bolton Institute
Deane Rd, Bolton BL3 5AB

Tel: 0204 28851 **Fax:** 0204 399074
Contact: Mrs B. Cockcroft, Registrar

Number of Undergraduates: 5500
Percentage of Mature Students: About 40%
Male/Female Ratio: About 3 : 2
Upper Age Limit for Mature Students: None

Learning Facilities: The libraries (on all three campuses) have about 100,000 books and 900 journals. There is a full range of audio-visual equipment and the Academic Computer Services department provides an Information Technology service to staff and students.

Creche Facilities: No
Mature Students Adviser: No, but there is an Access Officer who can advise on applications and qualifications; other counselling is available for all students through Student Services.
Accommodation: 800 single rooms are available in three halls; there are also 200 places in private houses managed by the Institute.

Bolton Institute is on three campuses in central Bolton and within easy reach of Manchester. The cost of living in Bolton is attractively low and students are entitled to the local 'leisure card', offering discounts on council-run leisure activities. The Institute maintains close links with local industry, which helps to keep its courses up-to-date and relevant.

The teaching day extends from 9 a.m. to 9.30 p.m., giving students considerable flexibility in the organisation of their timetables and making it possible for some full-time students to do all their class work between 10 a.m. and 3 p.m., which is obviously ideal for parents with children at school.

Degrees Available: BA, BEng, BSc.
Foundation courses lasting one year are available in Art and Design, Engineering, Civil Engineering and Textile Studies. Modular courses enable students to put together their own

programme, with either a single subject specialisation or a variety of subjects from Accountancy to Visual Arts. A maximum of twelve hours of 'class contact' per week is the norm.

Assessment: By course work and exams. Some courses include an individual research project in the final year.

How to Apply: Through ADAR for Art and Design courses, otherwise through UCAS. Bolton welcomes applications from mature students and has a policy of encouraging those with qualifications other than A levels and members of groups traditionally under-represented in higher education. While BTECs, GNVQs and a range of other qualifications are acceptable, emphasis is placed on judging the individual's ability to benefit from the course, in the light of their background and experience. For additional information, contact the relevant course tutor or the Access Officer in the Marketing and External Relations Unit.

Bournemouth University
Talbot Campus, Fern Barrow, Poole BH12 5BB

Tel: 0202 524111; 0202 314144 (admissions unit)
Fax: 0202 513293
Contact: Academic Secretary

Number of Undergraduates: 8000
Percentage of Mature Students: 8%
Male/Female Ratio: About 1 : 1
Upper Age Limit for Mature Students: None provided the application is realistic

Learning Facilities: The library has 120,000 books, subscribes to 1200 periodicals and is open seven days a week, including weekday evenings during term. There are a thousand computer work stations and the open learning facilities are open 24 hours a day. The facilities of the Language Unit are open to all.

Creche Facilities: Yes
Mature Students Adviser: Course administrators are trained to counsel mature students and a Mature Students' Guide is available.
Accommodation: Self-catering on-campus accommodation houses 240 first-year students out of an intake of 1800. There is plenty of university-approved hotel/boarding house

accommodation. While there are no special arrangements for married students, the Accommodation Officer will be happy to advise.

Bournemouth is a lively holiday town and most of the University is located on one attractively landscaped campus, about two miles from the centre. The recent 'greening' of the University means that most people are asked to travel to the campus other than by private car, and parking facilities are available only to those with special needs.

Bournemouth University also has four Associate Centres: the Bournemouth and Poole College of Further Education, the Isle of Wight College of Arts and Technology, Salisbury College and Yeovil College, where a number of foundation and first-year courses are taught.

Degrees Available: BA, BEng, BSc, LLB in the Departments of Applied Computing and Electronics, Conservation Sciences, Finance and Law, Management Systems, Marketing, Advertising and Public Relations, Media Production, Product Design and Manufacture, and Service Industries, and in the Institute of Health Services.

Four-year sandwich courses in such subjects as Engineering, Financial Services, International Marketing Management and Public Relations underline the University's close links with industry and the vocational emphasis of many courses.

Assessment: Many courses include a dissertation or major project in the final year. Placements in relevant industries are an integral part of all four-year courses (in Law, Accountancy, Engineering, etc). Shorter term practical experience forms part of some three-year courses e.g. Archaeology.

How to Apply: Through UCAS. The helpful booklet 'Applying to Bournemouth University as a Mature Student' (available from the Academic Secretary) points out that the UCAS form reflects the fact that the majority of applicants are school leavers with conventional qualifications. It advises mature applicants not to be put off by this, but to ensure that all relevant qualifications and experience are recorded; the 'further information' section is particularly important, as it gives mature students the opportunity to demonstrate that they have 'the knowledge needed to start and the motivation to succeed'.

Bournemouth is committed to 'the principle that you should not need to be taught again something which you have already thoroughly mastered at the right level'. Credit for previous study or work experience may enable you to start a course in the second year. Ask the Academic Secretary for the booklet 'Getting the

Credit' and, if appropriate, apply for exemption from the first
year's studies as soon as you apply for your course.

The University of Bradford
Bradford BD7 1DP

Tel: 0274 733466 **Fax:** 0274 383218
Contact: Dr Gina Mitchell, Access Unit

Number of Undergraduates: About 6000
Percentage of Mature Students: 22%
Male/Female Ratio: 13 : 12
Upper Age Limit for Mature Students: None

Learning Facilities: The library has nearly half a million books and
750 study places. There is a Computer Centre, which provides
computing facilities throughout the University; there are also
labs in the Departments of Engineering, Computing, Biomedical Sciences and Archaeological Sciences.

Creche Facilities: An on-campus nursery caters for 49 children
from six months to five years.

Mature Students Adviser: Yes, in the Access Unit. The University
also publishes a helpful 'Guide for Mature Students' and
arranges seminars for mature students at which you can raise
questions with academic staff and with mature students already
at the University.

Accommodation: Halls of Residence (part board or self-catering)
can accommodate all single first-year students who live more
than an hour's journey away. Married students can obtain lists of
private accommodation from the University.

*Bradford has been a University since 1966, but it grew out of the needs of
the local textile industry in the 19th century, became a College of
Technology in the 20th and its history is reflected today in the technical
and practical nature of many of its courses.*

*The University is situated on a campus close to the city centre and
considers itself part of the local community. Bradford has all the facilities
of a big city; it is the home of the wonderful National Museum of
Photography, Film and Television and the work of one of its most famous
sons, David Hockney, is celebrated in a converted mill in nearby
Saltaire.*

*Bradford is also a remarkably cheap place to live, not least because of
the vast range of unpretentious curry houses and other ethnic restaurants
for which the city is renowned.*

Degrees Available: BA in Arts or Social Science subjects (Bradford is one of the few places where you can do a degree in Peace Studies); BSc in a range of Science subjects with the emphasis on Biological Sciences, although there is a unique course in Electronic Imaging and Media Communications; also BSc in Midwifery, Physiotherapy and Radiography; BEng in all the usual specialisms, including a number of four- and five-year sandwich courses; many of the Engineering courses can be taken with Management Science.

There is a foundation course in Engineering, and other foundation courses are available through local colleges.

Part-time study is possible on some courses in the School of Social Studies or through the Associate Student Scheme, which allows you to enrol for individual course units.

Assessment: Varies from course to course, but usually combines exams with assessment of essays or practical work. Most courses are modular and assessed at the end of each unit.

How to Apply: Through UCAS.

Bradford welcomes applications from mature students and does a lot to help them. A wide range of non-traditional qualifications will be considered, as will relevant experience. You are likely to be invited for interview and will be expected to show 'awareness of concepts, issues and problems relating to the course for which you have applied' as well as commitment to study.

If you are applying for part-time study, write direct to the Admissions Tutor of the relevant department.

Bradford and Ilkley Community College
Great Horton Rd, Bradford BD7 1AY

Tel: 0274 753026 **Fax:** 0274 741060
Contact: Admissions Officer

Number of Undergraduates: 6200 full-time; 25,000 part-time
Percentage of Mature Students: About 43%
Male/Female Ratio: About 1 : 1
Upper Age Limit for Mature Students: None specified

Learning Facilities: Extensive libraries on both sites, providing specialist and general books, periodicals, audio-visual materials etc. There are also well-equipped language labs.

Creche Facilities: On both campuses, for children aged two- and-a-half to five years.

Mature Students Adviser: Not specifically, but advice is available to all students through Central Student Services. There is also an Access Unit (telephone 0274 753052/3) to advise those wishing to return to study after a break.

Accommodation: Self-catering Halls of Residence on both sites accommodate a total of about 500 students. About 30 rooms in the Bradford Hall are adapted for use by less mobile students or those who use a wheelchair. The Accommodation Office will help all students find rented accommodation, which is plentiful and cheap, but may be some distance from the campus (although public transport is good). No special provision for couples or families.

Bradford & Ilkley is one of the largest Colleges of Further and Higher Education in the UK and offers students training for employment in various professional and vocational fields. It started life as the Bradford Technical School, established by local industries in 1882, and has maintained its practical approach ever since. It also has long-established links with the University of Bradford, which validates its degrees.

Most of the teaching is done on the main campus on the west side of Bradford city centre; part of the School of Teaching and Community Studies is based at Ilkley, an attractive if sometimes bleak spa town about twenty miles away across the Moors.

Degrees Available: BA in Community Studies (four years, including professional training), in the Schools of Art, Design and Textiles, Business and Professional Studies and a Combined Studies degree in the School of Teaching and Community Studies; BEd (four years, leading to a qualification to teach at nursery or primary level).
Some courses in Business and in Community Health may be followed part-time.

Assessment: A combination of exams, course assignments and projects or field work.

How to Apply: Through ADAR for Art and Design, otherwise through UCAS. For part-time study, contact the appropriate Course Tutor for advice.
The College welcomes applications from prospective mature students who do not have traditional qualifications, provided they can show evidence of adequate study skills and appropriate experience. Bradford & Ilkley also operates a CATS scheme (see page 12), so credit can be given for prior learning.

Bretton Hall
West Bretton, Wakefield WF4 4LG

Tel: 0924 830261 **Fax:** 0924 830521
Contact: Admissions Co-ordinator

Number of Undergraduates: About 400
Percentage of Mature Students: About 15%
Male/Female Ratio: About 1 : 3
Upper Age Limit for Mature Students: None specified

Learning Facilities: The library stocks all books, journals and audio-visual material relevant to the curriculum, and provides a number of CD-Rom databases. The Learning Resources workshop has facilities for word-processing and desk-top publishing.

Creche Facilities: Day nursery for children aged two to five. You are advised to register with the Nursery Co-ordinator as early as possible.

Mature Students Adviser: A special advisory service is administered by the Access Tutor.

Accommodation: There are 11 hostels on campus; 40% of first-years are housed in these and the Accommodation Office finds places in rented accommodation for all other first-years. No special provisions for couples or families.

Bretton Hall is an 18th-century mansion supplemented by purpose-built facilities, set in landscaped parkland just outside Wakefield. Although the setting is semi-rural, a number of big cities are within easy reach.

The Hall, now a College of the University of Leeds, offers education of high standing in specialist, creative courses.

Degrees Available: BA in the Faculties of Art and Design and Performing Arts; BA with QTS (three years) in nursery or primary education. Specialist subjects on offer include Textile and Surface Pattern Design and Theatre Design and Technology.
All courses are modular and many may be studied part-time: contact the Admissions Registrar for details.

Assessment: Some courses still have formal exams, but most use continuous assessment of practical and creative work, performance, essays, dissertations, etc. In English there is a written exam for which you are given the paper a week in advance.

All modules are assessed separately, during and at the end of the year.

How to Apply: Through ADAR for Art and Design, otherwise through UCAS. You are welcome to contact the Access Tutor for general advice, or the Admissions Registrar if you know what you wish to study but would like to discuss your circumstances with a member of the appropriate department.

A pass in a kitemarked Access course or in the Leeds University mature students exam will be accepted as meeting the entry requirements.

Bretton Hall operates a CATS scheme (see page 12), so credit may be given for previous study.

University of Brighton
Mithras House, Lewes Rd, Brighton BN2 4AT

Tel: 0273 600900 (switchboard); 0273 642814/5 (application information) **Fax:** 0273 642825
Contact: Registry (Admissions)

Number of Undergraduates: About 11,000
Percentage of Mature Students: About 30%
Male/Female Ratio: About 1 : 1
Upper Age Limit for Mature Students: None

Learning Facilities: The seven main libraries hold a total of over half a million items and subscribe to over 2000 periodicals. There are comprehensive computing and audio-visual facilities on all campuses and laboratories and studios for all relevant courses.

Creche Facilities: Subsidised facilities are available on the Moulse-coomb and Falmer campuses, with a nursery due to open on the Eastbourne campus by 1994. Demand for places exceeds supply, so contact the Nursery Supervisor on 0273 642022 as soon as possible.

Mature Students Adviser: The Access Co-ordinator will advise on qualifications and applications, and a full range of counselling services is available to all students. The University also publishes a separate prospectus for mature students.

Accommodation: Over a thousand places are available in catering or self-catering Halls of Residence at Eastbourne and Brighton; the Accommodation Office also has a long list of rented accommodation in University-run houses and flats or in the private sector. All first-year students can be accommodated, and a hundred places in shared houses are reserved for first-years aged over 21.

The University of Brighton is spread over four campuses: one, known as Grand Parade, in the centre of Brighton itself, opposite the outrageous Royal Pavilion; two, Falmer and Moulsecoomb, the administrative centre, a couple of miles inland; and one at Eastbourne, about twenty miles away along the coast.

As befits its position so close to mainland Europe, the University has particularly strong international links: many courses incorporate study of a second language and/or a period of study abroad.

From 1994 a no-smoking policy will be in force on all sites.

Degrees Available: BA or BSc in the Business School and in the Faculties of Art and Design; Education, Sport and Leisure; Engineering and Environmental Studies; Health; and Information Technology; BEng; BA with QTS leading to a qualification to teach at nursery or primary level.

Foundation years are available in a number of specialisms within Engineering and Environmental Studies.

Some courses, particularly in Business or Engineering, contain a sandwich element of up to a year. A number of courses can be studied part-time – contact the Admissions Office for details.

Assessment: A combination of exams and continuous assessment, with project and practical work, dissertations and teaching practice taken into account as appropriate.

How to Apply: Through ADAR for Art and Design, otherwise through UCAS. For part-time study, contact the Admissions Office for advice and an application form. The University welcomes applications from mature students without traditional qualifications and will consider all such applications on their merits.

University of Bristol
The University, Bristol BS8 1TH

Tel: 0272 303030 **Fax:** 0272 251424
Contact: Undergraduate Admissions Office

Number of Undergraduates: 8384
Percentage of Mature Students: About 10%

Male/Female Ratio: 11 : 9

Upper Age Limit for Mature Students: 30 for Medicine, otherwise none

Learning Facilities: The library, which has over a million items and subscribes to 6000 periodicals, is open in the evenings and at weekends. There is a Computing Service and a Language Centre, both of whose facilities may be used by all students. Relevant departments have excellent labs and technical facilities.

Creche Facilities: The day nursery caters for children aged 18 months to five years and is open all year, except on Bank Holidays and other days when the University is closed.

Mature Students Adviser: Yes. There is a Mature Students' Advisory Centre open on Preview Day, during Intro Week and at intervals throughout the autumn term. There is also a Mature Students' Society.

Accommodation: The University guarantees to provide accommodation for all first-year students, most of them in catering or self-catering Halls of Residence. Some flats are available for married students and families, but priority for these is given to overseas students.

The University of Bristol was founded in 1876, although its Medical School dates back to 1833. It was the first university in the UK to offer Higher Education to women students on an equal footing with men. Nowadays it is much admired for the quality of its research, with seven departments having been declared 'world class' in a recent official survey, while many others were deemed 'national centres of excellence'. It has also recently embarked on an initiative to cater for the needs of deaf or hearing-impaired students.

Most of the University is on a single precinct just to the west of Bristol. Its Students' Union is one of the biggest in the country, with a huge variety of clubs and societies.

Degrees Available: BA in the Faculties of Arts and Social Studies; BSc; LLB; BEng; BDS; BVSc; MB, ChB.
Subjects recently introduced include Pathology and Microbiology, and Economics with study in Continental Europe.
All undergraduate courses are modular.
Part-time study is available through the Department of Continuing Education in a number of Arts and Social Studies subjects.

Assessment: Varies from department to department, but most use a combination of exams and continuous assessment, with dissertations, practicals or project work playing an important part in some subjects.

How to Apply: Through UCAS. The University welcomes applications from mature students, but expects them to show evidence of recent study (Access course, Open University credits, BTEC award, etc) to supplement relevant experience. If you wish to discuss your qualifications before submitting your application, contact the Admissions Officer on 0272 303982. Once you have received confirmation from UCAS that your application has been processed, you are encouraged to send your CV and any other information in support of your application direct to the Admissions Officer, quoting your UCAS registration number.

British School of Osteopathy
1–4 Suffolk St, London SW1Y 4HG

Tel: 071–930 9254 **Fax:** 071–839 1098
Contact: Registrar

Number of Undergraduates: About 320
Percentage of Mature Students: About 12%
Male/Female Ratio: About 1 : 1
Upper Age Limit for Mature Students: None specified

Learning Facilities: The specialist library holds about 7000 books and a range of slides and audio-visual materials. Audio-visual services are also available. There is an on-site clinic, seeing about a thousand patients a week, where the practical elements of the course are taught.

Creche Facilities: No
Mature Students Adviser: No, but confidential counselling is available to all students, and tutors are very approachable about academic problems.
Accommodation: None available through the School.

The British School of Osteopathy offers the only degree course in Osteopathy available in the UK. It has been in existence since 1917 and occupies a specially adapted building near Trafalgar Square. In addition to the physical skills of Osteopathy, the course teaches a holistic approach to the human body and gives students considerable experience in consulting patients and taking case histories.

Although the standard version of the course attracts a mandatory grant, the extended pathway as yet does not. In either case, your LEA will probably only pay 15% of your tuition fees. This means you could find yourself having to pay upwards of £4000 a year in tuition fees alone.

Degrees Available: BSc in Osteopathy (four years). An extended pathway version of the course was launched in November 1993 – this takes five years, with the first three done part-time at weekends and at summer and Easter 'schools', supplemented by distance learning.

On completion of either version of the course, you will be qualified to practise as an Osteopath in the UK.

Assessment: There are written and oral exams, practicals and projects, but the course is a very practical, vocational one – you can expect to have completed 1200 hours of clinical training by the end of the four years.

How to Apply: Direct, on a form available from the Registrar. There is no official closing date, but you are asked to apply at least a month before the course is due to start.

Applications from prospective mature students who do not meet the standard entrance requirements are welcome and will be considered on an individual basis. Successful completion of a suitable Access course or Open University credits may be deemed to satisfy the requirements; alternatively you may be asked to take a six-week Access course in chemistry, anatomy and/or physiology either through the School or at the University of Westminster. These courses are free and are normally held in the summer holidays just before the start of the course.

You should expect to be invited for interview before being offered a place.

———— ❈ ————

Brunel: The University of West London
Uxbridge UB8 3PH

Tel: 0895 274000 **Fax:** 0895 230883
Contact: Admissions Officer

Number of Undergraduates: About 4500
Percentage of Mature Students: About 14%
Male/Female Ratio: About 3 : 1
Upper Age Limit for Mature Students: None

Learning Facilities: The two main libraries (one on each campus) have a total of 350,000 items and subscribe to 1800 journals. Library services are available all day Monday to Friday and on

Saturday mornings; the Uxbridge library is also open on Saturday and Sunday afternoons for study only. There are comprehensive computing facilities, a Media Services department and an Experimental Techniques Centre providing specialist back-up for teaching and research in Science and Engineering.

Creche Facilities: Available for children aged one to five and open 50 weeks of the year (closed at Christmas and Easter). Apply early by contacting the Nursery Manager on 0895 239125, extension 144/5.

Mature Students Adviser: Not specifically, but every student has a personal tutor, and the full range of counselling services is available.

Accommodation: Brunel provides University accommodation for all first-year students, normally in one of thirteen catering or self-catering Halls (five at Uxbridge, eight at Runnymede), which between them have places for over 1800 students. There are also a number of self-catering University flats, and the Accommodation Office has a database of rented accommodation in the private sector. There are no special provisions for couples or families.
The cost of accommodation at Brunel compares favourably with most other parts of the country, which means it is very cheap by London standards.

Named after the great Victorian engineer, Brunel has been a university since 1966 and has an excellent record of graduate employment. Many of its courses are 'thin' sandwiches – i.e. they include two work placements of 15–30 weeks rather than one lasting a full year – and enable students to obtain experience of two very different aspects of the industry concerned.

Most of the University of Brunel is based at Uxbridge, west of London and close to the M4, M40 and M25; the Faculty of Education and Design is at Runnymede, about 11 miles south and housed in an imposing mansion overlooking the Thames.

Degrees Available: BA or BSc in the Faculty of Education and Design, including a qualification to teach Industrial Design and Technology; BSc or BEng in a very wide range of Science, Social Science, Technology and Engineering subjects, including a number of four-year sandwich courses; LLB, also with a four-year sandwich option.
There are foundation years in Science and Engineering.
All degree courses are modular. For information about part-time study, contact the Admissions Officer.

Assessment: A combination of exams and continuous assessment, with each module assessed separately during and at the end of the semester in which it is taught. Essays, seminar presentations and a major final-year project or dissertation will all be taken into consideration, and satisfactory performance on sandwich placements is essential.

How to Apply: Through UCAS.

Brunel welcomes applications from mature students without traditional qualifications. A wide range of alternatives, including Access courses, GNVQs and BTEC awards will be considered. The University operates a CATS and an APEL scheme (see page 12), and credit may be given for prior learning and/or experience. Contact the Department of Continuing Education (0895 235332 or 203186) for advice.

The University of Buckingham
Hunter St, Buckingham MK18 1EG

Tel: 0280 814080 **Fax:** 0280 824081
Contact: Admissions Office

Number of Undergraduates: About 850
Percentage of Mature Students: About 33%
Male/Female Ratio: About 5 : 4
Upper Age Limit for Mature Students: None

Learning Facilities: The library is open till 10 p.m. during the week and all day Saturday and Sunday. It has access to a number of databases as well as providing books, journals, bibliographies and newspapers. The University also has full computing facilities and an up-to-date Life Sciences complex with labs, dark room, greenhouse, fish tank house and insectary. The Language Learning Centre provides up-to-date facilities including computer-aided learning.

Creche Facilities: No, but there is a good nursery in town.
Mature Students Adviser: In some schools of study, but all students have a personal tutor and the University has a long record of success with mature students.
Accommodation: University accommodation is guaranteed to all first-years who apply by the closing date (you will be given plenty of notice of this). There is limited provision for couples, but not children. Contact the Accommodation Office as soon as possible if you need married accommodation.

Buckingham is the only independent University in Britain, which means it receives no financial support from the government and students are charged the full cost of their studies (in other universities, the government subsidises tuition, so even if you are not eligible for a grant and have to pay your own fees, they are substantially lower). In 1994 the annual fee is £8712, and if you are entitled to a grant, the contribution your LEA will make is £2020. That leaves a substantial sum – in fees alone, never mind living expenses – that you have to find yourself. Some scholarships and bursaries are available – contact the Admissions Office for details.

Buckingham's academic year is structured differently to that of other universities. It runs from January to December, comprises four terms and allows most degrees to be completed in two years. Experience has shown that this appeals strongly to mature students. Classes tend to be small, and Buckingham prides itself on giving individual attention and support to all its students.

The University is situated on two sites in the centre of this pleasant market town, which is within easy reach of London and Oxford.

Degrees Available: BA; BSc; BSc (Econ); LLB.

The range of subjects is not enormous, but there are some interesting possibilities, notably International Agribusiness Management; English and European Law with French, German or Spanish; and Law, Biology and the Environment.

Some courses involve a pre-sessional element (in the autumn term before January entry), which may mean improving your English or mathematical skills at Buckingham, or an intensive period of language study abroad; these courses are open to all students but are only eligible for a grant if they are an integral part of the course.

Assessment: Mainly final exams, but some course work is taken into consideration. For courses in the European Centre, you will spend six months abroad and prepare a project which will count towards your final mark.

How to Apply: Through UCAS, but you are advised to send a CV direct to the University at the same time. Because the academic years starts in January, UCAS deadlines are not strictly applied: contact the Admissions Office for advice if you are applying late. If you do not have traditional qualifications, your application will be considered on the basis of your educational and work background and experience. You may be asked to sit a test.

Buckingham encourages mature students from all over the world and you are welcome to visit the University for informal discussions before you apply: contact the Admissions Office to make an appointment.

Buckinghamshire College of Higher Education
Queen Alexandra Rd, High Wycombe HP11 2JZ

Tel: 0494 522141 **Fax:** 0494 524392
Contact: Assistant Registrar-Admin

Number of Undergraduates: About 2200
Percentage of Mature Students: Not specified
Male/Female Ratio: About 3 : 2
Upper Age Limit for Mature Students: None specified

Learning Facilities: Three main libraries provide extensive coverage of the subjects taught at the College and access to CD-Rom databases. They are open in the evenings and on Saturday. Information Technology Services provide resources and training for all students and Media Services offer audio-visual equipment and technical support.

Creche Facilities: No
Mature Students Adviser: Not specifically, but there is a full range of counselling and welfare support.
Accommodation: Nearly 600 places in catering or self-catering Halls of Residence, with priority given to first-year students. No special provision for couples or families.

Buckinghamshire College of Higher Education is on two campuses, the main one in the centre of High Wycombe, the other twelve miles away at Newland Park, in beautiful gentle countryside near Chalfont St Giles. Health Studies and some Business and Management courses are based at Newland Park, and students will not usually have to travel between the two sites.

A School of Science and Art was founded at High Wycombe in 1893 and the modern College has a strong tradition in design, specifically furniture design and graphic design. Buckinghamshire CHE is now a College of Brunel: the University of West London, which validates its degrees.

Degrees Available: BA in Art and Design, Arts, Business and Social Science subjects and in Nursing; BEng in Product Design Manufacture only; BSc in Building Processes and Management, Furniture Production and in the Faculties of Computing, Engineering and Technology, and Health Studies.
Degrees at the College cover a very wide range of subjects, from a programme in Arts, Media and Culture to Business Information Technology. A number are four-year 'sandwiches'.
There is a one-year, full-time foundation course in Art and Design.

There are opportunities for part-time study and an Associate Student Scheme.

Assessment: A combination of exams and continuous assessment, with a strong emphasis on creative work in Art and Design courses and a final-year project or dissertation required in most other subjects.

How to Apply: Through ADAR for Art and Design, otherwise through UCAS for full-time study. You should expect to be invited for interview and, in the case of Art and Design courses, to produce a portfolio of work. For part-time study, contact the College direct.

The College has arrangements for accrediting prior learning and/ or experience as part of the applications procedure for mature students – a brochure giving details is available from the appropriate Faculty Registrar. Applications from mature candidates without traditional qualifications will be considered on an individual basis.

Buckland University College
Ewert Place, Oxford OX2 7YT

Tel: 0865 53570 **Fax:** 0865 52961
Contact: Academic Registrar

Number of Undergraduates: About 80
Percentage of Mature Students: About 22%
Male/Female Ratio: 1 : 1
Upper Age Limit for Mature Students: None specified

Learning Facilities: The specialist library provides good coverage of books and journals relevant to the College courses. Students also have access to the library at Oxford Brookes University.

Creche Facilities: No
Mature Students Adviser: Counselling and welfare advice is available to all students.
Accommodation: The College will assist in finding suitable accommodation, usually within walking distance.

Buckland is an independent college with high academic standards and firm academic discipline – you are expected to turn up to lectures and to do the work on time. Small classes mean students benefit from individual attention and support where necessary.

Although the course attracts a mandatory grant, your LEA will only pay a percentage of your tuition fee – in 1993/4 you would have had to find £2385 yourself. You also have to register as an external student with the University of London, and pay a registration fee: Buckland will advise you on the procedure for this.

The College is in Summertown, a pleasant part of Oxford about a mile and a half north of the city centre. Because Buckland is small, its own social facilities are limited, but students benefit from the wealth of resources which cater for Oxford's huge student population.

Degrees Available: LLB, offered as an external degree of the University of London. Part-time study, with attendance on Saturdays only, is possible, and under those circumstances you should be able to complete the degree in four or five years.
A one-year foundation course is also available.

Assessment: By exams at the end of each year.

How to Apply: Direct to the College on a form obtainable from the Academic Registrar's office. Applications are accepted throughout the year. Mature students should show evidence of recent academic study: the University of London will normally accept a Grade C pass in a relevant A-level subject.

Camberwell College of Arts
Peckham Rd, London SE5 8UF

Tel: 071–703 0987 **Fax:** 071–703 3689
Contact: Richard Frost, College Admin Officer

Number of Undergraduates: 700
Percentage of Mature Students: 17%
Male/Female Ratio: 2 : 3
Upper Age Limit for Mature Students: None

Learning Facilities: The library has 40,000 volumes and a wide range of periodicals. There are extensive computer facilities and appropriate laboratory and studio facilities for each course.

Creche Facilities: At Camberwell's sister college within the London Institute, the London College of Printing (see page 22).

Mature Students Adviser: Welfare staff are trained to deal with problems likely to be met by mature students. The Central

Welfare Service is operated by the London Institute, but there is a satellite service on site.

Accommodation: Two Halls of Residence run by the London Institute (see page 227) accommodate only about 10% of first-year students. There is no provision for couples or families, but the Institute's Accommodation Office will try to help.

Formerly the Camberwell School of Arts and Crafts, the College was founded in 1898 and adopted its present name in 1988. It is part of the London Institute, which comprises a number of London's colleges of art, printing, fashion and distributive trades and has been entitled to award its own degrees since 1992. Courses are largely practical, backed up by tutorials in relevant history and theory. Prospective students are encouraged to visit the College before applying – contact the Registrar of the appropriate School (Applied and Graphic Arts or Art History and Conservation) for an appointment.

Degrees Available: BA in the School of Applied and Graphic Arts and the School of Art History and Conservation. Graphic Design may be studied part-time over four years.

There is also a one-year foundation course in Art and Design.

Assessment: Through regular formal assessment of practical and theoretical work.

How to Apply: Through UCAS for degrees in Art and Design and in Conservation; through ADAR for Ceramics, Graphic Design (full-time), Joint Honours Art and Design, and Silversmithing and Metalwork; direct to the School Registrar of the School of Applied and Graphic Arts for Graphic Design (part-time).

You may be required to submit a portfolio before being interviewed for admission to some courses.

Relevant work experience may be acceptable as an alternative to educational qualifications.

Camborne School of Mines (University of Exeter)
Redruth, Cornwall TR15 3SE

Tel: 0209 714866 **Fax:** 0209 716977
Contact: R.J. Hancock, Assistant Registrar

Number of Undergraduates: 350
Percentage of Mature Students: About 6%
Male/Female Ratio: 9 : 1

Upper Age Limit for Mature Students: None

Learning Facilities: The library has about 25,000 books and reports and subscribes to 230 periodicals. There are extensive computer and engineering labs, plus Materials Science and geological facilities and the School has experimental mines.

Creche Facilities: No

Mature Students Adviser: Not specifically, but all students have a personal tutor.

Accommodation: The School runs two self-catering hostels with 30 places for undergraduates and can advise on local rented accommodation of all kinds. About a quarter of first-year students are allocated School accommodation, but you are advised to apply early. There are 4 flats for married students.

Cornwall has long been famous for its tin mines and its china clay industry, so Camborne is ideally situated for the study of minerals. The School was founded in 1859 and now has a worldwide reputation in its field. It occupies a purpose-built site between the towns of Camborne and Redruth. The School is now part of the Faculty of Engineering at the University of Exeter, and students can benefit from the University's Careers Service and other facilities.

Degrees Available: BEng in Mining Engineering, Minerals Engineering, Industrial Geology, and Minerals Surveying and Resource Management.

Assessment: Fieldwork (some of it during the holidays) and laboratory work form an important part of all courses.

How to Apply: Through UCAS to the University of Exeter. The School welcomes applications from mature students and is happy to give any advice you may need on which course to take or whether your qualifications are likely to be suitable. Contact the Assistant Registrar before submitting a formal application.

The School points out that a sound education in Maths and Science is essential.

University of Cambridge

Intercollegiate Applications Office, Kellet Lodge, Tennis Court Rd, Cambridge CB2 1BJ

Tel: 0223 333308 **Fax:** 0223 66383

Contact: Above address, or the Admissions Tutor of the individual colleges

Please note that unless you are applying for an Organ Scholarship, you are no longer allowed to apply simultaneously to both Cambridge and Oxford

Number of Undergraduates: 10,408
Percentage of Mature Students: About 4%
Male/Female Ratio: About 3 : 2
Upper Age Limit for Mature Students: None

Learning Facilities: The University has about a hundred libraries, including college, faculty and departmental libraries; as a copyright library the University Library is entitled to receive a copy of every book published in the UK. There are also large collections of periodicals, maps, music, manuscripts and directories. The Language Centre has facilities for computer-assisted language learning.

Creche Facilities: There are various schemes to assist student parents with the cost of childcare and the Students' Union produces a useful leaflet giving details. Contact the Welfare Officer at Cambridge University Students' Union, 11–12 Trumpington St, Cambridge CB2 1QA, tel. 0223 356454, or the Admissions Officer of your proposed college, for a leaflet.

Mature Students Adviser: Not specifically, but careers, welfare and academic advice is readily available.

Accommodation: At Cambridge you are admitted to a College which will house you (either in College itself or in nearby University-controlled housing) throughout your undergraduate course. Lucy Cavendish (women only), St Edmunds and Wolfson Colleges cater for mature undergraduates; there may not be special facilities in other Colleges.

Cambridge is, of course, one of the great institutions of learning in the UK – and in the world. The oldest College, Peterhouse, was founded in 1284; the largest, Trinity, by Henry VIII in 1546; a handful date from the 1960s and 1970s. A Cambridge degree still carries an enormous amount of weight in the outside world, and its academic standards, both in its admissions policy and in the courses themselves, are high.

The Colleges are scattered through the town, with only Girton and Homerton any distance from the centre. The wide range of sporting and cultural facilities available, the stunning medieval architecture of many of the Colleges, and the beauty of the famous 'Backs' all add to Cambridge's attractions.

Degrees Available: BA in Arts and Humanities, Education, Engineering, Mathematics, Medicine and Veterinary Medicine, Natural Sciences and Social Sciences.

Cambridge offers an extraordinary range of Modern, Medieval and Classical Languages, with Arabic, Hebrew, Persian, Occitan, Hungarian and Polish among the less commonly found.

For BEd courses taught at Homerton College, see separate entry (page 183).

Assessment: A combination of exams and assessment of practical or performance work, essays or dissertations, depending on the subject. Oral ability is important in Modern Languages.

How to Apply: Through UCAS, but by 15 October, not 15 December as with most other universities. By that date you must also submit a (yellow) Mature Application Form to the Intercollegiate Applications Office or to your first choice of College (you can obtain the form from the Applications Office or from any College).

Mature applicants who do not have standard qualifications will be considered on their individual merits. In addition to motivation and personal qualities, you will be expected to show evidence of academic strength (normally of recent academic study) and the ability to cope with the demands of a degree course. You will almost certainly be invited for interview and may be asked to sit a test. The attitudes of Admissions Tutors vary enormously from College to College, so you are recommended to contact several for an informal chat before submitting your application.

You may apply to an individual College or submit an open application, but mature students are strongly advised to choose a College that has a sympathetic attitude to mature students and apply specifically to it. Some details about the Colleges are given in the University prospectus, and each College also produces a prospectus of its own. With very few exceptions, all subjects are available at all Colleges.

Canterbury Christ Church College of Higher Education
Canterbury CT1 1QU
Tel: 0227 782420/422/423
Contact: Admissions Office

Number of Undergraduates: 2500
Percentage of Mature Students: 30%

Male/Female Ratio: 1 : 3
Upper Age Limit for Mature Students: 45 for Nursing, Occupational Therapy and Radiography; otherwise none

Learning Facilities: The library has recently been extended and contains over 160,000 books. Students can also use the City Library, the cathedral library and the library of the University of Kent. A wide range of computer and audio-visual facilities are available at the College, as is a well-equipped Language Centre.

Creche Facilities: The College has an arrangement with a nearby playgroup, and the Canterbury Day Nursery is next door.
Mature Students Adviser: No, but welfare services are available to all students.
Accommodation: Campus accommodation is not offered to mature students. The Accommodation Office will help if required.

Canterbury Christ Church College offers degrees validated by the University of Kent. It is a friendly place with an excellent academic reputation and is located only a few minutes' walk from Canterbury Cathedral. These factors combine to make it one of the most popular Colleges of Higher Education in England. Christ Church has strong links with Europe and a number of students have the opportunity to study abroad.

Degrees Available: BA, BSc, BA (Ed). The BA (Ed) is a four-year course at the end of which successful students also obtain a Certificate of Education and emerge with Qualified Teacher Status. An interesting range of Arts and Science subjects is offered, including American Studies, Radio, Film and Television Studies and Tourism Studies as well as the more widely available English, Geography and History. BSc degrees can also be obtained in Diagnostic Radiotherapy and Occupational Therapy.
The BA and BSc Combined Honours courses can be followed part-time, either during the day or in the evening or both. Part-time degrees are normally completed in four to six years.

Assessment: Many courses offer the opportunity for an Individual Study (i.e. a long essay on an approved subject) in the final year. Teaching practice is an important part of the BA (Ed).

How to Apply: Through UCAS. Christ Church welcomes applications from mature students, who are normally expected to have education to A-level standard or to have completed an approved

Access course. Mature applicants with non-standard qualifications who want to study part-time receive sympathetic consideration.

University of Wales College of Cardiff
P.O. Box 494, Cardiff CF1 3YL

Tel: 0222 874412 **Fax:** 0222 874130
Contact: Undergraduate Admissions Office

Number of Undergraduates: About 9000
Percentage of Mature Students: About 6%
Male/Female Ratio: About 5 : 4
Upper Age Limit for Mature Students: None

Learning Facilities: The library, the largest in the University of Wales, has over half a million books, including specialist collections, and subscribes to 5000 periodicals. It has 2000 study places and is open in the evenings and on Saturdays. There are comprehensive computing facilities and 'state of the art' laboratory equipment, all the result of a recent massive spending programme.

Creche Facilities: Available 45 weeks a year for children aged from ten weeks to five years. Apply early by contacting the Dean of Students' Office, 47 Park Place, Cardiff.

Mature Students Adviser: Not specifically, but all students have a personal tutor and professional counsellors are available. The University also produces a brochure, 'Mature Students at Cardiff'.

Accommodation: With 16 Halls of Residence, both catering and self-catering, and a number of University-run flats and houses, Cardiff can offer accommodation to over 4000 students and guarantees a place for all first-years. There are a very few flats suitable for married first-year students, with or without children: contact the Residents Office as soon as possible, but do not move your family to Cardiff until you are sure of suitable accommodation.

University College Cardiff was founded in 1883 and it is now the largest of the colleges of the University of Wales. It is based in Cathays Park, a surprisingly attractive site for a city centre, with handsome 19th-century buildings and elegant tree-lined avenues. Like the city which surrounds it, the University is primarily English-speaking and all teaching is done in English.

Cardiff is a prosperous business centre which boasts excellent cultural and sporting facilities, from concerts in the magnificent St David's Hall to international rugby at the National Stadium.

Degrees Available: BA in Humanities and Social Studies; BA or BSc in Health and Life Sciences, with some four-year sandwich courses; BSc, BSc Econ or LLB in the Faculty of Business Studies and Law; BSc in Physical Sciences or BEng in Engineering and Environmental Design, also including a number of four-year sandwich courses; BPharm; BMus; BD.

A number of interesting subjects are on offer at Cardiff: these include Banking and Finance or Business Administration with a European language; Law with a European language or with Japanese; Architectural Engineering; International Transport; Marine Geography; Ecology and Environmental Management; Statistics with Management Science Techniques.

Foundation or preliminary years are available in Engineering, Life Sciences and Physical Sciences.

Assessment: A combination of written and/or oral exams and continuous assessment, including practical or project work, dissertation, etc.

How to Apply: Through UCAS. The University is happy to consider mature applicants without standard qualifications. Open University credits, Access courses and other alternative routes may be deemed to satisfy the entrance requirements. You are welcome to contact the Admissions Tutor of the department in which you wish to study for advice.

Cardiff Institute of Higher Education

P.O. Box 377, Llandaff Centre, Western Avenue, Cardiff CF5 2SG

Tel: 0222 551111 **Fax:** 0222 578427
Contact: Miss Sue Ryan, Information Officer, extension 4369

Number of Undergraduates: About 3500
Percentage of Mature Students: About 10%
Male/Female Ratio: About 1 : 1
Upper Age Limit for Mature Students: None specified

Learning Facilities: There are libraries and learning resources centres on the four main sites, providing 300,000 books and materials relevant to the courses taught there. Photographic, video and television facilities are available, as is the appropriate technical support. The Computer Services Unit provides networked computing facilities for all sites.

Creche Facilities: At Llandaff, for children aged 18 months to five years.

Mature Students Adviser: Not specifically, but counselling and advice is available through the Student Welfare Service.

Accommodation: Some 450 places are available in catering and self-catering residences; demand always exceeds supply, and priority is given to those whose homes are a long way from Cardiff and to those who apply early. The Accommodation Service will also help you find rented accommodation in the private sector. No special provisions for couples or families.

Teaching at the Institute takes place in six centres, of which the main ones are Colchester Avenue (Business Information and Management, and Tourism, Hospitality and Food) and Cyncoed (Education and Community Health). Art, Design and Technology are based at Howard Gardens, several faculties also use facilities at Llandaff and courses in Art Education and the foundation course in Art and Design are taught at Penarth Rd. However, Cardiff is a compact city, distances between sites are not great and bus links are good.

Quality of life is reckoned to be high in Cardiff – a recent survey conducted by Glasgow University rated it fourth among large cities and towns in the UK. As the Welsh capital, a centre for the arts, an expanding commercial centre and the home of several institutions offering Higher Education, its facilities are surprisingly good and wide-ranging for a city with a population of only about 300,000.

Degrees Available: BA or BEd leading to a qualification to teach at primary or secondary level – the BA is a four-year course, the BEd two years, designed for mature students who have completed a year of Higher Education; BA or BSc in the Faculties of Art, Design and Technology, Business Information and Management, Community Health Management or Tourism, Hospitality and Food; BEng in Electronics or in Manufacturing Systems and Manufacturing Management only.

Among the less common subjects available are various combinations of Recreation and Leisure, Tourism, Food Studies and Hotel Management in a modular degree scheme; also Podiatry,

Psychology and Communication, Speech and Language Therapy, and a number of specialisms in Three-Dimensional Design. There is a foundation course in Art and Design. Access courses in Computer Studies, Science and Technology are taught at the Institute: contact the Access Courses Officer for details.

A number of courses may be followed part-time, requiring attendance on one or two days and/or evenings per week. Contact the Information Office, Cardiff Institute of Higher Education, Freepost, Cardiff CF5 1ZZ, for details.

Assessment: A combination of exams and continuous assessment, with practical and project work, essays and dissertations taken into account as appropriate. Teaching practice is an integral part of Education courses.

How to Apply: Through ADAR for Art and Design, otherwise UCAS, but you are encouraged to contact the Institute to discuss your needs before submitting your application. Open days are held monthly throughout the year – contact Sue Ryan (see above) for details. The Institute does not necessarily expect mature students to meet its standard entry requirements, and welcomes applications from those on its own or other Access courses.

University of Central England in Birmingham
Perry Barr, Birmingham B42 2SU

Tel: 021–331 5000
Contact: Faculty Admissions Officer

Number of Undergraduates: 7000+ full-time; many part-time
Percentage of Mature Students: About 32%
Male/Female Ratio: 10 : 9
Upper Age Limit for Mature Students: None

Learning Facilities: The University has a total of eight main libraries, which means it provides one of the biggest learning resources in the Midlands. There are comprehensive computing and technical facilities reflecting recent investment in new equipment and laboratories.

Creche Facilities: Available in term-time for children aged two years or more.
Mature Students Adviser: Not specifically, but advice is available from academic staff, the Careers Office, Student Services etc, according to the nature of the problem.

Accommodation: The University has over a thousand single study-bedrooms in Halls of Residence and can accommodate all first-years who require a place. There are limited facilities for couples, but suitable accommodation is available through the Head Tenancy Scheme – contact the Property Office on 021–331 5191 for details.

The University of Central England grew out of Birmingham Polytechnic and a number of other schools, colleges and institutes, the oldest of which dates back 150 years. It is therefore spread over seven sites, of which the main one, the Perry Barr Campus, is just south of Birmingham city centre.

UCE courses are both flexible and practical, many having strong links with local industry. The Students' Union has particularly good facilities, and Birmingham itself offers concerts and exhibitions at the NEC and the magnificent new ICC Arena, as well as all the other attractions of a large city.

Degrees Available: BA or BSc in a variety of subjects in the Faculties of Art and Design, the Built Environment, Computing and Information Studies or Health and Social Sciences; BA or LLB in the Business School; BEd in Music; BA with QTS at primary level; BEng or BSc in the Faculty of Engineering and Computer Technology. Unusual subjects available at Central England include Criminal Justice and Policing, Environmental Planning with Conservation of the Built Environment or with Natural Resource Management, and Speech and Language Pathology and Therapeutics.

Foundation courses in Engineering are available at the University and at local colleges. Most first degree courses are modular and allow for part-time study.

Assessment: A variety of methods including exams, course work and practical work. All modules are assessed separately during and at the end of the semester in which they are taught.

How to Apply: Through ADAR for Art and Design, otherwise through UCAS for full-time study; for part-time study apply direct to the Admissions Officer of the relevant Faculty.

UCE is committed to providing access to Higher Education to students from a wide variety of social and cultural backgrounds and welcomes applications from prospective mature students without traditional qualifications. It will accept a wide variety of alternative qualifications and give credit for prior learning and/or experience.

———— ❊ ————

University of Central Lancashire
Preston PR1 2HE

Tel: 0772 201201 **Fax:** 0772 892935
Contact: Admissions Office

Number of Undergraduates: About 8500 full-time and 4800
  part-time
Percentage of Mature Students: Over 30%
Male/Female Ratio: About 1 : 1
Upper Age Limit for Mature Students: None

Learning Facilities: The library has over 300,000 volumes and
  subscribes to 1700 periodicals; it also provides a full range of
  audio-visual materials. Comprehensive computing facilities are
  available throughout the University and there are up-to-date
  technical facilities in relevant departments.

Creche Facilities: The pre-school centre caters for children aged
  two to five, during term-time only.
Mature Students Adviser: The Access Unit will advise on entry
  qualifications, and a counselling service is available to all
  students.
Accommodation: The University can house 1650 students in Halls
  of Residence and other University-run accommodation. Priority
  is given to first-years whose homes are not within reasonable
  commuting distance. The Accommodation Service will help
  other students find somewhere suitable to live, but there are no
  special provisions for couples or families.

The University of Central Lancashire has a positive Equal Opportuni-
ties policy, with particular concern for women returners and better
facilities than many for wheelchair users, the blind and the deaf. It has
strong links with a number of other colleges in the north-west, enabling
many students to take the first year of their course nearer to home. It also
has a policy of promoting awareness of environmental issues and of
purchasing 'green' products wherever possible. Smoking is permitted only
in designated areas and it is likely that all University buildings will
shortly become non-smoking.

   The University is situated within easy walking distance of the centre of
Preston, a busy market town on the main London-Glasgow railway line
and close to the M6.

Degrees Available: BA or BSc in the Faculty of Design and
  Technology or in Combined Honours, offering such diverse

subjects as Business French, German or Spanish, Deaf Studies, Horticulture, Pharmacology and Social Policy; also BA in the Business School and the Faculty of Cultural, Legal and Historical Studies; LLB; BSc in the Faculties of Health or Science; BEng.

Four-year 'sandwiches' are available in Fashion, Hospitality Management and various Business, Engineering and Technology courses.

Foundation years are available in Physics, Maths, Electronics and Mechanical Engineering; there is also a foundation year in Technology for Women and a one-year part-time course called New Opportunities for Women, aimed at women of any age over 18 who wish to prepare themselves for Higher Education or employment. Some foundation courses are also run at associate colleges.

Part-time study is available on all courses; many are specifically timetabled so that students need only attend classes on one day a week. For a part-time prospectus or details of foundation courses, contact Student Recruitment on 0772 892400.

Assessment: Varies from department to department, but usually includes both exams and continuous assessment, with final-year projects, seminar papers and practical and creative work, as appropriate. Satisfactory performance during work placement is essential for sandwich courses.

How to Apply: Through ADAR for Art and Design, otherwise through UCAS for full-time courses. For part-time courses, contact Student Recruitment (see above).

The University is committed to widening access to Higher Education and will consider a range of alternative qualifications and experience offered by mature applicants. A CATS scheme (see page 12) allows credit to be given for prior learning. You are welcome to contact the Access Unit on 0772 892738 to discuss your needs and opportunities before submitting a formal application.

Central St Martins College of Art and Design
Southampton Row, London WC1B 4AP

Tel: 071–753 9090 **Fax:** 071–242 0240
Contact: Relevant School Administrator

Number of Undergraduates: About 1800

Percentage of Mature Students: Not specified
Male/Female Ratio: Not specified
Upper Age Limit for Mature Students: None specified

Learning Facilities: The excellent specialist library has a total of 80,000 books, 250 journals and 100,000 slides. There is a Central Computing Unit with state-of-the-art computer-aided design technology, a photographic unit and media services department. The College also has a purpose-built theatre and art gallery. Students have access to the facilities of the London Institute and its other constituent colleges.

Creche Facilities: At the London College of Printing and Distributive Trades (see page 221).
Mature Students Adviser: Not specifically, but Student Services are available to give advice and support to all students.
Accommodation: Two Halls of Residence run by the London Institute (see page 227).

Central St Martins was founded through the merger of two of London's greatest art schools, the Central School of Art and Design and St Martins School of Art, both with traditions dating back to the 19th century and a record of excellence and distinguished graduates. The expertise of full-time staff who are practitioners in their field is supplemented by many visiting tutors.

Based on three main Central London sites – Art in Southampton Row, on the edge of Bloomsbury, Fashion and Textiles in Charing Cross Rd in Soho, and Graphic and Industrial Design in Long Acre in Covent Garden – the College is ideally placed to give students access to the capital's many museums and art galleries.

CSM is a constituent college of the London Institute.

Degrees Available: BA in the Schools of Art, Fashion and Textiles, and Graphic and Industrial Design. The course in Fashion has several options involving a year's sandwich element. The course in Fine Art may be followed part-time, in which case it will take five years to complete.
There is also a foundation course in Art and Design, which will normally be completed in one year full-time or two years part-time.

Assessment: Largely through creative project work.

How to Apply: Through ADAR except for the foundation course, for which you should apply direct to the School. Admission is by portfolio assessment and interview. Applications from mature students who can show evidence of creative abilities are welcomed.

Central School of Speech and Drama
Embassy Theatre, Eton Avenue, London NW3 3HY

Tel: 071–722 8183 **Fax:** 071–586 1665
Contact: Registry

Number of Undergraduates: About 600 students altogether
Percentage of Mature Students: About 5%
Male/Female Ratio: About 1 : 3
Upper Age Limit for Mature Students: Normally 25 for Acting, though older students may be admitted; otherwise none

Learning Facilities: The library holds about 24,000 books relevant to the School's courses and provides access to CD-Rom databases for further information. The Media Resources Unit provides computing facilities and technical support in video, sound and photography. The School has recently completed an extensive building project which has provided excellent new workshops and studios.

Creche Facilities: No
Mature Students Adviser: No, but the Student Services Co-ordinator is a trained counsellor who can be consulted by all students.
Accommodation: None available through the School, but the Student Services Unit has a list of hostels and runs an advice service.

The Central School was established in 1906 to provide training in speech and drama aimed principally at aspiring young actors. Its teaching has since evolved to include stage management, theatre design, teaching and speech therapy. The School is based at the Embassy Theatre in Swiss Cottage, where public performances are held throughout the year.

Central's degrees are validated by the Open University, but it also has close links with a number of the colleges of the University of London and with relevant professional bodies. Students therefore benefit from learning in a small community but have access to the resources of much larger institutions.

The School has a no-smoking policy.

Degrees Available: BA in Drama, Community and Education (with PGCE) or in Acting or Theatre Studies (Design); BSc in

Applied or Clinical Communication Sciences (four years, with a professional qualification).

There is also a foundation course in Art and Design.

Assessment: In Acting, by continuous assessment of performance-oriented work; otherwise by a mixture of exams and project work.

How to Apply: Through UCAS for Drama, Community and Education and Communication Sciences; through ADAR for Theatre Studies; direct to the school for the foundation course in Art and Design and for Acting – send for an application form, enclosing an A4 stamped addressed envelope. This should be returned by the end of March at the latest. Admission to the Acting course is by audition, for which you pay a fee (currently £25). For Theatre Studies you should expect to be invited for interview and to present a portfolio of work.

For the BSc course, a CATS scheme (see page 12) permits you to transfer credit from previous study.

Mature applicants are welcome on all courses, and are not necessarily expected to meet standard entry requirements – relevant experience and perceived ability to benefit from the training are considered important.

Charing Cross and Westminster Medical School (University of London)
The Reynolds Building, St Dunstan's Rd, London W6 8RP

Tel: 081–846 7202
Contact: Miss D.G. Carr, Admissions Officer

Number of Undergraduates: 850
Percentage of Mature Students: 9%
Male/Female Ratio: 1 : 1
Upper Age Limit for Mature Students: 30

Learning Facilities: The library has 30,000 books and 250 places. There are 31 computer work stations and science labs in all preclinical departments.

Creche Facilities: No
Mature Students Adviser: No
Accommodation: Two Halls of Residence and a number of student houses can accommodate all first-year students. There is no special provision for couples or families.

The new Chelsea and Westminster Hospital was opened in 1993, providing students of the School with the most modern medical teaching facilities in the UK. These include a closed-circuit fibre-optic colour TV teaching system which links the School's various teaching hospitals. The old Charing Cross and Westminster Medical Schools were founded in 1818 and 1834 respectively, so there is also a long tradition of caring for the sick and of teaching medicine.

Charing Cross and Westminster Medical School has its own Students' Union which runs social activities and co-ordinates a counselling service; the School is also part of the University of London, giving students access to the University library, careers service, Accommodation Office, etc.

Degrees Available: MB BS. There is also an Intercalated BSc Honours degree, an optional year's study between the preclinical and clinical parts of the main course.

Assessment: By exams and satisfactory completion of the clinical parts of the course.

How to Apply: Through UCAS. Graduates in non-medical subjects are considered, and one or two places a year are given to non-graduate mature students, but the requirements are the same as for school leavers – good A levels or equivalent.

Charlotte Mason College
Ambleside LA22 9BB

Tel: 05394 33066
Contact: Admissions Officer

Number of Undergraduates: 700
Percentage of Mature Students: Not specified, but increasing
Male/Female Ratio: About 1 : 9
Upper Age Limit for Mature Students: None specified

Learning Facilities: The library has over 80,000 volumes, an extensive collection of other learning materials and a CD-Rom information service. There is a Resources Centre providing audio-visual and reprographic back-up. Students may also use all the facilities of the Lancaster campus.

Creche Facilities: No
Mature Students Adviser: Not on site, but all Charlotte Mason students have a personal tutor, and academic, welfare, careers and medical advice is readily available.

Accommodation: Available for first-year students in small houses in the College grounds. Meals are provided. There are no special provisions for couples, although the College is aware of the needs of mature students and tries to provide an 'appropriate social mix' in each house. The Accommodation Office will help third- and fourth-year students find suitable accommodation, and students who are not resident in College may still take meals there if they wish.

Charlotte Mason College became the Ambleside campus and the Faculty of Teacher Education and Training of Lancaster University (see page 204) in 1992. It also became part of the Lancaster collegiate system: all students at the Ambleside campus are members of Charlotte Mason College. The Ambleside campus is in fact two sites, within a mile of each other, on the north shore of Lake Windermere. It is a beautiful setting with spectacular views.

Degrees Available: BA with Qualified Teacher Status (four years), at nursery or lower or upper primary level. The second year is normally spent at the main campus in Lancaster.

Assessment: A combination of exams and course work, balanced approximately 50 : 50, though this varies slightly depending on the course. Competence in teaching practice is vital and assessed on a pass/fail basis.

How to Apply: Through UCAS to the University of Lancaster. Like the rest of the University, Charlotte Mason welcomes applications from mature students and will accept a wide range of alternative qualifications. Prospective mature students are welcome to contact the Admissions Officer at Ambleside for more information and to arrange an advisory interview if this seems appropriate. You will not be admitted to an Education course without a formal interview.
See separate entry for the University of Lancaster (page 204) for more information.

Chelsea College of Art and Design
School of Art, Manresa Rd, London SW3 6LS
Tel: 071–351 3844 **Fax:** 071–352 8721

School of Design, 40 Lime Grove, London W12 8EA
Tel: 081–749 3236 **Fax:** 081–746 0784

Contact: School Administrators: Steve Farrow at the School of Art, Ann George at the School of Design

Number of Undergraduates: 592
Percentage of Mature Students: About 17%
Male/Female Ratio: 2 : 3
Upper Age Limit for Mature Students: None

Learning Facilities: The libraries have a total of 80,000 books and 150,000 slides, including a number of specialist collections. The College has excellent facilities for computer-aided design in addition to the normal word-processing and audio-visual resources.

Creche Facilities: No, but the London Institute runs a creche at the London College of Printing (see page 221) at the Elephant and Castle, some distance away across London.

Mature Students Adviser: Not specifically, but the London Institute runs a Central Welfare Service and there is a satellite welfare office on site at Chelsea.

Accommodation: The London Institute has two Halls of Residence; priority for places is given to first-years and to overseas students (see page 227 for more details). No special provision for couples or families.

Chelsea is a constituent college of the London Institute; students belong to the Institute's Students' Union and benefit from its facilities, careers advice, welfare service etc. Established in 1891, Chelsea has one of the finest reputations of any Art School, particularly in the field of sculpture, with Henry Moore and Graham Sutherland former teachers and Elisabeth Frink and Nicola Hicks former students. All its current teachers, both full-time and visiting, are distinguished practitioners of their arts.

Degrees Available: BA in Design or Fine Art, validated by the Open University. The Design degree is available through the conventional three years of study or by an accelerated route, two academic years of forty-five weeks each, starting in July.
There is also a foundation course in Art and Design, taught on a separate site near Chelsea Harbour.
Part-time study is possible on the Fine Art course.

Assessment: Mostly on practical creative work, with exams in art history and theory.

How to Apply: Through ADAR, except for the foundation course, for which you should apply direct on a form available from the

College Office at Manresa Rd. You will be expected to present a portfolio of work and applicants without traditional qualifications will be assessed on this and on relevant experience.

Cheltenham and Gloucester College of Higher Education
P.O. Box 220, The Park, Cheltenham GL50 2QF

Tel: 0242 532824/6
   0242 532825 (prospectus requests)
Contact: Mrs Gill Thatcher, Schools Liaison Officer

Number of Undergraduates: 4500 full-time, 2000 part-time
Percentage of Mature Students: About 30%
Male/Female Ratio: 2 : 3
Upper Age Limit for Mature Students: None – the College has a part-time student aged 76.

Learning Facilities: The libraries (one on each main site) have over 120,000 books, many additional resources such as government publications and audio-visual materials, and subscribe to nearly 1900 periodicals. There are comprehensive Media and IT services.

Creche Facilities: Two daycare centres for pre-school children, plus half-term facilities for children over the age of four.
Mature Students Adviser: Advice available through the Students' Union.
Accommodation: Full board and self-catering units are available, with about 60% of first-year students allocated College accommodation. Special arrangements may be made for couples.

Cheltenham and Gloucester CHE is based on three main sites in the attractive spa town of Cheltenham. Extensive building programmes are underway at all three sites, with new learning centres due to open in 1994 and 1995. Formed in 1990 from the merger of the Church of England College of St Mary and St Paul and the Gloucestershire College of Arts and Technology, the College retains the Christian tradition of the former and the dynamic, practical approach of the latter.

Degrees Available: BA and BSc in a wide variety of subjects including Business Studies with Hotel Management or Tourism Management; Education Studies; Financial Services; Professional Media; Performance Arts; Business Computer Systems; Business Information Technology; Earth's Resources; Environmental Policy. BEd (four years) leading to a qualification to teach at nursery or primary level. All degrees are offered on a modular basis, allowing a wide choice of subject and subject combinations. A number of four-year sandwich courses are available, and opportunities for part-time study plentiful.

Assessment: Each module is assessed separately, during and at the end of the semester in which it is taught. The emphasis is generally on continuous assessment. Teaching practice is an important part of BEd degrees.

How to Apply: Through ADAR for Art and Design, otherwise through UCAS for full-time study; direct to the College for part-time. The College offers advisory interviews to mature students, who should contact Gill Thatcher on 0242 532825 before making a formal application.

The College has a full CATS programme (see page 12) and credit may be given for previous studies and/or work experience.

Chester College of Higher Education
Cheyney Rd, Chester CH1 4BJ

Tel: 0244 375444 **Fax:** 0244 375444
Contact: Registry (Admissions)

Number of Undergraduates: Nearly 2000 full-time, about the same number on various part-time courses
Percentage of Mature Students: About 30%
Male/Female Ratio: About 1: 3
Upper Age Limit for Mature Students: None

Learning Facilities: The library contains over 150,000 items and is open in the evenings and on Saturday and Sunday afternoons. The Media Services Unit provides audio-visual and open access computing facilities, plus technical support. The College has its own residential centre at Murton in Cumbria, where fieldwork and, for Education students, residential courses with schoolchildren are based.

Creche Facilities: For children aged nought to five years, open Monday to Friday from 8 a.m. to 6 p.m.
Mature Students Adviser: Not specifically, but the Registry will advise on applications. Each student has a personal tutor and

counselling services are available to all. The College produces a
useful question-and-answer leaflet for mature applicants considering teacher training, and another on alternative entry to degree
courses.

Accommodation: The College provides 500 places in catering and
self-catering: nearly two-thirds of first-years can be given a place
in Hall. No special provisions for couples or families.

*Chester is the oldest teacher training college in the UK, having been
founded by the Church of England, with which it retains strong links,
and opened by Gladstone in 1842. It occupies a single campus about half
a mile from the historic city walls. The original Victorian buildings are
supplemented by modern teaching and leisure facilities.*

*The city of Chester is one of England's finest pieces of living history – it
was built as a Roman fortress to suppress the Welsh, and reminders of
Roman, medieval and Victorian life and architecture are visible
everywhere. The lovely River Dee runs through the centre of the city and
the best zoo in the country is three miles away.*

The College awards degrees of the University of Liverpool.

Degrees Available: BA in a range of Arts and Social Science
subjects; BSc in a more limited number of Science subjects; BEd
(four years) leading to a qualification to teach at upper or lower
primary level.

Assessment: A combination of exams and continuous assessment,
divided approximately 60/40.

How to Apply: Through UCAS, but you are advised to contact the
Registry first to obtain a mature student's pro forma. This is a
brief form asking for details of your education and experience:
after you have completed this and returned it to the College, you
may be offered an advisory interview. You will be expected to
show evidence of recent study beyond GCSE level, such as an A
level, a BTEC award or a relevant kitemarked Access course.
After you have submitted your formal application, you are likely
to be invited for interview before being offered a place.

City University
Northampton Square, London EC1V 0HB

Tel: 071–477 8000 **Fax:** 071–477 8562
Contact: Undergraduate Admissions Office

Number of Undergraduates: About 2500
Percentage of Mature Students: About 35%
Male/Female Ratio: About 2 : 1
Upper Age Limit for Mature Students: None

Learning Facilities: The main library is currently open five days a week only, but till 9 p.m. Monday to Thursday and till 8 p.m. on Fridays. These hours are under review and may be extended by the start of the 1994/5 session. The libraries stock a total of over 330,000 books and subscribe to 1800 periodicals; the main library has 500 study places. The Computer Unit provides a higher ratio of equipment and services per student than most other Universities. There is also a well-equipped Language Resources Centre available to all students.

Creche Facilities: No
Mature Students Adviser: No, but all students have a personal tutor and counselling and welfare services are available.
Accommodation: Halls of Residence can accommodate about 800 students and places are guaranteed to first-years who apply by 15 May and whose homes are not in Greater London. There are also a number of University flats and the Accommodation Office will help you find suitable accommodation, but there are no special provisions for couples or families.

City has been a University since 1966, but the Northampton Polytechnic, from which it grew, is a hundred years old in 1994. Its courses are practical in approach and the University prides itself on its high rate of graduate employment. Because it is comparatively small, classes also tend to be small and students benefit from individual attention. Although many courses offer students optional subjects in the later years, most, particularly those such as Engineering which are recognised by professional bodies, have a firm structure with a solid compulsory core.

City University is in the City of London, close to the Barbican and Sadler's Wells and with easy access to all the facilities of the capital. The main precinct, in Northampton Square, houses most of the University buildings; the Business School is based at Frobisher Crescent, a short walk away.

Degrees Available: BSc in Music, in Management and Design in Engineering and in the Schools of Science and of Business, Management and Systems; also BSc or BA in Social and Behavioural Sciences, including four-year courses in Clinical Communication Studies and in Nursing and Human Sciences; LLB in Business Law; BEng in a variety of specialisms, with a number of four-year sandwich courses.

City offers the unusual combinations of Journalism with Economics, Philosophy, Psychology or Sociology. The BSc in Music is a rare opportunity to combine performance with study of music from around the world and the technological aspects of modern sound.

'Open Studies' (Access) courses are available through the Department of Continuing Education and there is a foundation year in Science and Engineering.

Assessment: Exams are important, with those held at the end of the second and final years both counting towards your degree. Most courses also use an element of continuous assessment, especially in the form of a final-year project. On sandwich courses, satisfactory performance on work placements is essential.

How to Apply: Through UCAS, but mature students, particularly those on Access courses, are advised to contact the Student Recruitment Office in the Academic Registrar's Department first. Applications are considered on an individual basis and you should be prepared to show evidence of ability to benefit from the course you wish to follow. If you have not been in formal education for some years, you may be advised to take a suitable Access course first.

City College, Norwich
Ipswich Rd, Norwich NR2 2LJ

Tel: 0603 660011 **Fax:** 0603 760326
Contact: Pam Breckenridge, Access Centre

Number of Undergraduates: About 13,500 students in all, many following non-degree courses
Percentage of Mature Students: About 30%
Male/Female Ratio: 5 : 4
Upper Age Limit for Mature Students: None

Learning Facilities: The library has 65,000 books, 700 periodicals and a media library. There are also comprehensive computing facilities, language and science labs, specialised craft workshops and a study skills centre.

Creche Facilities: A day nursery is available during term-time for children aged up to five.
Mature Students Adviser: Yes, contact the Access Centre.
Accommodation: The College Hall of Residence accommodates

270 students, with priority given to first-years. There are no special provisions for couples or families.

Situated close to the centre of the lovely city of Norwich, City College has recently celebrated its centenary. It offers a wide range of Further and Higher Educational courses, the latter in association with Anglia Polytechnic University, which validates its degrees.

Degrees Available: BA in Combined Arts and Hospitality Management; BSc in Communication, Environmental Biology and Human Life Sciences. All courses can be followed part-time. Foundation or Access courses are available in Arts and Social Sciences, Natural Sciences and Technology.

Assessment: Degrees are modular and are assessed at the end of each unit.

How to Apply: Through UCAS, but you are welcome to contact the Access Centre (direct line 0603 663414, open all year) for an informal discussion before submitting your application.
All alternative entry qualifications are considered, as is relevant experience. Credit may be given for previous study. The College is very interested in applications from mature students, who are considered on an individual basis.

Colchester Institute
Sheepen Rd, Colchester CO3 3LL

Tel: 0206 761660 **Fax:** 0206 763041
Contact: Student Admissions Office

Number of Undergraduates: About 10,000 students on courses at various levels
Percentage of Mature Students: Between 33% and 50% on some courses
Male/Female Ratio: About 1 : 2
Upper Age Limit for Mature Students: None

Learning Facilities: The two main libraries, which are open long hours during term-time, hold a total of 125,000 items including books, audio-visual material and musical scores. CD-Rom databases are also available, and the Institute has extensive computing, computer-aided design and other technical facilities.

Creche Facilities: At the Colchester site, for children aged three to
   five.

Mature Students Adviser: The Adult Guidance Adviser in the
   Guidance Centre will advise on applications; all students have a
   personal tutor and counselling is available through the Student
   Welfare Office.

Accommodation: There are 185 places in Halls of Residence at the
   Clacton site, and a few flats at Colchester. The Accommodation
   Office keeps a register of accommodation for rent, but there are
   no special provisions for couples or families.

*Colchester Institute is a regional college of Anglia Polytechnic Univer-
sity, which validates its degrees. Its main campus is close to the centre of
Colchester, but the BA in Business Studies (Catering Management) is
taught at Clacton, a seaside campus whose facilities include the former
Grand Hotel. A free bus service runs between the two sites.*

   *Smoking is permitted only in certain parts of the Institute, and may
soon be forbidden altogether.*

   *The town of Colchester has a long history but also boasts many modern
facilities. It is within easy reach of London, Stansted Airport and the
East Anglian ports, so mainland Europe is not far away.*

Degrees Available: BA in Business Studies (Catering Management
   – either a four-year sandwich or a two-year course for students
   who already have a relevant HND), Design, Humanities or
   Music; BSc in Environmental Monitoring and Protection.
   Part-time study, including 'taster programmes' on some courses,
   is possible, as is open learning: details are available from the
   Enquiries Office on 0206 718000.
   The Institute also provides a fifteen-month Access course, which
   may be studied during the day or in the evening. Foundation
   courses are available in Art and Design, Engineering and
   Physical Education.

Assessment: Courses are modular, with each unit assessed separately. Projects, dissertations and practical work will be taken
   into account as appropriate, as will performance in work
   placement in the sandwich course.

How to Apply: Through ADAR for Design, otherwise through
   UCAS for full-time study; direct to the Institute for part-time,
   on an application form obtainable from the Enquiries Office.
   Colchester has a long and successful record with mature
   students: it welcomes applications from those without traditional qualifications and may give credit for relevant experience.

You are welcome to contact the Adult Guidance Adviser in the Guidance Centre to discuss your needs.

For the Design course you should expect to be invited for interview and to produce a portfolio of work.

Cordwainers College
182 Mare St, London E8 3RE

Tel: 081–985 0273 **Fax:** 081–985 9340
Contact: John Fleming, Courses Co-ordinator

Number of Undergraduates: 106
Percentage of Mature Students: 32%
Male/Female Ratio: About 1 : 5
Upper Age Limit for Mature Students: None

Learning Facilities: The library has 14,000 volumes and is increasing rapidly. There is a Learning Resources Centre, a computer suite, workshops with industry-standard equipment, design studios, a photographic studio and darkroom.

Creche Facilities: No
Mature Students Adviser: Yes
Accommodation: None available through the College at present, but this situation may change by 1995.

Cordwainers is a specialist college with courses at various levels in footwear, fashion accessories, leather crafts and saddlery. In its field it is recognised as one of the best, and has a good track record of graduates going into employment or successfully setting up their own businesses. Most of the UK's top footwear designers are trained here. The College is small enough to offer personal attention to each student's needs, yet large enough to have excellent, hi-tech facilities.

It is situated in Hackney, not far from London Fields and the Grand Union Canal, and within easy reach of central London.

Degrees Available: BA in Design and Product Development (in Footwear and Accessories), validated by the City University. There are also BTEC foundation courses in Art and Design (one and two years).

Assessment: Although there will be some written exams, the course is practical and closely linked to industry; an industrial project is a major part of final-year work, and as part of this you will be expected to write a dissertation of at least 12,000 words.

How to Apply: Through ADAR. You should expect to be invited for interview and to present a portfolio of work. Successful completion of an approved foundation course or BTEC National Diploma in Art and Design will be considered as an alternative to A levels; relevant work experience in the footwear or related industries may also be acceptable.

Courtauld Institute of Art (University of London)
Somerset House, Strand, London WC2R 0RN

Tel: 071–872 0220
Contact: Secretary to the Registrar

Number of Undergraduates: About 100
Percentage of Mature Students: About 18%
Male/Female Ratio: About 1 : 2
Upper Age Limit for Mature Students: None specified

Learning Facilities: The library has one of the most extensive collections of books, periodicals, catalogues and other materials on Art History in the UK. Through links with King's College the Institute also has extensive computing facilities.

Creche Facilities: No
Mature Students Adviser: No, but each student has a personal tutor.
Accommodation: Available through the University of London. Contact the Accommodation Office, University of London, Senate House, Malet St, London WC1E 7HU, telephone 071–636 2818.

The Courtauld has been teaching the History of Art since 1932 and has an international reputation in its field. The Institute and its Galleries are based in the splendid neo-classical Somerset House, on the Strand. Students benefit from small classes and discussion groups, but the Institute is also part of the University of London and students therefore have access to an enormous range of facilities.

The collection of the Courtauld Institute Galleries, based on the legacy of Samuel Courtauld but much expanded, is best known for great Impressionist and Post-Impressionist paintings by Monet, Manet, Renoir, Degas, Cézanne, Gauguin, Van Gogh and many more; there are also important works by Rubens, Tiepolo and Kokoschka.

Degrees Available: BA in the History of Art.

Assessment: Exams at the end of both second and third years, plus a major essay in each year.

How to Apply: Through UCAS, but you are also advised to send a full CV direct to the Institute. The Institute welcomes applications from mature students, who should show evidence of recent study in the Humanities (an appropriate Access course or Open University foundation course, Birkbeck College Diploma in the History of Art, etc). You will be considered on your individual merits and account will be taken of any special features.

GCSE level or equivalent in a modern language (normally French, German or Italian) is generally required, and although you may be accepted without this qualification you will be expected to attain the required standard of proficiency at an early stage of your course.

Coventry University
Priory St, Coventry CV1 5FB

Tel: 0203 631313 **Fax:** 0203 838793
Contact: Registry Services Manager

Number of Undergraduates: Over 14,000, about half of them full-time
Percentage of Mature Students: About 30%
Male/Female Ratio: About 2 : 1
Upper Age Limit for Mature Students: None

Learning Facilities: The library has more than a quarter of a million books and subscribes to 2000 periodicals; it is open until 8.45 p.m. Mondays to Thursdays, and for reference at the weekend. There are also a number of specialist collections, including the Lanchester Collection, the unpublished papers of Frederick Lanchester, the motoring and aeronautics pioneer. The University has over 1500 computer work stations and runs a computing advisory service. There are up-to-date laboratories and workshops for relevant courses.

Creche Facilities: For children under five, open 48 weeks a year. Apply early, as places are limited.
Mature Students Adviser: Not specifically, but a full range of counselling and welfare services is available.
Accommodation: All new students are guaranteed a place, in Halls of Residence, houses or flats. There are 62 twin flatlets in

Caradoc Hall, about three miles from the campus, and the Accommodation Office will help find suitable accommodation for families.

Although the Coventry College of Design was founded in 1843, Coventry is a new University with a forward-looking and practical approach. It has franchising links with over 20 colleges in the region through which you may be able to take the first year of a course at a college near your home, transferring to the University for the remainder. It also runs a Women and Work Programme, designed to coincide with school terms, for women who wish to return to education or employment. The programme covers such areas as basic computing skills, communication skills, looking for a job and personal and career development. The University occupies a single campus in the centre of the city.

Coventry was devastated by bombing during the war, and much of it, including Sir Basil Spence's famous cathedral, is less than fifty years old. However, some medieval traces remain and Coventry's most famous daughter, Lady Godiva, presides naked over the central shopping centre.

Situated on the main London-Birmingham railway line, Coventry is very easy to get to, with the NEC, Birmingham itself and the attractions of Stratford and the Warwickshire countryside within easy reach.

Degrees Available: BA, BSc and BEng in a wide range of subjects in the Faculties of Art and Design, the Built Environment, Engineering, Health and Social Sciences, International Studies and Law, Mathematical and Information Sciences, and Natural and Environmental Sciences, and in the Business School. All courses are designed to be flexible and allow you, in consultation with the academic staff, to build your own programme of study. Optional sandwich elements are available in some Engineering and Built Environment courses.
There is also a foundation course in Art and Design.
Many courses are designed to be suitable for part-time study. An Associate Student Scheme allows you to take one subject at a time for a nominal fee, while the mini-module scheme offers classes in the evenings and on Saturdays for those who wish to build up credits in small units before embarking on a full-scale course.

Assessment: Some courses have no exams at all, relying entirely on assessment of course and practical work, with a major final-year project or dissertation. Others combine these elements with formal exams.

How to Apply: Through ADAR for Art and Design, otherwise through UCAS for full-time study. For the foundation course or for part-time study on any course, apply direct to the University on a form available from the Academic Registry. Applications from prospective mature students will be assessed on their individual merits and a wide range of alternative qualifications and/or experience may be acceptable.

Cranfield University

see Royal Military College of Science (page 297) and Silsoe College (page 324)

Crewe & Alsager Faculty

Manchester Metropolitan University, Crewe Green Rd, Crewe CW1 1DU

Tel: 0270 589995 **Fax:** 0270 583433
Contact: Harry Mawdsley, Admissions and Marketing Tutor

Number of Undergraduates: 4000
Percentage of Mature Students: 25%
Male/Female Ratio: 1 : 1
Upper Age Limit for Mature Students: None

Learning Facilities: Each campus has a substantial library; between them they hold 200,000 books and subscribe to 1000 current periodicals. There are ample computing facilities as well as a television studio and audio-visual equipment.

Creche Facilities: No
Mature Students Adviser: Yes
Accommodation: 14 Halls of Residence accommodate 800 students and all first-years who require a place are usually offered one. No special provisions for couples or families.

The former Crewe & Alsager College of Higher Education became a faculty of the Manchester Metropolitan University in 1992, but is some forty miles from the rest of the University. Itself the product of the merger of two colleges, Crewe & Alsager operates on two campuses six miles apart and linked by regular free transport.

Degrees Available: BA in Crafts, Creative Arts, Humanities or Applied Social Studies (in the latter, students choose their own field of independent study in the final year); BEd leading to qualifications to teach at nursery, infant, junior or secondary level; BSc in Environmental Science and Sports Science only. There is also a foundation course in Design and Technology. Many degrees have a modular structure which is convenient for those who wish to study part-time: on this basis a three-year full-time course will normally take five years to complete.

Assessment: A combination of exams, continuous assessment and project work. Practical teaching ability is an important feature in BEd courses.

How to Apply: Through ADAR for Crafts, otherwise through UCAS. Early application is advised, and you are welcome to contact the Faculty first.

Normal entry requirements may be waived for mature students, and credit may be given for prior learning and/or experience.

Cumbria College of Art and Design
Brampton Rd, Carlisle, Cumbria

Tel: 0228 25333 **Fax:** 0228 514491
Contact: Registrar

Number of Undergraduates: About 800 altogether
Percentage of Mature Students: Not specified
Male/Female Ratio: Not specified
Upper Age Limit for Mature Students: None

Learning Facilities: The College has a new specialist library of books and slides, and excellent computing and media resources.

Creche Facilities: No
Mature Students Adviser: No
Accommodation: Not available through the College, but the Accommodation Officer keeps a list of suitable rented accommodation.

Cumbria College of Art and Design has expanded rapidly over the last few years, in terms of both numbers of students and courses on offer. The main site is just to the north of Carlisle itself, with Fine Art courses taught at the city-centre annex.

Carlisle is an attractive town whose older buildings are characterised by the distinctive local pink brick. Parts of the castle date back to Roman times, and Hadrian's Wall is within half an hour's drive, while the modern Sands Centre provides sporting facilities and attracts big-name bands and singers. The less exploited and more rugged northern part of the Lake District is within easy reach.

Degrees Available: BA in Fine Art, Design Crafts, Graphic Design, Media and Heritage Management, all validated by the University of Central Lancashire.
There is also a foundation course in Fine Art.

Assessment: Largely through creative project work, with a dissertation required in the final year of Fine Art and Media. The Heritage Management course combines academic study with practical, vocationally oriented training.

How to Apply: Through ADAR, except for Heritage Management and the foundation course, for which you should apply direct on forms available from the Registrar. Applications from mature students are welcome and will be considered on their individual merits. For the Art and Design-based courses you will normally be expected to have completed a BTEC foundation diploma in Art and Design, or equivalent, and you will be asked to show a portfolio of work.

Dartington College of Arts
Totnes TQ9 6EJ

Tel: 0803 863234
Contact: Registry

Number of Undergraduates: About 350
Percentage of Mature Students: About 40%
Male/Female Ratio: 2 : 3
Upper Age Limit for Mature Students: None specified, but the courses are physically demanding.

Learning Facilities: The library has large stocks of all kinds of recorded material and scores as well as books. There are workshops, a studio and performance space.

Creche Facilities: No
Mature Students Adviser: No
Accommodation: The College helps all students to find suitable accommodation. Priority in the on-site Halls of Residence is given to first-year students, but a wide range of rented

accommodation is available. No special provisions for couples or families.

Dartington College of Arts is set on the beautiful Dartington Hall Estate, with its modern facilities complemented by the medieval buildings and gardens. The estate is a mile outside Totnes, so some may find it isolated.

The College policy is that the arts should be practised side by side, so that, for example, Music is not studied to the exclusion of Visual Performance or Theatre. The teaching staff are recognised leaders in their fields, whose courses keep up-to-date with developments in the arts.

Dartington has a formal association with the University of Plymouth, which validates its degrees.

Degrees Available: BA with Single Honours in Music, Performance Writings, Theatre or Visual Performance, or Combined Honours in Performance Arts. The latter is a modular programme.

Assessment: A combination of exams and continuous assessment, involving practical work, seminar papers, portfolios, essays, dissertations, self- and peer-assessment, as appropriate.

How to Apply: Through ADAR or UCAS for the Visual Performance course, otherwise through UCAS. Dartington has a successful track record of training mature students, and those who do not possess traditional qualifications are encouraged to apply if they believe they have the necessary aptitude and ability. Admission is normally by audition and interview.

De Montfort University Leicester
The Gateway, Leicester LE1 9BH

Tel: 0533 551551 **Fax:** 0533 577533

De Montfort University Milton Keynes
Hammerwood Gate, Kents Hill, Milton Keynes MK7 6HP

Tel: 0908 695511 **Fax:** 0908 695581

Contact: Admissions Section (or Enquiry Office for prospectus only) on either campus

Number of Undergraduates: 12,688
Percentage of Mature Students: 10% of undergraduates, 38% overall

Male/Female Ratio: 5 : 4
Upper Age Limit for Mature Students: None

Learning Facilities: Two main libraries, one on each campus, hold a total of over 250,000 volumes and subscribe to 2266 periodicals. There is seating for 1111 students. Computer libraries are also available.

Creche Facilities: No

Mature Students Adviser: Student Services Welfare Officer. The University publishes a 'Guide for New Students' with lots of comforting information about what you have to do on your first day.

Accommodation: Mature students are normally expected to find their own accommodation, though a list of private accommodation is available from the Accommodation Office.

De Montfort University is on two sites, one close to the centre of Leicester, the other on a purpose-built campus on the outskirts of Milton Keynes. The latter was opened in 1992, and Milton Keynes' first graduates obtained their degrees in 1993. A regular bus service links the two campuses.

Students with special needs are particularly well catered for at Milton Keynes, as the campus was carefully designed to provide access for the disabled.

De Montfort is active in the linked college scheme (see page 4), so students from a number of local colleges (and from as far afield as Guernsey or York) can take the first year of their course close to home and then transfer to De Montfort.

Degrees Available: At Leicester: BA in Art and Design, Architecture and in Arts and Humanities subjects; BSc; BEng; LLB. Reflecting the cosmopolitan nature of the city, the Arts subjects offered include Contemporary Asian Studies, Jain Studies and South Asian Dance.
At Milton Keynes: BA or BSc in the Schools of the Built Environment, Business, Computing and Mathematical Sciences, and Engineering and Manufacture only.
A BA in Conservation and Restoration is awarded by De Montfort but taught at the Lincolnshire College of Art and Design (see page 212).
Many of these courses may be followed part-time.

Assessment: A combination of exams and course work, including projects (both individual and team) and practical work where appropriate.

How to Apply: Through ADAR for Art and Design, otherwise through UCAS, but mature students should contact the Admissions Tutor of the course they wish to pursue. Most courses will recognise alternative qualifications and appropriate experience.

University of Derby
Kedleston Rd, Derby DE22 1GB

Tel: 0332 622222 **Fax:** 0332 294681
Contact: Admissions Office

Number of Undergraduates: 8930
Percentage of Mature Students: 58%
Male/Female Ratio: 47 : 53
Upper Age Limit for Mature Students: None

Learning Facilities: There is a library on each of the main sites, with a total of 190,000 books, subscriptions to 1300 periodicals and a specialist collection of 80,000 slides on Art and Design-related subjects. There are comprehensive computing facilities and a Media Services department producing high-quality visual aids for teaching and research.

Creche Facilities: Available 50 weeks a year for children aged from two to five. Contact the Head of Nursery for details.

Mature Students Adviser: One of the Careers Advisers has special responsibility for mature students.

Accommodation: The University can accommodate 75% of those first-year students who live more than 15 miles from Derby in self-catering Halls of Residence. There are no provisions for couples or families, but suitable accommodation is available in the private sector. Contact the Residential Accommodation Office for help.

It is the University's intention to continue to expand its provision of student accommodation.

The University of Derby was formed from the union of a number of local Colleges of Higher Education and the Colleges of Radiography, Occupational Therapy, Nursing and Midwifery. As a result it occupies a number of sites, all within easy reach of each other in and around the city.

The University is committed to widening access to Higher Education to anyone it believes will benefit from it: integral to this policy are its work with the local Dyslexia Institute and the existence of a Deafness Studies Unit, providing services and hi-tech support for deaf and hard-of-hearing students.

Derby is a thriving city in the very centre of England, with a history dating back to Roman times and an industrial heritage that begins with England's first silk mill and carries on today with the manufacture of railway rolling-stock and Rolls-Royce aero-engines. Situated as it is on the edge of the Peak District, it also provides access to some of the most spectacular countryside in England.

Degrees Available: BA in the Faculty of Humanities and Social Science and in the Business School; BA or BSc in the Faculty of Art and Design; BEd leading to a qualification to teach at upper or lower primary level; BEng; BSc in the Faculty of Science and Technology and in the Institute of Health and Community Studies; LLB.

Many degrees in Science, Social Science, Art and Design and Humanities are modular and suitable for part-time study. Foundation courses are taught at Derby and at five local partner institutions.

Assessment: Modular courses are assessed unit by unit, using exams and course work, with emphasis on projects, practical work and performance, where applicable.

How to Apply: Through ADAR for Art and Design, otherwise through UCAS for full-time study. For part-time study, apply direct to the University on a form available from the Admissions Officer, c/o the Registry at the above address.

The University will consider applicants with any or no qualifications on an individual basis. It operates an APL scheme (see page 12) and actively encourages prospective mature students to regard previous experience as a qualification. It publishes a leaflet entitled 'Making Your Experience Count' and runs courses several times a year to help you put together a portfolio in support of your application for credit for prior experience or learning.

Doncaster College
Waterdale, Doncaster DN1 3EX

Tel: 0302 322122 **Fax:** 0302 738065
Contact: Registrar

Number of Undergraduates: 23,000 students on courses at all levels; of these, 2000 are full-time on BTEC or degree courses
Percentage of Mature Students: Not specified

Male/Female Ratio: Not specified
Upper Age Limit for Mature Students: None

Learning Facilities: There are well-stocked libraries on all sites. The College has 'state of the art' technical facilities for such specialist study areas as Mining and Resources Engineering.

Creche Facilities: At a nursery adjacent to the Waterdale site.
Mature Students Adviser: Not specifically, but students have a personal tutor and a college counsellor is also available.
Accommodation: 240 places are available at the High Melton site, but most students are local.

Doncaster College is the largest local provider of Further and Higher Education, with recognised expertise in specialist areas of technology, management and design. It is also a Community College, open to any student over the age of 16 and offering 600 Adult Education courses at over 70 venues across the borough.

The main site, Waterdale, is in central Doncaster, as is the Division of the Expressive Arts, based at Church View. Other courses are conducted at Bessacarr, three miles to the south, or High Melton, a rural campus six miles to the west.

The College's degrees are validated or offered on a franchise basis by Sheffield Hallam University.

Degrees Available: BA in Business Administration or Business Studies; BEng in Environment and Resource Management, Mining and Electrical or Mechanical Engineering, or Quarry and Road Surface Engineering.
There are foundation courses in Art and Design, Construction, Engineering, and Sport and Recreation; a number of Access courses are also available.
Part-time study, both day and evening, is possible on some courses, as is open learning. Contact the Department of Continuing Education on 0709 582427 x 263 for details.

Assessment: Varies from course to course, but with the emphasis on practical and industrial training.

How to Apply: Through ADAR for Design, otherwise through UCAS for full-time study; for part-time courses contact the College direct. Applications from mature students without standard qualifications are welcome and relevant experience may be taken into account in considering your application.

Duncan of Jordanstone College of Art
13 Perth Rd, Dundee DD1 4HT

Tel: 0382 23261 **Fax:** 0382 27304
Contact: Secretary and Registrar

Please see page 2 for general information on Scottish universities and colleges

Number of Undergraduates: 1367
Percentage of Mature Students: Not specified
Male/Female Ratio: 5 : 6
Upper Age Limit for Mature Students: None

Learning Facilities: The library, which is open until 8.30 p.m. Monday to Thursday in term-time, has 45,000 volumes and 188 current periodicals, 40,000 slides, a substantial collection of video tapes, slide-tape packages and maps. There are CD-Rom databases, and computer facilities are being installed.

Creche Facilities: None specific to the College, but students have access to the facilities of the University of Dundee.
Mature Students Adviser: Contact the Assistant Registrar in charge of Student Services
Accommodation: The College provides 170 places in self-catering residences and a range of private flats and houses are available through a Direct Leasing Scheme. About two-thirds of first-year students are allocated College accommodation. The University of Dundee will try to help couples and families find accommodation, but availability is limited.

Duncan of Jordanstone College of Art degrees are awarded through the University of Dundee, which is adjacent to the College and with which it has close links – although Duncan of Jordanstone has its own Students' Union, College students have access to the University Health Service, Careers Service and sports facilities.

Duncan of Jordanstone is the largest College of Art and Design in Scotland, and has an unusually broad range of expertise within that general field. It is particularly proud of the facilities of its new School of Television and Imaging, although this School does not at the moment offer undergraduate courses.

Degrees Available: BA in Fine Art; BDes in various aspects of Design, Textiles, Illustration, etc; BScArch leading to BArch; BSc in Town and Regional Planning and in Environmental Management.
The Arts and Design degrees are four-year programmes with a general foundation year common to all courses (except Interior

and Environmental Design, which has its own introductory year). BSc Honours courses are also four years.

The BScArch is awarded after three years; the BArch Honours after another three years, one spent in an architectural practice and two in further study.

Assessment: Most courses are assessed primarily on project work, though there will be exams on relevant aspects of theory, and final (sixth) year Architecture students are required to produce a dissertation.

How to Apply: Enquiries about Art and Design courses should be addressed to the Assistant Registrar, who will also supply application forms.

Applications for Architecture, Town and Regional Planning and Environmental Management courses should be made through UCAS to the University of Dundee and enquiries addressed to the Admissions Office there (see next entry).

Heads of Schools and Course Directors will give individual advice to mature students on request. The College participates in the Scottish Wider Access Programme (SWAP), which aims to give those without traditional qualifications the opportunity to prepare themselves for and enter Higher Education. It also recognises a number of Access courses: in some cases successful completion of these entitles you to a place on a course; in others it at least guarantees an interview.

If you do not have standard qualifications, you will have to satisfy the College that you have the motivation, potential and aptitude to follow your chosen course successfully. Evidence of previous achievements or work experience may be required, but credit may be given for these.

University of Dundee
Dundee DD1 4HN

Tel: 0382 23181 x 4028
Contact: Bill Baird, Director of Schools Liaison

Please see page 2 for general information on Scottish universities and colleges

Number of Undergraduates: 5720 full-time
Percentage of Mature Students: 21%
Male/Female Ratio: 51 : 49

Upper Age Limit for Mature Students: 30 for Medicine, otherwise none

Learning Facilities: The library has over 500,000 books and subscribes to 3800 periodicals. There is a sophisticated computer network, and an optional course in basic computer skills is offered to all students regardless of their field of study. The Language Laboratory is similarly open to all.

Creche Facilities: Playgroup for two- to five-year-olds, supervised by qualified staff. Apply early to ensure a place.

Mature Students Adviser: For Arts and Social Science students (who form the majority of the University's mature student intake). There is also an active Mature Students' Society.

Accommodation: All first-years who require University accommodation are allocated places in Halls of Residence or self-catering flats, which are cheaper than most others in the UK. A complex of 30 flats is available for students with families, but places are much in demand and cannot be guaranteed.

The University of Dundee came into being as a separate entity in 1967, but it had existed as part of the University of St Andrews for a hundred years before that. This mixture of youth and experience, coupled with the wide range of subjects on offer and the flexibility of courses, attracts students from all over the world. Dundee is proud of the opportunities it offers students to study abroad, both in the EC and in North America, and lays claim to being 'a European University at Dundee'. Its graduates also have one of the best records in the UK of finding employment.

The University is ten minutes' walk from the city centre, and all the facilities and accommodation are housed on a single campus.

Degrees Available: MA in Arts and Social Science subjects; BAcc; LLB; BSc; BEng; BDS; MB, ChB.

Courses in Food and Welfare Studies, Hotel and Catering Management, and in the School of Environmental Studies are taught at Duncan of Jordanstone College of Art (see previous entry).

Degrees in Medicine and Dentistry normally take five years of study, other honours degrees four years. However, as is normal in Scotland, it is possible to obtain a degree without honours in three years.

The University runs an Access to Science and Engineering course, and four versions of a course called New Opportunities – Return to Study, aimed at preparing students for entry to courses in the Faculties of Arts, Social Sciences and Law. These courses take one day a week for three nine-week terms.

Assessment: A combination of exams and continuous assessment, with essays and practical work, where relevant, counting towards the final marks.

How to Apply: Through UCAS. Applications from mature students are considered individually on their merits, although those wishing to study Medicine must have traditional qualifications. Although Dundee values the breadth of experience that mature students can contribute, the prospectus also points out that 'it is easier to accommodate mature students on courses where no previous knowledge of the subject is assumed (e.g Social Sciences or Law) than on courses (e.g. Medicine, Dentistry, Sciences, Engineering) where students are expected to have studied specific subjects . . . up to SCE Higher Grade or GCE Advanced Level Standard.'

The University is a member of SCOTCAT (see page 14), which means it has a policy of giving credit for previous studies, particularly other forms of tertiary education.

Dundee Institute of Technology
Bell St, Dundee DD1 1HG

Tel: 0382 308000 **Fax:** 0382 308877
Contact: Registry (0382 308080)

Number of Undergraduates: About 2000
Percentage of Mature Students: About 13%
Male/Female Ratio: About 7 : 3
Upper Age Limit for Mature Students: None

Please see page 2 for general information about Scottish universities and colleges

Learning Facilities: The library is open until 9 p.m. Monday to Friday and on Saturday and Sunday afternoons; it holds over 100,000 items and subscribes to 850 periodicals. There are extensive computing facilities, including computer-aided design, and a Media Centre providing media and reprographic back-up for teaching and research. All relevant departments have modern, well-equipped labs.

Creche Facilities: No

Mature Students Adviser: Counselling and support available through Student Services. There is also a Mature Students' Society.

Accommodation: Some 600 places are available in catering Halls of Residence or self-catering flats. Some residences are usually reserved for older students. The Accommodation Officer will help you find suitable rented accommodation in the private sector if necessary.

Dundee Institute of Technology was founded as the Dundee Technical Institute in 1888 and has long been considered an 'industrial University' – the high standard of its technical courses is widely acknowledged. The main Institute site is at Bell Street in the centre of Dundee, but there are three other sites within a few minutes' walk.

Dundee is a friendly, medium-sized city with a long history. It is one of Scotland's major centres for hi-tech industry; local links provide students at the Institute with useful vocational experience.

Degrees Available: BA in the Faculty of Management; BSc in a range of subjects including Community Health Studies and Nursing; BEng. Some Science and Engineering courses are 'sandwiches', requiring four to five years' full-time study for an honours degree.

Several first-degree courses may be followed part-time – see the prospectus and contact the relevant departmental office for details.

The Institute runs a number of foundation years aimed at preparing students for its undergraduate programmes; successful completion of one of these will guarantee you a place on a relevant course. Contact the Registry for details.

Assessment: A combination of exams and continuous assessment, with most courses requiring a major project in the latter part of the course. Some degrees are modular, with each unit assessed separately. For sandwich courses, satisfactory performance during work placement is essential.

How to Apply: Through UCAS for full-time courses; direct to the Institute for part-time. Forms for direct application may be obtained from the Registry and although applications are accepted at any time you are advised to apply as early as possible (from the September of the year before you wish to begin your course), as some courses will fill up quickly.

The Institute is committed to widening access to Higher Education and is happy to receive applications from prospective mature students who do not have formal qualifications. Those who are taking a foundation or Access course are particularly welcome, but all relevant qualifications and/or experience will be considered. A CATS scheme (see page 12) is being developed and will enable you to be given credit for previous learning. It is hoped that this will be in place by the start of the 1994/5 session. Contact the individual Course Leader for advice before submitting your application.

University of Durham
Old Shire Hall, Durham DH1 3HP

Tel: 091–374 2000 **Fax:** 091–374 3740
Contact: Deputy Registrar

Number of Undergraduates: 6617
Percentage of Mature Students: 11%
Male/Female Ratio: 11 : 10
Upper Age Limit for Mature Students: None

Learning Facilities: The library has 800,000 volumes and is open until 10 p.m. every day during term-time. The University has comprehensive computing facilities and offers computer literacy programmes to all undergraduates.

Creche Facilities: No
Mature Students Adviser: Not specifically, but the Student Support Centre exists to help any student who needs it.
Accommodation: All students at Durham belong to a college and normally live in during their first and final years.

Durham is a collegiate university with a very high academic reputation. Each college has members (students and staff) from all departments. A number of the colleges date from the 19th century, while the newest, Collingwood, opened in 1973. The oldest, University College, is partly housed in Durham Castle, just opposite the cathedral, which must make it one of the most attractive student residences in the UK. St Mary's College is for women; all the other colleges are mixed.

Degrees Available: BA in a range of Arts and Social Science subjects; BA in Education; BSc in Maths or Physics only; LLB; MEng (four-year course). Combined Studies courses in Arts and Social Sciences are broadly based, allowing students to take three subjects in each of three years. Joint and Single Honours courses offer a wide choice of main and subsidiary subjects, from Arabic or Classics to Community and Youth Work Studies.

Assessment: Largely exam based, although many courses include a final-year dissertation and practical work is assessed in relevant subjects.

How to Apply: Through UCAS. To obtain a place at Durham you must be accepted by a college as well as by the University. You can apply to an individual college or, if you have no preference, you can submit an open application. See the UCAS handbook and the University prospectus for more details. Mature students without conventional qualifications are considered carefully.

University of East Anglia
Norwich NR4 7TJ

Tel: 0603 56161
Contact: Rowena Armstrong, Admissions Office

Number of Undergraduates: 5302
Percentage of Mature Students: 40%
Male/Female Ratio: 1 : 1
Upper Age Limit for Mature Students: None

Learning Facilities: The library has 650,000 volumes and adds regularly to its stock of periodicals, music scores and government periodicals; it is open long hours, including evenings and weekends during term-time. The Computing Centre and library have more than 150 terminals between them and there are many others in the various schools of study. The Computing Centre also provides teaching and a help desk. There are fully equipped labs in all science schools, an audio-visual centre running courses in video and film production, and a TV studio equipped to broadcast standard.
The James Platt Language Centre, opened in 1992, provides some of the most innovative language teaching in the UK. The Sainsbury Centre for the Visual Arts, designed by Norman Foster, houses a spectacular collection ranging from indigenous African and pre-Columbian art to works by Henry Moore, Giacometti and Francis Bacon.

Creche Facilities: Nursery for children from six weeks to school age. There is a hardship fund for the benefit of student parents who need help with the fees. Places are limited, so apply early by writing to the manager.

Mature Students Adviser: Advice is available from the Student Union's permanent Welfare Officer and from the office of the Dean of Students.

Accommodation: University accommodation is allocated to all first-year students. Some houses or flats are available for couples, but early application is required. Accommodation in Norwich is reasonably cheap and easy to come by.

Perhaps best known for its courses in Creative Writing, with Malcolm Bradbury a former lecturer and Kazuo Ishiguro a former student, East Anglia offers a wide range of subjects in Arts, Science and Law. It is a largely purpose-built university situated on a single campus on the outskirts of Norwich. Improvements in road and rail services over recent years have made the region of East Anglia vastly more accessible to the outside world and added to the University's appeal.

Degrees Available: BA; LLB; BSc. Both BA and BSc degrees available in a wide range of subjects, including Danish, Norwegian and Swedish, Ecology or Environmental Science with a year in the USA and Mathematics with a year in Europe or Canada.

A limited number of BA and BSc courses may be followed part-time: contact the Admissions Office for details.

Foundation courses for students whose first language is not English, and for others who do not have conventional entrance qualifications, are available through a number of colleges in Norfolk and Suffolk. For details, write to the Admissions and International Office at the above address.

Assessment: A combination of exams and course work.

How to Apply: Through UCAS. Mature students are advised to contact the Admissions Office of their proposed School of Studies first: they will advise on whether previous qualifications or experience are likely to satisfy entrance requirements. A wide range of non-traditional qualifications is considered.

University of East London
Barking Campus, Longbridge Rd, Dagenham RM8 2AS
Stratford Campus, Romford Rd, London E15 4LZ

Tel: 081–590 7722 **Fax:** 081–849 3530

Contact: Lynne Chiswick, Head of Centre for Access and Advice or Tony Wailey, Mature Students Adviser, 081–849 3470
Number of Undergraduates: 9750
Percentage of Mature Students: 60% of full-time and sandwich students; 97% of part-time
Male/Female Ratio: About 1 : 1
Upper Age Limit for Mature Students: None (the oldest to date were 79)

Learning Facilities: The library has 300,000 books. There is a university-wide computer network and large numbers of PCs.

Creche Facilities: Two playgroups are available at moderate cost.
Mature Students Adviser: Yes. See above.
Accommodation: Campus Halls of Residence, flats and accommodation in private houses. Many students live locally and travel daily to the University. There are no special provisions for couples or families.

The University of East London is on two campuses within easy reach of central London. Because it has always had a high proportion of mature students, the University has a particularly flexible attitude to candidates without formal qualifications. The Access and Advice Unit exists to advise potential students, particularly mature students, and help them choose the right course. It publishes a number of useful leaflets on the assessment of prior learning and experience, and on choosing a course.

East London takes its equal opportunities policy seriously: there is an Access Co-ordinator for Asian Women and Girls, and the University does everything it can to help students with disabilities.

Degrees Available: BA; BEng; BSc; LLB.
  Degrees may be specialist (single subject), combined honours (normally in two subjects) or negotiated (a combination of subjects not offered in the prospectus but chosen by the student with the approval of the relevant staff): a modular scheme allows a great deal of flexibility, including opportunities for part-time study. There is a wide range of subjects available: Art and Design subjects include Visual Communication and Fashion: Design with Marketing; Arts offers Health Management, Media Studies, New Technology and European Studies, and Women's Studies, while in the Faculty of Science you can study Biomarketing and Management Environmental Monitoring, Integrated Electronic Design and Manufacture, and Surveying and Mapping Science among many others.
The University of East London has wide links with Access courses throughout the Greater London area and in Essex and Kent. Again, the Access and Advice Unit (see above) can help.

Assessment: Varies according to the nature of the course. Continuous assessment forms a substantial part of many courses, although most also have traditional exams.

How to Apply: Through ADAR for Art and Design, otherwise through UCAS for full-time study; direct for part-time. Popular courses fill up quickly, so early application is advised. A wide variety of alternative qualifications is considered and you are welcome to contact the Access and Advice Unit to discuss your application before submitting it formally.

Edge Hill University College
Ormskirk L39 4QP

Tel: 0695 575171
Contact: Head of Admissions

Number of Undergraduates: About 4000
Percentage of Mature Students: About 25%
Male/Female Ratio: About 2 : 5
Upper Age Limit for Mature Students: None specified

Learning Facilities: A new Learning Resources Centre opening in 1994 will have 250,000 items from books to databases and will provide 500 study places. There are full computing facilities, which all students are encouraged to use, and a Technical Services Unit providing TV, editing and audio-visual facilities.

Creche Facilities: Limited, for children aged two to five, but the College is hoping to expand its childcare provision for the 1994/5 session.

Mature Students Adviser: The Access and Equal Opportunities Unit will advise on application and qualifications; advice of all kinds is available to any student through Student Services.

Accommodation: 11 Halls of Residence have 500 places and priority is given to first-years and those with special needs: most Halls provide wheelchair access and there are a number of specially adapted study bedrooms. The Accommodation Team will help with rented accommodation, but there are no special provisions for couples or families.

Edge Hill is not a full-scale University but it is funded and assessed in the same way as all Universities in England and Wales, so is rightly confident that it is offering high quality education. The College is committed to equal opportunities, a fact that is reflected in the nature of many of its courses, and has a particularly strong Community Action group engaged in voluntary work in the local community.

The campus is on the outskirts of Ormskirk, a busy market town, and half an hour from the seaside resort of Southport. For those who want bigger cities, Manchester and Liverpool are within easy reach; for those who don't it is easy to get to the Lakes or the Peak District, and the Martin Mere Wildfowl and Wetlands Trust is only three miles away.

Degrees Available: BA or BSc with QTS for teaching a range of subjects at nursery or primary level (four years); BSc with QTS for teaching Business Education, Design and Technology or Maths at secondary level (two years, without honours, for mature students who already have an HNC or HND); BA or BSc in a range of Arts and Social Science subjects including Community and Race Relations, Afro-Asian Studies and Women's Studies.
The non-educational degrees are modular and may be studied part-time.

Assessment: A combination of exams and continuous assessment, with many courses requiring a major final-year project or dissertation. All units on modular courses are assessed separately, during and at the end of the year. For the teaching degrees strong emphasis is placed on practical experience in schools.

How to Apply: Through UCAS for full-time, direct to the College for part-time study. Applications from prospective mature students without traditional qualifications are welcome, and evidence of ability to benefit from the course is the main criterion for admission. This may take the form of recent study, such as professional qualifications or an Access course. You are invited to contact the Access and Equal Opportunities Unit on 0695 584269 to discuss your circumstances.

University of Edinburgh
Edinburgh EH8 9YL

Tel: 031–650 1000
    031–225 8400 (Faculty of Divinity only)

Number of Undergraduates: About 10,000
Percentage of Mature Students: About 10%
Male/Female Ratio: About 11 : 9
Upper Age Limit for Mature Students: None specified

Please see page 2 for general information about Scottish universities and colleges

Learning Facilities: The University of Edinburgh has one of the largest open-access libraries in the UK, with the vast core stock supplemented by specialist collections and rare books and manuscripts. It also has some of the best facilities for studying languages, and very up-to-date computing facilities including a high-speed fibre-optic network. Medical, veterinary and science facilities are first class. Telescopes and other technical support for the Department of Astronomy are housed in the nearby Royal Observatory.

Creche Facilities: No

Mature Students Adviser: Not specifically, but full counselling support is available to all students and, unique to Edinburgh, there is a Students' Union building reserved for the use of post-graduate and mature students. The University publishes a separate mature students' prospectus.

Accommodation: All first-year students whose homes are outside Edinburgh, who have a firm offer of a place and apply to the Accommodation Office by 1 September, are guaranteed accommodation, usually in traditional Halls or self-catering houses. There is a limited number of flats available for couples and families, but it is recognised that finding suitable, cheap accommodation in Edinburgh is a problem: you are strongly advised not to bring your family with you until you have sorted something out, and warned that this may take some time.

Founded in 1583, the sixth oldest University in the UK but the youngest of the four long-established Scottish ones, Edinburgh remains a prestigious place to obtain a degree. Most of the University is on two main sites in the centre of Edinburgh, including the administrative departments and the Faculty of Law in Old College, which once housed the entire University. The Faculties of Science and Engineering are at Kings Buildings, about two miles to the south.

The Scottish capital is a magnificent city. Whether you want to watch rugby at Murrayfield, visit the Royal Scottish Academy or the National Gallery, stroll along the Royal Mile, with Edinburgh Castle at one end and Holyrood House at the other, or stay on during the summer holidays to take in the Festival, it has something to offer.

Degrees Available: MA in a wide variety of Arts subjects, including an enormous number of Modern and Classical Languages (all of which, except French, can be studied from scratch); BA, BD or MA in the Faculty of Divinity; BVM & S;

MB, ChB; BMus in Music and in Music Technology; LLB with a
number of options including Accountancy, Celtic or a European
language; BEng/MEng, BSc or MPhys, again in a wide range of
subjects including Agricultural Science, Forestry and Astrophysics; BCom; BSc (Nursing); BSc or MA in the Faculty of
Social Science.
Some courses in the Faculties of Arts, Divinity, Music and Social
Science may be followed part-time and you should expect to take
from five to nine years to complete your degree.

Assessment: Final exams are important, but many courses also
include a major final-year project or dissertation.

How to Apply: Through UCAS. If you do not have traditional
qualifications, you are advised to write to the appropriate
Faculty before submitting your application, giving details of
your experience and qualifications, and of the course for which
you wish to apply. The University will consider an approved
Access course or other evidence of recent academic achievement,
but you should note that there is no relaxing of entry requirements for Medicine or Veterinary Medicine and competition for
places on many courses is extremely fierce.
The University is a member of SCOTCAT (see page 14), so credit
may be given for learning done elsewhere.

Edinburgh College of Art
Lauriston Place, Edinburgh EH3 9DF

Tel: 031–229 9311   **Fax:** 031–229 0089
Contact: Admissions Officer

Number of Undergraduates: About 600
Percentage of Mature Students: About 22%
Male/Female Ratio: About 3 : 7
Upper Age Limit for Mature Students: None specified

Learning Facilities: There are three main libraries, open until
8.30 p.m. Monday to Thursday during term-time but closed at
weekends. Between them they give in-depth coverage of all the
courses taught at the College, with periodicals, catalogues, reports,
slides, maps, etc., as well as books. Plans are afoot to expand the
existing computer facilities. The Department of Visual Communication provides audio-visual back-up and there are excellent studio,
workshop and laboratory facilities for all courses.

Creche Facilities: Only on the main Heriot-Watt campus.

Mature Students Adviser: No, but counselling services are available to all students.

Accommodation: Accommodation specific to the College is limited – contact the Accommodation and Welfare Officer for details, and for information about Heriot-Watt Halls of Residence.

Edinburgh College of Art can trace its origins back to 1760 and as such is one of the oldest establishments of its kind in the UK. Its current building, just behind the castle, was purpose-designed for the College in 1906 but now incorporates up-to-date facilities not only for drawing, painting, sculpture, and town and country planning (which has been part of the syllabus for 50 years), but for furniture and textile design, film and television work and animation.

The College in fact comprises two faculties of Heriot-Watt University – Environmental Studies and Art and Design – but retains its own site and distinctive identity.

Degrees Available: BA in a range of subjects within Art and Design, including Drawing, Painting, Sculpture, Design and Craft, and Visual Communications; BA or BArch in the Faculty of Environmental Studies.

The first year of study in Art and Design is common to all courses and may be regarded as a foundation year; if you have already completed this level of study you may be allowed to begin your course in the second year.

Assessment: The emphasis is very much on the student's practical and creative work, with some seminar presentations, essays and dissertations required in theoretical aspects of the course.

How to Apply: Through UCAS to Heriot-Watt University for Environmental Studies. For Art and Design, apply direct to the College on an application form available from the Registration Office. If you are applying for the foundation year, you should return the form by early January, for entry to the second year by 1 March. You will also be expected to submit a portfolio of work. As mature students will not necessarily be expected to have formal qualifications, it is important that you contact the College well before submitting your application to discuss your abilities and experience. You should expect to be invited for interview before being offered a place and you may be required to sit a special entrance exam.

Epsom School of Art and Design
Ashley Rd, Epsom KT18 5BE

Tel: 0372 728811
Contact: Registry

Number of Undergraduates: About 1000 students altogether, but an annual intake of 40 on the BA course.
Percentage of Mature Students: Varies
Male/Female Ratio: Varies
Upper Age Limit for Mature Students: None

Learning Facilities: The library has an extensive collection of specialist books, journals and catalogues as well as relevant audio-visual material. The Information Technology Resource is available to all students.

Creche Facilities: No
Mature Students Adviser: Not specifically, but the Student Services Officer can give advice or information, or refer you to someone else who can.
Accommodation: None owned by the College, but the Students Services Officer maintains a list of suitable local accommodation.

Epsom School of Art and Design was founded in 1896, but boasts up-to-date hi-tech facilities relevant to its courses. It is part of the Surrey Institute of Art and Design, which validates its degrees. Although it has offered a range of diplomas and HND courses for some time, the degree course has only been taught here since 1992.

The School is close to the centre of Epsom, an attractive town with good facilities and a famous racecourse. Easy access to London.

Degrees Available: BA in Fashion

Assessment: Project work is important throughout the course and you will be expected to produce a fashion collection in final year.

How to Apply: Through ADAR. You should expect to be invited for interview and asked to submit a portfolio of work.

University of Essex
Wivenhoe Park, Colchester CO4 3SQ

Tel: 0206 873666
Contact: Admissions Officer

Number of Undergraduates: 3800

Percentage of Mature Students: About 28%
Male/Female Ratio: 1 : 1
Upper Age Limit for Mature Students: None

Learning Facilities: The library has over half a million items and is open seven days a week, including weekday evenings, during term-time. The University also has full computing and language facilities.

Creche Facilities: A day nursery is open all year round for children under five: contact the office of the Dean of Students for details. A play scheme for school-age children is available at half-term.

Mature Students Adviser: Not specifically, but every student has a personal adviser and there is full counselling support.

Accommodation: Essex is able to accommodate 60% of its students in University accommodation and guarantees a place, usually in single rooms in self-catering units, for all unmarried first-years. There is limited accommodation for couples and families.

The University of Essex is situated in attractive parkland two miles from Colchester, the former capital of Roman Britain. Boadicea and the Emperor Claudius feature in the town's history, and part of the Norman castle still stands.

One of the attractions of Essex's degree courses is the opportunity to take four or five subjects (instead of the more normal three) in the first year. Throughout the course the keynote is flexibility, though there is less choice in Law or Engineering because of the requirements of the professional qualifications.

Degrees Available: BA in the Schools of Comparative Studies and Social Sciences; LLB; BA or BSc in the School of Mathematics and Computer Sciences; BEng or BSc in Science and Engineering, including a number of four-year sandwich courses.

Assessment: A mixture of exams and continuous assessment, with dissertations, practicals and project work taken into account as applicable.

How to Apply: Through UCAS. Essex has a long and successful record of teaching mature students, and will consider BTEC awards, Access courses, Open University credits or professional qualifications as alternatives to the standard entry requirements. You are welcome to write to the Admissions Officer, giving any additional information you think may be relevant to your application.

European Business School
Inner Circle, Regent's Park, London NW1 4NS

Tel: 071–487 7400
Contact: M. van Miert, Head of External Relations

Number of Undergraduates: 530
Percentage of Mature Students: 20%
Male/Female Ratio: 3 : 2
Upper Age Limit for Mature Students: None

Learning Facilities: The library has 35,000 volumes. There are computing facilities and a newspaper room.

Creche Facilities: No

Mature Students Adviser: Not specifically, but advice is available through the Student Services Department or the Careers Office.

Accommodation: There is some (expensive) on-campus accommodation, catering for 30% of first-year students and with no special provisions for couples. The School can provide help in finding outside accommodation.

The European Business School is a cosmopolitan place with students from all over Europe, and affiliated colleges allowing all students to spend time abroad. Courses are high-powered and the School has an excellent track record of successful graduates.

It is situated in Regent's Park, providing one of the most peaceful and attractive environments for study in London.

Degrees Available: BA in business-oriented subjects such as Accountancy, Finance, Information Technology and Public Administration, including study of two European languages (four years).
Courses are modular, allowing for part-time study.

Assessment: Courses are practical, with emphasis placed on communication and management skills and linguistic ability. Each unit is assessed separately.

How to Apply: Direct, at least two months before proposed entry. The School will consider A-level equivalent qualifications and give credit for prior learning and/or experience.

University of Exeter
Exeter EX4 4QJ

Tel: 0392 263035
Contact: Admissions Officer

Number of Undergraduates: 7000
Percentage of Mature Students: 11%
Male/Female Ratio: About 1 : 1
Upper Age Limit for Mature Students: None

Learning Facilities: The library has over 800,000 books and seating for 1040 people. There are 650 computer work stations for student use. Excellent purpose-built laboratories and technical facilities support courses in Science and Engineering.

Creche Facilities: A Family Centre is run jointly by the University and the Guild (Exeter's equivalent of the Students' Union).
Mature Students Adviser: Contact the Admissions Officer for advice on applications; counselling and other welfare services are available to all students.
Accommodation: All first year students are offered places in University accommodation, mostly in Halls but some in self-catering units. There are limited facilities for married students.

Exeter is one of the most popular universities in the country, offering high academic standards, an attractive campus close to the city centre, and easy access to the walkers' paradises of Exmoor and Dartmoor. Sports and entertainment facilities are particularly good and Exeter's main theatre, the Northcott, is on the campus. The foreign language centre is open to all students and many undergraduate courses now offer the opportunity for study in Europe.

See separate entries for courses in the Camborne School of Mines (page 105) and the affiliated College of St Mark and St John (page 308) and St Loye's School of Occupational Therapy (page 307).

Degrees Available: BA Combined or Single Honours; BA (Ed) or BSc (Ed); BEng; BSc Combined or Single Honours; LLB. After the first year of study, entry to a Modular Degree programme is available in the Faculties of Arts, Law and Social Studies: this enables students to devise an academic programme to suit their own needs, following one or two fields of study. Up to 25% of the programme may be dedicated to independent study leading to the presentation of a dissertation or portfolio. A detailed handbook about the modular degree is available from the Admissions Officer.

Suitably qualified applicants may be permitted to study part-time on all courses leading to BA, BEng, BSc and LLB degrees.

Assessment: Exams and continuous assessment. You will be told how important each form of assessment is for your particular course.

How to Apply: Through UCAS. Applications from mature students are considered on their merits, with academic background and experience since leaving school taken into account. Students who have completed a first year of study at another university or college, who have passed a University Certificate with merit or who have credits from the Open University may be allowed to enter the modular degree scheme in the second year.

Falmouth School of Art and Design
Woodlane, Falmouth TR11 4RA

Tel: 0326 211077
Contact: Irene Jenkins, Admissions Officer

Number of Undergraduates: 408
Percentage of Mature Students: 50%
Male/Female Ratio: 48 : 52
Upper Age Limit for Mature Students: None

Learning Facilities: The library has recently been rehoused in a purpose-built building and is open in the evenings during term-time. It contains a large reference section and specialist collections. There are workshops, studios, darkrooms and computer facilities appropriate to Falmouth courses.

Creche Facilities: Subsidised by the School and the NUS.
Mature Students Adviser: No, but there is a Student Information Line on 0326 211888.
Accommodation: Very limited and preference is given to younger students and those with special needs.

Falmouth has a high reputation in art, design and broadcasting; the School prides itself on strong links with industry and with practising professionals in its fields of interest. The School is 90 years old, but most of its studio and workshop facilities are in modern, purpose-built buildings. *Some courses are conducted at the Pool Annex in Redruth, 12 miles away from the main campus.*

Falmouth has no on-site leisure facilities, but the Cornish countryside and coastline are easily accessible and the Students' Union organises social events and employs a sports and recreation co-ordinator.

Degrees Available: BA in a limited number of subjects related to Art, Design and Broadcasting. The BA Honours in Fine Art may be followed part-time, making it a five-year course. A BTEC Diploma Foundation Art and Design course is available full- or part-time.

Assessment: Practical and project work play an important part in all courses.

How to Apply: Through UCAS or ADAR. All suitable candidates will be asked to submit a portfolio and attend an interview before being offered a place. Applicants without standard qualifications should be prepared to demonstrate experience, enthusiasm and commitment, with some evidence of current academic qualities. Credit may be given for suitable prior learning or experience.

Farnborough College of Technology
Boundary Rd, Farnborough GU14 6SB

Tel: 0252 391212 **Fax:** 0252 549682
Contact: Admissions Administrator

Number of Undergraduates: 114, in a total of over 10,000 full- and part-time students
Percentage of Mature Students: 33% of undergraduates
Male/Female Ratio: About 4 : 3 among undergraduates
Upper Age Limit for Mature Students: None

Learning Facilities: The library is well stocked and has computerised search facilities. There are campus-wide computing resources and purpose-built radio and TV studios.

Creche Facilities: Yes
Mature Students Adviser: Not specifically, but all students have a personal tutor and there is a full range of counselling and welfare support.
Accommodation: Contact the Accommodation Officer for details.

Farnborough College of Technology is a modern college with one of the largest non-university Business Schools in the UK. The College has strong links with industry and offers practical, vocational courses. The main building has won a number of design awards: opened in 1989, it features glass-covered walkways and indoor gardens. Smoking is not permitted anywhere within the College.

Degrees are validated by the University of Surrey.

Farnborough itself is close to the M3 and on the main London-Southampton railway line, so is easy to get to from anywhere in southern England.

Degrees Available: BA in Business Administration, Leisure Management or Media Production and Administration; BSc in Aerospace Engineering, Computing or Environmental Protection (with an optional sandwich element making it a four-year course).

Assessment: A combination of exams and continuous assessment.

How to Apply: Through ADAR for Media Production and Administration, otherwise through UCAS. You are welcome to contact the appropriate Director of Studies for an informal discussion before you apply.

University of Glamorgan Prifysgol Morgannwg
Pontypridd CF37 1DL

Tel: 0443 480480 **Fax:** 0443 480480
Contact: Mr B. Aldridge, Head of Department of Student Services

Number of Undergraduates: 8720 full-time, 2768 part-time
Percentage of Mature Students: 60%
Male/Female Ratio: 6 : 4
Upper Age Limit for Mature Students: None

Learning Facilities: The library has 140,000 books, 1000 periodicals plus slides, videotapes, etc. There are computer facilities, Media Services, laboratories and a theatre.

Creche Facilities: Open throughout the year for children aged one to five.
Mature Students Adviser: Yes
Accommodation: Some on-site accommodation; about three-quarters of first-year students can be given places. No special provision for couples or families.

The University of Glamorgan is on a single campus ten miles north of Cardiff, about a mile from the busy market town of Pontypridd, but easy to get to by road or rail. However, parking is difficult and you are advised not to bring a car. The setting is described in the prospectus as 'semi-rural'. Market days are one of Pontypridd's main attractions; the others include the remarkable 18th-century bridge across the Taff and the longest single railway platform in the UK.

The University has recently introduced a number of features aimed at encouraging women – staff and students – to participate fully in University life. There are late-night minibuses, improved lighting and security on the campus, and personal alarms have been issued.

Smoking is not permitted in any public areas except common rooms within the University's buildings.

Degrees Available: BA or BSc in a range of Arts, Social Science, Science and Engineering subjects; BEng; LLB.

Glamorgan offers a Combined Studies degree which allows for unusual mixes of subjects: Art, Building, Chemical Engineering, German, Information Technology, Public Administration and Theatre Studies all appear on the same list of options, though considerations such as timetabling may mean that not every possible combination is permitted. There is a particularly wide choice of Applied Science subjects and several options combining a Science subject with French or German.

There is also a Science foundation course.

Part-time study is possible on most courses.

Assessment: A combination of exams and continuous assessment, which may include practical and project work, essays, and self- and peer-assessment. Each module is examined separately, during and at the end of the semester in which it is taught.

How to Apply: Through UCAS for full-time study; direct to the University for part-time.

Professional qualifications, Access courses and relevant experience may be acceptable as alternatives to traditional entry requirements. The University operates a CATS scheme (see page 12), so credit may be given for prior learning.

------- ❊ -------

Glasgow University
Glasgow G12 8QQ

Tel: 041–339 8855 Fax: 041–330 4089
Contact: Registrar

Please see page 2 for general information about Scottish universities and colleges

Number of Undergraduates: 13,286
Percentage of Mature Students: 28%
Male/Female Ratio: 1 : 1
Upper Age Limit for Mature Students: None

Learning Facilities: The library has 1.6 million books and 2500
　　places. The University has one of the largest centres of
　　Computing Sciences in the UK; there are 650 computer work
　　stations for student use, laboratories in the science-based
　　departments, a language laboratory and engineering workshops.

Creche Facilities: A subsidised nursery is available for children
　　from three months to five years. Information and application
　　forms may be obtained from The Manager, University of
　　Glasgow Nursery, 63 Southpark Avenue.

Mature Students Adviser: No, but the full range of welfare services
　　is available for all students.

Accommodation: Available in Halls of Residence and self-catering
　　flats. All first-year students requiring accommodation are
　　allocated places. Some flats which are sub-leased to the
　　University may be suitable for families – contact the Accom-
　　modation Office for details.

*Glasgow University was founded in 1451 and its alumni include James
Watt, Joseph Lister, John Buchan and John Logie Baird. Today it has
120 departments and offers an enviable range of subjects and
combinations of subjects. It also prides itself on the advancement of
knowledge that can be credited to research carried out in all its eight
faculties. Most of the University is on a single campus to the west of the
city centre; the Veterinary Science faculty is situated four miles away.*

*　Glasgow's status as European City of Culture in 1990 brought many
of its qualities into the public eye for the first time. But the city has always
catered for a variety of cultural tastes, with an annual Mayfest and an
International Jazz Festival; it is also the home of the Scottish Opera, the
Scottish Ballet and the magnificent Burrell Collection of works of art,
Scotland's most important tourist attraction.*

Degrees Available: MA; BMus; BAcc; BArch; BD: Licentiate in
　　Theology; LLB; MA (Social Sciences), including a qualification
　　in social work; BEng or MEng; B Tech Ed; BDS; BN; BVMS;
　　MB, ChB; BSc; B Technol.

The range of subjects available at Glasgow is vast. It includes
such combinations as Film and Television Studies with Russian,
Polish with Politics, and Economic History with Scottish
Literature in the Faculty of Arts; Geography with Czech and
Politics with Celtic or vice versa in the Faculty of Social Sciences;
Naval Architecture and Ocean Engineering in the Faculty of

Engineering; Agricultural Botany and Archaeology with Computing Science in the Faculty of Science.

Some Access and foundation courses are available and there are limited opportunities for part-time study – contact the relevant Faculty Admissions Officer for details.

Assessment: Project and practical work play an important part in many courses.

How to Apply: Through UCAS for full-time study. The University is a member of SCOTCAT (see page 14), so credit may be given for studies undertaken elsewhere. If you wish to study part-time or to have previous studies taken into consideration, contact the Faculty Admissions Officer first.

Competition to study Veterinary Medicine is particularly keen.

Glasgow Caledonian University
City Campus, Cowcaddens Rd, Glasgow G4 0BA

Tel: 041–331 3000 **Fax:** 041–331 3005
Contact: Admissions Office

Please see page 2 for general information about Scottish universities and colleges

Number of Undergraduates: 5000+
Percentage of Mature Students: About 30%
Male/Female Ratio: 1 : 1
Upper Age Limit for Mature Students: None specified

Learning Facilities: The library has over 140,000 books, subscribes to 1500 periodicals and provides 650 study places. There are University-wide computing services, including specialist facilities in Science and Engineering labs.

Creche Facilities: For children aged six weeks to five years, with provision to cope with older children during holidays. Places are limited, but all full-time students are entitled to receive help with childcare fees, whether or not they use the University facilities. Contact the Student Services offices for details.

Mature Students Adviser: In the Department of Continuing Education. There is also a Mature Students' Society.

Accommodation: One Hall of Residence accommodating 137 students; otherwise the University leases local accommodation. No special provisions for couples or families.

Glasgow Caledonian was formed from the merger of Glasgow Polytechnic and Queen's College Glasgow. The main (City) campus is in the centre of Glasgow, with the Park Campus and Southbrae out of town to the west, but well served by public transport. Queen's College has a hundred-year-old tradition of providing training in health-related subjects, but the entire University boasts modern facilities and a forward-looking approach. It is also very much part of the Glasgow community and involved in a number of fund-raising and charitable projects.

Degrees Available: BA in the Faculty of Business; BEng; BSc in the Faculties of Health, and Science and Technology. A Combined Studies programme leading to a BA or BSc allows for some unusual subject combinations.

Many courses contain optional or compulsory 'thick' or 'thin' sandwich elements, so that it may take five years to obtain an honours degree. From the start of the 1994/5 session all courses will be modular. Some courses may be followed part-time and a separate prospectus is available.

The University is part of the Scottish Wider Access Programme (SWAP) and has links with a number of Access courses; it also runs an evening Access course in Science, Engineering and Technology. Successful completion of such a course guarantees you a place on an agreed degree programme.

Assessment: A combination of exams and continuous assessment of course work, practicals and clinical work, as appropriate, with the emphasis on the practical/vocational side. Satisfactory performance in work experience is essential.

How to Apply: Through UCAS for full-time study, direct to the University for part-time.

Glasgow Caledonian is committed to widening access to Higher Education for all, and mature students without formal qualifications are positively encouraged. Previous study and/or experience will be taken into account: the University is part of SCOTCAT (see page 14) and has a framework for assessing prior experiential learning (see page 12).

Glasgow College of Building and Printing
60 North Hanover St, Glasgow G1 2BP

Tel: 041–332 9969 **Fax:** 041–332 5170
Contact: Student Services Section

Number of Undergraduates: Over 5500 students altogether on a variety of courses. About 1300 of these are full-time.

Percentage of Mature Students: About 15%
Male/Female Ratio: About 6 : 1 overall
Upper Age Limit for Mature Students: None specified

Learning Facilities: The library has over 20,000 books and subscribes to 190 periodicals, giving in-depth coverage of the subject areas covered in College courses. There are computing facilities, audio-visual equipment and a closed-circuit TV service. Students also have access to the facilities of Glasgow Caledonian University.

Creche Facilities: Through Glasgow Caledonian University.
Mature Students Adviser: Not specifically, but all students have a personal tutor and the Student Support Co-ordinator is there to advise any student who needs help.
Accommodation: Limited, through Glasgow Caledonian University.

Formed in 1972 from the merger of the Colleges of Building and Printing, this is now the largest and most respected college of its kind in Scotland. Most of its courses lead to SCOTVEC awards or Scottish Vocational Qualifications, but three degree courses are taught in association with Glasgow Caledonian University. Students will attend classes at both institutions.

The College is right in the centre of Glasgow, with ready access to all the facilities of Scotland's largest city.

Degrees Available: BSc in Building Engineering and Management, Building Surveying or Quantity Surveying (all four-year sandwiches). The course in Quantity Surveying may be taken part-time.
The three courses share a common first year.

Assessment: A combination of exams and continuous assessment. Satisfactory performance in work placements is essential.

How to Apply: Through UCAS to Glasgow Caledonian University.

Glasgow School of Art
167 Renfrew St, Glasgow G3 6RQ

Tel: 041–353 4500
Contact: Academic Registrar

Number of Undergraduates: About 1200

Percentage of Mature Students: Not specified
Male/Female Ratio: 1 : 2
Upper Age Limit for Mature Students: None specified

Learning Facilities: A specialist library, plus modern studios and laboratories with facilities for computer-aided design. Students also have access to the resources of the University of Glasgow.

Creche Facilities: No
Mature Students Adviser: No, but advice and welfare services are available to all students.
Accommodation: Some cheap accommodation is available in a local hostel; otherwise you will have to find somewhere to rent in the private sector.

The School is housed in the centre of Glasgow, in the Mackintosh Building, the Art Nouveau masterpiece of architect Charles Rennie Mackintosh. Founded in 1840, it is now an Associate College of the University of Glasgow, which validates its degrees.

Degrees Available: BA in Design or Fine Art; BArch; BEng in Product Design Engineering.
Part-time study is possible in the School of Architecture.

Assessment: These are practical, largely studio-based courses with the emphasis on creative work.

How to Apply: Through UCAS to the University of Glasgow for full-time studies in Architecture and Product Design Engineering; otherwise direct on a form available from the Academic Registrar. Suitable applicants will be invited for interview and asked to present a portfolio of work. The School is looking for creative people who can show enthusiasm and the ability to follow the courses successfully.

Goldsmiths' College (University of London)
New Cross, London SE14 6NW

Tel: 081–692 7171
081–694 9927 (prospectus only)
Contact: Eamon Martin, Assistant Registrar

Number of Undergraduates: About 1000 full-time, many more part-time
Percentage of Mature Students: About 54%

Male/Female Ratio: 1 : 3
Upper Age Limit for Mature Students: None

Learning Facilities: The library stocks over 200,000 items, including musical scores and a substantial audio-visual collection, and subscribes to over 1500 periodicals. During term-time it is open until 8.45 p.m. Mon.–Fri., and on Sat. mornings. Students can also use the main University of London library.
Comprehensive computing facilities are available for all students, there is a Media Resources workshop and technical support provided by the Department of Media and Communications.

Creche Facilities: For children aged from three months to five years. Places are limited, so apply early.

Mature Students Adviser: Advice on applications may be obtained from the Department of Advanced and Continuing Education, and counselling services are available to all students.

Accommodation: Over 1000 places are available in catering or self-catering Halls of Residence, all within reasonable distance of the College; most first-years whose homes are not within commuting distance can be accommodated. The Accommodation Office will help you find privately rented accommodation, but the College has no special provisions for couples or families.
Students may also apply for a place in the University of London's Inter-Collegiate Halls: contact the University of London Accommodation Office, Senate House, Malet St, London WC1E 7HU, telephone 071–636 2818.

Goldsmiths' was founded in 1891 to promote 'technical skill, knowledge, health and general well-being among men and women of the industrial, working and artisan classes' and, although it would probably phrase this rather differently nowadays, the College is still known for the practical and vocational nature of its courses and for its accessibility to all members of the community. It is the most recent College to join the federation of the University of London, which validates its degrees.

Situated on a single campus in a not very attractive part of South East London, Goldsmiths' is very easy to get to and from. It has a friendly, cheap Students' Union, with lovely Greenwich and all the facilities of the capital on its doorstep.

Degrees Available: BA; BMus; BSc; BA with QTS (four years), leading to a qualification to teach at primary level in a range of subjects and at secondary in Design and Technology only.
Part-time study is available through the Associate Student Scheme. The College also offers a wide range of Access courses

and courses in study skills – contact the Department of Advanced and Continuing Learning for details.

Assessment: Courses are modular, with each unit being assessed separately, during and at the end of the year. The balance of assessment varies from course to course, but most use seen and unseen exams, essays, dissertations, practical work, etc, as appropriate. Teaching practice is an integral part of Education degrees.

How to Apply: Through ADAR for courses in Art and Design, otherwise through UCAS for full-time study; direct to the College for part-time and Access courses. Goldsmiths' has always encouraged mature students, though it should be stressed that competition for places is strong. The College operates both a CATS and an APEL scheme (see page 12) which means that prior learning and/or experience can be taken into account. Successful completion of a kitemarked Access course will be recognised as satisfying the entry requirements.

You are welcome to contact the Department of Advanced and Continuing Education for further information and advice.

University of Greenwich
Wellington St, Woolwich, London SE18 6PF

Tel: 081–316 8000 (switchboard)
081–316 8590 (course enquiries)
Contact: Course Enquiries Officer

Number of Undergraduates: Over 15,000
Percentage of Mature Students: About 27%
Male/Female Ratio: About 3 : 2
Upper Age Limit for Mature Students: None

Learning Facilities: Libraries on each campus have a total of 250,000 books, plus tens of thousands of slides, cassettes, videos, etc. There is a computer lab on each campus with a total of about a thousand terminals; individual faculties also have dedicated computing facilities.

Creche Facilities: Subsidised
Mature Students Adviser: Yes
Accommodation: Halls of Residence can accommodate all first-year students who apply by a given deadline. Contact the Accommodation Service for details. Most mature students live locally, but can be helped to find accommodation if required.

The University of Greenwich grew out of the merger of several well-established South London polytechnics and colleges; as a result it has one of the best academic reputations of the 'new' universities. It is based on eight campuses scattered across South and East London.

Degrees Available: BA; BEng; BSc; LLB; BEd specialising in early years, primary, junior or secondary teaching.
A BA in Garden Design and a BSc in Horticulture are available at the associated Hadlow College of Agriculture and Horticulture, Hadlow, Kent; and a BA in Media and Communications at West Kent College, Tonbridge, Kent.
Foundation and Access courses are available, and part-time study possible. Most courses are modular. The first year of some courses is run at one of the University's numerous associate colleges.

Assessment: Most courses employ a combination of exams and continuous assessment, although the balance varies from subject to subject. Each unit of a modular course is assessed separately, during and at the end of the semester in which it is taught.

How to Apply: Through UCAS, but after your application has been acknowledged you should write direct to the University, quoting your UCAS reference number and giving information in support of your application. It is advisable to apply for the most popular courses (Law, Business Studies, Psychology and Education) by the UCAS deadline of 15 December, though the University will consider mature applicants all year round. There is no official deadline for application for part-time courses, but many fill up between Easter and August. The University issues a useful leaflet advising mature students on completion of the UCAS form.
Greenwich assesses applications on the basis of the student's ability to benefit from the course. All relevant education and/or experience is considered.

Gwent College of Higher Education
Allt-yr-yn Avenue, Newport NP9 5XA

Tel: 0633 432432 **Fax:** 0633 432006
Contact: Admissions Office, P.O.Box 101, Newport NP6 1YH

Number of Undergraduates: 1800 full-time, many more part-time

Percentage of Mature Students: 72% of total student population
Male/Female Ratio: 47 : 53
Upper Age Limit for Mature Students: None

Learning Facilities: The library has 130,000 books, 550 periodicals and 300 study places. There are also extensive computing facilities, media resources, studio, TV and radio facilities.

Creche Facilities: Provided free by the Guild of Students during school holidays only.

Mature Students Adviser: The College has two Careers Officers, both of whom are trained to counsel mature students.

Accommodation: 700 single study-bedrooms with shared kitchen facilities. All first-year students are allocated College accommodation. No special provision for couples or families.

The main campus is in the village of Caerleon, three miles from Newport. The Business School and the Faculty of Technology are at Allt-yr-yn, a modern purpose-built campus close to the centre of Newport, while the School of Art and Design is based in an impressive Edwardian building at Clarence Place, also in the centre of town.

The beautiful Usk and Wye rivers, the proximity of the Black Mountains and the Brecon Beacons make Gwent an ideal place to study for those who love the outdoors; the Roman remains which have been excavated to reveal a massive amphitheatre and the widely held belief that Caerleon was the site of King Arthur's Camelot attract those interested in history and legend.

Degrees Available: BA in Combined Studies, Cultural and Critical Studies or in subjects within the School of Art and Design; BEng in Electronic and Instrumentation Systems only (three years full-time or four years sandwich); BSc; BEd – either a four-year course preparing students to teach at primary level, or a two-year course for mature students who already have an HND, to teach Design and Technology, Science or Maths at secondary level. There are extensive opportunities for part-time study.

Assessment: A combination of exams and continuous assessment, including practical and creative work where appropriate, and in some courses a final-year project or dissertation.

How to Apply: Through ADAR for Art and Design, otherwise through UCAS for full-time study. For part-time, contact the College direct. Access courses, BTEC awards, City and Guilds and relevant experience may be accepted as alternative qualifications. Mature students will be expected to show motivation and the ability to study.

Harper Adams Agricultural College
Newport, Shropshire TF10 8NB

Tel: 0952 820280 **Fax:** 0952 814783
Contact: Mrs G. Podmore, Admissions Secretary, direct line 0952 815000

Number of Undergraduates: 1300
Percentage of Mature Students: 23%
Male/Female Ratio: 7 : 3
Upper Age Limit for Mature Students: None

Learning Facilities: The library is purpose-built and open long hours. It contains about 32,000 books and subscribes to 700 periodicals. The College also has a computer centre, a modern suite of laboratories, engineering workshops and a farm.

Creche Facilities: No
Mature Students Adviser: The Senior Warden
Accommodation: Six Halls of Residence accommodate 530 students; there are also College houses and other approved accommodation. All first-year students can be accommodated. 'Special' provision for couples can be arranged via the Warden.

Harper Adams is a University Sector College with a national and international reputation in its specialist field – the provision of courses for the industries, services and professions associated with rural land. It is appropriately based in rural Shropshire, surrounded by good-quality agricultural land. All courses include environmental considerations hand-in-hand with commercial practice.

Degrees Available: BEng and BSc in Agriculture and related subjects. A one-year, full-time foundation course also offered.

Assessment: All degree courses are modular, assessed during and at the end of the semester in which the module is taught. A combination of exams and course work, especially practical work 'on the farm', is used.

How to Apply: Through UCAS, but if at the same time you apply direct to the College on a form available from the Admissions Office, your application will be processed more quickly. Mature applicants are considered on their merits, with prior experience and/or qualifications taken into account. You should expect to be invited for interview before being offered a place.

The College operates a CATS scheme (see page 12) and an Associate Student Scheme (see page 27).

Harrogate College
Hornbeam Park, Harrogate HG2 8QT

Tel: 0423 879466 **Fax:** 0423 879829
Contact: College Information Officer

Number of Undergraduates: About 1400 full-time, 7000 part-time on all levels of course
Percentage of Mature Students: Not specified
Male/Female Ratio: Not specified
Upper Age Limit for Mature Students: None

Learning Facilities: The library and learning resources centre closes at 4.30 p.m. on Fridays but stays open until 8 p.m. Monday to Thursday and is also open on Saturday mornings. Audio-visual and computing facilities are available.

Creche Facilities: Yes, open 50 weeks a year.
Mature Students Adviser: No, but all students have a personal tutor and there are counselling and welfare services.
Accommodation: None available through the College, but plentiful in Harrogate: the College General Office maintains a list of suitable accommodation for rent.

Harrogate College offers over 600 courses of a practical and vocational nature in Further Education and Training, and has excellent facilities to support them. Its one degree course is new for 1994/5.

The town of Harrogate grew up round its spa and although it now tends to attract conference-goers and tourists rather than those suffering from gout, its imposing Victorian buildings give it a rather old-fashioned look. It is on the edge of the glorious Yorkshire Dales, and within easy reach of both Leeds and York.

Degrees Available: BA in Study in Art and Design, validated by the University of Bradford.
There is also a foundation course in Art and Design.

Assessment: Through a combination of practical creative work and formal tests in theoretical aspects of the course.

How to Apply: Through ADAR for the degree course, direct for the foundation course. Mature students are not necessarily expected to meet the standard entry requirements, and credit may be given for prior learning and/or experience.

Institute of Health Care Studies (University of Wales)
University Hospital of Wales, Heath Park, Cardiff CF4 4XW

Tel: 0222 747747 **Fax:** 0222 747763
Contact: Admissions Officer

Number of Undergraduates: An intake of about 100 a year over three schools
Percentage of Mature Students: About 27%
Male/Female Ratio: 1 : 3
Upper Age Limit for Mature Students: 45

Learning Facilities: There is a large library and appropriate computing and clinical facilities.

Creche Facilities: Available at the University Hospital of Wales (see page 364).
Mature Students Adviser: Not specifically, but each student is assigned to a personal tutor and the Institute runs a counselling service for all students.
Accommodation: All first-year students who require it can be given a place in Institute accommodation. There are no special provisions for couples or families.

The Institute of Health Care Studies comprises three schools: the South East Wales School of Radiography, the Cardiff School of Physiotherapy and the Welsh School for Occupational Therapy. It is on the same site as the University Hospital of Wales in central Cardiff, but clinical teaching is carried out in a number of hospitals in South East Wales. The individual schools are small, allowing for personal attention to students' needs and progress, and the academic reputation of the courses is high.

Degrees Available: BSc in Occupational Therapy, Physiotherapy and Diagnostic Radiography. Degrees are validated by the University of Wales and, in the case of Physiotherapy, by the Chartered Society of Physiotherapy.

Assessment: By written and clinical exams; in Occupational Therapy you will also be required to write a dissertation in your final year. Clinical work is extremely important on all courses.

How to Apply: Through UCAS. Non-standard qualifications are considered on an individual basis. Access courses, BTEC awards and Open University units in science subjects may be acceptable. You must show evidence of recent study and have a science background equivalent to that of school-leavers with A levels. You are advised to send a CV to the relevant school in support of your application.

Heriot-Watt University
Riccarton, Edinburgh EH14 4AS

Tel: 031–449 5111 **Fax:** 031–449 5153
Contact: Admissions Officer

Please see page 2 for general information on Scottish universities and colleges

Number of Undergraduates: About 4500 at the main campus, almost as many again at other sites (see below and separate entries)
Percentage of Mature Students: About 17%
Male/Female Ratio: About 2 : 1
Upper Age Limit for Mature Students: None

Learning Facilities: During the term the main library is open till 9 p.m. Monday to Friday and from 9 a.m. to 5 p.m. at the weekend. It specialises in the subjects taught at the University and prides itself on in-depth coverage. Students can gain access to over a thousand databases through the University network. Comprehensive computing facilities are available to all students, and the University has pioneered research and development of computer-based learning. There are also excellent technical facilities for all Engineering and Science courses.

Creche Facilities: Yes, but places are limited so apply early.
Mature Students Adviser: Not specifically, but the full range of counselling and welfare services is available to all students.
Accommodation: There are over a thousand places in University Halls or flats, catering or self-catering, and 90% of first-years who come from outside Edinburgh can be accommodated. You have to apply to the University Welfare Services team for a

brochure and application form – this is not sent out automatically. There are no special provisions for couples or families and finding suitable cheap accommodation can be a problem. Contact the Welfare Services as early as possible for help.

Heriot-Watt came into being in 1966 as a technological university, but grew out of a 19th-century institute for technical education whose name commemorates two of the great figures of Scotland's technological history. Over the last ten years the University has invested £50 million in the 'state of the art' facilities of its new campus at Riccarton, a 380-acre landscaped site on a country estate just west of Edinburgh. The campus has been designed with the needs of the disabled in mind and there is wheelchair access throughout.

Three other colleges with long-established reputations in vocational and practical teaching – Moray House (for education), the Edinburgh College of Art and the Scottish College of Textiles – have recently become faculties of Heriot-Watt, and the University continues to expand and to maintain its reputation for high-quality specialised research.

Degrees Available: BA in the Faculty of Economic and Social Studies or in Landscape Architecture; BArch; BEng in a range of specialisms including Energy Resource Engineering and Offshore Engineering; BSc in a wide range of subjects including Building, Colour Chemistry, and Optoelectronics and Laser Engineering. In addition to the Science and Technology-based courses for which it is famous, Heriot-Watt also has excellent facilities for language study and offers courses in interpreting and translating.
From 1994 all courses will be modular.
For courses taught at the Edinburgh College of Art, Moray House and the Scottish College of Textiles, see separate entries on pages 154, 240 and 319.

Assessment: Each module is completed within a ten-week term and is assessed separately during and at the end of that term. Exams are supplemented by assessment of essays, lab work, reports, etc., as appropriate.

How to Apply: Through UCAS, but you are advised to contact the Admissions Tutor of the relevant department first to discuss your circumstances and to seek advice about whether or not your qualifications will be acceptable.
Heriot-Watt welcomes applications from prospective mature students who are taking Access courses or from those who can

demonstrate, through recent study, work experience or professional qualifications, that they are likely to be able to follow the course successfully. The University is part of SCOTCAT (see page 14), so will give credit for prior learning.

University of Hertfordshire
College Lane, Hatfield AL10 9AB

Tel: 0707 284000
Contact: Sandra Simpson, Mature Students Adviser

Number of Undergraduates: 14,000
Percentage of Mature Students: 50%
Male/Female Ratio: 1 : 1
Upper Age Limit for Mature Students: None

Learning Facilities: There are four libraries, one on each main campus. In term-time they open at least twelve hours a day during the week and on Saturday and Sunday afternoons. There are also ample computing facilities and language labs. Library and Media Services pride themselves on their use of new technology to accommodate students' study needs. The University also has its own observatory for the teaching of Astronomy.

Creche Facilities: Available on the Hatfield and Wall Hall campuses, for children aged between two and five years.
Mature Students Adviser: Sandra Simpson. There is also a Mature Students' Society and the University runs pre-entry workshops to help mature students cope with returning to study.
Accommodation: The University can accommodate 3000 students in Halls of Residence, and places are allocated to all first-years who require accommodation. There are some double rooms and a few flats for single parents.

The University of Hertfordshire consists of four campuses – in Hatfield, Hertford, St Albans and Wall Hall (about two miles from Watford). The St Albans campus is in the centre of the city; the others are spacious, attractively landscaped, green sites. The School of Art and Design is at St Albans; the Business School at Hertford; Engineering, Health and Human Sciences, Natural Sciences and Information Sciences at Hatfield; Humanities and Education at Wall Hall. Hertfordshire is a young university with modern facilities and a flexible and helpful approach to mature students.

Degrees Available: BA in Arts and Social Science subjects, and in Art and Design; BEd; BEng; BSc; LLB. A number of part-time and four-year sandwich courses are available, some of them taught in part or in whole at one of the University's Associate Colleges.

A general Access course and Access to Science and Technology are taught at Associate Colleges, as are foundation courses in Science and Engineering.

Assessment: A mixture of exams and continuous assessment, with a major final-year project or dissertation in most courses.

How to Apply: Through UCAS for most degree courses; through ADAR for Art and Design. If you wish to study part-time, apply direct to the University Registry. The University will consider the full range of alternative academic qualifications and relevant work experience; it also runs a CATS scheme (see page 12), so credit may be given for previous study.

For further information on credit transfer and adult guidance, contact Sandra Simpson on 0707 285220; for information on Access courses, contact Ailsa Herbert on 0707 285212.

Heythrop College (University of London)
Kensington Square, London W8 5HQ

Tel: 071–580 6941 **Fax:** 071–795 4200
Contact: Annabel Clarkson, Academic Registrar

Number of Undergraduates: 122
Percentage of Mature Students: 60%
Male/Female Ratio: 2 : 1
Upper Age Limit for Mature Students: None

Learning Facilities: The library has 250,000 volumes, including one of the finest collections of works on theology and philosophy in the UK. It is open until 7 p.m. Monday to Friday in term-time and holidays, and all day Saturday during the term. The College also has appropriate computer facilities.

Heythrop is an independent college within the University of London. Students therefore have the advantages of belonging to a small community, plus the benefits of membership of the University of London Students' Union and the opportunity to register with the University of London Central Institutions Health Service and Careers Advisory Service. Being so small, Heythrop has limited sports and social facilities of its own, but students may use those of nearby Imperial College.

Heythrop undergraduates cover a wide age range and integration between older and younger students is very good.

Heythrop's history dates back to 1641, when a college was established in Louvain in France for the education of English Jesuit students. After the French Revolution the college was moved to England, eventually becoming part of the University of London in 1970 and occupying its new site in a quiet square behind Kensington High St in 1993. It prides itself on high academic standards, underlined by the system of weekly one-to-one tutorials which are compulsory for all first-year students.

Creche Facilities: No

Mature Students Adviser: No, but a counselling service is available to any student who needs it.

Accommodation: The University of London Intercollegiate Halls of Residence have places for 2500 students, and all first-year students at Heythrop who wish for accommodation are offered places. There is some provision for couples. Contact the University of London Accommodation Office, Senate House, Malet St, London WC1E 7HU, telephone 071–636 2818.

Degrees Available: BA in Biblical Studies, Philosophy and Philosophy and Theology only; BD in Theology.
There are opportunities for part-time study – contact the Academic Registrar for details.

Assessment: The emphasis is on exams, but some courses also require an extended essay in the final year.

How to Apply: Through UCAS. Heythrop gives sympathetic consideration to mature applicants who are taking or have completed a recognised Access course, and to those with a variety of other non-standard qualifications.

Hinckley College of Further Education
London Rd, Hinckley LE10 1HQ

Tel: 0455 251222 **Fax:** 0455 633930
Contact: Mrs Pauline Taylor, Lecturer

Number of Undergraduates: 15 for the degree course; many more on other courses at various levels
Percentage of Mature Students: Not specified
Male/Female Ratio: All female so far on the degree course
Upper Age Limit for Mature Students: None

Learning Facilities: The library is small but expanding, and the College supplies transport for students wishing to use the De Montfort University library. There is a computer-aided design suite and appropriate industrial laboratories.

Creche Facilities: Yes
Mature Students Adviser: Yes
Accommodation: None available through the College, though accommodation can usually be arranged in the town.

Hinckley's one degree course was first offered in 1992; the College otherwise provides a wide range of Access and foundation courses, GCSE, A level and technical courses, full- or part-time.

Hinckley gives students the opportunity to study in a quiet and friendly environment but is only 13 miles from De Montfort University Leicester, where a wider range of facilities is available. De Montfort also validates the Hinckley degree course.

Degrees Available: BSc in Knitwear Design and Production. This is a modular course allowing for part-time study.

Assessment: Each unit is examined separately, by continuous assessment, project assessment and end-of-semester exams.

How to Apply: Direct, although non-mature students apply through ADAR. Applications should ideally be in by 30 April; any received after that date will be considered if places are still available.

Holborn College
200 Greyhound Rd, London W14 9RY

Tel: 071–385 3377 **Fax:** 071–381 3377
Contact: Admissions Officer

Number of Undergraduates: 800
Percentage of Mature Students: About 6%
Male/Female Ratio: 1 : 1
Upper Age Limit for Mature Students: None

Learning Facilities: The library has about 12,000 volumes. There is also a computer laboratory.

Creche Facilities: No
Mature Students Adviser: No, but academic counsellors and the welfare officer are available to advise all students.

Accommodation: There is no College accommodation, but plenty of privately rented accommodation of various types is available locally.

Established in 1970 as a specialist independent Law School preparing students for the University of London LLB and professional examinations, Holborn College now also offers degrees in Business Studies validated by the University of London. In 1991 it became an Associate College of the University of Wolverhampton, which now also validates an LLB course at Holborn. The College is 'recognised as efficient by the British Accreditation Council', having been one of the first independent colleges to put itself forward for inspection (independent colleges are not required by law to do this); it was also the first educational establishment to win the Queen's Award for Export Achievement, because of the international nature of its work.

The College has no medical or sports facilities, but these are readily available in the area and the College organises a variety of extra-curricular activities. It is situated in Fulham, within easy reach of all London has to offer.

Degrees Available: LLB validated by London or Wolverhampton; BSc (Econ) in Accounting, Management Studies or Economics and Management Studies validated by London.
The College also offers a flexible distance-learning LLB course for students who are unable to attend classes. This must be completed within seven years, but usually takes much less. It is possible to change from full- to part-time study or from distance learning to the internal degree programme and vice versa at any time during the course.

Assessment: A combination of exams and continuous assessment, although exams are very important. Each course follows a College Course Planner, which contains a syllabus, reading list and details of what students should be concentrating on week by week.

How to Apply: Direct to the College at least six weeks before the start of the course. Application forms are available from the Admissions Officer. Do not wait for exam results before applying.
Standard entry requirements (i.e. A levels or equivalent) may be waived, in the case of Wolverhampton, if there is a 'reasonable expectation' that you will be able to follow the course success-fully. The College also has a flexible attitude to assessing prior learning and/or experience. For the University of London

degrees, evidence of mature age study is usually required – i.e. Access courses, BTEC awards, etc.

Homerton College
Cambridge CB2 2PH

Tel: 0223 411141 **Fax:** 0223 411622
Contact: Admissions Secretary

Number of Undergraduates: About 600
Percentage of Mature Students: About 5%
Male/Female Ratio: About 1 : 10
Upper Age Limit for Mature Students: None specified

Learning Facilities: Large specialist library, computing facilities, a dance centre and laboratories, plus all the facilities of the University of Cambridge.

Creche Facilities: No, but help with childcare expenses may be available to student parents.
Mature Students Adviser: No, but counselling and other support is available through the University.
Accommodation: Most first-years have rooms in College; there are no special provisions for couples or families.

Homerton is an Approved Society of the University of Cambridge; in most respects it functions like the other colleges, although its admissions procedure is different – see below. Arts degrees with a Certificate of Education are available through other Cambridge colleges, but the BEd degree is only available through Homerton.

The College is out of town but – as you might expect at Cambridge – within easy cycling distance.

Degrees Available: BEd (four years) with a qualification to teach at lower or upper primary level.

Assessment: Exams in the specialist subject and in Education. Satisfactory performance in teaching practice is essential.

How to Apply: If you are applying to any other Cambridge college as well, follow the application procedure outlined under the University of Cambridge (page 106). If Homerton is the only Cambridge college to which you are applying, follow the standard UCAS procedure and note that the UCAS deadline of

15 December, rather than the Cambridge Intercollegiate one of 15 October, applies.

Homerton welcomes applications from mature candidates, particularly those on approved Access courses: the normal entry requirements may be waived in these cases. You are welcome to contact the Admissions Tutor to discuss your circumstances before submitting a formal application, and you should expect to be invited for interview before being offered a place.

The University of Huddersfield
Queensgate, Huddersfield HD1 3DH

Tel: 0484 422288 **Fax:** 0484 516151
Contact: Assistant Registrar (Admissions)

Number of Undergraduates: Nearly 8000 full-time, over 3000 part-time (day and evening)
Percentage of Mature Students: 57%
Male/Female Ratio: About 3 : 2
Upper Age Limit for Mature Students: None specified

Learning Facilities: The main library has over 300,000 items, with an expanding audio-visual collection and access to CD-Rom databases. It is open long hours, including weekends. There are comprehensive computing and audio-visual facilities.

Creche Facilities: Very cheap, for children aged six weeks to five years. The nursery is managed by a local children's nursery association, which can also provide after-school and holiday care for older children.

Mature Students Adviser: Not specifically, but the help of qualified counsellors is available to all students.

Accommodation: Over a thousand places in catering and self-catering Halls of Residence, mainly on or near the main campus, with priority given to first-year students. There are no special provisions for couples or families, but private rented accommodation is plentiful and cheap and the Accommodation Office will help all students find somewhere suitable to live.

Most of the University is on a single campus, Queensgate, in the centre of Huddersfield, with the School of Education based at Holly Bank, about two miles out of town. Although the facilities are modern, a number of the buildings date from the 19th century, when the Huddersfield Technical College was established. This expanded steadily, grew into the poly in the 1940s and became a University in 1992.

Huddersfield is a typical industrial town of the region, with its history rooted in textile mills and transportation by canal. For those who want big-city facilities, it is very close to Leeds and the M62, which also brings Manchester within easy reach. The surrounding Pennine countryside is some of the most striking in England.

Degrees Available: BA in Accountancy, Architectural Studies (International), Applied Social Studies, Surface Pattern and in the Schools of Business, Music and Humanities; BSc in Textile Design, Product Design and in the Schools of Applied Sciences and Human and Health Sciences; also BA or BSc in the School of Computing and Mathematics; BMus; LLB; BEng; BEd – two-year courses for those who already have an HND, leading to a qualification to teach at secondary level only.
Many courses include a sandwich element, and it is hoped that it will soon be possible to include some work experience on all courses. There are one-year foundation courses in Accountancy, Science and Engineering.
A CATS scheme (see page 12) is currently being developed and all courses will soon be modular – many already are. Many courses can be followed part-time – contact the Assistant Registrar (Admissions) for details.

Assessment: Varies from course to course, but generally a combination of exams and continuous assessment, including practical work and work placements. Some courses include a major project in the final year. On modular courses each unit is assessed separately, during and at the end of the year.

How to Apply: Through ADAR for Surface Pattern, Textile Design and Product Design; otherwise through UCAS for full-time study. For foundation courses or part-time study, you should apply direct to the University on a form obtainable from the Assistant Registrar (Admissions).
Mature applicants without traditional qualifications will be assessed on their individual merits; relevant experience will be taken into consideration, but evidence of recent study, usually in the form of an Access course or Open University credits, is desirable. You should expect to be invited for an interview before being offered a place.

University of Hull
Hull HU6 7RX

Tel: 0482 46311
Contact: Schools and Colleges Liaison Officer

Number of Undergraduates: 5971
Percentage of Mature Students: 12%
Male/Female Ratio: 1 : 1
Upper Age Limit for Mature Students: None

Learning Facilities: The library has over 800,000 books and seating for 1600 readers. There is a computer centre and a language centre with computer-assisted language learning.

Creche Facilities: Enthusiastic and well-organised, accommodating children from three months to five years. The Students' Union issues a Nursery Handbook with information for parents.

Mature Students Adviser: No, but the usual welfare services are available.

Accommodation: The University owns or manages a number of Halls of Residence, flats and houses, and all first-year students can be accommodated. There are very limited facilities for couples.

The academic departments of the University of Hull are situated on a single campus about two miles out of town, with some university accommodation as much as three miles away. Not the easiest place in the country to get to, Hull is nevertheless a popular, fast-growing and friendly university. Philip Larkin used to be the librarian here and the University library now houses an important Larkin Collection.

Degrees Available: BA in a range of Arts and Social Science subjects, including Dutch and Scandinavian Studies as well as the more commonly found languages; BMus; BSc in Accounting and in Science subjects; BSc (Econ); LLB; BEng in a number of subjects including Engineering Design and Manufacture, Optoelectronics and Laser Systems Engineering and Ecological and Environmental Engineering. There is also a four-year BSc course called Engineering Europe, which includes a choice of six European languages, and another in Engineering Science, which is aimed at applicants who do not have Science A levels.
There are opportunities for part-time study – contact the Department of Adult Education for details. Credit given for previous study and/or work experience means that it is sometimes possible to enter a course in the second year.

Assessment: A mixture of exams and continuous assessment, varying from course to course.

How to Apply: Through UCAS. Mature students may like to contact the relevant department direct before making a formal application. Although applications should ideally be submitted by the UCAS deadline of 15 December, they will be considered throughout the year.

A wide variety of qualifications of a similar standard to A level will be considered.

University of Humberside

Admissions Processing Unit, Registry, Milner Hall, Cottingham Road, Hull HU6 7RT

Tel: 0482 440550 **Fax:** 0482 471343

Contact: Student Services for general information and to be referred on to someone who can handle a more specific enquiry

Number of Undergraduates: 10,971
Percentage of Mature Students: About 53%
Male/Female Ratio: 1 : 1
Upper Age Limit for Mature Students: None

Learning Facilities: The library has 180,000 volumes, 1400 journals and 900 reading spaces. There are comprehensive computing facilities with a thousand work stations, media services including TV and radio studios, and Engineering and Food Science labs.

Creche Facilities: Not at present, but may become available in the near future.

Mature Students Adviser: One of the Careers Officers has special responsibility for mature students.

Accommodation: There are 452 places in Halls of Residence, reserved for first-year students and those with special needs. There are also 469 places in self-catering accommodation and many more in University-approved rented accommodation. About 60% of first-years are allocated a place. The University Accommodation Service can give advice to couples and families on finding somewhere suitable to live.

The University of Humberside is based on four sites, three within easy reach of each other in Hull and the School of Food, Fisheries and Environmental Studies about 30 miles away, across the Humber Bridge, in the famous fishing port of Grimsby.

Humberside is considered by many to be a great place to be a student. It is certainly cheaper than average. It has a history dating back to Roman and Viking times, though its first big date is 1066 – King Harold fought the Battle of Stamford Bridge here before heading south to

Hastings. Nowadays, Hull is perhaps better known as the home of two major rugby league teams, but other sporting and leisure activities are also well catered for.

Degrees Available: BA in the School of Art, Architecture and Design; BA, BSc or BEng in the Business School; BA or BSc in the Schools of Food, Fisheries and Environmental Studies and Social and Professional Studies.
Foundation courses are available in Food Science and Engineering; the University is also a member of the local Authorised Validating Agency for Access courses and can recommend a course to prospective students wishing to follow this route. Successful completion of one of these courses will guarantee you a place at Humberside.
Part-time study is available on many courses.

Assessment: A combination of exams and continuous assessment. Many courses are largely practical, with the emphasis on creative work, project work and case studies where applicable.
By 1994 most courses will be modular and each unit will be assessed separately during and at the end of the semester in which it is taught.

How to Apply: Through ADAR for Art and Design, otherwise through UCAS for full-time courses; for part-time study apply direct to the University on a form available from the Admissions Processing Unit, University of Humberside, FREEPOST, Hull HU6 7BR, telephone as above. If sending to the University for an application form, please specify the title of the course for which you wish to apply. For Art, Design and Architecture, expect to be invited for interview and to present a portfolio of work.
Humberside welcomes applications from prospective mature students with non-standard qualifications and will treat each one on its individual merits. Any alternative qualifications and/or experience may be acceptable. The University runs both a CATS and an APEL scheme (see page 12).

Imperial College of Science, Technology and Medicine (University of London)
South Kensington, London SW7 2AZ

Tel: 071–589 5111 **Fax:** 071–225 2528
Contact: Admissions Office

Number of Undergraduates: About 4550
Percentage of Mature Students: About 3%
Male/Female Ratio: About 3 : 1, but the numbers of women are increasing
Upper Age Limit for Mature Students: None specified

Learning Facilities: The libraries, which include the library of the Science Museum, house specialist collections relating to Imperial courses. Their stock totals over 300,000 volumes and they are open in the evenings and on Saturdays. The libraries have up-to-date technology for accessing information of all kinds, there are full computing facilities and excellent laboratories and technical support for all courses.

Creche Facilities: Available for children aged six months to five years. There is always a waiting list, so telephone the Nursery Manager on extension 3356 as soon as possible.
Mature Students Adviser: Not specifically, but there are qualified student counsellors and the full range of support.
Accommodation: Imperial guarantees a place for all first-year students, either in its own Halls of Residence (about a thousand places) or in the University of London's Intercollegiate Halls. To apply to the latter, contact the University of London Accommodation Office, Senate House, Malet St, London WC1E 7HU, telephone 071–636 2818. Imperial also has a few shared rooms and small flats.

Imperial College is a constituent college of the University of London. It was founded in 1907 by Royal Charter, although it was formed from the merger of several older colleges, the eldest of which, the Royal College of Chemistry, was established by Albert, the Prince Consort, in 1845.

The Royal Charter stated that the College 'aims to give the highest specialised instruction, and to provide the fullest equipment for the most advanced training and research in various branches of science, especially in its application to industry', and as the prospectus says, these aims remain very much unchanged. Science is taken seriously at Imperial – so much so that one of its social clubs is the T.H. Huxley society, in memory of the great Victorian biologist.

Imperial College is on a 16-acre site in South Kensington, near Hyde Park and museum land.

Degrees Available: BEng or BSc in a wide range of scientific and technological subjects, including Associateship of the City and Guilds of London Institute, the Royal School of Mines or the Royal College of Science.

Assessment: Formal exams combined with assessment of projects, seminar papers, practical work, essays, etc.

How to Apply: Through UCAS. Mature applicants without traditional qualifications will be considered on an individual basis and expected to show sufficient competence in the chosen field to undertake the degree course successfully. You are advised to contact the Admissions Tutor in the relevant department for advice before submitting your application.

Jews' College (University of London)
Albert Rd, London NW4 2SJ

Tel: 081–203 6427 **Fax:** 081–203 6420
Contact: Clive A. Fierstone, Academic Registrar

Number of Undergraduates: 22
Percentage of Mature Students: 27%
Male/Female Ratio: 5 : 3
Upper Age Limit for Mature Students: None

Learning Facilities: The library, which has 80,000 volumes, is closed on Saturdays but open on Sunday mornings. Computer facilities are available to all students.

Creche Facilities: No
Mature Students Adviser: No, but there is a counselling service available to any student who needs it.
Accommodation: Limited, especially for women students and offered on a first-come, first-served basis. There are no provisions for couples or families.

This tiny college – there are only 54 post-graduate students in addition to the 22 undergraduates – is situated in Hendon, one of the most predominantly Jewish areas of London, with innumerable kosher shops and restaurants. The College offers certificates, diplomas and post-graduate degrees as well as its one Bachelor's degree, and concentrates exclusively on Jewish Studies. Some graduates go on to study for the rabbinate, but the BA is accepted by employers in computing, accountancy, law and almost every field requiring graduate entrance. Because the College is so small, students benefit from individual attention and are better able to progress at their own pace than they would be in a larger institution.

Jews' College is part of the University of London, but has its own Students' Union and is home to the UK branch of Yavneh Olami, the worldwide Organisation of Religious Students.

Degrees Available: BA in Jewish Studies.
A preliminary year of study may be necessary for those with insufficient background in Jewish Studies to benefit fully from this course.

Assessment: Exams and continuous assessment, with a 5000-7000 word essay counting as one unit in the final year.

How to Apply: Normally through UCAS, but mature students without conventional qualifications should write direct to the College. Each application is considered on its merits. Relevant prior learning may enable you to enter a course in the second year.
A level Hebrew (classical or modern) is preferred, but the requisite knowledge of the language can be gained in the preliminary year.

Keele University
Staffs ST5 5BG

Tel: 0782 621111 **Fax:** 0782 613847
0782 632343 (Department of Academic Affairs)
Contact: Undergraduate Admissions Office

Number of Undergraduates: 3500
Percentage of Mature Students: About 20%
Male/Female Ratio: 1 : 1
Upper Age Limit for Mature Students: None specified

Learning Facilities: The library is very large and includes a substantial map collection; it is open every day and during the evenings in semester-time. There are extensive computing facilities, a Media and Communication Centre providing audio-visual services, laboratories and access to clinical facilities for relevant courses.

Creche Facilities: For children aged three months to five years, with 50 places for students' children. The nursery officially closes at 5.15 but arrangements can be made to look after children whose parents have lectures later than this. Places are in great demand, so apply early.

Mature Students Adviser: Not specifically, but the usual range of welfare services is available to all students.

Accommodation: Available for all first-years, usually in self-catering Halls of Residence. There are a small number of flats and houses suitable for families, but early application is essential.

Keele is situated on an enormous (600-acre) campus in the middle of the Potteries, two miles from Newcastle-under-Lyme and five from Stoke. The campus has banks and shops which supply most everyday needs. Despite being in the middle of nowhere, it has the M6 and the railway hub of Crewe not far away, so is easy to reach from all over the UK.

Keele has been a university since 1962 and has a well-established research base; bearing the multi-disciplinary nature of today's workplace in mind, it also offers an enormous variety of subject combinations.

Degrees Available: BA in a very wide range of Arts and Social Science subjects; BA with Certificate of Education enabling you to teach at primary or secondary level (four years); BSc in Biomedical Sciences or Diagnostic or Therapeutic Radiography, or in a limited number of Science subjects.

In addition to all the usual subjects, Keele offers such rarities as Astrophysics, Criminology and Electronic Music. Most courses are joint honours, with unusual combinations like Russian Studies and Biology, Geology and Law, or Classical Studies and International Politics being permitted.

Most courses may be extended to four years to include a foundation year.

All courses are modular.

A BSc in Physiotherapy validated by Keele is taught mainly at the Oswestry and North Staffordshire School of Physiotherapy.

Assessment: A combination of exams and continuous assessment, with each module assessed separately during and at the end of the semester in which it is taught.

How to Apply: Through UCAS, but you are welcome to write to the Undergraduate Admissions Office in support of your application. Please do not do this until you have received a serial number from UCAS (see page 48), and quote this in your letter.

Keele gives careful and sympathetic consideration to all applications from prospective mature students, but you will have most chance of success if you can show evidence of recent academic study. If you are applying for admission to a four-year course (including the foundation year), you will not necessarily be expected to have the specific subject knowledge that would be required for entry to the three-year course, but you should still be able to show academic ability and potential.

Keele operates a CATS scheme (see page 12), so credit may be given for prior learning.

University of Kent at Canterbury
Canterbury CT2 7NZ

Tel: 0227 764000 **Fax:** 0227 452196
Contact: Admissions Officer

Number of Undergraduates: 4500
Percentage of Mature Students: 10–15%
Male/Female Ratio: About 5 : 4
Upper Age Limit for Mature Students: None

Learning Facilities: The library holds nearly a million items, including books, pamphlets and microforms; it subscribes to 3200 periodicals covering every subject taught at the University, and has a number of specialist collections ranging from EC publications to rare books in literature and theology. Students also have access to the archive collection at Canterbury Cathedral. The Computing Laboratory provides a network of terminals throughout the campus, and all students are encouraged to take some form of computing course. There are up-to-the-minute facilities for language study, and specialist labs and workshops for relevant subjects.

Creche Facilities: For children aged six weeks to five years. The Students' Union subsidises fees for student parents on low incomes. You are advised to apply about six months before you wish to take up a place. Write to The Supervisor, The Oaks, Giles Lane, Canterbury CT2 7LX.

Mature Students Adviser: The School of Continuing Education will advise on applications and qualifications; there are confidential counselling and welfare services for all students, and a Mature Students' Society. The Faculty of Social Sciences issues an information sheet for mature students which gives both general guidance and specific advice about applying for individual courses.

Accommodation: Places are guaranteed for all first-year students who apply by 15 August. Finding suitable accommodation for families can be difficult – contact the Accommodation Office for help as early as possible, and do not plan to move your family until you are sure you have somewhere suitable to live.

The University of Kent at Canterbury is on an attractive hillside campus within walking distance of the city centre – it holds its degree award ceremonies in the cathedral.

Kent is a collegiate University and all students are admitted to one of four colleges, which have their own teaching and study facilities, accommodation and social lives. One of the colleges, Keynes, has specially adapted accommodation for the disabled.

Although Kent, founded in 1965, is a comparatively young university, it has an established academic reputation, with many of its teaching staff conducting research in the forefront of their fields. Its youth is reflected in its flexible approach: courses are designed to offer students as much choice as possible. It also has some of the strongest links with Europe of any UK university. And, commendably, it states its equal opportunities admissions policy prominently on the inside front cover of the prospectus rather than tucking it away in the small print.

Degrees Available: BA in an interesting range of Humanities and Social Science subjects, including African and Caribbean Studies, Development Studies, Economic Analysis, History and Policy, Film Studies, and Theology and Religious Studies with a year in Jerusalem; BA, BSc or BEng in the Faculty of Information Technology, which includes the Institute of Mathematics and Statistics; BSc in the Faculty of Natural Sciences; LLB including a number of options involving the law and/or language of a European country.

Many courses involve a sandwich element, and many include the possibility of studying a modern language.

All courses may be followed part-time and although there is no overall time limit, some must be completed within six years lest material become out of date. There are also some purpose-designed part-time courses which hold classes in the evenings – contact the School of Continuing Education for details.

Many courses include a foundation year for those who do not have A levels in appropriate subjects, and the University runs its own Access courses – again, contact the School of Continuing Education.

Assessment: A combination of exams and continuous assessment, including dissertations, projects and practical work. Final-year exams are by far the most important element in most courses, with something between 70 and 90% of your total marks earned from them.

How to Apply: Through UCAS for full-time study, direct for part-time. Applications from prospective mature students who can show commitment and evidence of recent study are very welcome. Each application is considered on its individual merits and credit is given for prior learning.

Kent Institute of Art and Design

School of Visual Communication, Oakwood Park, Maidstone ME16 8AG

Tel: 0622 757286 **Fax:** 0622 692003
Contact: Registry

School of Fine Art, New Dover Rd, Canterbury CT1 3AN

Tel: 0227 769371 **Fax:** 0227 451320
Contact: Admissions Office

Rochester upon Medway College
Fort Pitt, Rochester ME1 1DZ

Tel: 0634 830022 **Fax:** 0634 829461
Contact: Admissions Office

Number of Undergraduates: 1330
Percentage of Mature Students: About 25%
Male/Female Ratio: 1 : 1
Upper Age Limit for Mature Students: None

Learning Facilities: The library has over 77,000 books, plus videos, a slide library, etc. There are comprehensive computing facilities and well-equipped studios.

Creche Facilities: No
Mature Students Adviser: No, but welfare services are available to all students.
Accommodation: Limited College accommodation provides places for 27% of first-year students, with no provision for couples or families. Most students live in private rented accommodation.

The Kent Institute of Art and Design was founded in 1987 from the merger of three older Colleges of Art, and retains its three separate sites. All are close to their respective town/city centres.

The Institute has expanded its range of degree courses over the last few years and has excellent facilities for teaching its specialist subjects. Degrees are validated by the University of Kent at Canterbury.

Degrees Available: At Maidstone: BA in Communication Media. At Canterbury: BA in Architecture or Fine Art. At Rochester: BA in European Fashion (four-year sandwich) or Three-Dimensional Design.
Foundation courses are available and part-time study is possible.

Assessment: These are practical courses with the emphasis on creative work and personal projects.

How to Apply: Through UCAS for Architecture, European Fashion or Three-Dimensional Design; otherwise through ADAR.
Credit may be given for previous learning and/or experience, but this varies from course to course. Contact the relevant college for further details.

King Alfred's
Winchester SO22 4NR

Tel: 0962 841515 **Fax:** 0962 842280
Contact: Admissions Officer

Number of Undergraduates: About 2000
Percentage of Mature Students: About 25%
Male/Female Ratio: About 1 : 3
Upper Age Limit for Mature Students: None

Learning Facilities: The library stocks 100,000 items and sub-scribes to 500 periodicals. In addition the School Resources Collection supplies a wide variety of books, audio-visual materials, teaching kits, etc as back-up to students on teaching practice. The College has comprehensive computing facilities, audio-visual resources, a television centre and a modern theatre and Arts Centre.

Creche Facilities: For children aged three to five, during term-time only.
Mature Students Adviser: The Mature Students' subcommittee holds regular meetings.

Accommodation: 550 places in Halls of Residence or flats can accommodate all first-year students who live more than 25 miles from Winchester and who apply before the end of June. There are four flatlets suitable for married students.

King Alfred's is a University Sector College affiliated to the University of Southampton, which validates its degrees. It sits on a hill overlooking the historic city of Winchester, ten minutes' walk away. Founded over 150 years ago as a training centre for Anglican schoolmasters, it now welcomes students of all faiths or none but retains a strong Christian identity.

Degrees Available: BA in a few Joint Honours programmes; BA or BSc in Combined Studies; BA with QTS for primary teaching (four years); BEd for teaching Design and Technology or Maths at secondary level (two years, for mature students who already have an HND or HNC).
Those who wish to study part-time are welcome on the Combined Studies programme.

Assessment: Most courses are modular and each unit or area of study is assessed separately 'in ways appropriate to its content'. The emphasis is on continuous assessment; not all courses have formal exams. Teaching practice is an integral part of Education degrees.

How to Apply: Through UCAS. Mature applicants are welcomed and a range of alternative qualifications, including Open University credits or successful completion of an Access course, may be accepted. Relevant experience will also be taken into account. You are invited to contact the Admissions Office for advice and information before submitting a formal application. The College is developing a CATS scheme (see page 12) which means you will be able to receive credit for relevant prior learning.

--------- ❊ ---------

King's College London (University of London)
Strand, London WC2R 2LS

Tel: 071–836 5454 **Fax:** 071–836 1799
Contact: Relevant School Office

Number of Undergraduates: 6750
Percentage of Mature Students: About 22%

Male/Female Ratio: 1 : 1
Upper Age Limit for Mature Students: None

Learning Facilities: The library has over 800,000 books, subscribes to some 3000 periodicals and has a number of specialist
collections. There are comprehensive computing facilities,
audio-visual aids and a Language Centre offering general and
specialist courses. Students are also eligible to use the library of
the University of London.

Creche Facilities: No

Mature Students Adviser: Not specifically, but the College
produces a helpful 'Guide for Mature Students', and advice for
all students is available from confidential counselling staff,
academic advisers, the Careers Office, etc, depending on the
nature of the problem.

Accommodation: The College has a number of Halls of Residence
and 75% of places are reserved for first-years. The property
section of the Accommodation Office will help with rented
accommodation. Limited accommodation is available for married students. Students may also apply for a place in one of the
University of London's Intercollegiate Halls: contact the
University of London Accommodation Office, Senate House,
Malet St, London WC1E 7HU, telephone 071–636 2818.

*King's College is a constituent college of the University of London, based
in the Strand but with a number of smaller campuses scattered across
London. Founded in 1829 with strong links with the Church of England,
King's now welcomes students of any faith or none, but continues to hold
regular multi-denominational Christian services in its handsome 19th-
century chapel. In addition to its degree programmes, King's offers a
unique further qualification: the Associateship of King's College, which
is awarded to any student who successfully completes an optional series of
lectures encouraging you to think systemically about ethical and
philosophical questions.*

Degrees Available: BA in a range of Arts subjects; BMus; LLB
including options in European, French or German Legal
Studies; BSc with Postgraduate Certificate in Education; BEng
or BSc (Eng); BPharm; BSc in the Management Group, the
Nursing Group, Life Sciences, Mathematical and Physical
Sciences, and in Environmental Health, Nutrition and Dietetics, Physiotherapy and Radiography (the last four are all four-
year courses including the relevant State Registration). In the
Nursing Group, the BSc in Nursing is a four-year course, in

Community Nursing and Midwifery three years, all including professional qualifications.

The preliminary courses in Natural Sciences, which may be considered foundation years for Medicine and Dentistry (see next entry), are also taught at King's. Foundation courses in Life Science, Physical Science or Engineering are available in association with the City of Westminster College: contact the Senior Tutor at the School of Life, Basic Medical and Health Sciences, King's College London, Kensington Campus, Campden Hill Rd, London W8 7AH for details.

Most undergraduate degree courses are modular, making them suitable for part-time study.

Assessment: Written exams normally count for at least 60% of the final mark, though most courses also assess essays, linguistic ability, practical work and projects, depending on the subject. In modular courses, all units are assessed individually, during or at the end of the relevant semester.

How to Apply: Through UCAS, but write to the appropriate School Office first, giving details of your qualifications and experience: they will be able to advise you as to whether these are likely to be acceptable.

King's welcomes applications from mature students and will consider a wide range of alternative qualifications and/or experience on an individual basis. You should expect to be invited for interview before being offered a place.

King's College School of Medicine and Dentistry (University of London)
Medicine, Bessemer Rd, London SE5 9PJ
Tel: 071–274 6222 x 4017

Dentistry, Caldecot Rd, London SE5 9RW
Tel: 071–326 3079
Contact: Admissions Office at relevant site

Number of Undergraduates: About 500 in Medicine, 272 in Dentistry
Percentage of Mature Students: About 12%
Male/Female Ratio: 4 : 3
Upper Age Limit for Mature Students: About 35

Learning Facilities: The specialist library at Denmark Hill has 30,000 books and bound journals. Students also have access to the main King's College library and the University of London library. There is a computer unit, research laboratories and dental clinics. Clinical teaching is done at local medical and dental hospitals.

Creche Facilities: Yes
Mature Students Adviser: Not specifically, but welfare and counselling services are available to any student who needs them.
Accommodation: See King's College, above

The School is part of King's College London, which in turn is part of the University of London. King's College Hospital has a distinguished history – Joseph Lister did much of his research into antiseptics there. The first two (preclinical) years of the Medicine and Dentistry courses are taught largely at King's College in the Strand (see previous entry), giving students the chance of mixing with students from a wide range of other disciplines. Clinical teaching (years three to five) is mostly based at the King's College Hospital and Dental School in South London.

Degrees Available: BDS; MB BS; both five years.
There is also an Intercalated BSc, an optional one-year course which may be taken between the preclinical and clinical parts of the main degree.
The School also offers a one-year Preliminary Course in Natural Sciences, successful completion of which guarantees a place on the Medicine or Dentistry course.

Assessment: Exams and assessment throughout the clinical part of the course.

How to Apply: Through UCAS.
Good A levels or equivalent are usually required. The Preliminary Course in Natural Sciences encourages applications from prospective students with A levels in non-science subjects.

Kingston University
Penrhyn Rd, Kingston upon Thames KT1 2EE

Tel: 081–547 2000 **Fax:** 081–547 7178
Contact: Admissions Office

Number of Undergraduates: 11,370
Percentage of Mature Students: About 32%
Male/Female Ratio: 3 : 2

Upper Age Limit for Mature Students: None

Learning Facilities: Four libraries have a total of 350,000 books, 300 current journals and 965 study places. There are 1800 computer terminals, CD-Rom databases, appropriate science and language laboratories.

Creche Facilities: Available for children aged two to five.

Mature Students Adviser: Not as such, but there is plenty of support from both academic and non-academic staff.

Accommodation: Self-catering single rooms on campus accommodate about 78% of first-year students. Most mature students at Kingston are local, but the Accommodation Office will give any help that may be necessary.

Formed from the joining together of a polytechnic, a College of Art, a College of Technology and a College of Education, Kingston University now has 36 Schools and Departments within its six faculties, and prides itself on its vocational bias: the percentage of its graduates who find full-time employment is well above the national average. It has a friendly approach to mature students and publishes a number of useful leaflets about part-time and Access courses.

The University is on four main sites, well connected by bus services and combining the advantages of pleasant green surroundings with easy access to London. Kingston itself is mentioned in the Domesday Book and Kingston upon Thames is the oldest of London's four royal boroughs. Hampton Court and Kew Gardens are the principal local attractions.

Degrees Available: BA in Arts subjects, Architecture and Landscape Studies and in the Schools of Fashion, Fine Art, Graphic Design, Surveying and Three-Dimensional Design; BEd for teaching the 3–8 or 7–12 age ranges; BEng; BSc; LLB, including the option of European and International Legal Systems. Sandwich courses are available in Science and Engineering.

The Faculty of Science operates a modular degree scheme, allowing students a wide choice of combinations of subjects and the ability to change specialisation if they wish.

Kingston also runs a part-time Combined Studies course (BA or BSc) aimed specifically at mature students: subjects available range from Economics to the History of Art, Architecture and Design. Most courses take two evenings a week and you can expect to obtain your degree after five or six years. Other part-time courses are available in all six faculties.

The University is part of the Surrey and South West London Access Agency and a wide variety of Access courses are run at nearby colleges. Foundation courses in Accountancy, Art and

Design, Science and Engineering are taught at the University itself.

Assessment: Modular degrees are assessed unit by unit. Most courses combine exams and continuous assessment, with a major project or dissertation in the final year. In some courses in the Faculty of Design, 80% of the degree is assessed on practical work, with only 20% dependent on end-of-year exams.

How to Apply: Through ADAR for courses in the Faculty of Design; otherwise through UCAS for full-time study, but contact the Admissions Office for advice before submitting your application or if you wish to study part-time. A range of non-standard qualifications and/or experience may be accepted and the University is developing a CATS scheme (see page 12) to formalise arrangements for credit transfer.

Laban Centre for Movement and Dance
Laurie Grove, New Cross, London SE14 6NH

Tel: 081–692 4070 **Fax:** 081–694 8749
Contact: Dr Marion North, Director

Number of Undergraduates: 200
Percentage of Mature Students: 6%
Male/Female Ratio: 1 : 4
Upper Age Limit for Mature Students: None, but the course is physically demanding.

Learning Facilities: The Centre holds the main specialist library for dance in the UK. There are theatres, music and sound rooms, lighting design and costume design workshops, etc. Students also have access to the Goldsmith's College library, which is adjacent to the centre.

Creche Facilities: No
Mature Students Adviser: Yes
Accommodation: None available through the Centre, but it publishes a list of local accommodation. If you need help in finding somewhere suitable to live, contact the Centre by the middle of August before the start of your course.

Rudolf Laban was one of the most influential figures in European modern dance and dance scholarship. The Laban Centre was founded with his advice and assistance in 1945, provided the UK's first BA Honours degree in Dance Theatre in 1976 and is now recognised as one of the three leading providers of dance education and training in the country. It is a small but cosmopolitan community whose staff and students are committed to achieving the highest standards in dance.

The course attracts only a discretionary grant, and the basic tuition fee for the first year of the BA course in 1994/5 is £6950. If you are refused a grant, the Centre will help you appeal and has had some success in the past in persuading LEAs to change their minds.

Degrees Available: BA in Dance Theatre, following one of two routes: either Performance (for those who wish to be professional dancers) or Critical and Cultural Studies (for those who want an academic degree specialising in Dance). The degree is validated by the City University.

Assessment: By exams and continuous assessment of essays, projects etc. For the Performance route, performance plays an increasingly important part as the course progresses.

How to Apply: Direct, on a form available from the Admissions Officer. Applications are accepted throughout the year.
Mature applicants, particularly those with relevant experience, are welcome but may be asked to submit a written piece of work for assessment. You are welcome to contact the Centre for further information or advice before applying.

St David's University College Lampeter
(University of Wales)
Lampeter SA48 7ED

Tel: 0570 422351 **Fax:** 0570 423423
Contact: Dr C. Hughes, Assistant Registrar

Number of Undergraduates: 1305
Percentage of Mature Students: 18%
Male/Female Ratio: 1 : 1
Upper Age Limit for Mature Students: None

Learning Facilities: The library has 150,000 books, pamphlets and volumes of periodicals, with scope for expansion to 200,000. It is open 70 hours a week during term-time. There is a purpose-built Media Centre, designed principally to train students in sub-titling and television production. Computing, audio-visual services and a language lab are also available.

Creche Facilities: Subsidised creche for children aged one year plus.

Mature Students Adviser: No, but welfare and counselling services are available to all students.

Accommodation: Most first-year students are offered a place in a Hall of Residence: mature students need to apply for this (school leavers do not), so write to the Accommodation Officer as soon as possible. The Accommodation Officer can assist couples to find accommodation, but none is available in College.

With the exception of Oxford and Cambridge, Lampeter is the oldest University College in England and Wales. With rail services at Carmarthen and Aberystwyth upwards of twenty miles away and the M4 rather further, it is not the most accessible seat of learning in the world, but it is set in a small market town in a beautiful part of rural Wales and the nearby salmon river and nesting red kites attract many nature lovers. The College, part of the University of Wales, is small but expanding and has some excellent modern facilities.

Lampeter lies in a Welsh-speaking area and although most teaching is done in English, the prospectus is in both languages, as are all the College's signs, forms and publications.

Degrees Available: BA (single or joint, with an emphasis on classical' subjects such as Ancient History, Archaeology, Greek and Roman Civilisation or Hebrew, and on religious and philosophical subjects); BD.

There are courses in Welsh and in Welsh Studies. German, classical Greek, Hebrew and Latin are available for beginners; Lampeter is also the only College is Wales where you can study a Scandinavian language (in this case Swedish) to degree level.

Assessment: A mixture of exams and continuous assessment, with dissertations and essays important in most courses.

How to Apply: Through UCAS. Lampeter welcomes applications from mature students and will consider kitemarked Access courses as an alternative to standard entry requirements.

For further advice about Access courses, contact the College's Centre for Continuing Education.

Lancaster University
University House, Lancaster LA1 4YW

Tel: 0524 65201; 0524 592015 (Admissions Office)
Contact: Undergraduate Admissions Officer

Number of Undergraduates: About 7000
Percentage of Mature Students: About 25%
Male/Female Ratio: About 1 : 1
Upper Age Limit for Mature Students: None

Learning Facilities: The library has over 850,000 items, subscribes to over 3000 periodicals and can accommodate 820 readers. The Computer Centre provides campus-wide facilities and offers advice to all students.

Creche Facilities: The pre-school centre has places for 53 children. Parents on low incomes may be entitled to substantially reduced fees. Phone extension 4561 for more details.

Mature Students Adviser: Kathleen Biro on extension 4291. The University publishes one of the best mature students' guides around and offers free effective learning programmes on such subjects as better essay writing, oral presentation and exam preparation.

Accommodation: The University guarantees to accommodate all first-year students who need a place in one of its Colleges. There are mature areas within each college, a few adult flatlets and some family accommodation. Contact the Accommodation Office early for more details.

Lancaster is now a two-campus University, with a main site about three miles from the centre of Lancaster itself and the Lake District Campus at the former Charlotte Mason College in Ambleside (see separate entry, page 120). All students belong to a College, which is the focus of academic and social life as well as providing accommodation.

In addition to being very encouraging to mature students, Lancaster welcomes applications from students with special needs, and has close links with the Spastics Society and a number of other disability organisations. The campus is compact and relatively free of traffic. Wheelchair access is available in most of the teaching and public buildings. The University is also well equipped to accommodate visually impaired students. Contact the Special Needs Adviser for more information.

Degrees Available: BA in a wide range of Arts and Social Science subjects, including Economics or Linguistics or Politics or Religious Studies with Japanese Studies: these are four-year courses involving a year at a Japanese University; BBA (four years including either a work placement or studies in a European language with a year abroad); BEng, with one three-year course offering a period in the USA or Canada; BMus; BSc in a wide range of subjects, a number of which also offer the possibility of study in North America; LLB, either a three-year course in Law or a four-year one in European Legal Studies.

For the BA with Qualified Teacher Status, see separate entry for Charlotte Mason College (page 120).

Courses are not modular, but all students take three subjects in their first year and can defer decisions about single or combined major degrees until the end of that year. Part-time study is available on all first-year courses except Primary Education, and on some later courses. There is also an Associate Student Scheme (see page 27).

Assessment: All courses combine exams with continuous assessment. This may involve practical work, field work, work experience, projects and dissertations, as appropriate.

How to Apply: Through UCAS for full-time courses, but you are welcome to write direct to the Undergraduate Admissions Office at the same time, including any supplementary information you feel would be useful to your application. If you wish to study part-time or become an Associate Student, contact the Undergraduate Admissions Office for more information on the options available.

Mature students are welcomed at Lancaster and a wide range of non-traditional qualifications may be accepted. The University, together with the University of Central Lancashire, validates courses in the Open College Network of the North West (see page 25) and units completed on these courses, or successful completion of a kitemarked Access course, may be deemed to satisfy the entry requirements. Prior learning and/or experience is assessed on an individual basis, as is the possibility of credit transfer.

University of Leeds
Leeds LS2 9JT

Tel: 0532 333999
Contact: Assistant Registrar, Taught Courses Office

Number of Undergraduates: About 12,500
Percentage of Mature Students: About 8%

Male/Female Ratio: About 6 : 5
Upper Age Limit for Mature Students: None specified

Learning Facilities: The library is one of the largest university libraries in the UK, with over 2+ million items and 2500 study places. There are also a number of substantial faculty libraries. There are comprehensive computing and audio-visual facilities, a well-equipped Language Centre offering courses in 40 languages and modern laboratories for all relevant courses. The Workshop Theatre is used for teaching theatre and drama within the Department of English.

Creche Facilities: For 50 children aged between three months and five years, with a play scheme during school holidays for those aged five to 12. Places for the under-twos are limited and you are advised to apply early.

Mature Students Adviser: The Mature Entry Scheme Officer (see below) administers the matriculation exam; the Student Access Office will advise on applications, and there is a Welfare Office in the Students' Union.

Accommodation: There are over 5500 places in Halls or University-owned houses or flats and all first-year students will normally be offered a place. Finding suitable cheap accommodation for couples and families can be difficult and you should contact the Accommodation Office for help as soon as you know you are likely to be moving to Leeds.

Leeds received its University charter in 1904, having grown out of an older Medical School and College of Science and Technology. It is one of the largest universities in England, has a very strong research base and particularly impressive computing facilities.

The University has made considerable efforts to accommodate students with disabilities: there is wheelchair access to most buildings and support for those with sight or hearing problems. It also runs a Women's Centre which provides women with emergency accommodation and organises an evening minibus service.

The University occupies a large precinct near the centre of the city, although some of the Halls of Residence are four miles away. Leeds itself is a large, prosperous city with excellent sports, culture and shopping facilities and the West Yorkshire Moors within easy reach.

Degrees Available: BA in a very wide range of Arts and Social Science subjects, including Arabic, Chinese, Japanese and Russian; also BA or BBroadcasting in Broadcasting Studies; LLB, including options with French, Chinese Studies or Japanese Studies (four years); BEng in a wide variety of specialisms including Fire Engineering and Fuel and Energy Engineering; BSc in Biological Sciences, Physical Sciences, Geological Sciences or Maths; BChD; MB ChB.

There is also an optional one-year intercalated BSc course which students of Medicine and Dentistry may take between the pre-clinical and clinical parts of their studies.

The University offers an expanding part-time degree programme: many of the normally full-time courses may be followed part-time and there are also purpose-designed courses, some of which hold classes in the evenings. Contact the Office of Part-time Education, telephone 0532 333212, for more details.

Assessment: With the exception of Medicine and Dentistry, most courses are modular and each unit is assessed separately during and at the end of the semester in which it is taught. A combination of exams and continuous assessment is used: in some departments as much as 40% of the degree is assessed through course work. Medicine and Dentistry rely heavily on exams throughout the course, with some use of continuous assessment; a good performance in clinical work is also vital.

How to Apply: Through UCAS. Mature students must satisfy the University's basic entrance requirements, but in the absence of traditional qualifications this can be done by successful completion of a kitemarked Access course or by passing a special matriculation exam held in May. Further information can be obtained from the Mature Entry Scheme Officer, Mr J.B. Garner, in the Department of Civil Engineering, telephone 0532 332272.

Before submitting a formal application you are welcome to contact the Admissions Tutor of the course you wish to follow to discuss your individual needs.

Leeds Metropolitan University
Calverley St, Leeds LS1 3HE

Tel: 0532 832600 **Fax:** 0532 833114
Contact: Course Enquiries Office

Number of Undergraduates: About 7000 full-time, nearly 10,000 part-time
Percentage of Mature Students: About 45%
Male/Female Ratio: 1 : 1
Upper Age Limit for Mature Students: None

Learning Facilities: The three main libraries have a total of about half a million books, subscribe to 2000 periodicals and provide 1100 study spaces. Full computing and media services are available on both campuses, and courses such as Science, Engineering, Health and Art and Design courses benefit from first-rate labs, workshops and equipment. The University also has its own highly regarded art gallery and studio theatre.

Creche Facilities: Not on campus, but the Childcare Co-Ordinator in the Student Office will help student parents make suitable arrangements for their children.

Mature Students Adviser: Not specifically, but a full range of welfare services is available through the Student Office. The UCAS booklet 'A Mature Student's Guide to Higher Education' is available from the Course Enquiries Office, which will also advise on applications.

Accommodation: About 800 places are available in Halls of Residence, and these are normally reserved for first-years. The Accommodation Office and Unipol, a housing agency supported by both Leeds universities and their Students' Unions, will help other students find somewhere suitable to live. Reasonably priced rented accommodation is easier to come by in Leeds than in many other cities with large student populations.

Leeds Metropolitan University is on two campuses: Beckett Park in Headingley, three miles out of town to the north, houses the Departments of Education, Informatics, Leisure and Tourism, and is famous for its excellent sporting facilities; all other courses and the administrative functions of the University are based at Calverley St in the city centre.

As is often the case with a 'new' University that grew out of a number of local technical colleges, Leeds Metropolitan offers many vocational or professionally oriented courses which aim to equip its graduates to find employment in their chosen field, and the University's teaching and research are closely linked to industry.

Degrees Available: BA in the Business School, the School of the Environment and in the Faculties of Cultural and Education Studies, and Health and Social Care; BEd; BSc in Health, Science and Information; BEng, including a new course in Electronics, Music and Media Technology; LLB.

Many courses include a sandwich element and/or a period of study overseas.

The BEd may be a four-year course leading to a qualification to teach at either primary or secondary level, or a two-year course for secondary teaching only, aimed at mature students who have relevant post-A level education and experience.

Foundation courses in Accounting are taught at the City campus; in Electronic and Electrical Systems Engineering and in Manufacturing Systems Engineering at Wakefield District College, about ten miles away.

Most courses are modular and allow for part-time study.

Assessment: The emphasis on exams varies from department to department: most courses rely heavily on practical work, case studies, projects, assignments, dissertations etc. Satisfactory performance in teaching practice or the work placement element of a course is essential.

How to Apply: Through ADAR for Art and Design; otherwise through UCAS for full-time study. For part-time study, apply direct to the University on a form available from the Course Enquiries Office. The University will accept a broad range of qualifications as satisfying the entry requirements, including Access courses or Level 3 NVQs. It is also keen to encourage applicants who have developed skills or knowledge through work or life experience as well as through formal education. You will be expected to show commitment to the course of study and the ability to benefit from it. The University operates a CATS scheme (see page 12), so credit can be given for prior learning.

University of Leicester
University Rd, Leicester LE1 7RH

Tel: 0533 522522 **Fax:** 0533 522447
Contact: Admissions Office (0533 522295)

Number of Undergraduates: 6364
Percentage of Mature Students: 18%
Male/Female Ratio: 1 : 1
Upper Age Limit for Mature Students: None

Learning Facilities: The library has over a million volumes and 800 study spaces for students. Electronic information services are also available for student use. There is a Computing Centre with a Computer Help Desk.

Creche Facilities: Not on campus, but students who have to use private nursery facilities may be given some financial support. The Mature Students' Association organises a playgroup at half-term.

Mature Students Adviser: In the Students' Union. There is an active Mature Students' Association.

Accommodation: The University runs Halls of Residence and self-catering accommodation, allocating places to all first-years who want them. There are some self-contained flats suitable for couples.

Five of the six Halls are two miles from the campus, but there is a frequent bus service and the University supplements this with its own service at peak times and a women's minibus at night.

Established (with six students) as part of London University in 1921, Leicester was granted its own charter in 1957. Situated on a single campus close to the centre of this ethnically diverse and environmentally conscious city, it has played a pioneering role in research into subjects as diverse as genetic fingerprinting and football hooliganism.

In the 1990s, Leicester is more welcoming to mature students than many other 'old' universities and has a very flexible approach to part-time study. It also publishes a leaflet entitled 'Information for Mature and Part-Time Students' which is particularly useful on financial matters.

Degrees Available: BA and BSc with single, joint or combined honours; BA in Social Sciences; BSc (Econ); BEng; LLB; MB, ChB.

By autumn 1994 all these courses, except those in the Faculty of Medicine, will have adopted a modular structure.

Part-time study is well established at Leicester and it is already possible to do as few as one or two units per year, attending classes either during the day or in the evening. You can expect to take four to eight years to complete a degree on this basis.

Foundation courses are available in Science, Mathematics and Computer Science, and Engineering – contact the Admissions Office for details.

Assessment: In the modular scheme, work on each module is assessed as the course progresses. This entails essays, dissertations, practicals and/or field work, as appropriate to each subject. Some courses also retain traditional exams.

How to Apply: Through UCAS for full-time degree courses; direct to the Admissions Office for part-time study or foundation courses.

Access Courses and other non-standard qualifications may be acceptable, as each application is considered individually on its merits. Motivation, experience, employment, interests and any other evidence that you will be able to benefit from the course are all taken into account. Mature students are likely to be invited for interview before being offered a place.

Leicester participates in the Midlands regional CATS scheme (see page 12), so credit may be given for previous study.

——— ❋ ———

Lincolnshire College of Art and Design
Lindum Rd, Lincoln LN2 1NP

Tel: 0522 512912
Contact: Student Admissions Registry

Number of Undergraduates: About 120 in a student body of nearly 2000
Percentage of Mature Students: Not specified
Male/Female Ratio: About 1 : 2
Upper Age Limit for Mature Students: None

Learning Facilities: The library has about 10,000 books and 7000 slides. It is open late on Thursdays only, and closed at weekends. Computing and audio-visual facilities are also available.

Creche Facilities: No, but facilities are available at the neighbouring North Lincolnshire College.
Mature Students Adviser: No, but counselling services are available to all students and will be increased for the 1994/5 session.
Accommodation: In student houses and private homes, available for about 300 students. Contact the Accommodation Officer for details.

In addition to its Further and Higher Education courses, Lincolnshire College manages a number of additional learning support programmes in the city centre. For a smallish college it provides an impressive range of student services. Plans to merge with De Montfort University in 1994 should lead to growth in many areas.

Degrees Available: BA in Conservation and Restoration or Graphic Design and Illustration, validated by De Montfort University. Students may also take the first year of degree courses in Visual Arts (Fine Art), Fashion Design or Knitwear Design and Production at Lincoln, transferring to De Montfort in Leicester to complete their studies.

There is also a foundation year in Art and Design leading to a BTEC Diploma.

Students on all programmes are encouraged to undertake and industrial placement in the course of their studies.

Assessment: A combination of formal assessment and practical, studio-based work.

How to Apply: Through ADAR. You should normally have completed or be about to complete a BTEC or other suitable foundation course, and you will be expected to present a portfolio of work.
For the foundation course, apply direct to the College on a form available from the Student Admissions Registry.

The University of Liverpool
P.O. Box 147, Liverpool L69 3BX

Tel: 051–794 2000 **Fax:** 051 708 6502
Contact: Admissions Sub-Dean of the appropriate Faculty

Number of Undergraduates: 9264
Percentage of Mature Students: 17%
Male/Female Ratio: 6 : 5
Upper Age Limit for Mature Students: None

Learning Facilities: There are two main library buildings providing 1100 study places; their stock totals over a million items, including rare books and specialist collections on the Mersey poets and the Spanish Civil War. There are numerous computer work stations to which all students have access, a hi-tech language centre and well-equipped labs and workshops for appropriate courses.

Creche Facilities: Yes
Mature Students Adviser: Margaret Morris
Accommodation: All prospective first-year students who apply to Liverpool as first choice and confirm acceptance of a place by September are allocated a place in University accommodation; most other first-years are also accommodated. There are no special provisions for couples or families, but Liverpool Student Homes, a joint initiative with Liverpool John Moores University, will help.

The University of Liverpool was founded in 1881, although some parts of it are older, and has built up a fine research record. It is one of the more flexible of the 'old' universities towards the needs of mature students: the recent appointment of a Mature Students' Adviser is only one sign of new initiatives being taken.

The University occupies a single city-centre precinct, although the Halls of Residence are three miles away in an attractive setting near Sefton Park.

Degrees Available: BA in a range of Arts and Social and Environmental Studies subjects; BSc in a wide range of Earth Sciences, Life Sciences, Maths and Physics-related subjects; also BSc in Radiography, Orthoptics and Physiotherapy; BDS; BNS; BVSc; MB, ChB; LLB in Law with French or German; BEng, including a four-year course in Engineering with Management and European Studies, which entails a year abroad.

Liverpool offers an interesting variety of subjects and subject combinations: some of the more unusual are Oriental Studies (specialising in Akkadian, Egyptology or Hebrew), Human Movement Science, and Radiation Physics and Environmental Science.

A foundation course is available in Engineering, and the BA in Social Sciences may be studied part-time.

Assessment: Through exams and continuous assessment of essays, projects, presentations, etc.

How to Apply: Through UCAS.

The alternative qualifications that may be accepted vary from department to department, but most accept Access courses and Open University credits. The University has its own Mature Matriculation exam which you may be asked to take. Credit may be given both for previous study and for relevant experience.

You are welcome to discuss your circumstances with the Mature Students' Adviser or the Course Admissions Tutor before submitting a formal application.

--------- ❊ ---------

Liverpool Institute of Higher Education
P.O. Box 6, Stand Park Rd, Liverpool L16 9JD

Tel: 051–737 3000 **Fax:** 051–737 3100
Contact: Deputy Registrar (Admissions)

Number of Undergraduates: 2700
Percentage of Mature Students: About 22%
Male/Female Ratio: About 1 : 3
Upper Age Limit for Mature Students: None specified

Learning Facilities: The library has over 200,000 books, subscribes to 900 periodicals and provides access to CD-Rom databases. Students may also use the University of Liverpool library. There are full computing facilities, audio-visual materials and technical support.

Creche Facilities: For children aged two to five, with half-term provision for children up to 12.

Mature Students Adviser: Not specifically, but every student has a personal tutor, the Institute runs a counselling service and each department has a Study Skills Co-Ordinator who can give advice specific to your course.

Accommodation: The Institute has 900 study-bedrooms in the main College buildings or in Halls of Residence, and all first-years who require a place can be accommodated. No special provisions for couples or families.

Liverpool Institute of Higher Education was formed in 1980 from the merger of the Catholic Christ's and Notre Dame College and the Anglican S. Katharine's College, both dating back to the 19th century. While the Institute welcomes students of all faiths or none, it remains committed to the Christian ideals on which these colleges were founded. The two colleges now occupy one campus in a suburb three miles to the east of Liverpool city centre. Degrees are validated by the University of Liverpool and the two institutions have close academic links.

Students with special needs are well catered for at Christ's and Notre Dame; wheelchair access at S. Katharine's College is more difficult.

Degrees Available: BA in a wide range of Arts, Social Science and Science subjects; BEd with QTS (four years) for teaching at nursery to upper primary/middle school age.

Single subject degrees are available only in Design, American Studies, European Studies and Theology and Religious Studies; otherwise BA and BSc courses are all Combined Honours. All programmes are modular.

A one-year kitemarked Access course in Education is available to all students over the age of 20, but targeted at members of ethnic minorities, which are generally under-represented in teacher training. Priority is given to applicants who live locally and there are no course fees.

Part-time study is available on many courses.

Assessment: A combination of exams and continuous assessment, including practical or creative work, seminar papers, teaching practice and a final-year project or dissertation where relevant.

How to Apply: Normally through UCAS for full-time courses, except Design, which is through ADAR. However, if you are applying for the Design course and have not completed or are not taking a suitable foundation course, you should first contact the

Admissions Office at the above address, telephone 051–737 3295. Suitable candidates will be interviewed and expected to show a portfolio of work.

Mature applicants for other full-time courses should, in addition to completing their UCAS form, obtain a Mature Student's Supplementary Information Form from the Institute. This enables you to supply more details about your background and experience than you can fit on to the UCAS form.

If you do not have formal qualifications, are not taking an Access or Open University course or equivalent and have been out of formal education for some time, the Institute has a mature entry process which may involve you taking a special exam designed to ensure that your literacy skills are adequate for the course you wish to follow. It also offers an optional preparatory course leading up to this exam: this concentrates on such areas as essay writing and exam techniques, but also aims to build your confidence in your own ability to study at degree level.

For part-time study, contact the Admissions Office for an application form, which should be returned direct to the Institute by 15 December.

Liverpool John Moores University

St Nicholas Centre, Great Orford St, Off Mt Pleasant, Liverpool L3 5YD

Tel: 051–231 2121 **Fax:** 051–707 1938
Contact: Admissions

Number of Undergraduates: 10,900
Percentage of Mature Students: 44%
Male/Female Ratio: 7 : 6
Upper Age Limit for Mature Students: None

Learning Facilities: The library contains 550,000 items and 1200 study places. There are substantial computer facilities and recently refurbished labs in all Engineering and Science areas.

Creche Facilities: Free, but very limited number of places. Mature Students Adviser: Contact the Education Advice Unit. Accommodation: There are 1400 places in Halls of Residence, which can accommodate about 40% of first-years. No special provisions for couples or families.

Liverpool John Moores University's entry is one of the longest in the UCAS handbook, covering nine pages (for comparison, Glasgow covers

*eight, Birmingham six and Oxford and Cambridge less than three each).
There are also three courses in Design and Visual Art which are covered
by ADAR. The range of subjects and choice of combinations available is
truly staggering. Picking a few at random, there are courses in
Mechanical and Marine Engineering; Applied Community Studies and
Food and Nutrition; Applied Psychology and Criminal Justice; Dance
and Literature, Life and Thought; Marketing and Media and Cultural
Studies; Human Resource Management and French (or German).
German, Japanese, Russian and Spanish may all be taken from scratch.*

*The University has two main city-centre campuses, one housing the
Schools of Engineering, Science and Social Science, the other Arts and
Business Studies. Education and Community Studies are based on a
smaller campus about three miles out of town.*

Degrees Available: BA; BSc; BEng all in a vast range of subjects
(see above); LLB; BEd for teaching at the upper primary or
secondary level. Many courses are available part-time; there are a
number of four-year sandwich courses, largely in Engineering or
Applied Science subjects; foundation courses are available in
Art, Engineering and Accounting.

The first year of many courses is taught at one of a number of
local colleges, with students transferring to Liverpool John
Moores for their second and following years.

Assessment: Because the University runs an Integrated Credit
Scheme, students have the option to design their own courses
and each unit or module is assessed separately during or at the
end of the semester in which it is taught. A combination of exams
and continuous assessment is used.

How to Apply: Normally through UCAS or ADAR, but mature
students who live locally and are only applying to Liverpool John
Moores should obtain an application form from the Admissions
Office and apply direct.

Any alternative qualifications are considered, and students may
apply for Accreditation of Prior Learning (see page 12).

The University of London
Senate House, Malet St, London WC1E 7HU

Tel: 071–636 8000

*The University of London is a federation of 58 Colleges and Institutes,
ranging from large, broadly based Colleges like UCL and King's to tiny*

specialists like the Jews' College. It was founded in 1836 when the government awarded a joint charter to the rival King's and University Colleges, but many Colleges, particularly the medical schools, have informal origins much older than that. Today the University offers over 1500 degree courses, has over 60,000 full-time students and 10,000 teaching staff.

Students who enrol at one of the constituent Colleges automatically become students of the University of London at the same time. They can use the central library, which is one of the largest of any academic institution in the UK. It has 1.3 million books, including many unique specialist collections – the Goldsmiths' Library alone, which specialises in economic and social history, has 65,000 items dating from the 15th to the 19th centuries.

Students of the University of London may also apply for a place in one of its Intercollegiate Halls of Residence (contact the Accommodation Office at the above address, telephone 071–636 2818), and take advantage of its huge centralised Careers Advisory Service.

The following constituent Colleges of the University of London have separate entries in this book:

Birkbeck College
Charing Cross and Westminster Medical School
Courtauld Institute of Art
Goldsmiths' College
Heythrop College
Imperial College of Science, Technology and Medicine
Jews' College
King's College London
King's College School of Medicine and Dentistry
London Hospital Medical College
London School of Economics and Political Science
School of Oriental and African Studies
School of Pharmacy
Queen Mary and Westfield College
Royal Academy of Music
Royal College of Music
Royal Free Hospital School of Medicine
Royal Holloway
Royal Veterinary College
St Bartholomew's Hospital Medical College
St George's Hospital Medical School
St Mary's Hospital Medical School
School of Slavonic and East European Studies
Trinity College of Music

——— ❋ ———

London Bible College
Green Lane, Northwood HA6 2UW

Tel: 0923 826061 **Fax:** 0923 836530
Contact: Dean

Number of Undergraduates: About 230 full-time
Percentage of Mature Students: Not specified, but students' ages
range from 18 to 70, with an average age of 29
Male/Female Ratio: About 3 : 2
Upper Age Limit for Mature Students: None, but if you do not
meet the standard entry requirements you will not be admitted
unless you are at least 23.

Learning Facilities: The library, with 23,000 books and subscriptions to over a hundred periodicals, is one of the best of its
kind in the UK. Five word-processors are available for undergraduate use and the Resources Room supplies audio-visual
material, Bible study material etc.

Creche Facilities: No
Mature Students Adviser: No, but teaching staff and a professional
counsellor are available to help any student.
Accommodation: There are 130 places in Halls of Residence on
campus, but no special provisions for couples or families.

*The London Bible College has 50 years' experience of training students
for the Christian ministry and, in return for a high level of commitment,
aims to impart a thorough knowledge and understanding of the Bible and
an enhanced spiritual life. It states its doctrinal position thus: 'The
College stands within the conservative evangelical tradition and is
committed to the full inspiration and authority of Scripture.' Worship is
central to all life at the College, not just to study.*

*The degree course attracts a mandatory grant, but because the College
is private this will not cover all your tuition fees: you will have to find over
£2000 yourself for the 1994/5 session.*

*The College is set in leafy grounds in a pleasant suburb on the fringes of
London, close to the M1, M25 and M40.*

Degrees Available: BA in Theology, validated by Brunel University. There are also opportunities for distance learning and for
part-time study.

Assessment: Exams and continuous assessment, divided about
50/50.

How to Apply: Direct to the College on a form available from the
Dean. This should be returned, along with your registration fee

(currently £20), two photos and a medical certificate (the College supplies a form to be completed by your doctor), not later than March of the year you wish to begin your course. A substantial part of the application form is devoted to questions about your own faith and your reasons for wishing to study Theology. You are asked to name three referees, one of whom is a leader of your local church, and much will depend of the reference he/she gives you.

Mature students who do not satisfy the general entry requirements but have appropriate experience may be admitted. You are welcome to ask for an informal interview with a member of staff before submitting your application: please telephone the receptionist for an appointment.

London College of Fashion
20 John Princes St, London W1M 0BJ

Tel: 071–629 9401 **Fax:** 071–495 1547
Contact: Registrar of the School of Fashion Management (for the Product Development course) or Registrar of the School of Fashion Promotion

Number of Undergraduates: About 2200
Percentage of Mature Students: Not specified, but 16% overall in the London Institute
Male/Female Ratio: Not specified
Upper Age Limit for Mature Students: None

Learning Facilities: Three specialist libraries hold a total of 40,000 books and subscribe to 200 relevant periodicals. There are comprehensive computing and audio-visual facilities, computer-aided design and manufacture equipment, studios, workrooms and a specialist fashion theatre with permanent catwalk. Students also have access to the facilities of the other colleges of the London Institute.

Creche Facilities: At the London College of Printing and Distributive Trades (see next entry).
Mature Students Adviser: Not specifically, but the London Institute has a Central Student Service Department at 388-396 Oxford St, London W1R 1FE, telephone 071–491 8533, open all year round, and the various College sites have Satellite Student Services available Monday to Friday during term time. Professional counsellors and other support are also available.

Accommodation: Available through the London Institute. Contact the College's Student Information Assistant (telephone 071–493 0212) or the Institute's Accommodation Office (071–491 8533) for details.

The London College of Fashion is the only specialist institution providing education and training for the fashion industries, and has some of the finest facilities of their kind in the world. It operates on five sites, three just off Oxford St, one near the Barbican and one in Curtain Rd in the City, all former or current centres of the 'rag trade'. Degree courses are taught at the Oxford Street sites, but students are encouraged to visit the other sites and take advantage of their facilities.

The College's roots go back to the early part of this century, and it is now part of the London Institute (see page 227).

Degrees Available: BA in Product Development for the Fashion Industries (four-year sandwich, recently renamed from Clothing) or in Fashion Promotion, validated by the Open University.
There is also a one-year introductory course in Clothing.

Assessment: Exams and continuous assessment, including projects.

How to Apply: For 1994 entry to Fashion Promotion, through ADAR; for 1995 entry through UCAS. For Product Development, through either UCAS or ADAR. If you do not have traditional qualifications, contact the relevant Registrar for advice first.

London College of Printing and Distributive Trades
Elephant and Castle, London SE1 6SB

Tel: 071–735 8484 **Fax:** 071–582 0882
Contact: The relevant School Officer (see below)

Number of Undergraduates: About 1600
Percentage of Mature Students: Not specified, but 16% overall in the London Institute
Male/Female Ratio: About 3 : 2
Upper Age Limit for Mature Students: None

Learning Facilities: The Department of Learning Resources provides a wide range of books and other materials appropriate to the College's courses. There are audio-visual materials, a CD-Rom network and excellent technical facilities.

Creche Facilities: At the Elephant and Castle; open all year round for children aged three months to five years.

Mature Students Adviser: Not specifically, but the London Institute has a Central Student Service Department at 388-396 Oxford St, London W1R 1FE, telephone 071–491 8533, open all year round, and the various College sites have Satellite Student Services available Monday to Friday during term time. Professional counsellors and other support are also available.

Accommodation: Limited College accommodation is available in Halls of Residence run by the London Institute, whose Accommodation Office will help students find somewhere suitable to live. Apply early.

The London College of Printing and Distributive Trades is part of the London Institute, which is now entitled to award degrees in its own name. The College consists of six schools on three main sites scattered across London. Three of the schools and the College administration are based at the Elephant and Castle, which is easy to reach from the centre of London and from many parts of South-East London and Kent. The BA in Retail Management is taught at Davies St in the West End, just off Oxford St, and the BA in Communications Media at the Backhill site in Clerkenwell, near the City and Kings Cross.

All College courses are practical and have strong ties with industry. The expertise of the full-time staff is supplemented by visiting lecturers who are practising professionals in their fields.

Degrees Available: BA in Graphics and Media Design (three years full-time or a four-year sandwich), Communication Media, Printing Management or Retail Management. These courses are offered in the Schools of Graphic Design, Media, Printing Technology and Retail Studies respectively.
Access and foundation courses are available.

Assessment: A combination of exams and course work, including personal projects or portfolios. The degree in Retail Management is made up of units, each of which is assessed individually.

How to Apply: Through ADAR for Graphic and Media Design; otherwise through UCAS. Applicants without standard qualifications may be accepted if they have completed an appropriate Access course or if they can demonstrate their ability to follow the course successfully. Contact the relevant Course Director if you would like to discuss your individual case.

You should expect to be invited for interview before being offered a place and may be asked to produce a portfolio of work.

------ ❋ ------

London Contemporary Dance School

16 Flaxman Terrace, London WC1H 9AT

Tel: 071–387 0152 **Fax:** 071–383 4851

Contact: School Office

Number of Undergraduates: 120
Percentage of Mature Students: 7+%
Male/Female Ratio: 1 : 8
Upper Age Limit for Mature Students: None, provided they are physically able to cope with the training

Learning Facilities: The School has a specialist library, and dance studios, a music studio and The Place Theatre for performance.

Creche Facilities: No
Mature Students Adviser: All students have a personal tutor.
Accommodation: None available through the School.

In addition to providing contemporary dance and choreography training of a very high standard, the School is closely linked to the London Contemporary Dance Theatre. A high percentage of graduates have gone on to a professional career with the Dance Theatre and elsewhere, but students are expected to work extremely hard and only the dedicated will succeed.
The School is centrally situated, close to King's Cross and Euston.

Degrees Available: BA in Dance.

Assessment: Largely through performance, though there are theoretical courses too.

How to Apply: Direct to the School by June at the latest, but application as early as October of the year before you wish to begin the course is strongly recommended. Admission is by interview and audition, with a special entry paper for mature students. Applications for credit transfer or for previous experience to be taken into account are considered on an individual basis.

------ ❋ ------

London Guildhall University

India House, 139 Minories, London EC3N 1NL

Tel: 071–320 1000 **Fax:** 071–320 3134
Contact: Admissions Office

Number of Undergraduates: 5680 full-time, about the same number part-time
Percentage of Mature Students: 48%
Male/Female Ratio: 52 : 48
Upper Age Limit for Mature Students: None

Learning Facilities: The University has six libraries providing books, journals, audio-visual material and databases. There are comprehensive computing facilities and specialist workshops, labs and studios.

Creche Facilities: Two nurseries, one at Commercial Rd, one at Tower Hill. The Students' Union also aims to provide a temporary creche during half-term.

Mature Students Adviser: Contact the Higher Education Access Centre (see below). The University publishes a useful Mature Students' Guide.

Accommodation: Two Halls of Residence accommodate 480 students; one is self-catering, the other provides meals. Wheelchair access is available at the latter. Priority in allocating places is given to first-years, but University accommodation cannot be guaranteed. If you need help in finding somewhere to live, contact the Student Accommodation Service at Calcutta House, Old Castle St, London E1 7NT as soon as possible – details of accommodation will not be sent to you automatically.

The London Guildhall University, formerly the City of London Poly, is the product of a number of older institutions. Its most recent acquisition is the former London College of Furniture, which has enabled it to offer a number of specialist courses in Furniture Design. Its long-established courses in Silversmithing and Jewellery are recognised as among the best in their field.

London Guildhall has three faculties – Arts, Design and Manufacture, Business and Human Sciences – spread over six sites within about a mile of each other in the City of London and Whitechapel. Whatever your interests, the City is a fascinating place to be: St Pauls, the Tower, Docklands, Petticoat Lane and the Barbican Centre are all nearby.

Degrees Available: BA and BSc in a variety of subjects. Students can choose a specialist subject from the start, or follow a modular programme which allows them to defer a decision or to attain a joint honours or Combined Studies degree. In some subjects there is the option to take the first two years of the modular programme at South Thames College in Wandsworth.
Many courses can be followed part-time, some on an evenings-only basis.

Assessment: A combination of exams and continuous assessment, with projects and practical work, essays and oral presentations all taken into account where applicable. Each unit in the modular programme is assessed separately, during and at the end of the semester or year in which it is taught.

How to Apply: Through ADAR or UCAS if you are applying to more than one institution. If you are applying to London Guildhall only, write to the University direct. If they offer you a place, this will need to be confirmed through the clearing house in due course.

London Guildhall welcomes applications from mature students on kitemarked Access courses or 'Return to Study' courses. The Higher Education Access Centre gives guidance to those considering returning to study after a gap and advises on Access courses, presenting a portfolio, credit transfer and Accreditation of Prior Learning (APL, see page 12). Write to the Higher Education Access Centre, Calcutta House, Old Castle St, London E1 7NT, or phone 071–320 1201 or 247 7845.

London Hospital Medical College
(University of London)
Turner St, London E1 2AD

Tel: 071–377 7611 **Fax:** 071–377 7677
Contact: Admissions Office

Number of Undergraduates: 151 (96 in the Medical School, 55 in the Dental School) are admitted each year
Percentage of Mature Students: 4%
Male/Female Ratio: 4 : 3
Upper Age Limit for Mature Students: 30

Learning Facilities: The library at the London has over 30,000 books and scientific journals as well as 130 study places. In addition, students have access to the Queen Mary and Westfield College library (see page 277), the British library and other University of London libraries. There are computer and audio-visual facilities, well equipped laboratories and closed-circuit television which allows lecture theatres to be linked to operations in the hospital. The College museum has over 8000 pathological specimens.
Creche Facilities: No
Mature Students Adviser: No

Accommodation: Students at the London are well catered for: College accommodation is plentiful, convenient and cheaper than at most other Colleges of the University of London. All first-year students who require it are allocated College accommodation.

The London Hospital Medical College, founded in 1785 adjacent to what is now the Royal London Hospital, is the oldest medical school in England and Wales. It has been part of the University of London since 1900, and the Dental School was founded in 1911. The hospital's distinguished history includes associations with Dr Barnardo; with Langdon Down, who first described what came to be known as Down's Syndrome; and with Sir Frederick Treves and John Merrick, the Elephant Man.

The preclinical courses in both Medicine and Dentistry are taught at nearby Queen Mary and Westfield College; for the clinical courses students return to the London.

Students at the College see a very broad mix of cases. Communication skills are an important feature of the courses and academic standards are high.

Degrees Available: MB, BS; BDS. An intercalated one-year BSc degree is available to about 30 students a year.

Queen Mary and Westfield College runs an Access course called QMWay, which is recognised by the London, but only one medical and one dental place a year are available to students who have completed this course.

Assessment: For the first five terms medical and dental students follow a preclinical course of which about 60% is common to both disciplines. Assessment is by exams, project work and some in-course assessment.

Both clinical courses entail practical experience, but final exams are the major form of assessment.

How to Apply: Through UCAS. The General Medical and Dental Councils lay down strict standard entry requirements, and mature students without conventional academic qualifications will find that opportunities at the London are limited. A levels or equivalent are essential; the entrance requirements for Medicine and Dentistry are not as flexible as they are for many other courses.

London Institute
388–396 Oxford St, London W1R 1FE

Tel: 071–491 8533

The London Institute, a federation of five constituent colleges with a total of about 22,000 students, is the largest provider of education in Art, Design and related areas in Europe. It was formed in 1986, although the individual colleges are all much older, and granted the right to award its own degrees in 1992. Degrees are awarded in the joint names of the Institute and the relevant college.

Students at any one of the constituent colleges may use the libraries and other academic facilities of all five colleges. They also automatically become members of the Institute's Students' Union, with access to its accommodation service and two Halls of Residence, careers advice, welfare provisions, etc. In addition to the Central Student Service Department, there is a satellite' Student Services Office at each college.

The following are the constituent colleges of the London Institute, which all have separate entries in this book:

Camberwell College of Arts
Central St Martins College of Art and Design
Chelsea College of Art and Design
London College of Fashion
London College of Printing and Distributive Trades

London School of Economics and Political Science (LSE – University of London)
Houghton St, London WC2A 2AE

Tel: 071–405 7686 **Fax:** 071–831 1684
Contact: Assistant Registrar (Undergraduate Admissions)

Number of Undergraduates: About 2600
Percentage of Mature Students: About 20%
Male/Female Ratio: About 4 : 3
Upper Age Limit for Mature Students: None

Learning Facilities: The library is the principal national library for the Social Sciences, with over three million items and a thousand study places. The School has ample computing facilities and a well-equipped Language Studies Centre.

Creche Facilities: For children aged six months to five years, open 46 weeks a year. Student parents with financial difficulties may be able to get help with fees.

Mature Students Adviser: Not specifically, but advice and counselling are readily available to all students. A booklet entitled 'LSE: Entry at 21+' can be obtained from the Assistant Registrar (Undergraduate Admissions).

Accommodation: The School has three Halls of Residence and a number of houses and 'cluster' flats. All first-year students whose homes are outside the Greater London area are guaranteed a place, and priority is also given to those with disabilities. There are some double rooms in shared houses. Students may also apply for a place in the University of London Intercollegiate Halls – contact the University of London Accommodation Office, Senate House, Malet St, London WC1E 7HU, telephone 071–636 2818.

LSE is a specialist School with a worldwide reputation for teaching and research in the Social Sciences. A spokesperson from the School is frequently interviewed on national news in times of governmental crisis, and many LSE graduates go on to successful careers in politics or international relations.

LSE's location is part of its attraction for students who want to feel 'part of the real world' – tucked away behind the Law Courts, it is on the border between the Cities of Westminster and London, the seat of politics and the seat of finance.

The School has a commitment to improving facilities for those with disabilities: wheelchair access is possible in most teaching buildings and some accommodation, while there is also support for those with sight or hearing difficulties.

Degrees Available: BA in Anthropology and Law, European Studies, Geography, History, Philosophy or Social Anthropology; BSc or BSc (Econ) in a range of subjects relating to Economics, Politics and Society, including Russian Government, History and Language; also BSc in Statistical and Mathematical Sciences; LLB including options with French or German law.

Assessment: Mostly by formal exams, but some optional courses may be examined by an extended essay.

How to Apply: Through UCAS. Mature applicants will not necessarily be required to fulfil the general entry requirements, and applications from those on recognised Access courses are very welcome.

Loughborough College of Art and Design
Radmoor, Loughborough LE11 3BT

Tel: 0509 261515 **Fax:** 0509 265515
Contact: Admissions Officer

Number of Undergraduates: 550
Percentage of Mature Students: About 8%
Male/Female Ratio: About 2 : 3
Upper Age Limit for Mature Students: None specified

Learning Facilities: The library has 50,000 books and an extensive slide collection. There are excellent specialist studios and workshops for all courses.

Creche Facilities: A limited number of places on a first-come, first-served basis – apply early.

Mature Students Adviser: No, but counselling services are available to all students.

Accommodation: Halls of Residence, both catering and self-catering, can accommodate nearly 300 students. Priority is given to first- and final-year students. There are no special provisions for couples or families, but the Accommodation Office keeps a list of registered lodgings, whose rents compare favourably with those in many other parts of the country.

Loughborough is the only specialist college north of London offering Higher Education courses in Art and Design, and recent awards won by its students prove that it is one of the most successful in the country. Its courses are taught by practising professionals who combine artistic expertise with a clear understanding of the job market.

The campus is just across the road from Loughborough University of Technology (see next entry), and the two student bodies belong to the same union and share many social and sporting facilities.

Degrees Available: BA in Fine Art, Textile Design or Three-Dimensional Design, validated by Nottingham Trent University. Specialisms available include Printmaking, Furniture, and Silversmithing and Jewellery. Validation for a new course in Illustration is pending; if this is granted, the course will be available for the 1994/5 session.
There is also a foundation course in Art and Design.

Assessment: Largely on practical, creative work, with an interim assessment in February and a final one at the end of the academic session.

How to Apply: Through ADAR, except for Illustration and the foundation course, for which you should apply direct on a form obtainable from the Admissions Officer. You will normally be expected to have undertaken a suitable foundation course, and you will be invited to attend for interview and present a portfolio of work.

Applicants who do not fulfil the standard entry requirements may be admitted in special circumstances or if they show exceptional ability or flair. You are advised to have an informal discussion with the Admissions Officer before submitting a formal application.

------ ❋ ------

Loughborough University of Technology
Loughborough LE11 3TU

Tel: 0509 263171 **Fax:** 0509 265687 (Central Admissions)
Contact: Howard Jones, Senior Assistant Registrar, The Student Office

Number of Undergraduates: 6650 full-time
Percentage of Mature Students: 16%
Male/Female Ratio: 2 : 1
Upper Age Limit for Mature Students: None

Learning Facilities: The library has 600,000 volumes and over 400 study places. There is a 24-hour computing facility with 1500 access points between Central Computer Services and the various departments.

Creche Facilities: A registered and subsidised day nursery for children up to the age of five is run by the Students' Union.

Mature Students Adviser: Contact Howard Jones, as above. There is a Mature Students' Association, and a useful booklet entitled 'An Introductory Guide for Mature Students', which is strong on financial aspects, teaching methods and study skills.

Accommodation: Some 70% of Loughborough undergraduates live on campus, in Halls of Residence or University flats. All first-year students who do not live within reasonable travelling distance are automatically allocated catering accommodation for the first term (there is no need to apply).

Some of the flats have shared rooms, but there is no special provision for couples or families: contact the Accommodation Office as early as possible if you need assistance.

Loughborough has one of the highest reputations in the UK for the use of information technology – it is not far from achieving its declared aim of having at least one computer work station for every four students, and it has a policy of giving all students the opportunity to obtain the basic skills to benefit from these facilities.

It is also considered one of the best places to study Engineering, perhaps because courses in the School of Engineering have particularly strong links with industry. Certainly the percentage of Loughborough graduates who enter full-time employment immediately after graduation has been above the national average for some years.

Degrees Available: BA, BSc and BEng, with the possibility of a four-year sandwich course leading also to a Diploma in Professional or Industrial Studies or to a Certificate of Education. There is a one-year foundation course in Science and Engineering.

The choice of Arts subjects is limited, but Loughborough offers a broad range of Science and Engineering options, including Chemical Engineering with Environmental Protection or with Food Bioprocessing; Automotive Engineering; Chemistry and Physical Education and Sports Science; and Information Technology and Human Factors.

Assessment: Varies enormously from course to course. A few depend largely on exams, some exclusively on continuous assessment. Most employ a combination of the two, with essays, projects and practical work being assessed where applicable. Teaching practice is a vital part of those degrees which are combined with a Certificate of Education, but the certificate is awarded separately and has no bearing on the class of your degree.

How to Apply: Through UCAS. Applications from mature students are welcome and all sorts of prior learning and/or experience may be considered. You should be able to show that you have the ability to sustain a degree course successfully.

LSU College of Higher Education
The Avenue, Southampton SO9 5HB

Tel: 0703 228761 **Fax:** 0703 230944
Contact: Mrs Elizabeth Cotton, Academic Secretary, The Registry
Mrs Sue Oakley, Assistant Principal, Student Services

Number of Undergraduates: 1745
Percentage of Mature Students: About 25%

Male/Female Ratio: About 1 : 4

Upper Age Limit for Mature Students: 45–50 depending on circumstances for teaching courses; otherwise none

Learning Facilities: The library has about 100,000 items and subscribes to 450 periodicals. The College also has a Media Resources Centre, closed-circuit television used in teaching, and a range of computer work stations.

Creche Facilities: The day nursery on campus is open all year except Bank Holidays and the Christmas period. Apply early as places are much in demand.

Mature Students Adviser: No, but there is a full-time counselling team. The College also publishes a booklet entitled 'Student Support Services' which is full of helpful advice on problems any student is likely to face.

Accommodation: The College runs 20 hostels/houses and tries to offer accommodation to all first-year students who require it, though it cannot guarantee places for late applicants. There are no special provisions for couples or families.

LSU stands for La Sainte Union and the College was founded nearly a hundred years ago as a Catholic teachers' training centre. It has diversified greatly, in terms both of the courses of study available and of the cultural and religious background of its students, but it maintains its fundamental values and principles. The mission statement in its prospectus emphasises its commitment to the idea of community, to the development of the whole person and to relationships of mutual respect.

LSU is an accredited college of the University of Southampton, which validates its degrees. It is situated near the centre of Southampton but benefits from close proximity to the attractive green space known as The Common.

Degrees Available: BA or BSc; BA or BSc with Qualified Teacher Status (at lower or upper primary level, four years); BTh.
The range of Science subjects is limited, but does include a BSc in Podiatry, which enables graduates to become state-registered chiropodists.
A part-time BA in Combined Studies is also available: you would normally take up to three courses (involving three hours a week formal study each) at a time, leading to a degree in four to six years. Contact the Registrar for details.

Assessment: A combination of exams and continuous assessment. The BTh involves a final-year dissertation; in other courses field work, practical work or facility in a foreign language are assessed as appropriate. Teaching practice is an important part of degrees including QTS.

How to Apply: Through UCAS.

LSU welcomes applications from mature students without traditional qualifications and considers these on an individual basis. Evidence of recent study such as an Access course, foundation course or BTEC award in an appropriate subject is usually required. For courses leading to a teaching qualification, GCSE/GCE or equivalent in English Language and Maths is essential.

A CATS scheme (see page 12) will be in place from September 1994.

University of Luton
Park Square, Luton LU1 3JU

Tel: 0582 34111 **Fax:** 0582 418677
Contact: Admissions Office

Number of Undergraduates: 6443
Percentage of Mature Students: 47%
Male/Female Ratio: About 1 : 1
Upper Age Limit for Mature Students: None

Learning Facilities: The University has a new Learning Resources Centre combining library (140,000 volumes), computerised information services and extensive computing facilities.

Creche Facilities: Yes, for children aged from two to five.
Mature Students Adviser: Yes
Accommodation: University accommodation can house just over a third of first-year students. There are no special provisions for couples or families.

Luton is the UK's newest University, having attained that status in the autumn of 1993. It has recently spent a lot of money on new facilities, including the Learning Resources Centre and a 25-seat auditorium. The main campus is in the centre of Luton, as are two smaller campuses which accommodate the Faculties of Humanities and Design and Technology; the Faculty of Management is at Putteridge Bury, about four miles away and housed in a magnificent mansion whose gardens were designed by Gertrude Jekyll.

The University has a no smoking policy which is firmly enforced.

Degrees Available: BA and BSc in Arts, Business, Social Science, Science and Technology; LLB. Some of the less usual subjects available include Architectural Technology, Freshwater Ecotoxicology and Human Factors in Computing. Degrees are modular and therefore suitable for part-time study.

There are foundation courses in Business, Health and Social Studies, Humanities, Built Environment, Computing, Engineering and Science.

Assessment: Usually by a combination of continuous assessment and exams, although some courses have no exams at all. Essays, projects, practical work and case studies are all assessed where appropriate. Each unit is assessed individually, during and at the end of the semester in which it is taught.

How to Apply: Through UCAS. Suitable applicants without formal qualifications are interviewed and assessed on work and life experience. Credit may be given for prior learning. You are welcome to contact the Admissions Unit for advice before submitting your application form, or to discuss your application once it has been submitted.

University of Manchester
Manchester M13 9PL

Tel: 061–275 2000 **Fax:** 061–273 5306
Contact: Admissions Office
Number of Undergraduates: Over 14,000
Percentage of Mature Students: About 9%
Male/Female Ratio: About 4 : 3
Upper Age Limit for Mature Students: None

Learning Facilities: The library, which incorporates the John Rylands Collection, is one of the finest University libraries in England, with a total of nearly three and a half million books and subscriptions to 6000 periodicals. It also has a collection of over a million manuscript or archival items. The library is on two main sites – the Main Library on campus and the Deansgate Building in the centre of town.

There are first-rate laboratory and technical facilities for relevant courses, including the Radio Astronomy Observatory at Jodrell Bank for students of Physics with Astrophysics. The University also boasts excellent cultural facilities in the form of the

Manchester Museum, the Whitworth Art Gallery and the University Theatre, all on or adjacent to the campus.

Creche Facilities: Run by the Students' Union.

Mature Students Adviser: Yes. Contact the Registrar's Department on 061–275 3286.

Accommodation: A number of Halls of Residence and the large 'student village', Owens Park, can accommodate all first-years who are attending university for the first time, provided they confirm acceptance of a place at the University and apply to the Accommodation Office by the end of August. There are a number of flats suitable for couples and families, and the University is continually expanding its accommodation provisions.

Founded in 1851, Manchester is the oldest and largest of the English civic universities, and the city has an enormous student population. It has thrown off its grimy Industrial Revolution image, has the best cultural facilities in the North (not to mention at least one of England's greatest football teams) and is reckoned to be a great place to be a student. Perhaps its finest claim to academic fame is that Ernest Rutherford split the atom here, but the teaching and research standards across all its wide range of subjects are extremely high.

Manchester is a campus university, situated just to the south of the city centre.

Degrees Available: BA or BSocSci in a variety of Arts and Social Science subjects, including Comparative Religion, Middle Eastern Studies and a wider than usual choice of Modern Languages; BA in Architecture or in Planning and Landscape; Mus B; BA (Econ) or BEcon Sc; BA or BSc with QTS in Combined Studies (Human Communication and Communication Disorders), Leisure Management or Speech Pathology; BA Accounting and Law; LLB, including a course in English and French Law; BSc in a wide range of subjects in the Faculty of Science and the School of Biological Sciences, including Artificial Intelligence, Chemistry with Patent Law, and Psychology and Neuroscience; BEng in the usual specialisms plus Nuclear Engineering and Structural Engineering with Architecture; BDS; BNurs; MB, ChB.

Most Science and Engineering courses contain an optional or compulsory sandwich year, or the possibility of including a Modern Language study with a year abroad.

Most courses, with the exception of Dentistry and Medicine, are either already modular or becoming modularised.

Enquiries about the expanding programme of part-time study should be addressed to the Office of Continuing Education and Training on 061–275 2047.

Assessment: The emphasis is on exams, but most courses include an element of continuous assessment, and in some final-year courses you may be allowed to submit a dissertation and/or project instead of taking an exam. Competence in practical or clinical work or teaching experience is an integral part of relevant degrees.

How to Apply: Through UCAS. Mature applicants without standard qualifications are welcome to contact the individual departments to discuss their circumstances before submitting a formal application.

———— ❋ ————

Manchester Metropolitan University
All Saints, Manchester M15 6BH

Tel: 061–247 2000 **Fax:** 061–247 6311
Contact: Jean Roebuck, External Liaison Officer

Number of Undergraduates: 23,591
Percentage of Mature Students: 61%
Male/Female Ratio: 4 : 5
Upper Age Limit for Mature Students: None

Learning Facilities: The total library stock is one million books and periodicals. Most libraries are open until 9 p.m. Monday to Thursday and till 7 p.m. on Fridays in term-time. The All Saints library also opens from 10 a.m. to 4 p.m. on Sundays. The University has computer networks, language centres, CD-Rom facilities and video workshops.

Creche Facilities: A nursery run jointly with Manchester University.

Mature Students Adviser: Jean Roebuck. The University also publishes a user-friendly brochure, 'Guidelines for Mature Students', which is particularly helpful on the worries students returning to study after a gap might have about lectures, essays and exams.

Accommodation: 1400 places are available in Halls of Residence; the majority are allocated to first-year students. No special provisions for couples or families.

The former Manchester Polytechnic gained university status in 1992 and while it is committed to high quality education it retains much of the

*flexibility common in the 'new' universities. About a third of its students
are part-time and many courses are based on units, allowing a wider
choice of subjects and method of study.*

*The Main (All Saints) campus is just south of Manchester city centre,
with the Aytoun, Elizabeth Gaskell and Hollings campuses a short
distance away and the Didsbury campus some five miles to the south.*

Degrees Available: BA in Arts, Social Science and Art and Design
subjects, including Business in Europe, Applied Human Communication, Illustration with Animation and Television Production and Design; BEd leading to a teaching qualification at
primary or secondary level; BEng; BSc, again in a range of
subjects – Applied Consumer Science and Speech Pathology and
Therapy are among the less usual ones; LLB.

A Combined Studies Degree Programme provides considerable
choice for students wishing to major in Applicable Mathematics,
Applied Physics, Geography or Mathematics: Environmental
Studies, European Studies and Printing and Photographic
Technology are among the subsidiary subjects available if you
choose this route.

There are in-house foundation courses in Art and Design, and in
most aspects of Science and Engineering.

Many courses are available part-time.

For courses at the Crewe and Alsager Faculty, see separate entry
(page 134).

Assessment: In most subjects a combination of exams and
continuous assessment; in Art and Design practical and project
work is important, though if you wish to follow a more
traditional academic route there may be scope for you to do so.

How to Apply: Through ADAR for Art and Design; otherwise
through UCAS for full-time study; for part-time contact the
relevant Course Tutor direct. Prospective mature students are
also welcome to discuss their circumstances with the course tutor
before submitting a formal application. Credit may be given for
relevant experience and/or prior learning.

Matthew Boulton College of Further and Higher Education

Sherlock St, Birmingham B5 7DB

Tel: 021–446 4545 **Fax:** 021–446 4324
Contact: Podiatric Course Tutor

Number of Undergraduates: About 80 on the degree course, out of a total student body of up to 8000, 1700 of them full-time

Percentage of Mature Students: Not specified

Male/Female Ratio: About 5 : 3 of all full-time students

Upper Age Limit for Mature Students: None

Learning Facilities: There is a well-stocked library supplying the needs of all the College's courses. Substantial recent expenditure on a Chiropody teaching suite and specialist electronics lab means that the Podiatry teaching facilities are first-rate.

Creche Facilities: For children aged one to five. Places are limited – apply early.

Mature Students Adviser: No, but all students have a personal tutor and counselling and other advice are readily available.

Accommodation: None available through the College, though there is a YWCA just across the road. Most students are from the Birmingham area.

The Birmingham School of Chiropody and Podiatric Medicine was established in 1946 and is now part of the Faculty of Science, Health and Environment of Matthew Boulton College. Matthew Boulton is primarily a College of Further Education, offering over 200 courses including GCSEs, A levels, BTEC awards, Access courses and professional and business courses. It is close to the centre of Birmingham, within walking distance of New Street Station.

Degrees Available: BSc in Podiatric Medicine, offered in association with the University of Sunderland. This is available as a three-year course or, for those without A levels or equivalent in appropriate subjects, a four-year course including a 'Year 0' or foundation year. During the foundation year, every effort is made to timetable classes within school hours.

Assessment: Exams in theoretical aspects of the course, but there is a strong emphasis on clinical expertise.

How to Apply: Through UCAS. If you do not have Science A levels or equivalent, you are advised to apply for the four-year course and you may be asked to take a short test in English and Maths.

——— ✳ ———

Middlesex University

All Saints, White Hart Lane, London N17 8HR

Tel: 081–362 5000

0800 181170 (prospectus help line)

Contact: Admission Enquiries

Number of Undergraduates: 14,000
Percentage of Mature Students: About 60%
Male/Female Ratio: About 1 : 1
Upper Age Limit for Mature Students: None

Learning Facilities: The library has over 400,000 books and a collection of slides, videos, records etc. It subscribes to over 2000 periodicals and provides 1300 study places. There are comprehensive computing facilities across all campuses, including computer-aided design; a 'state of the art' Microelectronics Centre and other up-to-the-minute technological facilities; and modern workshops and studios for Art, Design and Performing Arts.

Creche Facilities: At Trent Park, Tottenham and Enfield campuses, open during term-time only. Trent Park and Tottenham also operate half-term play schemes for children up to 12. Contact the Childcare Co-Ordinator (telephone 081–362 6208) as early as possible to book a place: she will help you find alternative child care if the University nurseries are full.

Mature Students Adviser: Not specifically, but all students have a personal academic tutor, and the full range of welfare services is available.

Accommodation: There are over a thousand rooms in Halls of Residence, with priority given to first-years away from home for the first time, but demand is much greater than supply. Accommodation Services keep a register of suitable accommodation for rent in the private sector. No special provisions for couples or families.

Middlesex University is scattered over six main sites in North London: Art and Design courses are taught at the Cat Hill, Quicksilver Place and Bounds Green campuses; Engineering and Technology also at Bounds Green, Performing Arts and Education at Trent Park, Business at Hendon and a mix of subjects at Tottenham, which also houses the administrative offices.

The diversity of the courses is reflected in the different styles of the campuses: Trent Park is an 18th-century manor house in elegant parkland, while Bounds Green is purpose-built and high-tech.

The University is expanding rapidly and prides itself on its increasing international links. It is nevertheless very much part of the community it serves, with 15% of its students coming from the three local boroughs and a further 25% from the rest of London.

Degrees Available: BA in a wide range of subjects in Art, Design and Performing Arts, Business, Humanities or Social Science; BA with QTS at primary or secondary level (secondary in Music or Design and Technology only; both available as two-year courses for mature students who already have an HND or equivalent); BEng; BSc in a number of subjects, the more unusual ones including Artificial Intelligence, Ecology and Ecotechnology, and Human-Computer Interface Design; LLB. All degree courses are modular and many may be part-time.

Assessment: A mixture of course work and exams, with each unit assessed separately during and at the end of the semester in which it is taught.

How to Apply: Through ADAR for most Art and Design courses, otherwise through UCAS for full-time courses. (For a number of courses in Art, Design and Performing Arts you must apply through UCAS or you can apply through either ADAR or UCAS – check the prospectus for clarification on the individual course.) If you live locally and are applying to Middlesex only, you can apply direct – contact the Admissions Enquiries Office for details and a form. Part-time applications should also be made direct. Middlesex has a very high proportion of mature students and welcomes applications from those without traditional qualifications who can show strong motivation. A wide range of alternative qualifications, including Access courses, are acceptable and credit may be given for prior learning and/or experience. If you do not have formal qualifications you are likely to be invited for an interview before being offered a place.

Moray House

Institute of Education, Heriot-Watt University, Holyrood Campus, Holyrood Rd, Edinburgh EH8 8AG

Tel: 031–556 8455 **Fax:** 031–557 3458
Contact: Dr David Jenkins, Registrar

Number of Undergraduates: 1480
Percentage of Mature Students: 25%
Male/Female Ratio: 2 : 5
Upper Age Limit for Mature Students: None

Learning Facilities: The library has 140,000 books and subscribes to 900 periodicals. There is a full range of computer facilities, educational television service and audio-visual resources.
Creche Facilities: No

Mature Students Adviser: No, but wide-ranging help for all students is available through Student Services.

Accommodation: There is accommodation for 500 students in Hall of Residence, and all first-years who wish it are normally allocated a room. No special provision for couples or families.

Moray House has been a College of Education for 150 years and became part of Heriot-Watt University in 1991. The main campus is in Edinburgh Old Town, while the Scottish Centre for Physical Education, Movement and Leisure Studies (formerly Dunfermline College of Physical Education) has its own campus about six miles to the west. Although Old Moray House dates from the 17th century, most of the College's buildings are purpose-built and its facilities are modern.

Degrees Available: BEd for teaching at primary level; BEd in Technology, Physical Education or in Teaching English to Speakers of Other Languages; BA in Recreation; BA Ordinary in Community Education or in Social Work.

Foundation courses for Primary Teaching, Technology and Community Education are available at local FE Colleges.

Assessment: Work placement and/or practical experience are an important part of all courses.

How to Apply: Direct, to the Registrar at the above address, by 15 December of the year preceding entry. Access courses, HNCs and HNDs may be considered as alternative entry qualifications. For some courses, such as social work, mature students should be prepared to convince the selection panel that they can cope with the academic side of the course.

Credit may be given for previous study and/or relevant experience – details from John Landon, Senior Lecturer, Modular Masters at the above address, telephone 031–558 6371/6097.

Myerscough College
Myerscough Hall, Bilsborrow, Preston PR3 0RY

Tel: 0995 640611 **Fax:** 0995 640842
Contact: Academic Registry

Number of Undergraduates: About 50 on the degree course, in a total student body of 1400+.
Percentage of Mature Students: Not specified
Male/Female Ratio: Not specified

Upper Age Limit for Mature Students: None specified

Learning Facilities: The library gives in-depth, up-to-date coverage of the subjects taught. There are farms, glasshouses, a nursery and excellent specialist laboratories and computing equipment. Students also have access to the facilities of the University of Central Lancashire.

Creche Facilities: No

Mature Students Adviser: Contact the Admissions Officer, or the resident warden of the campus.

Accommodation: A number of purpose-built study-bedrooms are available, with priority given to first-year students. There are no special provisions for couples or families, but privately rented accommodation is plentiful and the Student Welfare and Accommodation Officer will help.

Myerscough is a specialist college offering courses at various levels for 'all engaged in agriculture, horticulture and the direct use of animals, plants and the land, for sport, recreational and leisure purposes'. It celebrates its centenary in 1994 and its courses are backed by a well-established research base. The College is on three sites, but Horticulture is taught at the main Myerscough Centre, in rolling countryside about six miles north of Preston, and at the University of Central Lancashire.

Degrees Available: BSc in Horticultural Technology and Management, offered jointly with and validated by the University of Central Lancashire (four-year sandwich course).

Assessment: The course is unit-based and each unit is assessed separately by a mixture of course work (practical work, projects, essays, case studies etc) and exams, in the ratio of about 30 : 70.

How to Apply: Through UCAS to the University of Central Lancashire. Mature applicants without formal qualifications are welcome and will be judged on their ability to benefit from the course. Relevant experience will be taken into consideration, and the course is part of the University CATS scheme (see page 12), so credit may also be given for prior learning. You are likely to be invited for interview before being offered a place.

Napier University
219 Colinton Rd, Edinburgh EH14 1DJ

Tel: 031–444 2266 **Fax:** 031–455 7209
Contact: Admissions Office

Please see page 2 for general information about Scottish universities and colleges

Number of Undergraduates: About 6000 full-time, 3000 part-time

Percentage of Mature Students: About 33%

Male/Female Ratio: 3 : 2

Upper Age Limit for Mature Students: None, but it is unusual for the Journalism course to accept older applicants because of the limited opportunities in the industry.

Learning Facilities: The University has three libraries with a total of 145,000 books, 1800 periodicals and 790 study places. They are open seven days a week during the term. There are also comprehensive computer facilities on all three campuses.

Creche Facilities: Yes

Mature Students Adviser: Yes

Accommodation: Limited: less than 10% of first-years are allocated accommodation in University Halls or flats. There is no special provision for couples or families, but a wide range of private accommodation is available in residential areas close to the campuses.

All Napier courses are designed to provide practical as well as academic training and the University has close links with the nearby industrial area known as Silicon Glen. The recently introduced modular scheme provides flexibility in choice of subjects, but Napier still emphasises formal teaching and clearly defined study structure. You are expected to turn up for lectures.

Napier is based on three main campuses to the west of Edinburgh city centre, linked by public transport and by University minibuses. The Student Union facilities are disappointing, though efforts are being made to improve them; on the other hand the sporting facilities are excellent and students have all the attractions of Scotland's capital on their doorstep.

Degrees Available: BA in the Faculty of Applied Arts and in the Business School; BSc in Industrial Design (Technology) and in a limited number of Science and Engineering subjects; BEng.

Among the less widely available subjects offered are Export Studies and Languages, Hospitality (specialising in either Hotel Catering Management or Tourism Management), Civil and Transportation Engineering, Polymer Engineering and Rural Resources.

All degrees are modular and a Combined Studies CATS degree (see page 12) of BA or BSc is also available.

Foundation courses are available through local Further Education Colleges. Part-time study is possible.

Assessment: Varies from course to course, but most use both exams and continuous assessment. Satisfactory performance in work placements and practical work are important on relevant courses.

How to Apply: Through UCAS, but you are welcome to contact the relevant Faculty Adviser of Studies to discuss your individual needs before submitting a formal application.

Napier will consider any alternative qualifications and/or experience which demonstrate that you have the ability to benefit from Higher Education and are suitably prepared for the proposed course.

National Extension College
18 Brooklands Ave, Cambridge CB2 2HN

Tel: 0223 316644 **Fax:** 0223 313586
Contact: Customer Services, 0223 450215

Please note: Grants for NEC courses, as for all distance learning courses, are discretionary. See page 30 for more details

Number of Undergraduates: Over 15,000 are enrolled annually on a range of courses from GCSE to degrees and professional qualifications.

Percentage of Mature Students: Not specified, but the vast majority.

Male/Female Ratio: About 1 : 1
Upper Age Limit for Mature Students: None

Learning Facilities: You will be expected to buy books: a list of those required will be sent to you.

Creche Facilities: N/A
Mature Students Adviser: All students have a personal tutor.
Accommodation: N/A

The National Extension College is an independent educational charity which has specialised in distance learning for over 30 years. Its courses are ideal for those who wish to develop their career prospects but are obliged, because of employment or other commitments, to study at their own pace; they are also particularly popular with women who wish to return to work after having a family but need to build up skills and confidence.

Once you have enrolled you are assigned to a personal tutor who sets and marks assignments and generally supervises your studies. At the end of the course you sit formal exams at the University of London.

The basic registration fee for the NEC is £130; in addition degree course students pay £25 per assignment card – one of these covers each assignment your tutor marks and means that you only pay for tuition when you need it. You will also have to pay an initial registration fee at the University of London; an annual fee to keep your registration up to date; and exam entry fees when the time comes. Contact the External Programme of the University of London (address below) for details.

Degrees Available: BA; LLB; BSc in Economics; BD. These are all external degrees from the University of London.

Assessment: Your tutor will set you assignments and mark them as you send them in.

How to Apply: Contact the Degree and Professional Service of the NEC on 0223 450230/1 for an application form, which should be returned to the College. You must also apply direct to the External Programme, University of London, Senate House, Malet St, London WC1E 7HU, telephone 071–636 8000 x 3150. You will normally be expected to satisfy the general entry requirements of the University of London, but these may be waived in the case of mature students. You may be asked to complete an approved course of preliminary study before being accepted on to the degree programme.

National Hospital's College of Speech Sciences
Chandler House, 2 Wakefield St, London WC1N 1PG

Tel: 071–837 0113 **Fax:** 071–713 0861
Contact: Admissions Tutor

Number of Undergraduates: 190
Percentage of Mature Students: 38% and increasing every year
Male/Female Ratio: Between 1 : 20 and 1 : 25
Upper Age Limit for Mature Students: Not officially, but the course is of four years' duration and a working life of 10–15 years minimum after graduation is considered reasonable. Therefore, although the College has students in their forties, it is unlikely to accept applicants much older than that.

Learning Facilities: The College has a specialist library of about 4000 books and 70 journals subscriptions. Students also have access to the University College London libraries (about one and a quarter million books) and to the library of the University of

London. The College has a computer room, listening lab, video viewing facilities and voice measurement instrumentation facilities. Students can also use the comprehensive lab facilities of UCL.

Creche Facilities: Through UCL
Mature Students Adviser: Not specifically, but all students have a personal tutor.
Accommodation: Through UCL

At undergraduate level the National Hospital's College of Speech Sciences collaborates with the Department of Phonetics and Linguistics at University College London, and applications are considered jointly. The Speech Sciences course is strongly vocational and graduates of the College are qualified to work as Speech Therapists in the public or private sector.

For further information about facilities, see separate entry for University College London (page 362).

Degrees Available: BSc in Speech Sciences (four years), taught jointly with University College London.

Assessment: The course is organised into units, which are assessed separately. Some depend entirely on written exams, others use continuous assessment of laboratory, clinical and project work.

How to Apply: Through UCAS to University College London. Applications from mature students are welcomed and considered on their individual merits. A wide range of alternative qualifications is considered and evidence of recent study is preferred: many students enter the course after successful completion of a Science-based Access course. You should expect to be invited for interview and may be asked to do a short test.

Nene College
Moulton Park, Northampton NN2 7AL

Tel: 0604 735500 **Fax:** 0604 720636
Contact: Admissions Department of the individual course

Number of Undergraduates: About 6000 full-time, 4000 part-time on degree or HND courses
Percentage of Mature Students: About 10%

Male/Female Ratio: About 1 : 1
Upper Age Limit for Mature Students: None specified

Learning Facilities: The library has over 175,000 books, subscribes to 900 periodicals and houses a School Experience
Collection containing 5000 audio-visual items to support Education studies. Extensive IT facilities and Media Services are also
available and there are specialist laboratories for relevant
courses.

Creche Facilities: For children aged two and a half to five. Places
are very limited, so apply early.
Mature Students Adviser: The Head of Continuing Education will
advise on applications, and counselling and welfare services are
available to all students.
Accommodation: About 25% of first-years are accommodated in
study-bedrooms on the Park campus and the College finds
private rented accommodation for the rest. The Accommodation
Office will do its best to help you find somewhere suitable to live,
but there are no special provisions for couples or families.

*Most of the College is on a single campus on the outskirts of
Northampton; Art, Design and Technology are based at St George's
Avenue, about two miles away.*

*Northampton is famous as a hub of the shoe industry: the Central
Museum exhibits the shoes Queen Victoria wore at her wedding, and
ballet shoes worn by Nijinsky and Margot Fonteyn. Midway between
London and Birmingham and easy to reach from either, Northampton is
a bustling town with four major market days a week and plenty of
cultural, leisure and sporting facilities: Silverstone motor-racing circuit is
about 15 miles away and for those who prefer something quieter the Nene
Valley countryside is underrated and refreshingly uncrowded.*

Degrees Available: BA or BSc in the Faculties of Design and
Industry; Education, Health and Science; Humanities and
Social Sciences; and Management and Business; BEd with QTS
for teaching at lower or upper primary level; LLB.
The rather unusual range of subjects on offer includes Energy
Management, Leather Technology, Social and Behaviour
Sciences, and Performance Arts. There is a Combined Studies
programme leading to either a BA or a BSc: this is a modular
course and may be followed part-time. You may also enrol for a
single subject as a 'taster'. Contact the Combined Studies Office
for more details.

Assessment: A combination of exams and continuous assessment. Each module in the Combined Studies programme is assessed separately. Where applicable, competent performance at teaching practice or clinical work is essential.

How to Apply: Through ADAR for courses in Art and Design, otherwise through UCAS for full-time study; direct to the College for part-time. Nene actively encourages applications from prospective mature students who can show commitment and the ability to benefit from the course; those who are taking Access courses are welcome, and relevant experience will be taken into consideration.

NESCOT
Reigate Rd, Ewell, Epsom KT17 3DS

Tel: 081–394 1731 **Fax:** 081–394 3030
Contact: Louise Clewlow, Academic Registry

Number of Undergraduates: 650 full-time
Percentage of Mature Students: 6%
Male/Female Ratio: 2 : 1
Upper Age Limit for Mature Students: None

Learning Facilities: The library has over 40,000 books and 220 places. There are central computing facilities linked to 120 terminals, nine computing suites, CD-Rom databases, language lab, science labs, an acoustics lab and TV and photographic studios.

Creche Facilities: No
Mature Students Adviser: No, but there is an APEL/APL co-ordinator (see page 12) who will advise on what experience or non-standard qualifications may be accepted. All students have a personal tutor, and there is a confidential counselling service.
Accommodation: The College runs only two self-catering hostels and places are mostly reserved for overseas students. No provision for couples or families.

The former North East Surrey College of Technology is on two sites in a pleasant part of suburban Surrey within easy reach of central London and only a couple of miles from Epsom Downs race course. Although the range of subjects available at degree level is limited, there are two modular degrees (in Biological Sciences and Building Technology)

offering a certain amount of flexibility.
All NESCOT buildings and vehicles are no smoking.

Degrees Available: BA in Business Studies; BSc in Biological
Sciences, Biological Imaging, Building Technology, Computer
Studies, Electronic Imaging or Environmental Management.
The College runs foundation courses for all undergraduate
degrees. There is a wide range of part-time courses.
Degrees are validated by the Open University or by the
University of Surrey.

Assessment: Practical work is an important part of most courses.
Each unit in the modular programmes is assessed separately,
during and at the end of the semester in which it is taught.

How to Apply: Normally through UCAS for full-time degree
courses, but prospective mature students should contact the
Registry first. For part-time study, apply direct to the College.
All applications are considered on an individual basis and prior
learning and/or experience may be taken into account. The
College operates a CATS scheme and has an APL system (see
page 12).

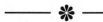

New College, Durham
Framwellgate Moor Centre, Durham DH1 5ES

Tel: 091–386 2421 (switchboard)
091–384 2813 or 2825 (admissions) **Fax:** 091–386 0303
Contact: Admissions Officer

Number of Undergraduates: 610 on diploma and degree courses,
out of a total of over 10,000 students on full- or part-time courses
in Further or Higher Education.
Percentage of Mature Students: 30% of undergraduates
Male/Female Ratio: About 2 : 3 among undergraduates
Upper Age Limit for Mature Students: None specified

Learning Facilities: The library has over 100,000 books and audio-
visual items, and subscribes to 550 periodicals. There are
computing facilities, media services, a language lab, a mock
travel agency and podiatric theatre and clinic.

Creche Facilities: On Fridays only
Mature Students Adviser: No, but counselling is available for all
students.

Accommodation: All first-years can be accommodated in hostels on the Neville's Cross site. There are no special provisions for couples or families.

New College is situated one two sites just outside Durham which are easily reached by public transport. Most of the Higher Education teaching takes place in the attractive neo-Georgian buildings at Neville's Cross, to the west of the city.

Students at New College benefit from the fact that Durham has a very large student body, with a diversity of cultural, social and sporting facilities. They are also on the fringes of one of the loveliest cities in England, and of some splendid unspoiled countryside.

Degrees Available: BSc in Podiatry with State Registration, in association with the University of Sunderland.

The first years of a BSc in the Management of Technology, a BA modular credit scheme and a foundation year in Science or Computing may all be studied at New College, before transfer to Sunderland for the rest of the course. Similarly, the first year of a BA in Tourism may be taken here and the course completed at the University of Newcastle.

Assessment: For Podiatry, a combination of exams and practical work. For other courses, exams and course work will both count towards the final mark.

How to Apply: Through UCAS, to New College for Podiatry, to Sunderland or Newcastle for the other degrees.

New College will consider Access courses, BTEC awards or appropriate experience and is particularly keen that prospective students for the Podiatry course show a high degree of motivation.

University of Newcastle upon Tyne
Newcastle upon Tyne NE1 7RU

Tel: 091–222 6000 **Fax:** 091–222 6139
Contact: Mrs L. Braiden, Assistant Registrar

Number of Undergraduates: About 9350
Percentage of Mature Students: 14%
Male/Female Ratio: About 4 : 3
Upper Age Limit for Mature Students: None

Learning Facilities: The library has 800,000 books and 5000 periodicals. It is open during the evenings and for longer hours at exam time. There are computer work stations in all departments on campus, a language centre and extensive laboratories. The Hatton Art Gallery is attached to the Department of Fine Art and the Museum of Antiquities (with a fine collection of material relating to Hadrian's Wall) to the Department of Archaeology.

Creche Facilities: The Students' Union sponsors 10 places for children up to the age of three at a local private nursery. These are always in great demand, so early booking is essential.

Mature Students Adviser: Not specifically, but each student has a personal tutor who is there to help with academic or other problems.

Accommodation: Halls of Residence, University houses and flats accommodate about 4500 students, and a place is guaranteed to all first-years who apply by 16 July and firmly accept an offer from the University by 7 September. There are a few University flats available for married students, and these tend to be let to couples who are both students at the University. Contact the Housing Office for details.

Newcastle is a large and expanding university situated on a single site on the fringes of the city centre. It prides itself on its academic standards, modern facilities and care for its students' welfare. By 1994 all courses will have been modularised, allowing for greater flexibility in optional programmes and possibly more scope for part-time study and for credit transfer.

The University has a particularly helpful approach to mature students, producing in addition to its prospectus a guide to accommodation, a guide for mature and non-traditional applicants and a student welfare handbook, which includes a section on study skills that will be especially helpful to those returning to study after a break.

Degrees Available: BA in Arts subjects and in the Faculty of Social and Environmental Sciences; BSc in the Faculty of Science and the new Faculty of Agricultural and Biological Sciences; BSc in Speech in the Faculty of Education; BEng in a wider than average range of subjects, including Marine Technology; LLB; BDS; MB, BS; BSc in Midwifery.

A few courses, notably English and Natural Resources, may be followed part-time.

There are foundation courses in all Engineering and some Science subjects.

The University also has links with a number of local colleges which run kitemarked Access courses.

Assessment: The emphasis is still on exams, with some continuous assessment of course work, projects or dissertations depending on subject.

How to Apply: Through UCAS, but you should also write to the Admissions Tutor giving further information such as your CV, details of Access courses, etc.

It is the University's policy that 'each faculty shall aim to fill at least 15% of its places with applicants from non-traditional backgrounds or qualifications'. It welcomes applications from 'all candidates with recent evidence of interest in and capacity for study' and undertakes to give every candidate individual consideration.

Newman and Westhill Colleges

Newman College, Genners Lane, Bartley Green, Birmingham B32 3NT

Tel: 021–476 1181 **Fax:** 021–476 1196
Contact: Registrar

Westhill College, Hamilton Building, Weoley Park Road, Selly Oak, Birmingham B29 6LL

Tel: 021–472 7245 **Fax:** 021–415 5399
Contact: Registrar at Newman; Mrs Inga Bulman, Deputy Principal (Students) at Westhill

Number of Undergraduates: About 1900: 900 at Newman, 1000 at Westhill
Percentage of Mature Students: 20+%
Male/Female Ratio: About 1 : 3 at Newman, 1 : 2 at Westhill
Upper Age Limit for Mature Students: About 40 for BEd courses, otherwise none

Learning Facilities: The two College libraries have a total of 160,000 books and subscribe to 500 periodicals. Both Colleges have audio-visual resources and computer facilities. The Church Education Resources Centre, based at Westhill, is a unique resource for visitors, students and church groups.

Creche Facilities: The Colleges Nursery Centre at Selly Oak, close to Westhill, caters for children aged from six weeks to five years.
Mature Students Adviser: Several tutors share this responsibility.
Accommodation: Halls of Residence can accommodate all first-year students who require a place. There are no special provisions for couples or families.

Newman and Westhill Colleges are affiliated to the University of Birmingham, which validates their degrees. They are about two miles apart, close to the University and about five miles from the centre of Birmingham. Although the Colleges are independent of each other, they work closely together and staff and students regularly move between the two.

Westhill was founded in 1907, by a group representing the main Free Churches, on a site provided by the Cadbury family, chocolate manufacturers and philanthropists. The College's attractive wooded grounds are still part of the Bournville estate.

Newman was founded in 1968 by the Catholic Education Council. Its buildings are modern and purpose-built.

The governing bodies and stated aims of both Colleges still reflect their religious backgrounds and all their degrees prepare students for work in 'caring' professions – teaching, community work or the Church.

Degrees Available: BEd leading to a qualification to teach at nursery or primary level (four years); BHum; BPhil (Ed) in Community and Youth Studies; BTheol (three or four years). The BPhil (Ed) is taught at Westhill only; all other courses are available at either College.

Part-time study is possible on some courses.

Assessment: A combination of exams, continuous assessment and project work. Teaching practice is an integral part of the BEd courses.

How to Apply: Through UCAS, but at the same time you should contact the Registrar of the College you would like to attend for details of the Colleges' special mature entry scheme. This involves a short preliminary essay, two interviews and a written test.

Both Colleges welcome mature applicants who do not have standard qualifications and may accept completion of a kite-marked Access course as satisfying the entry requirements.

Norfolk Institute of Art and Design
St George St, Norwich NR3 1BB

Tel: 0603 610561 **Fax:** 0603 615728
Contact: Individual Course Director

Number of Undergraduates: About 400
Percentage of Mature Students: 56%

Male/Female Ratio: About 3 : 4
Upper Age Limit for Mature Students: None specified

Learning Facilities: Libraries on the two sites hold a total of 24,000 books and subscribe to 150 journals, specialising in the Art and Design of the 19th and 20th centuries; Norwich has a slide collection of about 120,000 items, Great Yarmouth 25,000. There are computing facilities and well-equipped workshops on both sites, with audio-visual back-up at Norwich and computer-aided design at Great Yarmouth.

Norfolk Institute was formed in 1989 from the merger of two much older art schools, one in Norwich and one in Great Yarmouth. The Institute continues to occupy both sites, but all first degree courses are taught at Norwich.

Norwich is an inspirational place to study Art and Design: there is a fine collection of painting (especially landscape painting), sculpture and craft in the castle, and the Sainsbury Centre, designed by Norman Fowler, combines uncompromising late 20th-century architecture with a spectacular display of modern and primitive art.

Creche Facilities: No
Mature Students Adviser: No, but counselling services and other forms of advice are available to all students.
Accommodation: Limited, available at Norwich campus only and reserved for first-year students. Contact the College Accommodation Service if you need help finding somewhere suitable to live.

Degrees Available: BA in Cultural Studies, Fine Art, Graphic Design or Visual Studies, validated by Anglia Polytechnic University.
The Cultural Studies programme may be followed part-time, in which case you can expect to complete your degree in five years. There is also a foundation course in Art and Design.

Assessment: The emphasis is on continuous assessment, with studio work bearing 80% of the marks and theoretical work (which includes a final-year dissertation) 20% in practical courses.

How to Apply: Through UCAS or ADAR for Cultural Studies or Visual Studies, otherwise through ADAR. Visual Studies is a new course, not included in the 1994 UCAS Handbook, and for 1994 entry you may also apply direct to the College.
Gifted mature applicants who show strong commitment to the course and the ability to benefit from it are welcome. You should

expect to be invited for interview and to submit a portfolio of work before being offered a place.

North East Wales Institute of Higher Education
Plas Coch, Mold Rd, Wrexham LL11 2AW

Tel: 0978 290666 **Fax:** 0978 290008
Contact: Admissions Office

Number of Undergraduates: 2000
Percentage of Mature Students: 12%
Male/Female Ratio: 48 : 52
Upper Age Limit for Mature Students: None

Learning Facilities: A new library is under construction (see below). There are comprehensive computing facilities and full laboratory and technical facilities appropriate to the courses.

Creche Facilities: On all campuses. The nursery at Cartrefle campus caters for children aged two to five; all the others will take them from the age of six months.
Mature Students Adviser: Within Student Services
Accommodation: Halls of Residence or managed accommodation provide places for 70% of first-year students. No special provisions for couples or families.

The Institute is currently based on two main campuses and a number of smaller sites in central Wrexham, but a massive building programme is underway to create a single campus at the existing Plas Coch site. A major feature of this will be a new library and Learning Centre which will provide IT and Media Services. It is hoped that the library will be ready for use by autumn 1994.

NEWI is also expanding its curriculum and hopes to attain University status by the year 2000. It has a bilingual policy and although all courses are taught in English, some are also available through the medium of Welsh.

Degrees Available: BA in the Faculties of Art and Design and Humanities; BEd leading to qualifications to teach at all primary levels and at secondary level with a specialisation in Business/ Information Technology only; BN; BEng; BSc.

Degrees in Nursing, Education and Humanities are validated by the University of Wales.

Some Science and Engineering courses take four years and involve two years' study at the University of Wales at Swansea or Bangor, at the University of Salford or at UMIST.

Access courses in Science and in Humanities are available.

The Institute is currently introducing a modular degree programme and many courses can be followed part-time.

Assessment: Varies from course to course: most involve a high proportion (50% or more) of continuous assessment, projects and practical work. Each module is assessed separately.

How to Apply: Through UCAS for full-time study; direct to the Admissions Office for part-time.

All applicants are considered, and prior learning, non-academic qualifications and/or relevant experience may all be acceptable. The Institute runs a CATS scheme and is developing a system for APEL (see page 12).

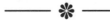

University of North London
Holloway Rd, London N7 8DB

Tel: 071–607 2789 **Fax:** 071–753 5075
Contact: Course Enquiries Office on 071–753 5066/7

Number of Undergraduates: 9903
Percentage of Mature Students: About 70%
Male/Female Ratio: About 5 : 6
Upper Age Limit for Mature Students: None

Learning Facilities: The libraries have a total stock of 340,000 books and subscribe to 2000 periodicals. During term-time they are open until 8.30 p.m. during the week, and two campus libraries also open on Saturdays from 10 a.m. to 2.45 p.m. The University provides a thousand computer work stations.

Creche Facilities: There are three well-equipped childcare facilities catering for children aged two to five. These are licensed for a total of 60 children, which gives the University one of the largest provisions for childcare of any Higher Education institution in the UK. Nonetheless there is usually a waiting list, so you are advised to make enquiries as early as possible.

Playgroups for children aged 5-11 are organised at half-term on all three main sites.

Mature Students Adviser: Nikki Marsh, based in the Marketing and Communications Office, 071–753-5074.

Accommodation: Two Halls of Residence, a small hostel and purpose-built flats accommodate 870 students. From 1994 it will be possible to house all first-year students living more than 25 miles away, provided they apply before July. There is no special provision for couples or families, but the Accommodation Office will endeavour to help all students find somewhere suitable to live.

The University of North London is on three main sites within easy reach of each other, centred round the A1 (Holloway Rd). A large majority of the students are mature, and the University makes every effort to help and encourage mature applicants. In addition to the standard Undergraduate Prospectus, and the Part-Time Prospectus mentioned below, there is a glossy Mature Students' Guide covering all the problems and questions likely to occur to potential mature students, and detailing the copious Access, foundation and return-to-study courses available at local colleges.

Degrees Available: BA or BSc in a range of Arts, Social Science and Science subjects; BA in Architecture; BEd with Qualified Teacher Status for teaching at primary level; BEng; LLB. Subjects available under the Combined Honours in Humanities scheme include Caribbean Studies, Irish Studies and South Asian Studies. North London also operates an interfaculty scheme which allows students to choose combinations of subjects that are not often permitted elsewhere.

A wide range of Access and foundation courses are taught at nearby colleges. Because most degrees are taught on a modular basis, there is ample opportunity for part-time study. The University publishes a part-time prospectus, available from the Course Enquiries Office.

Assessment: A combination of exams and continuous assessment, with project and practical work where relevant. Each module is assessed separately at the end of the semester in which it is taught.

How to Apply: Through ADAR for Interior Design, otherwise UCAS for full-time study, but if you are applying only to North London you should apply direct. Although you do not then have to stick to the UCAS deadline, you run the risk that popular courses will be full if you leave it too late. You should also apply direct if you wish to study part-time.

The University of North London has a policy of encouraging students who would not traditionally enter Higher Education, so all qualifications and work or life experience are considered individually. For some courses, you may be asked to produce written work and discuss it at an interview.

The University runs a CATS scheme (see page 12) – if you would like your previous studies or work experience to be taken into account, or just want advice on this area, contact the Interfaculty Studies Office.

You should be aware that some Business courses require Maths GCSE and that all teacher training courses require both English and Maths GCSE or equivalent. If you do not have this qualification, you may be able to take a suitable exam offered by the University.

Northern School of Contemporary Dance

98 Chapeltown Rd, Leeds LS7 4BH

Tel: 0532 625359 **Fax:** 0532 374585
Contact: Administrator

Number of Undergraduates: 135
Percentage of Mature Students: 24%
Male/Female Ratio: About 2 : 3
Upper Age Limit for Mature Students: None

Learning Facilities: The College has its own library, audio-visual equipment and a large collection of videotapes and recordings. There is also a theatre for student and outside use.

Creche Facilities: No
Mature Students Adviser: No
Accommodation: None available through the College

The Northern School of Contemporary Dance has a very high reputation in its field and a high percentage of its graduates find work as dancers or in related fields. Applicants do not necessarily need a great deal of experience, as commitment and potential are considered more important. The physical side of the course is demanding and the College believes that excellence can only be attained through a combination of artistic understanding and technical expertise.

The College does not run a Health Service, but there is a physiotherapist on the staff and students register with local GPs.

Degrees Available: Bachelor of Performing Arts (Dance), validated by the University of Leeds.

There is a one-year foundation course which prepares students for vocational dance training or for degree-level study in the Performing Arts.

Assessment: 75% practical dance achievement; 25% what the prospectus describes as 'academic underpinning'.

How to Apply: Direct. Contact the Administrator for a prospectus and application form. Admission is by audition and, if that is satisfactory, by interview. The last auditions take place in June for entry the following autumn.

The College normally expects applicants to have A levels or equivalent, but there is a Special Entry Examination for those who do not have standard qualifications.

———— ❊ ————

University of Northumbria at Newcastle
Ellison Building, Ellison Place, Newcastle upon Tyne NE1 8ST

Tel: 091–227 4064 **Fax:** 091–227 4707
Contact: Registry for prospectus; Unilink for advice (091–227 4066)

Number of Undergraduates: 10,225 full-time, 3826 part-time
Percentage of Mature Students: 54%
Male/Female Ratio: 1 : 1
Upper Age Limit for Mature Students: None

Learning Facilities: The library on the main campus occupies a nine-storey building and has half a million books. Smaller libraries on the other campuses run a next-day book-obtaining service for students. Over a thousand microcomputers and terminals are distributed around the campus.

Creche Facilities: Two nurseries, one on the City Centre campus and one at Coach Lane, cater for children aged two and a half to five. Playgroups for school-aged children may be organised at half-term if there is sufficient demand.

Mature Students Adviser: Yes. The University also publishes an excellent Mature Students' Guide, which gives advice on Access courses, credit transfer, grants and loans, etc, and contains lots of useful addresses.

Accommodation: Usually allocated only to full-time first-year students who do not live locally (about 50%). A few family units are available. Private rented accommodation is easy to find in Newcastle, and the Accommodation Service will help.

The University of Northumbria at Newcastle is on four campuses: the largest in Newcastle city centre, and the others at Coach Lane, on the outskirts of the city, in Carlisle and at Longhirst in rural Northumberland. Carlisle and Longhirst specialise in Business Studies and Management.

One of the most unspoiled counties in England, Northumberland offers scenic beauty and historical interest, with easy access to Lindisfarne, the Border castles and Hadrian's Wall. Newcastle itself is considered a great place to be a student, with a strong tradition of local music and thriving pubs and clubs.

Degrees Available: BA in Arts and Art and Design subjects; BEd in general primary or specialised secondary teaching; BEng; BSc in Science, Social Science and paramedical subjects (Midwifery, Nursing Studies, Occupational Therapy and Physiotherapy); LLB including an option in French Law.

There are a number of part-time courses which can be studied say one day or two evenings per week and lead to a degree in up to six years. The University publishes a separate prospectus on part-time courses.

Before the start of each academic year, the University, in association with local colleges, runs a kitemarked Access course, the Higher Education Foundation Course. This is aimed at people wishing to continue their education after a break and concentrates on building up confidence and developing study skills. There are also one-year full-time foundation courses in Accountancy and in Engineering and Science.

Assessment: Normally through a mixture of exams and continuous assessment, though some practical courses such as Design for Industry have no formal exams. Depending on the course, projects, field work and essays or dissertations may play a major part.

How to Apply: Through UCAS for most full-time degrees; through ADAR for the majority of courses in Art and Design. For part-time courses, you should obtain a standard University application form from the Registry and apply direct to the School/Faculty concerned.

Most courses will consider non-standard qualifications. The University operates a CATS scheme (see page 12), so credit may be given for former studies. Relevant work experience may also be taken into account.

University of Nottingham
University Park, Nottingham NG7 2RD

Tel: 0602 515151
Contact: Admissions Office

Number of Undergraduates: About 10,000 full-time
Percentage of Mature Students: About 10%
Male/Female Ratio: About 3 : 2
Upper Age Limit for Mature Students: None specified

Learning Facilities: The University library, which houses over a million books, subscribes to over 5000 periodicals and is constantly being expanded, comprises five specialist libraries dedicated to the various faculties. Nottingham also has a Department of Manuscripts and Special Collections with two million original documents from medieval to modern. There are comprehensive computing facilities, a high-tech language centre with 3000 tapes in 30 languages and first-rate laboratory and technical facilities for relevant subjects. There is a new Arts Centre on campus, with an excellent small art gallery, and the collections of the University Museum supplement the teaching of Archaeology.

Creche Facilities: Playgroup for children aged two and a half to five.

Mature Students Adviser: Not specifically, but a wide network of welfare and counselling services exists. A booklet entitled 'University of Nottingham Entry at 21+' is available from the Registrar, and there is a Mature Students' Guild in the Students' Union.

Accommodation: Twelve catering Halls of Residence can accommodate nearly 3000 students and self-catering flats a further 1100. All first-years who live outside Nottingham and apply to the Accommodation Office by 1 August are guaranteed a place. Private rented accommodation for couples and families is limited – contact the Accommodation Office for information.

The University of Nottingham owes its attractive campus about three miles out of town to the generosity of Jesse Boot (founder of the chemist's), who donated an estate of his own when the University College needed to move to larger premises after the First World War. It has continued to expand, and now boasts some of the finest research and teaching facilities in the country.

Most of the teaching takes place on campus, but the Faculty of Medicine is based at the Queen's Medical Centre just across the road, and the School of Agricultural and Food Sciences at Sutton Bonington, about ten miles away to the south.

Degrees Available: BA in the Faculties of Art or Law and Social Sciences; LLB; BSc in the Faculties of Science or Agricultural and Food Sciences; BEng; BM, BS; BN; BPharm.

All courses except those in Architecture and Medicine are modular and many BA degrees can be taken part-time, over a period of five to seven years.

Courses in the Faculties of Science, Engineering and Agricultural and Food Sciences may include a sandwich placement or a year at a university in Europe or America; an element of French, German, Italian, Japanese, Russian or Spanish study may form part of a number of three-year Engineering degrees.

An intercalated one-year BMedSci may be taken by medical students between preclinical and clinical parts of the course.

A BSc in Physiotherapy validated by the University is taught at the Nottingham School of Physiotherapy.

Assessment: Varies from course to course, but most include both exams and continuous assessment, with each module assessed separately. Where relevant (e.g. in Medicine, Nursing and Science and Engineering subjects) competent performance in clinical or practical work is essential.

How to Apply: Through UCAS for full-time study, to the Registrar for part-time. Applications from prospective mature students are welcome, and BTEC awards, Access courses or Open University credits may be deemed to satisfy the entry requirements.

If you do not have traditional qualifications, you should also write to the Admissions Tutor of the course you wish to follow, giving information about your interests and experience in support of your application. You may be invited for interview, required to sit a test, or asked for examples of previous work.

Nottingham Trent University
Burton St, Nottingham NG1 4BU

Tel: 0602 418418 **Fax:** 0602 484266
Contact: Academic Registrar

Number of Undergraduates: About 13,500 full-time, 3800 part-time

Percentage of Mature Students: 39%

Male/Female Ratio: 9 : 7

Upper Age Limit for Mature Students: None

Learning Facilities: There are two main libraries, one on each campus, plus a specialist reference library for Business and Law. They are open until 9 p.m. during the week (Clifton campus library closes at 5 on Fridays), 9–5 on Saturdays and for reference only on Sunday afternoons. Between them they stock over 400,000 books and subscribe to 2500 periodicals. There are comprehensive computing facilities throughout the University.

Creche Facilities: For 70 children, which is very much larger than most other University nurseries, but demand for places still exceeds supply, so apply early. There is also a half-term play scheme for older children.

Mature Students Adviser: Not specifically, but the Co-Ordinator/ Adviser in the Centre for Access and Continuing Education will advise on applications. Counselling services are available and all students have a personal tutor. The Centre for Adult and Continuing Education publishes a Mature Students' Guide and a number of booklets on Higher Education, Access, credit transfer, accrediting prior experience, etc. It also organises pre-enrolment meetings, 'welcomes', and monthly meetings designed to offer support to mature students.

Accommodation: It is University policy to accommodate all full-time first-year students who require a place in a Hall of Residence, but in practice many mature students at Nottingham Trent live at home and most of those that move to Nottingham prefer smaller units such as University houses and flats. There are no special provisions for couples or families, but some are planned for the future.

Nottingham Trent is an extremely popular University – for 1992 entry it received an average of 15 applications for each available place. Nottingham itself is an attractive and lively medium-sized city with a large student population and correspondingly good, cheap facilities of all kinds. Whether your interest is Robin Hood, D.H. Lawrence, first rate cricket and football or getting out of town to the Derbyshire Dales or the Peak District, Nottingham has something to offer.

The University is on three sites, with five of the eight Faculties based at the City site; Humanities and Science are at Clifton, about four miles out

of town to the south; and Education is in a nearby Georgian manor house, Clifton Hall.

Degrees Available: BA in a range of Art and Design, Humanities and Social Science subjects; BEd leading to a qualification to teach at primary or secondary level (some of the secondary courses are two-year, for mature students who already have an HND); BEng; BSc; LLB.

The subjects on offer cover a very broad spectrum, from Knitwear Design to Integrated Engineering. A Combined Studies programme leading to a BA or BSc allows for unusual combinations of subjects.

A number of courses, particularly in Business, Engineering, Environmental Health and Law, have optional or compulsory sandwich elements which mean they last four years.

Foundation courses in Science and Engineering are available both at the University and at local franchised colleges.

A wide range of courses is available part-time – contact the relevant Faculty Office for details.

Assessment: A mixture of exams, assessment of course work and projects. Teaching practice and satisfactory completion of work placements are integral to the relevant courses.

How to Apply: Through ADAR for Art and Design, otherwise through UCAS for full-time courses; direct to the University for part-time.

Nottingham Trent has a large number of mature students, recognises many alternative qualifications and gives credit for prior learning and/or experience. You are welcome to contact the Centre for Adult and Continuing Education for an informal discussion before submitting your application.

Oak Hill College
Chase Side, Southgate, London N14 4PS

Tel: 081–449 0467 **Fax:** 081–441 5996
Contact: Admissions Officer

Number of Undergraduates: 80
Percentage of Mature Students: 100%
Male/Female Ratio: 4 : 3
Upper Age Limit for Mature Students: None specified

Learning Facilities: The library has 18,000 books and a wide range of periodicals to support the subjects taught.

Creche Facilities: Yes

Mature Students Adviser: Not specifically, but there is a resident chaplain and members of the faculty are available to help with any problems that may arise.

Accommodation: Available on campus for most students, in either study-bedrooms or shared houses.

Oak Hill is a Church of England College within the evangelical tradition of the Church, but welcomes applicants from all denominations. Founded in the 1930s, it is now an accredited College of Middlesex University, which validates its degrees. It welcomes involvement from students' families, inviting spouses to attend lectures free of charge and providing recordings of lectures for families to use at home.

Oak Hill has spacious, attractive grounds in a residential area of North London, with easy access to the centre of town and to the M25.

Degrees Available: BA in Theological and Pastoral Studies.

Assessment: The course is modular and each unit is assessed separately at the end of the semester in which it is taught. The final year includes a dissertation. Work placements giving practical experience of the Ministry are an integral part of the course; so are the assignments and project connected with this work.

How to Apply: Direct to the College on a form available from the Admissions Officer. Mature applicants with appropriate experience will be considered on their individual merits. If you are undertaking the course with a view to going into the Christian Ministry, one of your referees must be the minister of your Home Church. You should expect to be invited for interview, and will be welcome to stay overnight and take the opportunity to find out as much as possible about the College.

The Open University
Walton Hall, Milton Keynes MK7 6YZ

Tel: 0908 653231

Contact: The OU has 13 regional centres in the UK, each with its own Enquiry and Admission Service: check your phone book for the one nearest you. Failing that, contact the Central Enquiry Service, P.O. Box 200 at the above address.

Number of Undergraduates: About 100,000
Percentage of Mature Students: The vast majority
Male/Female Ratio: Varies
Upper Age Limit for Mature Students: None

Please note: Grants for Open University courses, as for all distance learning courses, are discretionary. See page 30 for more details.

Learning Facilities: The basic materials you need for your course will be sent to you, along with a list of any books or other materials you should buy.

Creche Facilities: N/A
Mature Students Adviser: All students are assigned to a tutor who is both their academic supervisor and a source of support and advice if required.
Accommodation: N/A

The Open University has been offering a wide range of distance learning since 1969 and has a commitment to provide Higher Education for anyone who wants to learn. Although you study at home, you have a personal tutor with whom you have regular contact, you may have group tutorials at which you meet other students, and the OU has 250 study centres in the UK where personal teaching and counselling are available.

To obtain a degree, you need to study six full credits. Each credit entails about 12–15 hours' study a week over a nine-month period. If you are unable to make this sort of commitment, you can take half-credit courses instead. Material to enable you to do the necessary work will be sent to you through the post.

In 1994 a foundation course costs about £260 and most full-credit courses either £310 or £475. In addition, you will have to buy books and other materials (costs vary enormously from course to course) and you may have to pay to attend a summer school for up to a week (about £200 with full board).

Degrees Available: BA or BSc in a range of subjects from Art History to Electronics.
There are foundation courses in Arts, Social Sciences, Mathematics, Science and Technology: each counts as a full credit towards the total required for your degree.

Assessment: Throughout each course you are expected to complete assignments which count towards your final mark. At the end of the course there is a three-hour exam.

How to Apply: Direct, on an application form obtainable from the OU regional centre most convenient to you. Degree courses normally start in February and run until October; you should apply at the latest by the end of September of the year before you wish to start, and preferably by February/March. Admission is on a first come, first served basis and there is always more demand than there are places available.

You do not normally have to have formal qualifications to undertake a degree course. If you have already done some studying at Higher Education level, you may be given credit for this.

Oxford University
Colleges Admissions Office, University Offices, Wellington Square, Oxford OX1 2JD

Tel: 0865 270207 **Fax:** 0865 270708
Contact: Secretary

Number of Undergraduates: 9866
Percentage of Mature Students: 2%
Male/Female Ratio: About 3 : 2
Upper Age Limit for Mature Students: None

Please note that unless you are applying for an Organ Scholarship, you are no longer allowed to apply simultaneously to both Cambridge and Oxford

Learning Facilities: The library resources are vast: in addition to the University libraries (which include the famous Bodleian, see below), faculties, departments and colleges have libraries of their own. The University has computing facilities and a Language Teaching Centre.

Creche Facilities: Four colleges (Balliol, St Anne's, Somerville and Wolfson) run their own nurseries. A University nursery with 74 places is due to open in mid-1994. Students on low incomes will be able to apply for subsidies.

Mature Students Adviser: No, but the full range of counselling and welfare services is available.

Accommodation: Prospective students at Oxford apply to and are accepted by a college, which houses them for at least two years of a three-year course. Accommodation is mostly in single study-bedrooms. A limited amount of college/university accommodation is available for couples or families, but demand is always greater than supply.

Oxford is, of course, one of the great learning institutions in England – and the world. It is also one of the oldest universities in Europe, having been in existence since the 12th century. University College was founded in 1249 and 16 others of the existing Colleges date back to before 1600, including Christ Church, founded in 1546 by Cardinal Wolsey. The Bodleian Library, established in 1409, is entitled to receive a free copy of every book published in the UK and contains well over 2.5 million books.

The Oxford Colleges are scattered around the town and the beauty of their architecture – particularly that of Magdalen College and of Oxford Cathedral, which is part of Christ Church – is part of Oxford's attraction.

An Oxford degree still carries an enormous amount of weight in the outside world, and its academic standards are high.

Degrees Available: BA in Arts and Social Studies, in Science or in Science and Arts; MEng (a four-year course with a first year common to all specialities); BFA; BM, BCh; degrees in Metallurgy/Science of Materials.

Oxford has a School of Oriental Studies which offers Arabic, Chinese, Egyptology and Sanskrit among other specialisations; there is also a wide choice of Modern Languages including Czech with Slovak, Modern Greek and Portuguese.

Assessment: Largely exam-based, at end of first and final years.

How to Apply: Through UCAS, but you must also complete the Oxford Application Card (obtainable from the address above) and return it to the Oxford Colleges Admissions Office by 15 October in the year before you wish to start your course.

If you are not taking A levels or the equivalent, or if you took them more than five years ago, you should apply to sit the University's own entrance exam: details are given in the Undergraduate Prospectus, or you can contact the Admissions Office or your first choice of college for advice. Alternatively, apply to Manchester College, which accepts only mature students, but offers a limited choice of degree courses. Manchester has a special written paper which applicants sit.

Although Oxford is committed to increasing its number of mature undergraduates, at the moment it has very few.

Oxford Brookes University
Gipsy Lane, Headington, Oxford OX3 0BP

Tel: 0865 741111
　　0865 483039 (for prospectus only)
Contact: Admissions Officer 0865 483040

Number of Undergraduates: 8000 full-time, 4500 part-time

Percentage of Mature Students: About 30% on the modular course; fewer elsewhere

Male/Female Ratio: About 1 : 1

Upper Age Limit for Mature Students: None – some students on the modular scheme are in their 70s.

Learning Facilities: Between them the two main libraries (one on each campus) house nearly 300,000 books, subscribe to 23,000 periodicals and provide nearly 800 study places. Gipsy Lane library is open seven days a week during term, Wheatley library six. Specialist collections include a full set of British Standard Specifications and Codes of Practice, and the John Fuller Collection devoted to catering, hospitality and gastronomy.

There are comprehensive information services and computing facilities, and modern purpose-built labs.

Creche Facilities: For children aged two to five, open 48 weeks of the year. There is also a half-term play scheme for children aged 5–14. Write to the Nursery Manager for an application form and return it as soon as possible.

Mature Students Adviser: Yes, in the Student Services Centre. Prospective students can attend a mature students' counselling and advice session – contact the Modular Course Co-Ordinator on 0865 483048 for details. The University also publishes a particularly helpful and encouraging Mature Students' Guide. In the first term of each session study skills workshops are offered to all students who want them.

Accommodation: Catering and self-catering Halls and hostels accommodate over 2000 students and priority is given to first-years. Limited accommodation for couples or for single parents (but not large families) is available through the Housing Association.

Refusing to be overshadowed by its distinguished neighbour, Oxford Brookes has built up an enviable reputation for academic excellence. Its modular scheme remains the largest in the UK, offering students a choice of over a thousand units in almost innumerable combinations.

Most of the University is on the Gipsy Lane campus, on the eastern fringes of Oxford, with the Schools of Business and Education about five miles away to the east, at Wheatley. Health Care students also spend part of their time at the prestigious John Radcliffe Hospital. Parking is extremely difficult and students are advised not to bring cars.

Degrees Available: BA in Architectural Studies, Business Studies or European Business Studies; BEng in Engineering, Electronic

Engineering or Mechanical Engineering; BSc in Estate Management. All other courses – for a BA, BSc, BEd, BEng or LLB – are modular and allow single or double honours in a very diverse range of subjects including Building, Cartography, Fine Art, Health and Exercise Science, Hotel and Catering Management, Languages for Business, Midwifery, Nursing and Technology Management. Oxford Brookes is also one of very few institutions in the UK to offer degree-level qualifications in Publishing and in Retailing.

All modular programmes may be followed part-time and you can expect to complete your degree in about five to seven years. There is also an Associate Student Scheme which allows you to study up to three modules before enrolling on a full-scale course. There are foundation courses in Art and Design and in Engineering.

Assessment: A combination of exams and continuous assessment, with each unit of the modular courses assessed separately during and at the end of the term in which it is taught. Field work, practical work and clinical competence are all assessed where applicable.

How to Apply: Through ADAR for Fine Art (you will be asked to submit a portfolio), otherwise through UCAS for full-time study; for part-time or for foundation courses contact the Registry for a direct application form. While direct applications are accepted throughout the year, you are advised to apply by February at the latest.

Applications from prospective mature students, especially those with evidence of recent study such as an Access course, are very welcome, and you are invited to contact the University to discuss your circumstances before submitting a formal application.

University of Paisley
High St, Paisley PA1 2BE

Tel: 041–848 3000 **Fax:** 041–887 8012
Contact: Admissions Office

Please see page 2 for general information on Scottish universities and colleges

Number of Undergraduates: 4814
Percentage of Mature Students: 23%

Male/Female Ratio: 53 : 47
Upper Age Limit for Mature Students: None

Learning Facilities: The library has 120,000 volumes and over 1200 current periodicals. During term-time it is open until 9 p.m. Monday to Friday and all day on Saturday. There is a Computer Centre with comprehensive facilities and an Educational Development Unit, which includes a television studio, photographic darkrooms, audio-visual equipment, etc.

Creche Facilities: Nursery places are available during term time.
Mature Students Adviser: No, but counselling and welfare services are available to all students.
Accommodation: Five Halls of Residence accommodate about 300 students and preference is given to first-year students who do not live within commuting distance. There are also a number of University flats. Some double study-bedrooms are available in the Halls and some shared places in the flats.

The University of Paisley grew out of a Technical College and School of Art founded nearly a hundred years ago, and attained university status in 1992. The campus is in the centre of the town, with the Students' Union and some accommodation off-campus but nearby.

Paisley is only seven miles from Glasgow, but retains its own identity. Its ecclesiastical connections can be traced back to the sixth century and it boasts a magnificent abbey, part of which dates from 1163. In the aftermath of the Industrial Revolution it became a flourishing textile centre and is the home of the Paisley pattern.

Degrees Available: BA in Combined Studies and in Social Science and Business-orientated subjects; BSc in a range of subjects including Construction Management, Land Economics, and Quality Management and Technology; BEng.
On most Science and Engineering courses there is an optional sandwich element which extends the normal four-year course to four and a half or five years.
Many courses can be followed part-time.

Assessment: A combination of exams and continuous assessment of written and practical work as appropriate, including a major research-based project in the final year of most courses.

How to Apply: Through UCAS.
Paisley welcomes applications from prospective mature students, particularly those who have 'shown an interest in their educational advancement and an aptitude for academic study'. The University is a participating member of the Scottish Wider

Access Programme (SWAP, see page 20) and accepts one year's full-time study of SCOTVEC modules as an alternative to the traditional entry qualifications. Previous work experience may also be taken into account. A CATS scheme (see page 12) allows you to follow a flexible degree programme and gives credit for previous study.

School of Pharmacy (University of London)
29–39 Brunswick Square, London WC1N 1AX

Tel: 071–753 5800 **Fax:** 071–278 0622
Contact: Registrar

Number of Undergraduates: About 400
Percentage of Mature Students: About 4%
Male/Female Ratio: About 9 : 11
Upper Age Limit for Mature Students: None specified

Learning Facilities: The School has an excellent specialist library, Computer Unit and Multimedia Unit. Students also have access to the main University of London library and to the nearby Bloomsbury Science Library.

Creche Facilities: No
Mature Students Adviser: No, but students have access to the welfare services of the University of London.
Accommodation: Available in the University of London's Intercollegiate Halls. Contact the Accommodation Office, Senate House, Malet St, London WC1E 7HU, telephone 071–636 2818 for details. No special provisions for couples or families.

The School was founded in 1842 by the Pharmaceutical Society when the society itself was in its infancy. Most members of the teaching staff are engaged in research which is recognised as being of an exceptionally high standard and means that the courses are absolutely up-to-date. They also have practical applications, as students have experience in pharmacy in industry, hospitals and the community.

The School is situated in Bloomsbury, close to the main buildings of the University of London.

Degrees Available: BPharm; BSc in Toxicology and Pharmacology (four-year sandwich).

Assessment: A combination of exams and continuous assessment of practical and other course work.

How to Apply: Through UCAS. The School welcomes applications from mature students who do not have standard qualifications – contact the Registrar for information and advice before applying.

University of Plymouth
Drake Circus, Plymouth PL4 8AA

Tel: 0752 600600 **Fax:** 0752 232141
Contact: Access Co-Ordinator, 0752 232382

Number of Undergraduates: 18,400
Percentage of Mature Students: 47%
Male/Female Ratio: 11 : 9
Upper Age Limit for Mature Students: None

Learning Facilities: The University has libraries on all four sites, with a total of over 350,000 books and subscriptions to 2800 periodicals. There are also computing facilities and audio-visual and media support for students and teachers.

Creche Facilities: On the Plymouth campus, catering for three- to five-year-olds. Places are limited, so apply early.
Mature Students Adviser: Yes
Accommodation: The University has 1260 places in Halls of Residence and hopes to have a further 430 by September 1994. About a third of first-year students can be allocated a place. There are no Halls serving the Exeter campus, but the University manages houses and flats and the Accommodation Office will advise you. No special provisions for couples or families.

Born out of the Polytechnic of the South West, itself an amalgam of various older Devon colleges, the University of Plymouth came into being in 1992. It is situated on four sites scattered about South Devon (see below for which courses are taught where). All have their own social and sporting facilities and easy access to the famous Devon moors and to the coast – indeed, the Exmouth campus is within sight of the sea.

Plymouth has rapidly established its reputation at University level, with a particularly high rating in Environmental Sciences. It is also a popular and friendly place with a flexible and welcoming attitude to mature students.

Degrees Available: At Plymouth: BA in the Business School; BEng; LLB; BSc in a vast range of subjects including Fisheries Technology, Marine Technology, Maritime Business and Ocean Science as well as all the common Science and Social Science subjects.

At Exeter: BA in the Faculty of Arts and Design; at Exmouth: BEd leading to a qualification to teach at upper or lower primary level; at Seale-Hayne (Newton Abbot): BSc in the Faculty of Agriculture, Food and Land Use.

A number of courses in the Business School and in the Faculty of Technology are four-year sandwich programmes.

There are foundation courses in Agriculture, Marine Studies, Science and Technology, and opportunities for a wide range of study at partner colleges throughout Devon and Somerset.

Many courses are modular and can be followed part-time.

Assessment: Each unit of a modular course is assessed separately, during and at the end of the semester in which it is taught. Practical, creative and project work and performance on teaching practice will be taken into account where relevant.

How to Apply: Through ADAR for Arts and Design courses, otherwise through UCAS for full-time courses. If you want more advice before submitting a formal application, or for information about part-time study, contact Continuing Education at the address above, telephone 0752 232382.

The University has traditionally welcomed a high proportion of mature students and will give consideration to all qualifications and/or experience that are relevant to the course in question. Plymouth operates a CATS scheme (see page 12), so credit may also be given for prior learning.

You should expect to be invited for an interview.

University of Portsmouth
University House, Winston Churchill Ave, Portsmouth PO1 2UP

Tel: 0705 876543 **Fax:** 0705 843082
Contact: Assistant Registrar (Admissions)

Number of Undergraduates: About 10,000 full-time, 2000 part-time
Percentage of Mature Students: About 22%

Male/Female Ratio: About 4 : 3
Upper Age Limit for Mature Students: None specified

Learning Facilities: The main library holds half a million volumes and a growing audio-visual collection. It subscribes to 3000 periodicals, is open for 76+ hours a week during term-time and has over 800 study places. There are comprehensive computing facilities, a Television Centre providing multi-media support for teaching and research, and a Language Centre whose resources are available to all students. Art, Design and Media, Science and Engineering courses benefit from specialist workshops and laboratories with sophisticated equipment.

Creche Facilities: Available for children aged six months to five years, open Monday to Friday all year round. Contact the Nursery Supervisor, The Quadrant, Mildam, telephone 0705 876561 as early as possible to book a place. The Students' Union also runs a half-term play group for children at primary school.

Mature Students Adviser: The full range of counselling and welfare services is available to all students. The UCAS booklet 'Stepping Up: A Mature Student's Guide to Higher Education' is available from the Academic Registrar's office.

Accommodation: Eight Halls of Residence – some catering, some self-catering – can accommodate over 1100 students; about 25-30% of first-years are allocated a place. The Accommodation Office will help other students find places in approved lodgings or privately rented flats and bedsits. There is very little provision for couples or families.

Portsmouth is a new University but grew from a School of Science and Art founded in 1870 and has steadily expanded its activities over the last 120-odd years: it became the Southern Regional College of Technology in 1957 and a polytechnic in 1969. It has always been very much part of the community it serves, but attracts many students from further afield seeking courses which bring recognition from various professional bodies.

Most of the University is scattered about various sites in central Portsmouth, none of them very far apart; however, the Business School and the School of Educational Studies are at Milton and Langstone respectively, a couple of miles away down the road to Southsea, and the School of Health Studies is at Cosham, three miles inland.

Portsmouth is, of course, a maritime city whose naval history dates back to the time of the Crusades and where the recently salvaged Tudor ship Mary Rose and Nelson's Victory can still be seen. On the other hand, the devastation wrought by Second World War bombing means that much of the city is less than 50 years old and it boasts modern facilities for shopping, sport and entertainment.

Degrees Available: BA, BSc or BEng in an interesting range of subjects including Art, Design and Media, Architecture, East Asian Studies, Engineering Geology and Geotechnics, International Finance and Trade, and Land Management as well as the usual subjects and specialisms in Humanities, Social Science, Business, Engineering and Science. There is also a two-year BEd course leading to a teaching qualification in Secondary Science only, for students who already have some post-A level experience.

Foundation studies are available in Business, Engineering and Science. The foundation year in Engineering is taught at the University, in Business and Science at Chichester College of Technology, about 16 miles away.

Most Engineering courses include an optional sandwich year.

Part-time study is possible on some courses, mainly in Health Studies, Community Studies, Nursing and related subjects.

Portsmouth is moving towards a semester-based modular structure for most courses.

Assessment: The emphasis varies from course to course, but most involve both exams and continuous assessment, taking into account seminar papers, practical and creative work, dissertations and projects where relevant. A number of courses include 'open' exams for which you see the papers in advance.

How to Apply: Through UCAS for full-time courses, except for Art, Media and Design which may be through UCAS or ADAR. For part-time study, apply direct to the University on a form obtainable from the Assistant Registrar (Admissions).

Mature applicants who do not satisfy the standard entry requirements are welcome, but you are asked to contact the Admissions Tutor of the relevant department to discuss your qualifications and the opportunities open to you before submitting a formal application. Successful completion of an approved Access course may be deemed to satisfy the entry requirements, and prior learning and/or experience will be taken into account.

Queen Margaret College, Edinburgh
Clerwood Terrace, Edinburgh EH12 8TS

Tel: 031–317 3000
      031–317 3247 (Admissions) **Fax:** 031–317 3526
Contact: Admissions Officer

Number of Undergraduates: About 2000 full-time, 2000 part-time

Percentage of Mature Students: About 9%
Male/Female Ratio: 1 : 4
Upper Age Limit for Mature Students: None specified

Learning Facilities: The library has 80,000 books and relevant periodicals. Information Technology is an integral part of most College courses and there are eight well-equipped computer workshops. The Educational Resource Centre provides audio-visual and photographic facilities.

Creche Facilities: No

Mature Students Adviser: No, but all students may consult the student counsellor.

Accommodation: Catering or self-catering Halls of Residence on campus can accommodate over 400 students. No special provision for couples or families, but the Accommodation Office can advise on rented accommodation in the private sector.

Founded in 1875 as the Edinburgh School of Cookery, QM is on an attractive green site – formerly the grounds of a stately home – about four miles from Edinburgh. The Scottish capital, in addition to being a major tourist attraction and a great centre for the arts, has an enormous student population and provides all the facilities that this entails.

The College is best known for its health care courses and offers one of the widest ranges of programmes in the UK in this field.

Degrees Available: BA or BSc in subjects relating to Health, Food and Consumer Studies, Hospitality and Tourism, and Media and Dramatic Studies.
Part-time study is possible – contact the College for details.

Assessment: A combination of exams and continuous assessment, with seminars, laboratory work, reports and performance on work placements all taken into account.

How to Apply: Through UCAS for full-time, direct to the College for part-time. Mature applicants, particularly on an approved Access course and/or with experience, are very welcome.

Queen Mary and Westfield College
(University of London)
Mile End Rd, London E1 4NS

Tel: 071–975 5555
071–975 5511 (admissions office) **Fax:** 071–975 5500
Contact: Admissions Office

Number of Undergraduates: 5500
Percentage of Mature Students: 13%
Male/Female Ratio: 7 : 5
Upper Age Limit for Mature Students: None

Learning Facilities: The library has nearly half a million volumes and a thousand study places. There are some of the best computing and IT facilities of any UK University, an Audio-Visual Unit and a Language Learning Centre with well-equipped language labs. Students may also use the main University of London library.

Creche Facilities: For children aged three months to five years. Open throughout the year except College closure days and Bank Holidays. Contact the Nursery Supervisor, Amanda Jerman, on 081–983 4717 for details.

Mature Students Adviser: Yes

Accommodation: The College has nearly 1400 places in Halls of Residence and self-catering accommodation. These are situated near Epping Forest, about seven miles north of the campus – a 35-minute journey by public transport. About 41% of first-years are allocated places. One Hall of Residence is designated for mature and post-graduate students; double rooms in other residences are let to married students, subject to availability. Students are also eligible to apply for a place in one of the University of London's Intercollegiate Halls: contact the QMW Accommodation Office for details.

Queen Mary and Westfield College is one of the largest colleges of the University of London, founded in 1989 from the union of two long-established seats of learning. A programme of building and development is nearing completion and the College now has many impressive modern facilities surrounding its original 19th-century building.

Degrees Available: BA in the Faculty of Arts, with the emphasis on Modern European Languages; BDS; BEng in a range of specialisations, a number of them with a Modern Language option; BSc; BSc (Econ); MB BS; LLB including options in German or European Law.
For details of the MB BS degree, see London Hospital Medical College (page 225).
There are Access courses to Medicine, Science and Engineering, and a foundation programme in Engineering.

Assessment: Most courses, other than those in Dentistry, Law and Medicine, are modular and each unit is assessed separately during and at the end of the semester in which it is taught. Assessment methods vary from course to course and may include exams, practical and field work, essays, oral exams, etc.

How to Apply: Through UCAS. QMW welcomes applications from mature students without traditional qualifications. You should be able to show evidence of ability and commitment to study e.g. successful completion of an Access course or professional qualifications. Relevant work experience may also be considered.

You are welcome to contact the Admissions Office for advice before submitting your application form.

Queen's University of Belfast

University Rd, Belfast BT7 1NN

Tel: 0232 245133 **Fax:** 0232 247895
Contact: Admissions Office

Number of Undergraduates: Over 9000
Percentage of Mature Students: About 4%
Male/Female Ratio: About 6 : 5
Upper Age Limit for Mature Students: None specified

Learning Facilities: The Queen's library is one of the best in the UK, with a collection of over a million items built up over 150 years. In addition to the main library there are specialist faculty libraries for Agriculture and Food Science, Medicine, and Science and Engineering. All are open in the evening during the week in term-time and for part of the Easter holidays. There are campus-wide computing services (providing one work station for each five students) and facilities for language study open to all students; the Northern Ireland Technology Centre, which has recently benefited from large-scale investment in facilities for computer-aided design and manufacturing; a Palaeoecology Centre which specialises in studies of the environment, chronology and fauna since the last Ice Age and has superb facilities for precision carbon-dating; an Electron Microscope Unit and an Observatory.

Creche Facilities: No
Mature Students Adviser: No, but counselling services are available to all students.

Accommodation: Places for over 2000 students are available in catering Halls of Residence or self-catering flats and 'centres'. Most first-years can be accommodated, but there are no special provisions for couples or families.

Queen's College Belfast was established by Queen Victoria in the 1845 and was at the time one of only three colleges in Ireland. It became a university in 1908 and has a long-established reputation for high-quality teaching and research. In addition to the technical facilities mentioned above, it is the only university in the UK to have its own international arts festival, with theatrical and musical contributions of every kind by major performers.

The University is situated on a single campus in an attractive suburb about a mile from the centre of Belfast, next to the Botanic Gardens.

Degrees Available: BAgr or BSc in the Faculty of Agriculture and Food Science; BA in a wide range of Arts subjects, many with a 'classical' emphasis – Archaeology, Byzantine Studies, Celtic, Classical Civilisation, Scholastic Philosophy, etc – but also including Irish Studies and (uniquely) Ethnomusicology; BSc in Industrial Management or in a range of subjects in the Faculties of Architecture and Planning, Finance and Information, and Science; BSSc in Economics and Social Sciences; BEng; LLB with a number of options including languages; BDS; BMedSci; MB, ChB, BAO; BD; BTh.

Students of Medicine and Dentistry may take a one-year intercalated BSc or BMedSci between the preclinical and clinical parts of the course.

Foundation years are available in Agriculture and Food Science, Engineering and Science.

All courses, except some in the Faculty of Medicine, are modular.

The Queen's Faculty of Education offers a Post-Graduate Certificate in Education, but also has an association with two local Colleges of Education which provide four-year BEd degrees. For information about these, contact The Academic Registrar, St Mary's College, 191 Falls Rd, Belfast BT12 6FE or The Senior Tutor (Admissions), Stranmillis College, Belfast BT9 5DY. Do not apply through UCAS.

Assessment: Mostly by examination at the end of each unit's semester or at the end of the year; for some modules you are required to undertake a project rather than sit an exam.

How to Apply: Through UCAS. Queen's welcomes applications from mature students and will take experience and non-academic achievement into account. You will also be expected to show evidence of recent study, probably in the form of an Access or foundation course, Open University credits, BTEC award, etc.

Rapid Results College

Tuition House, 27/37 St George's Rd, London SW19 4DS

Tel: 081–947 2211
 081–947 7272 for pre-enrolment enquiries **Fax:** 081–946 7584
Contact: Customer Services Manager

Please note: Grants for Rapid Results College courses, as for all distance learning courses, are discretionary. See page 30 for more details.

Number of Undergraduates: Difficult to assess: perhaps 10,000–15,000 active at any one time on courses at all levels.
Percentage of Mature Students: The vast majority
Male/Female Ratio: Varies
Upper Age Limit for Mature Students: None

Learning Facilities: You will be sent all the material you need to complete your course successfully. You may be expected to read newspapers or journals, but not to buy books or other equipment.

Creche Facilities: N/A
Mature Students Adviser: Every student has a personal tutor who is available at any time to discuss problems and progress.
Accommodation: N/A

The Rapid Results College has been providing distance learning since 1928 and has a record of 400,000 exam successes. Your study programme is drawn up to suit your individual needs and the time you have available. You will be expected to complete regular assignments, which are marked and returned to you with comments and suggestions. Tuition for the four-year LLB course costs £1820; you will also have to pay a registration fee at the College and at the University of London.

The College also offers a number of courses leading to professional qualifications in e.g. Accountancy, Banking and Marketing.

Degrees Available: LLB. This is an external degree from the University of London, normally taken over a minimum of four years.

Assessment: Exams in June of each year.

How to Apply: Direct to the External Programme, University of London, Senate House, Malet St, London WC1E 7HU, telephone 071–636 8000 x 3150. If you do not have standard qualifications, your application will be considered on its individual merits.

Ravensbourne College of Design and Communication
Walden Rd, Chislehurst BR7 5SN

Tel: 081–468 7071 **Fax:** 081–295 1070
Contact: Academic Registrar

Number of Undergraduates: 644
Percentage of Mature Students: 27%
Male/Female Ratio: 11 : 9
Upper Age Limit for Mature Students: None

Learning Facilities: The library contains 30,000 books, 8000 video programmes, 50,000 slides and 40 CD-Roms. It also subscribes to 180 periodicals and is open until 7.30 p.m. on Mondays to Thursdays. There are workshop and computer facilities and the recently completely studios in the School of Television and Broadcasting are to industry standard with up-to-date equipment.

Founded in the 1960s from the merger of two much older art schools, Ravensbourne is an independent, specialist college on a new, purpose-built campus. For the last ten years it has concentrated on training students for employment in the fields of design and broadcasting. The School of Television and Broadcasting offers exclusively BTEC HND courses, but overall the College is recognised as having some of the finest facilities of their kind in the country. Its teachers all work actively in the areas in which they teach, so the approach of the courses is professional and practical.

Because the College is small it has few on-site sports or social facilities, but the Students' Union organises regular events. The facilities of Central London are within easy reach, as is the National Sports Centre at Crystal Palace.

Creche Facilities: No
Mature Students Adviser: Not specifically, but advice and counselling is available for all students.

Accommodation: Halls of Residence about a mile from the new campus accommodate 105 students, with priority being given to new students coming from a long way away. About a third of first-year students are allocated College accommodation. There is no special provision for couples or families.

The College is awaiting planning permission for new, on-site Halls of Residence.

Degrees Available: BA in Visual Communication Design, Three Dimensional Design and Fashion. These are all full-time degrees validated by the Royal College of Art.

There are also one-year foundation courses in Fine Art, Three Dimensional Design, Fashion and Graphic Design.

Assessment: The courses are largely practical and creative with no more than 20% of the time being spent in lectures or other formal teaching sessions. Assessment is on practical work throughout the course, with strong emphasis on final-year shows and projects. All students follow a course in Historical and Theoretical Studies and submit a dissertation in their final year.

How to Apply: Through ADAR for degree courses. For foundation courses, apply direct to the College by the end of January.

You will be expected to attend an interview and present a portfolio of work.

University of Reading
P.O. Box 217, Reading RG6 2AH

Tel: 0734 875123 **Fax:** 0734 874722
Contact: Miss D. Buss, Schools Liaison Officer

Number of Undergraduates: 6883 full-time
Percentage of Mature Students: 22%
Male/Female Ratio: About 1 : 1
Upper Age Limit for Mature Students: None

Learning Facilities: The library has over 900,000 books and pamphlets and subscribes to almost 5000 periodicals. There is a Music Library, a library devoted to aspects of Education, and the library of the Institute of Agricultural History which has 40,000 books and pamphlets on all aspects of its specialism.

There are plentiful, up-to-date computer facilities, with informal courses available through the Computer Services Centre. There are also four well-equipped language labs and good laboratory and technical facilities for relevant courses.

Creche Facilities: The Student Union runs a nursery for children aged between three and five – this is open from nine to five 50 weeks a year. In addition there is a University playgroup open in the mornings only during term-time.

Mature Students Adviser: Yes. There is also a Mature Students' Society and the University publishes a 'Guide for Mature Applicants', obtainable from the Faculty Admissions Offices.

Accommodation: 14 Halls of Residences and a number of University-supervised student houses accommodate 4500 students in total. All new students who have firmly accepted a place at Reading and who have returned an accommodation application form (sent when you accept your place) by the end of May are offered a place in Hall. Other first-years are likely to be offered 'University landlady accommodation' at the start of the autumn term and may move into Hall as places become available. There is some accommodation for married students and the Mature Students' Advisory Group will help.

Most of Reading University is situated on the Whiteknights campus, about a mile and a half south of the city centre. It is an attractive site with mature trees and a conservation area in what was once the estate of a medieval manor. Reading's Faculty of Agriculture and Food is one of the largest and best established in the UK, and the University owns over 2200 acres of farms for teaching and research purposes.

Degrees Available: BA in the School of Letters and Social Sciences; BA or BA (Ed) in the School of Education and Community Studies; LLB, with options in French Law or Legal Studies in Europe; BSc or BEng in the Schools of Agriculture and Food, Science, and Urban and Regional Studies.

Education Studies courses last four years and include a specialisation in early or late primary years.

In addition to most of the usual subjects, Reading offers some less familiar combinations, including Food Manufacture, Management and Marketing; Linguistics and Language Pathology; Typography and Graphic Communication; Psychology and Cybernetics; and Physics and Electronics with French, German or Italian.

Part-time courses, taught either during the day or in the evening, are available in a number of Arts subjects: you could normally complete a degree in five to seven years. Contact the Director of Part-Time Studies, Department of Extended Education, London Rd, Reading RG1 5AQ for a prospectus and further details.

Assessment: A combination of exams and continuous assessment, with many courses still depending largely on exams. Practical work is particularly important in Science and Engineering courses, and in Art and Music, while many Letters and Social Science courses involve a dissertation in the final year.

How to Apply: Through UCAS. Reading welcomes applications from prospective mature students with non-standard qualifications and considers each one on its merits, accepting a wide variety of alternative routes. You will be expected to produce evidence of your ability to cope with the chosen course. You may also be asked to sit a special entrance test and you are likely to be invited for interview before being offered a place.

Credit is sometimes given for relevant experience and the University is currently developing a CATS scheme (see page 12).

University College of Ripon and York St John
Lord Mayor's Walk, York YO3 7EX

Tel: 0904 656771 **Fax:** 0904 612512
Contact: Admissions Officer

Number of Undergraduates: About 2800 (900 at Ripon, 1900 at York).
Percentage of Mature Students: Not specified, but increasing
Male/Female Ratio: About 1 : 3 overall, with a higher percentage of women at Ripon.
Upper Age Limit for Mature Students: None specified

Learning Facilities: The libraries hold a total stock of over 200,000 books plus extensive non-book stock, and subscribe to a thousand journals. During term-time the libraries are open until 9.30 p.m. Monday to Thursday, till 5 p.m. on Friday, and on Saturday mornings. There are comprehensive computing and media services on both sites. Relevant courses have well-equipped laboratories, workshops or studios.

Creche Facilities: On both sites. The nursery at York is open from 8 a.m. to 6 p.m., that at Ripon only from 9 till 11.30 a.m. and 1 to 3.30 p.m.
Mature Students Adviser: Yes: contact Liz Maynard on the above number.

Accommodation: Nearly 700 places in Halls of Residence, plus College-run houses and flats, can accommodate most first-year students. There is no special provision for couples or families, but the Accommodation Office will assist all students in finding somewhere suitable to live.

The ancestor of Ripon and York St John was founded by the Church of England in York in 1841 to train teachers 'to bring education to the poor and underprivileged'. A breakaway women's college was established in Ripon 20 years later, and the two reunited in 1975. Although it is now a multicultural and multi-faith College, it remains committed to the Christian principles on which it is based. Having enjoyed a long association with the University of Leeds, in 1990 Ripon and York St John became a full college of the University, which validates its degrees.

Both arms of the College occupy Victorian buildings supplemented by modern teaching and accommodation blocks. The York campus comprises five sites in or near the centre of the city, with the main one at Lord Mayor's Walk, in the shadow of the Minster. The Ripon campus is in spacious parkland half a mile from the city centre.

Students do not normally have to travel between York and Ripon in the course of their studies, but the College operates a frequent term-time bus service between the two cities.

Degrees Available: BA or BSc with QTS in Design and Technology at secondary level or a range of subjects at upper or lower primary level; BA or BSc in Arts and Social Science subjects; BHSc in Occupational Therapy.

The Secondary Education degree can be completed in two years by mature students with suitable post A-level qualifications and/or experience.

Part-time study is possible on the BA or BSc programmes.

Assessment: BA and BSc courses are modular and semester-based, with each unit assessed separately. All these courses contain a compulsory element of 'work-related studies', which involves both theoretical study and work experience. Many courses contain additional practical elements, be they teacher training, pastoral work in Theology and Religious Studies or 'hands-on' experience in Drama and Television, and satisfactory performance in these areas is essential. Most courses also involve a 'special study' which means writing an extended report or dissertation.

How to Apply: Through UCAS for full-time, direct to the College on a form available from the Registrar for part-time.

Applications from prospective mature students are welcome. Successful completion of a recognised Access course is likely to be deemed to satisfy the entrance requirements; alternatively the College offers a Mature Matriculation exam, taken in May, and a short course beforehand to help you prepare for it. Contact the College for information before submitting your UCAS application.

Robert Gordon University
Schoolhill, Aberdeen AB9 1FR

Tel: 0224 262000 **Fax:** 0224 263000
Contact: Admissions Office 0224 262102/3
Information Centre 0224 262180

Please see page 2 for general information about Scottish colleges and universities

Number of Undergraduates: 5304
Percentage of Mature Students: 8%
Male/Female Ratio: 53 : 47
Upper Age Limit for Mature Students: None

Learning Facilities: The University has a central library and nine site libraries holding a total of 160,000 books and subscribing to 1400 periodicals. There are 620 study places in the main library. Most libraries are open late several nights a week during term-time; the Central and Hilton Place libraries also open at weekends. Computer facilities and CD-Rom technology are available throughout the University. Well-equipped laboratories and workshops support relevant courses.

Creche Facilities: Available for a nominal charge.
Mature Students Adviser: No, but there is a counselling service available to all students.
Accommodation: Halls of Residence, both full board and self-catering, and student flats can accommodate 86% of first-year students. There are no special provisions for couples or families.

Robert Gordon was a successful Aberdonian businessman who bequeathed his fortune to establish a school for educating young boys. Established in 1750, it developed into a college in 1881, a Technical College in 1903 and underwent various incarnations and mergers before attaining University status in 1992. Its practical and technical background is still reflected in the nature and content of its courses.

Most of the University's eight sites are within easy reach of each other in central Aberdeen; the Schools of Architecture and Surveying and the Gray's School of Art are together on the Garthdee campus, a little way out of town.

Degrees Available: BA in the Faculty of Management; BA or BSc in the Faculties of Health and Food, and Design; BSc or BEng in the Faculty of Science and Technology. Many courses include an optional sandwich element of up to a year.
Unusual subjects available include Cost Engineering, Design for Industry and Interior Architecture. Courses in practical or vocational subjects such as Nutrition and Dietetics or Quantity Surveying include State Registration or exemption from some professional exams.
There is a foundation course in the Faculty of Science and Technology.
Many degrees are modular and part-time study is possible.

Assessment: Courses are practical and vocation/employment oriented, so performance during work experience is important. In most cases students will undertake personal projects. In modular degree programmes, each unit is assessed separately during and at the end of the semester in which it is taught.

How to Apply: Through UCAS for full-time courses other than Art and Design. For Art and Design courses, obtain an application form from the Admissions Office and return it direct to the University (this form is used jointly by all four of the major Scottish Art Schools, but should be returned to your first choice). For part-time courses, contact the Admissions Office for information and advice.
Robert Gordon is committed to the concept of wider access to Higher Education. It is implementing a CATS scheme (see page 12), so credit may be given for prior learning; work experience, special aptitudes and motivation will all be taken into account.

Roehampton Institute
Roehampton Lane, London SW15 5PU

Tel: 081–392 3000 **Fax:** 081–392 3131
Contact: Admissions Officer

Number of Undergraduates: 4250
Percentage of Mature Students: About 20%

Male/Female Ratio: About 1 : 4
Upper Age Limit for Mature Students: None specified

Learning Facilities: Each college has its own library, with a total of over 400,000 items and subscriptions to 1500 periodicals. Computing facilties have increased enormously in the last year. The Media Services Centre provides audio-visual facilities and support, and Central Television Services include studios, workshops and a sound studio.

Creche Facilities: Shared with the local health authority and on two sites – the Froebel Institute and Queen Mary's University Hospital. Places are limited, so apply early.

Mature Students Adviser: No, but there is a Mature and Day Students' Society, and welfare and counselling services are available to all students.

Accommodation: Halls and Institute-run houses can accommodate most first-year students, though not all, and places are allocated on a first-come, first-served basis. No special provisions for couples or families.

Roehampton Institute comprises four Colleges – Froebel Institute College, Digby Stuart College, Southlands College and Whitelands College – within a two-mile radius of each other in South-West London. The four main Institute buildings are all listed and set in surprisingly spacious gardens.

The four Colleges were founded separately in the 19th century; three were originally Christian institutions dedicated to the training of Christian teachers, while the Froebel Institute's purpose was to promote the ideas of the German educationalist Friedrich Froebel, who effectively invented the kindergarten.

The Institute is now affiliated to the University of Surrey, which validates its degrees.

Degrees Available: BA with QTS for teaching at nursery or lower or upper primary levels; BA or BSc Joint or Combined Honours, or Single Honours in Marketing and Modern Languages (four years), Humanities, Psychology and Counselling, or Biological Sciences.

All degree programmes are modular and most, except the BA with QTS, can be followed part-time. Contact the Admissions Office in the Registry for details.

Assessment: A combination of exams and continuous assessment, with the balance varying from course to course. Practical work, projects, seminar papers, essays and dissertations may all be taken into account as appropriate and teaching practice is an integral part of the Education degrees. Each module is assessed separately, during and at the end of the semester in which it is taught.

How to Apply: Through UCAS for full-time study, direct to the Admissions Office for part-time. Applications from prospective mature students who do not have traditional qualifications but can demonstrate their ability to cope with the demands of the course and to benefit from it are welcome. A CATS scheme and arrangements for APEL (see page 12) mean that credit can be given for prior learning and/or experience.

Under certain circumstances it may be possible to start your degree in February, at the beginning of the second semester. Contact the Admissions Office for details.

Rose Bruford College of Speech and Drama
Lamorbey Park, Sidcup DA15 9DF

Tel: 081–300 3024 **Fax:** 081–308 0542
Contact: Admissions Officer

Number of Undergraduates: 240
Percentage of Mature Students: About 42%
Male/Female Ratio: 1 : 1
Upper Age Limit for Mature Students: None specified

Learning Facilities: The library has 28,000 books and musical scores, 10,000 slides and a substantial audio-visual collection, providing in-depth coverage of the College's courses. There are specialist workshops and the College has its own theatre, the Barn, in which student productions are held.

Creche Facilities: No
Mature Students Adviser: No, but all students have a personal tutor.
Accommodation: None available through the College, but the Accommodation Officer will endeavour to ensure that all students find somewhere suitable to live.

Rose Bruford founded the College which bears her name in 1950, and it has become one of the UK's foremost theatrical schools, pioneering degree courses in performance and technical aspects of the theatre. These courses demand commitment and flexibility, promoting expertise in TV, film and radio as well as the theatre.

In addition to its main site, an elegant mansion in the south-east London suburb of Sidcup, the College has premises in Greenwich which provide classroom, rehearsal and performance space. All students spend time on both sites.

Given the notorious levels of unemployment in the theatre, the College is understandably proud to be able to say that 76% of its graduates over the last five years have been successful in finding work in their chosen professions.

Degrees Available: BA in Theatre for Actors, Writers or Directors, or in Technical Theatre, validated by the University of Kent. New courses in Lighting Design, Theatre Design and Music Technology will become available for the 1994/5 session.

Assessment: Continuous assessment of performance, project, practical and research work. There are no formal exams.

How to Apply: Direct to the College on an application form available from the Admissions Officer. The form gives you plenty of space to describe relevant experience and theatrical ambitions. A section of the form should be detached and passed to your referee, who should return it direct to the College. There is no official closing date for applications, but you are advised to return the form and your application fee (currently £25) by the end of March.

Applications for the Theatre Design course may also be made through ADAR.

The College takes a broad view of qualifications and experience and will treat applicatons from prospective mature students on their individual merits. Admission for all students is by interview; for the Actors' course there is also an audition and candidates for other courses will be asked to take part in workshops and/or produce pieces of written work.

Royal Academy of Music
Marylebone Rd, London NW1 5HT

Tel: 071–873 7373 **Fax:** 071–873 7394
Contact: Academic Registrar

Number of Undergraduates: 300+
Percentage of Mature Students: About 11%
Male/Female Ratio: About 9 : 11
Upper Age Limit for Mature Students: None specified

Learning Facilities: Recent improvements have given the Academy all the facilities students could wish for, including a specialist library containing 120,000 items – scores, orchestral parts and audio-visual material as well as books; there is an opera theatre and a concert hall, a high-quality stock of keyboard instruments, recording studios, electronic studios and ample rehearsal space. Practice facilities are open until 8.45 p.m. Monday to Friday during term-time. Students also have access to the resources of King's College London and of the University of London.

Creche Facilities: No

Mature Students Adviser: The Academy has its own counsellor, who may refer students to the services of King's College.

Accommodation: The Academy has 44 places in its own Hall of Residence and access to the accommodation provision of King's College. Contact the Estates Manager if you need help in finding somewhere suitable to live.

The Royal Academy of Music was founded in 1822 and now lives in an Edwardian building which its prospectus describes as striking and The Student Book *likens to a pink wedding cake. It is undeniably in a convenient situation, minutes from Oxford St in one direction and Regent's Park in the other.*

The Academy is very much an international commuity, with a good 20% of its students coming from overseas. It has a long tradition of training successful musicians and of recruiting top members of the profession to its teaching staff – Sir Arthur Sullivan, Sir Henry Wood and Sir John Barbirolli head the list of legendary artists who have been associated with the Academy, while percussionist Evelyn Glennie, ENO soprano Susan Bullock and the members of the Vanburgh String Quartet are among its 1980s graduates.

Degrees Available: BMus (Performance) – four years

Assessment: This is a practical, performance degree aiming at the highest possible standards in the chosen principal study.

How to Apply: Direct to the Academy on a form available from the Academic Registrar. Mature applicants who do not meet the entry requirements but show exceptional abilities will be considered on their merits. The closing date for applications is 1 October for all principal studies except conducting, when the deadline is 1 February. You should include your audition fee, currently £40 – this will be returned if you are not considered suitable for interview. Auditions, which include a written paper, are held in early December (March for conductors) – the Academy prospectus gives excellent guidelines on what is expected of you.

Royal Agricultural College
Cirencester GL7 6JS

Tel: 0285 641404 **Fax:** 0285 650219
Contact: Registrar
Number of Undergraduates: About 650
Percentage of Mature Students: 6%
Male/Female Ratio: 7 : 2
Upper Age Limit for Mature Students: None specified

Learning Facilities: The library provides in-depth coverage of agriculture-related subjects and the reading rooms are open until 11 p.m. during term-time. The College farms over 300 acres of contrasting land which provide students with practical experience; it also has well-equipped specialist laboratories.

Creche Facilities: No
Mature Students Adviser: No, but the Student Welfare Officer may be consulted by any student.
Accommodation: There are 305 places in on-campus accommodation, enough to accommodate most but not all first-years. The College will send a list of other lodgings to those not allocated a place.

Founded in 1845, the Royal Agricultural College was the first specialist Agricultural College in the English-speaking world, and its remains at the forefront of its field. Its courses place strong emphasis on technology and on the business side of agriculture; many contain an international element and the College has an impressive list of links with European Colleges of Agriculture and with countries in the Far East and elsewhere where it runs training and advisory programmes.

The College is situated in beautiful Cotswold countryside and has its own Students' Union Club (in a 16th-century tithe barn) and sports and social activities; students may also take advantage of the facilities of the universities which collaborate on their courses (see below).

Degrees Available: BSc in Agriculture and Land Management, Crop Production Ecology and Management, International Agricultural and Equine Business Management, International Agribusiness Management and Rural Land Management.

All courses except Rural Land Management may be extended to four years by the inclusion of a sandwich element, and you will be expected to find relevant employment during some of the holidays.

The College also offers a one-year foundation programme.

Assessment: A combination of project work, case studies and exams. The course in Rural Land Management places more emphasis on exams.

How to Apply: Through UCAS to the various universities with which the courses are associated: Buckingham for Agriculture and Land Management, International Agricultural and Equine Business Management and International Agribusiness; Bath for Crop Production; Reading for Rural Land Management. For the foundation programme, apply direct to the College on a form available from the Admissions Secretary.

The College encourages students without formal qualifications, but degree courses assume some prior knowledge and experience: if you do not have Science A levels or relevant experience, you may be well advised to apply for the foundation year first. You are welcome to contact the Registrar for advice.

Royal College of Music
Prince Consort Rd, London SW7 2BS

Tel: 071–589 3643 **Fax:** 071–589 7740
Contact: David Harpham, Admissions Tutor

Number of Undergraduates: About 380
Percentage of Mature Students: Not specified
Male/Female Ratio: About 3 : 4
Upper Age Limit for Mature Students: None, but achievement and ability of prospective students must be commensurate with age

Learning Facilities: The library has about 350,000 volumes. The College also has a museum of instruments.

Creche Facilities: No
Mature Students Adviser: Not specifically
Accommodation: Some hostel facilities available. About 25% of first-year students can be accommodated. No special provisions for couples or families. Suitable cheap accommodation in London may be difficult to find.

The Royal College of Music, founded in 1883, has always had an extremely high reputation in the field of musicianship. Its former pupils include Benjamin Britten, Ralph Vaughan Williams, Julian Bream and Joan Sutherland; in addition to a high-calibre permanent staff, many of whom are actively engaged in the music profession, it frequently welcomes distinguished musicians as visiting teachers.

The College is in South Kensington, London's museum land, with easy access to everywhere. It has its own Students' Association, and students can also use the facilities of nearby Imperial College.

Degrees Available: BMus

Assessment: On performance
How to Apply: Direct. The *only* criterion for entry is an extremely high standard of performance.

Royal Free Hospital School of Medicine
(University of London)
Rowland Hill St, London NW3 2PF

Tel: 071–794 0500 x 4258 **Fax:** 071–794 3505
Contact: Medical School Registry

Number of Undergraduates: About 500
Percentage of Mature Students: About 13%
Male/Female Ratio: 1 : 1
Upper Age Limit for Mature Students: None in theory; in practice it is unusual for applicants over 30 to be admitted

Learning Facilities: The School has a modern library, computing facilities, laboratories, substantial collections of Anatomy and Pathology specimens and up-to-date teaching and audio-visual equipment. The library is open until 10 p.m. Monday to Friday, and all day on Saturday. Students also have access to the University of London library.

Creche Facilities: No
Mature Students Adviser: No
Accommodation: The School's Hall of Residence can accommodate 78 students and first-years are given priority. The University of London also runs Halls of Residence, and you should apply to the Accommodation Officer, Senate House, Malet St, London WC1E 7HU, telephone 071–636 2818. It is acknowledged that finding cheap accommodation in London can be a problem.

The Royal Free Hospital has a distinguished history, having pioneered the care of the destitute in London, accepted patients during the great cholera epidemic of 1832 and been awarded the title 'Royal Free' by Queen Victoria on her accession to the throne in 1837. The Medical School, founded in 1874, was the first to admit women students and has more recently led the field in research into liver and kidney disease.

Situated in desirable Hampstead, minutes from the famous Heath, the School combines high academic standards with a pleasant living and working environment.

Degrees Available: MB, BS. There is also a one-year intercalated BSc degree which may be taken between the preclinical and clinical parts of the course.

Assessment: Assessment tests are held throughout the course, with final examinations at the end of the fifth year. Satisfactory performance in clinical work is essential.

How to Apply: Through UCAS. Although all applications are considered on their individual merits, most students admitted to the School have A levels or equivalent in three out of Biology, Chemistry, Maths and Physics. Good GCSEs in Physics, Maths and English Language are essential, and otherwise acceptable candidates who do not have A level in a biological subject are asked to do preliminary reading and attend a short course in September before the course proper begins.

Royal Holloway, University of London
Egham TW20 0EX

Tel: 0784 434455 **Fax:** 0784 437520
Contact: Schools Liaison Office

Number of Undergraduates: 4227
Percentage of Mature Students: 18%
Male/Female Ratio: 44 : 56
Upper Age Limit for Mature Students: None

Learning Facilities: Three libraries have a total of half a million volumes, 1800 periodicals and 600 study spaces. There are comprehensive computing facilities and well-equipped science and language labs.

Creche Facilities: Yes
Mature Students Adviser: No, but there are counsellors available to help all students. The College publishes a helpful guide for mature students, and there is a Mature Students' Society.

Accommodation: All first-years and about half the final-year students can be allocated College accommodation, mostly in catering or self-catering Halls of Residence. There are no special provisions for couples or families.

Royal Holloway and Bedford New College, to give it its full title, was founded in 1985 from the merger of two 19th-century women's colleges which have been part of the University of London since 1900. The merger has made Royal Holloway one of the largest of the London Colleges, and it is certainly in one of the pleasantest situations – twenty miles out of town on the fringes of Windsor Great Park. Almost all the facilities are on one site, with one of the Halls of Residence a mile or so away.

The campus is dominated by the splendid Founder's Building. Built by the founder, Mr Thomas Holloway, in an extravagant mood, it is modelled on the Loire chateau of Chambord. It now houses the administrative departments, part of the library, a magnificent picture gallery and an understandably popular Hall of Residence.

Degrees Available: BA; BMus; BSc. A good range of Arts and Science subjects is offered. Most courses are modular.

A foundation year in Science is run in conjunction with five local FE colleges, and successful completion guarantees a place on an appropriate degree course at Royal Holloway.

Part-time study is possible in special circumstances – contact the Academic Registrar to put your case.

Assessment: Emphasis is still on exams in the final year, but all units are assessed separately and continuous assessment of essays and practical work is taken into account on most courses.

How to Apply: Through UCAS, but you are encouraged to make informal contact first: write to the Admissions Tutor of the relevant department. Royal Holloway welcomes applications from prospective mature students and looks for evidence of recent academic study to show that you are competent to undertake the course. All suitable alternative qualifications will be considered, and credit transfer may be possible if the syllabuses allow for a smooth progression.

Royal Military College of Science (RMCS)
Cranfield University, Shrivenham, Swindon SN6 8LA

Tel: 0793 785400/1 **Fax:** 0793 783966
Contact: Admissions Office

Number of Undergraduates: 450, many more post-graduates
Percentage of Mature Students: 43% overall at Cranfield
Male/Female Ratio: 20 : 1
Upper Age Limit for Mature Students: None specified

Learning Facilities: The library has 100,000 books, including specialist collections, and subscribes to 400 periodicals. There are excellent computing, laboratory and technical facilities, including wind tunnels and vehicle test tracks.

Creche Facilities: No
Mature Students Adviser: No
Accommodation: All first-year students can be accommodated in Halls of Residence, in College houses or in the Officers' Mess. There are no special provisions for couples or families.

RMCS Shrivenham is part of Cranfield University, until recently the Cranfield Institute of Technology, and traces its ancestry back to 1772 when a school was founded at Woolwich to study ballistics and explosives. The College has a contractual arrangement with the Ministry of Defence and provides scientific and technical education to members of the armed forces, the civil service and industry. The number of civilian students has increased markedly in recent years and now makes up about half the undergraduate population.

The College lies in attractive country between Swindon and Oxford, in the Vale of the White Horse.

Degrees Available: BEng; BSc in Applied Sciences, Computing and Management and Radiography.

Assessment: A combination of exams and continuous assessment of laboratory and course work.

How to Apply: Through UCAS to Cranfield University, but you are welcome to contact the Admissions Tutor first to discuss your application. Mature applicants without traditional qualifications are considered on their individual merits, and are required to show evidence of their ability to follow the course.

Royal Northern College of Music
124 Oxford Rd, Manchester M13 9RD

Tel: 061–273 6283 **Fax:** 061–273 7611
Contact: Academic Registrar

Number of Undergraduates: 443
Percentage of Mature Students: Not specified
Male/Female Ratio: 1 : 1
Upper Age Limit for Mature Students: None

Learning Facilities: The library has 65,000 volumes (books and
music) and a large audio collection. There is a professional-
standard recording studio, electronic music room, practice
rooms, rehearsal room, etc.

Creche Facilities: No
Mature Students Adviser: No, but there is a comprehensive
counselling service for all students.
Accommodation: The College has a Hall of Residence with places
for 180 students, which means it can normally accommodate all
first-years who require a place. There are no special provisions
for couples or families.

*For 20 years the RNCM has concentrated on preparing gifted students
for careers in music, whether performance or composition. Master classes
by distinguished professionals are a regular feature of all courses.*

*The College's vocational approach is underlined by the fact that
students give over a hundred public concert and opera performances a
year, many of which are reviewed in national papers. A wide range of
professional productions and exhibitions also take place in the College
auditoria.*

*The RNCM is close to the University of Manchester and to the centre
of the city, which is renowned for some of the best live music and theatre in
England.*

Degrees Available: GMusRNCM (Graduate in Music of the Royal
Northern College of Music); GRNCM (Graduate of the Royal
Northern College of Music). The former carries honours degree
status, the latter pass degree. A course offered jointly with the
University of Manchester allows students of the MusB course
there to study for a Diploma of the RNCM at the same time.
There is also a Diploma in Professional Performance
(PPRNCM).
All these courses normally last four years full-time.

Assessment: Apart from the PPRNCM course, all undergraduate
degrees have an academic component with formal exams.
However, performance is the most important aspect of all
courses.

How to Apply: Direct to the College on an application form
obtainable from the Secretary for Admissions, which should be

returned by 1 October of the year before you wish to begin your course. Selection is by interview and audition some time between October and January, and you will have to pay an audition fee (currently £30). Details of what is required for the audition, which vary according to the field in which you wish to specialise, are given in the College prospectus.

If you are applying for the joint course, you should also apply to the University of Manchester through UCAS.

The basic entry requirements for the GMusRNCM are two A levels, normally including Music; for the GRNCM five GCSEs, or 'acceptable equivalents'.

Royal Scottish Academy of Music and Drama
100 Renfrew St, Glasgow G2 3DB

Tel: 041–332 4101 **Fax:** 041–332 8901
Contact: Secretary and Treasurer

Number of Undergraduates: About 300
Percentage of Mature Students: About 25%
Male/Female Ratio: About 2 : 3
Upper Age Limit for Mature Students: Normally 30

Learning Facilities: The library specialises in the subjects taught at the Academy and provides recorded material, musical parts and scores as well as books. There is excellent teaching accommodation, including practice rooms, recording studios and a language lab.

Creche Facilities: No
Mature Students Adviser: No, but counselling and academic support is available to all students.
Accommodation: A few places are available in a hostel run by Queen's College Glasgow and in accommodation administered by the YMCA. Suitable, cheap accommodation is much in demand in Glasgow and you are advised to start looking as soon as you have been accepted for entry to the Academy. The Senior Administrative Assistant has a list of addresses. There is no special provision for couples or families.

Scotland's only conservatoire has been in existence for nearly 150 years but has recently moved to new premises with up-to-the-minute facilities. These include theatres and a concert hall, all equipped to professional standard, where student productions and performances are staged.

The Academy's staff are practising professionals and their teaching is supplemented by that of prestigious visiting lecturers. Degrees are validated by the University of Glasgow.

Degrees Available: BA in Musical Studies or Dramatic Studies; BEd (Music) – four years with QTS for teaching at secondary level. The Dramatic Studies course is broadly based, but is not designed to train actors. A three-year course leading to a Diploma in Dramatic Art is available for those who wish to act professionally.

Part-time study in performance in the School of Music is available to students of exceptional ability.

Assessment: The emphasis is very much on practical skills and performance.

How to Apply: Direct, on an application form available from the Admissions Office of the relevant School (Music or Drama). Admission is by interview and audition. Auditions for Music are held in November and March, and the forms should be returned by 15 October or 31 January *at the latest* – you are strongly advised to apply earlier. For Drama auditions are held between January and June and the closing date for applications is 31 March. For both Schools, your application must be accompanied by a non-returnable registration fee, currently £35.

If you are applying for the BEd, you should obtain an application form from The Course Co-Ordinator, BEd (Music), St Andrew's College of Education, Glasgow G61 4QA, telephone 041–943 1424, and return it by 15 December. Entrance exams are held in the spring term.

Mature applicants who do not satisfy the general entrance requirements may be admitted if they can show that they have the attainment and capacity to benefit from the course.

Royal Veterinary College (University of London)
Royal College St, London NW1 0TU

Tel: 071–387 2898 **Fax:** 071–388 2342
Contact: Registrar

Number of Undergraduates: About 350
Percentage of Mature Students: About 10%
Male/Female Ratio: 2 : 3
Upper Age Limit for Mature Students: None specified, but you need to be physically fit

Learning Facilities: The College library at Camden supplies the needs of preclinical students and includes historical collections and a veterinary museum. The main library of 16,000 books, pamphlets and journals, is at Hawkshead. Both are closed at weekends, but Camden is open for study and reference until 7 p.m. and Hawkshead normally until 10 p.m. Monday to Friday during term-time. Students also have access to the main University of London library and other libraries within the University.

Along with a number of other London-based colleges, RVC is a member of the Bloomsbury Computing Consortium and has state-of-the-art computing facilities on both sites. Both campuses also have animal hospitals and clinics giving students 'hands-on' experience of treating animals throughout their course and the College has specialist research and teaching facilities which are second to none.

Creche Facilities: No

Mature Students Adviser: No, but all students have a personal tutor, and advice of various kinds is available through the College and the Students' Union.

Accommodation: Not available in Central London, but students can apply for places in the University of London Intercollegiate Halls of Residence, most of which are within easy walking distance: contact the University of London Accommodation Office, Senate House, Malet St, London WC1E 7HU, telephone 071–636 2818. Priority in these Halls is given to first-year students. Applications must be received by 31 May, so do not wait until you have exam results or a firm offer of a place. The Accommodation Office can also provide details of accommodation suitable for couples and families. Again, apply early.

The College has rooms for 90 students in two Halls at Hawkshead, where priority is given to students on the clinical part of the course.

The Royal Veterinary College, founded in 1791, is by far the oldest of the universities offering Veterinary degrees and the only one which specialises entirely in Veterinary Medicine. Students spend most of the first two years of their course in Camden Town, just north of Central London, transferring to the field station at Hawkshead in Hertfordshire for the remaining three years.

Degrees Available: BVetMed. An optional one-year intercalated BSc may be taken between the preclinical and paraclinical parts of the course.

Assessment: Mainly by exams, written, oral and practical, at the end of the second, third, fourth and fifth years, but you are also required to produce a 5000-word report in the course of your final year.

How to Apply: Through UCAS. Three Science A levels or equivalent are normally required for entry and, although applicants who hold alternative qualifications are considered on their individual merits, you are unlikely to be offered a place if you fall far short of this target. You may also be asked to show evidence that you have spent some time 'seeing practice' with a veterinary surgeon.

University of St Andrews
College Gate, St Andrews KY16 9AJ

Tel: 0334 76161 x 2150/1/2 **Fax:** 0334 76404
Contact: Dr M.I.S. Hunter, Director of Admissions

Please see page 2 for general information on Scottish universities and colleges

Number of Undergraduates: About 4100
Percentage of Mature Students: About 8%
Male/Female Ratio: About 47 : 53
Upper Age Limit for Mature Students: None

Learning Facilities: The main library has over 750,000 books, periodicals, microfilms and audio-visual material. The University also has comprehensive computing facilities, a Language Teaching Services building and a number of notable collections – of anatomical and zoological specimens, scientific instruments and geological specimens – used for teaching and research.

Creche Facilities: Yes – contact the Director of Undergraduate Recruitment for details

Mature Students Adviser: Not as such, but a mature student quoted in the prospectus says, 'Staff are increasingly aware of the problems of mature students and I have found them very approachable.'

Accommodation: About two-thirds of St Andrews students are housed in University accommodation; all first-years who require a place can normally be given one, usually in a Hall of Residence. No special provisions for couples or families.

St Andrews is the oldest university in Scotland, having been recognised by Papal Bull in 1413. The main site – St Salvator's Quadrangle, known as the Quad – contains the magnificent 15th-century Collegiate Church, regarded as one of the finest medieval buildings in Scotland. The Quad is on the northern side of the city, close to the sea and the Royal and Ancient golf course. The other two main sites are the nearby St Mary's College, which houses the Faculty of Divinity, and the North Haugh, about a mile to the west, for Physical and Mathematical Sciences.

Perhaps because St Andrews is such a small city (the population is about 16,000) and the staff and students of the University have for so long made up such a high proportion of its residents, University and Town interests and events blend in a way that is rarely found in larger University cities.

Degrees Available: MA in a wide range of Arts and some Social Science subjects; BSc in Medical Science and in a wide range of Science subjects; BD.

The less usual subjects on offer include European Integration Studies, Hebrew and New Testament, Islamic and Medieval History, Astronomy (Astrophysics), Logic and Philosophy of Science, Experimental Pathology, and Marine and Environmental Biology.

Students wishing to study part-time because of other commitments are actively encouraged, and help is given in arranging timetables and workloads. Contact the relevant Faculty Officers and Advisers of Studies well in advance for advice.

Assessment: The emphasis is still on exams, though practical, laboratory and field work is assessed where applicable. Some courses require a final-year dissertation.

How to Apply: Through UCAS. St Andrews participates in SWAP (the Scottish Wider Access Programme, see page 20), which is committed to encouraging adults to enter Higher Education. Mature students do not therefore have to have traditional qualifications. You should expect to be invited for interview, where your individual circumstances will be considered. Contact the University's Wider Access Co-Ordinator, Dr Ian Hunter, for advice and information.

St Bartholomew's Hospital Medical College
(University of London)
West Smithfield, London EC1A 7BE

Tel: 071–601 8834
Contact: Miss Catherine Dobbing, Admissions Officer

Number of Undergraduates: 350 on site, plus 250 on the preclinical course at Queen Mary and Westfield College (see page 277)

Percentage of Mature Students: About 15%

Male/Female Ratio: 1 : 1

Upper Age Limit for Mature Students: Normally 30, but the College occasionally accepts students slightly over this limit.

Learning Facilities: The library has 80,000 books and subscribes to 280 periodicals. Students may also use the main library of the University of London. There are computing facilities, on which students can be trained if required, an Audio-Visual department, a Medical Illustration department and a Museum of Pathological Specimens.

Creche Facilities: No

Mature Students Adviser: Not specifically, but all students have a personal tutor.

Accommodation: The College guarantees all first-year and final-year students a place in its Hall of Residence. There are also self-catering flats which may be suitable for couples.

Saint Bartholomew's Hospital has been in existence since 1123 and is the only one of the medieval hospitals in London to occupy its original site. A formalised Medical School came into being in the late 18th century, although medical students are known to have been attached to the hospital since 1663.

Despite its long history, Barts has modern teaching facilities and a wealth of important research is carried on there.

A constituent college of the University of London since 1900, Barts has strong links with the London Hospital Medical College and with Queen Mary and Westfield College, where the preclinical course is taught. An unusual feature of its medical course is the stage between preclinical and clinical studies, where for two terms students concentrate on aspects of behavioural science and medical ethics. A recently devised curriculum also moves students away from traditional lecture-based learning towards more autonomous study.

Degrees Available: MB BS. There are also two optional intercalated one-year courses: the BSc, which may be taken after the second, third or fourth year of study, or the BMedSci, which may be taken after the fourth year provided you have not already taken the BSc.

Assessment: There are formal written and clinical exams throughout the course. At the moment a lot of emphasis is placed on exams taken at the end of the final year, but the system is currently under review.

How to Apply: Through UCAS. One student is accepted each year from the QMWay Access Course run at Tower Hamlets College under the auspices of Queen Mary and Westfield College (see page 277); otherwise good A levels or equivalent are expected.

St George's Hospital Medical School
(University of London)
Cranmer Terrace, London SW17 0RE

Tel: 081–672 9944 x 55992 **Fax:** 081–672 6940
Contact: Admissions Officer

Number of Undergraduates: 785
Percentage of Mature Students: About 8%
Male/Female Ratio: About 4 : 3
Upper Age Limit for Mature Students: None officially, but it is most unusual for students over 35 to be admitted.

Learning Facilities: The library specialises in combined health sciences and houses 70,000 journal volumes and 26,000 monographs; it subscribes to 800 periodicals and provides 400 study places. Students also have access to the main University of London library. The Medical School is purpose-built and has modern, well-equipped labs; clinical studies are carried out at the adjacent St George's Hospital, at other local hospitals and in the community.

Creche Facilities: No
Mature Students Adviser: No, but all students have a personal tutor and access to the services of the Student Counsellor.
Accommodation: The School has 13 purpose-built houses which comprise a self-catering Hall of Residence with 250 places. All first-year students can be accommodated. Students are also eligible to apply for places in the University of London's seven intercollegiate Halls of Residence. Contact the University of London Accommodation Office, Senate House, Malet St, London WC1E 7HU for details. Applications from prospective students must be received by 31 May, so do not wait until you have exam results or a firm offer of a place. The Accommodation

Office can also provide details of accommodation suitable for couples and families. Again, apply early.

St George's Hospital was founded in 1733 and has always taught medical students. It has a number of distinguished names on its list of former staff and students, among them Edward Jenner of smallpox vaccination fame. After over 200 years at Hyde Park Corner, the hospital and school moved to its new, purpose-built accommodation in Tooting in the 1970s.

Degrees Available: MB BS. There is also an intercalated one-year BSc degree which students may take between the preclinical and clinical parts of their course.

Assessment: Written and clinical exams.

How to Apply: Through UCAS. Competition for places is severe and, although each application is considered on its merits, it is unlikely that those without good A levels or equivalent will be accepted. Mature applicants who do not have these qualifications are advised to contact the Entrance Requirements Department of the University of London, Senate House, Malet St, London WC1E 7HU for advice.

St Loye's School of Occupational Therapy
Millbrook House, Millbrook Lane, Topsham Rd, Exeter EX2 6ES

Tel: 0392 219774 **Fax:** 0392 435357
Contact: Admissions Officer

Number of Undergraduates: About 330
Percentage of Mature Students: About 33%
Male/Female Ratio: 1 : 4
Upper Age Limit for Mature Students: None specified

Learning Facilities: The library has 8500 books and subscribes to 100 periodicals – this makes it a substantial specialist centre for Occupational Therapy. The reference area is open in the evenings. The School has comprehensive computing facilities, a professional-standard video studio and a 'state of the art' laboratory.

Creche Facilities: No
Mature Students Adviser: No, but counselling services are available to all students.

Accommodation: School accommodation is limited, but the Accommodation Office sends all new students a list of private rented accommodation and will help you find somewhere suitable to live.

St Loye's is the largest School of Occupational Therapy in Europe and has an established reputation for excellence in its field. Its main building is a spacious country house which has been extended to provide the up-to-date technological facilities for which the School is renowned. Members of the teaching staff are at the forefront of research in Occupational Therapy, so students benefit from their up-to-the-minute knowledge.

St Loye's is close to the centre of Exeter and enjoys close links with the University.

Degrees Available: BSc in Occupational Therapy, validated by the University of Exeter.

Assessment: Exams, a research project, a dissertation and assessment of performance during clinical placements.

How to Apply: Through UCAS. Mature applicants who can show evidence of recent study (Access course, Open University credits etc) are welcome and relevant experience will be taken into account. All candidates are expected to show enthusiasm for the course and some knowledge of what Occupational Therapy entails. You should expect to be invited for interview before being offered a place.

College of St Mark and St John
Derriford Rd, Plymouth PL6 8BH

Tel: 0752 777188 **Fax:** 0752 761120
Contact: Admissions Officer

Number of Undergraduates: 1815
Percentage of Mature Students: 30%
Male/Female Ratio: About 1 : 2
Upper Age Limit for Mature Students: Varies from course to course: for vocational courses normally about 50 at time of admission

Learning Facilities: The library has 115,000 volumes and subscribes to 630 periodicals. There is a computer service and laboratories/practical work areas appropriate to the various courses.

Creche Facilities: A recently established play scheme.

Mature Students Adviser: Not specifically, but Student Services provide counselling and welfare support for any student who needs them.

Accommodation: The College has houses on site, Halls of Residence and approved lodgings. All first-year students who require it are allocated some form of College accommodation. The placing of mature students is given consideration, but there are currently no special provisions for couples or families.

The College is affiliated to the University of Exeter, which validates its degrees. It occupies a very pleasant campus five miles outside Plymouth, with easy access to Dartmoor National Park and the Devon and Cornwall coasts.

Degrees Available: BA in Art and Design and in an interesting variety of Arts and Social Science subjects (Theology and Philosophy can be combined with Information Technology or Development Studies; Media Studies with English, Geography or Public Relations, for example); BEd (four years) leading to a qualification to teach at either primary or secondary level. Some courses may be followed part-time.

Assessment: A combination of exams and continuous assessment, with teaching practice playing a major part in BEd degrees.

How to Apply: Through UCAS. A wide variety of alternative qualifications (BTEC awards, GNVQs, Open University credits, Access courses, etc) are considered and relevant work experience may also be taken into account.

------ ❀ ------

S. Martin's College
Lancaster LA1 3UD

Tel: 0524 63446 **Fax:** 0524 68943
Contact: Teresa Abramson, Academic Registrar

Number of Undergraduates: 2200
Percentage of Mature Students: 27%
Male/Female Ratio: 3 : 7
Upper Age Limit for Mature Students: None for academic degrees; for professional degrees you should normally be under 50 at the time of graduation.

Learning Facilities: The library has 150,000 volumes. There are four laboratories of microcomputers and all students have the opportunity to acquire basic skills. The College also has science labs, a well-equipped Art department, drama and dance studios and audio-visual equipment.

Creche Facilities: Well-equipped childcare facility for children aged two to four. Book early as places are limited.

Mature Students Adviser: Not specifically, but the Student Welfare Officer, Academic Registrar and Head of Student Services are all available to help, depending on the nature of the problem.

Accommodation: The College runs six Halls of Residence and can normally offer a place to all first-year students. There are no special provisions for couples or families.

S. Martin's was founded by the Church of England and retains its commitment to 'follow ecumenical Christian principles', though it welcomes students of other faiths or of none. It is a College in the University sector – effectively a mini-University – and its degrees are validated by the University of Lancaster. Students at the College can use many of the University's resources, although they have their own Students' Union and sports facilities.

Situated on a single campus close to the centre of Lancaster, the College has a long-standing tradition of voluntary work for charities and in the local community. Chaplaincy activity also plays an important role in student life for those who wish to be involved.

In addition to preparing students for the 'caring professions', S. Martin's has a reputation for producing excellent modern language teachers.

Degrees Available: BA in Arts and Social Science subjects; also in Christian Ministry, Heritage Management, Performing Arts and Community and Youth Studies; BA or BSc with QTS for nursery, primary or secondary teaching (these courses are normally four years, but a limited number of places are available on an 'accelerated route' programme which is completed in three, and there are two-year courses in Mathematical Education and Physical Sciences Education with QTS for those who have already completed some study at Higher Education level); BSc in Maths, Science and Technology, Psychology, Sports Science, Midwifery, Nursing, Occupational Therapy or Radiography. A modular Combined Studies programme allows for considerable flexibility in the choice of options.

Some courses, including those leading to QTS, may be taken part-time: you should expect to complete the normal four-year degree in five or six years.

The College does not run foundation courses, but these may be taken through the Open College of the North West. Contact the Academic Registrar for details.

Assessment: A combination of exams, continuous assessment and self-and peer-assessment. Teaching practice is important in QTS degrees, as is project work in such subjects as Design and Technology, performance in Music, Drama and Dance, and clinical work in the School of Health.

How to Apply: Through UCAS, but you are welcome to contact the Academic Registrar first for an informal discussion and perhaps an advisory interview.

A wide range of alternative qualifications and relevant experience may be taken into account. S. Martin's welcomes mature students who integrate well on all courses – 31% of the 1992 undergraduate intake and 29% of the 1993 were over 21.

St Mary's College
Strawberry Hill, Twickenham TW1 4SX

Tel: 081–892 0051 **Fax:** 081–744 2080
Contact: Judy Adams, Admissions Officer

Number of Undergraduates: 1850
Percentage of Mature Students: 11%
Male/Female Ratio: 1 : 2
Upper Age Limit for Mature Students: None

Learning Facilities: The library has 150,000 books and subscribes to 700 periodicals. It is open until 9 p.m. Monday to Friday during term-time, and on Saturday morning in periods of teaching practice and leading up to summer exams. There are comprehensive computing facilities available to all students and a Learning Resources Centre offering audio-visual support, a colour television studio, mobile video recording facilities and an editing suite.

Creche Facilities: No
Mature Students Adviser: No, but all students have a personal tutor and may consult Student Welfare Services for advice about any problems.
Accommodation: Some accommodation is available in the main College building, and there are four Halls of Residence on campus. This totals 540 places. Priority is given to first-years, of

whom about 75% (most of those who require accommodation) are allocated places. There are no special provisions for couples or families.

St Mary's was established as a Roman Catholic teacher training college in 1850, and although its student intake and its range of courses has broadened greatly since then, its mission still includes the provision of teachers for Catholic and other Christian schools. Its degrees are validated by the University of Surrey, of which it is now a constituent college.

The main College building is a Grade 1 listed building, an 18th-century Gothic mansion built by the writer Horace Walpole and considered one of the finest examples of the Gothic Revival period. It is in the pleasant borough of Richmond is south-west London, with the centre of town only half an hour away and Hampton Court, Kew Gardens and Richmond Park within easy reach.

Degrees Available: BA in English, History and Theology and Religious Studies; BA with QTS (four years) leading to a qualification to teach at secondary or upper primary level; BSc in Environmental Science. A Combined Honours programme allows a wider choice of subjects and combinations, including Drama, Irish Studies and Sports Therapy.
The modular structure of the courses allows for part-time study in all courses.

Assessment: Each module is assessed separately, by means of exams and continuous assessment of essays, practical work, problem solving and teaching practice, as applicable.

How to Apply: Through UCAS. The College will accept a variety of non-standard qualifications. It is part of the South West London Access Agency and welcomes students who have completed recognised Access courses. It has a flexible entry policy, particularly with regard to mature students: any prospective students who think their qualifications and experience equip them to follow a degree course successfully should write to the Registrar for advice. Credit may also be given for prior learning.

------- ✳ -------

St Mary's Hospital Medical School
(University of London)
Norfolk Place, Paddington, London W2 1PG

Tel: 071–723 1252 **Fax:** 071–724 7349
Contact: Secretary to the Delegacy

Number of Undergraduates: About 600

Percentage of Mature Students: Between 5 and 10% (normally about 10 admitted a year)

Male/Female Ratio: About 1 : 1

Upper Age Limit for Mature Students: None officially, but you are unlikely to be accepted if you are over 30

Learning Facilities: The library has over 30,000 volumes, provides 150 study places and is open for study till 10 p.m. on weekdays, with a full librarian service till 9 p.m. There is a collection of over 40,000 slides and prints, comprehensive computing and audio-visual services and excellent laboratory and clinical facilities. Students also have access to the resources of Imperial College and the main University of London library.

Creche Facilities: Through Imperial College.

Mature Students Adviser: No, but all students may use the services of the Student Counsellor.

Accommodation: The Medical School has its own residences, providing 255 places. First-year students living away from home for the first time are guaranteed a place, either here, in Imperial College accommodation or in one of the University of London's Intercollegiate Halls. The Medical School encourages preclinical students to apply for places in the Intercollegiate Halls so that they can mix with students from other Colleges and faculties. Information about these Halls is available from the University of London Accommodation Office, Senate House, Malet St, London WC1E 7HU, telephone 071–636 2818, which will also try to help married students or those with families find somewhere suitable to live. Students of the Medical College may also seek help from the Accommodation Office at Imperial (see page 188).

It was at St Mary's that Alexander Fleming discovered penicillin; it is also the 'royal' hospital where the Princess of Wales gave birth to her children. The Medical School was founded in 1854, became part of the University of London in 1900 and now occupies a building in Paddington which dates from the 1930s but is continually being extended and equipped with modern facilities.

Since 1988 St Mary's Hospital Medical School has been a constituent college of the Imperial College of Science, Technology and Medicine.

Degrees Available: MB BS. There is also an intercalated one-year BSc course which students may take between the preclinical and clinical parts of their studies.

Assessment: Written and clinical exams, plus a fourth-year project and in-course assessment.

How to Apply: Through UCAS. If you do not have good Science A levels or equivalent you are advised to contact the Officer for Entrance Requirements of the University of London, Senate House, Malet St, London WC1E 7HU for advice, but you should be aware that competition for places is severe.

University of Salford
Salford M5 4WT

Tel: 061–745 5000
Contact: Admissions Officer

Number of Undergraduates: 3677
Percentage of Mature Students: About 20%
Male/Female Ratio: 7 : 3
Upper Age Limit for Mature Students: None

Learning Facilities: The library has 300,000 volumes and 900 study places; it is open in the evenings during the week. There are full computing services and excellent language-study facilities.

Creche Facilities: Shared with University College Salford and available for children aged two to five during term-time only.

Mature Students Adviser: Not specifically, but the Access Liaison Officer will advise on applications and the full range of counselling and welfare services are available.

Accommodation: Salford is well served in this respect, with a number of Halls and a large Student Village. All first-years who apply by 8 September are guaranteed a place, and most students who want to can spend at least one other year in University accommodation. There are 57 one-bedroom and 57 two-bedroom flats suitable for couples and families.

Salford is proud of its record of applying knowledge to real life in its courses – it was, for example, one of the first Universities to offer a BSc in Modern Languages.

The recent redevelopment of Salford Quays has brightened up this industrial city and the University is on a pleasant campus within walking distance of the centre of Manchester. The area has a vast student population – over 7500 in Salford alone and many thousands more in Manchester itself – with all the facilities that this brings with it.

Degrees Available: BA or BSc in Arts, Social Science or Business subjects; BSc in Information Technology or in a range of Science subjects, including what the prospectus describes as a 'green' degree in Applied Environmental and Resource Science; BEng in some interesting specialisms including Aeronautical Engineering and Robotic and Electronic Engineering.

Most scientific and Engineering courses include an optional one-year sandwich element.

All first degree courses are modular.

There is a foundation year in Engineering. Part-time study is possible in Sociology (day time) or Politics and Contemporary History (evenings): an Honours degree will normally take five years on this basis.

Salford has also pioneered the concept of 2 + 2 courses, whereby you take the first two years of a course at a local college and gain an HND before transferring to Salford to complete the course. There is also a 1 + 2 course, available in Information Technology only, in which the first year is taken at Leigh College and the final two years at Salford.

Assessment: Mainly exams, but also assessment of essays, oral presentations, projects etc. Each unit is assessed separately.

How to Apply: Through UCAS for full-time courses. Salford welcomes applications from prospective mature students, particularly those on recognised Access courses, and will assess your experience, personal qualities and ability to complete the course successfully.

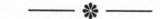

University College Salford
Frederick Rd, Salford M6 7PU

Tel: 061–736 6541
     061–745 3273 (admissions office) **Fax:** 061–745 8386
Contact: Central Admissions Office

Number of Undergraduates: About 800 full-time, many more part-time
Percentage of Mature Students: 40%
Male/Female Ratio: 1 : 1
Upper Age Limit for Mature Students: None

Learning Facilities: The library has 54,000 books and subscribes to 700 periodicals. There are computing services, language labs and technical support for relevant departments.

Creche Facilities: For children aged two to four, during term-time only.

Mature Students Adviser: No, but the full range of welfare services is available to all students.

Accommodation: There are 800 places in Halls of Residence and the University also rents student houses which may be suitable for couples or families. Privately rented accommodation in Salford is comparatively cheap.

The forerunner of University College Salford, until recently the Salford College of Technology, was founded in 1896 and the College has a long tradition of providing practical, vocationally oriented courses. Most teaching takes place on a single site in the centre of Salford, with Performing Arts and Media, and Design and Technology not far away on their own sites.

The University College's degrees are validated by the University of Salford, with which it has close links.

Degrees Available: BA in subjects connected with Art and Design, the Performing Arts and Media, and the leisure industries; BEng; BSc in some applied Sciences and paramedical subjects such as Physiotherapy, Podiatry, and Prosthetics and Orthotics. Many courses can be followed part-time.

Assessment: A combination of exams and continuous assessment. All courses involve work placements, and satisfactory performance on these is essential.

How to Apply: Through ADAR for Art and Design, otherwise through UCAS for full-time study; for part-time apply direct on a form available from the Central Admissions Office. University College Salford has a large number of mature students and welcomes applications from those with non-tradional qualifications who show commitment and evidence of recent study.

University College Scarborough
The North Riding College
Filey Rd, Scarborough YO11 3AZ

Tel: 0723 362392 **Fax:** 0723 370815
Contact: Mrs Gaylyn Fox or Dr E.J. Payne Ahmadi

Number of Undergraduates: 980
Percentage of Mature Students: 18%

Male/Female Ratio: 1 : 5
Upper Age Limit for Mature Students: 50 for teacher training, otherwise none.

Learning Facilities: The library has 70,000 books and is open six days a week. There are a computer technology suite, science labs, theatre studio, concert room, art studios and a gym.

Creche Facilities: No
Mature Students Adviser: Not specifically, but each student has a personal tutor.
Accommodation: About 25% of first-years can be accommodated in study bedrooms on site and most others in University-run accommodation: either local hotels used as Halls of Residence, or self-catering flats. There are no special provisions for couples or families.

Known until recently as the North Riding College, University College Scarborough is now an independent Higher Education Corporation and a constituent College of the University of Leeds, which validates its degrees and with which it has a long-standing academic association.

The College is situated on a single campus about a mile from the centre of Scarborough, with magnificent views over the cliffs. In addition to being famous as a holiday resort, Scarborough is the home town of the playwright Alan Ayckbourn, whose plays receive their first performances here, at the Stephen Joseph Theatre-in-the Round.

Road and rail links with the rest of the country have improved significantly over recent years, so although Scarborough remains a smallish town surrounded by largely unspoiled countryside, it is far from inaccessible.

Degrees Available: BA or BSc with Qualified Teacher Status entitling you to teach at nursery and lower primary or at upper primary level – specialist subjects are Biological Studies, Maths and Music only (please note: this is a recent government-enforced cut-back and the UCAS Handbook for 1994 entry lists subjects that are no longer available). The second year of this course is spent at the University of Leeds.

There is also a BSc in Environmental Science and Conservation and a Combined Studies BA majoring in Applied Social Studies, Art and Design, Theatre Studies, English, History or Religious Studies.

Part-time Continuing Education courses are available in association with the University of Leeds – contact the Registry for details.

Assessment: All programmes except those with QTS are modular and each unit is assessed separately during and at the end of the semester in which it is taught. A combination of exams and continuous assessment is used, including oral and practical exams, seminar papers, essays or dissertations, as applicable. Teaching practice is an important element of Education degrees.

How to Apply: Through UCAS. A range of alternative qualifications (Access course, GNVQs, BTEC award, etc) may be acceptable. Applications from prospective mature students without formal qualifications are welcome, although GCSE or equivalent in English Language and, for teaching courses, Maths is essential. Mature applicants will be judged on their merits but may be asked to sit an exam.

Scottish Agricultural College

Auchincruive, Ayr KA6 5HW

Tel: 0292 520331

581 King St, Aberdeen AB9 1UD
Tel: 0224 480291

West Mains Rd, Edinburgh EH9 3JG
Tel: 031–667 1041

There is also a FREEPOST address: SAC Academic Registrar, FREEPOST, SAC Auchincruive, Ayr, KA6 5HW; and a FREE-PHONE number: 0800 269453.

Contact: Students Service Manager at Auchincruive, or the Education Liaison Officer or Senior Tutor at any of the three sites

Please see page 2 for general information on Scottish universities and colleges

Number of Undergraduates: 183 in a total student body of 1000+ full-time, many more part-time over the three sites
Percentage of Mature Students: About 5%
Male/Female Ratio: 4 : 1
Upper Age Limit for Mature Students: None specified

Learning Facilities: There are specialist libraries on each of the three sites, and college farms on which all students gain practical experience.

Creche Facilities: Yes – contact Student Services at Auchincruive for details.

Mature Students Adviser: Not specifically, but course tutors and welfare staff are available to give help and advice all students who require them.

Accommodation: Some College accommodation available, and the College will try to help all students to find somewhere suitable to live. Contact the Student Services Manager at Auchincruive in the first instance.

The Scottish Agricultural College came into being in 1990 following the merger of the three major existing Colleges of Agriculture in Scotland. It is still based at the three sites – in Aberdeen, in Edinburgh and three miles outside Ayr – occupied by its predecessors, and runs courses at various levels in close association with Aberdeen, Edinburgh, Glasgow, Napier, Robert Gordon and Strathclyde Universities. Students spend part of their time at the university concerned and part at the nearest SAC campus.

SAC courses are designed to combine traditional land-based skills with the increasing demands of technology and the leisure industries.

Degrees Available: BSc or BTechnol in courses related to Agriculture, Aquaculture, Horticulture, Food Production and Manufacture, Leisure and Recreation Management and Rural Resources.

The College operates a CATS scheme (see page 12) which enables most courses to be followed part-time.

Assessment: Courses are practical and student-centred, with seminars, assignments, case studies and performance at work placements all counting towards your degree.

How to Apply: Through UCAS to the University of Aberdeen for Aquaculture or Rural Business Management; to Napier for Rural Resources; to Strathclyde for Horticulture; to Glasgow for Plant and Animal Science, Food Production and Land Use, Food Production, Management and Marketing, or Leisure and Recreation Management.

See separate entries for these universities for further advice on applications.

———— ❋ ————

Scottish College of Textiles
Netherdale, Galashiels TD1 3HF

Tel: 0896 3351 **Fax:** 0896 58965
Contact: Miss S. Kelly, Admissions Office

Please see page 2 for general information on Scottish universities and colleges

Number of Undergraduates: 732
Percentage of Mature Students: 12%
Male/Female Ratio: 1 : 2
Upper Age Limit for Mature Students: None

Learning Facilities: The library has 17,000 books and 70-80 study places. The College also has computing facilities, language labs, audio-visual equipment and superb specialist technical resources.

Creche Facilities: No
Mature Students Adviser: The Student Welfare Officer has particular expertise in advising mature students.
Accommodation: Halls of Residence on campus; college flats nearby. College accommodation is normally available for all first-years who need it. No special provision for couples or families.

The Scottish College of Textiles has been in existence since 1883 and although it is now a Faculty of Heriot-Watt University, which awards its degrees, it retains its own identity on a modern campus just outside Galashiels in the Scottish border country. It boasts some of the best facilities in Europe in its field, and has one of the best academic reputations.

Degrees Available: The following are all four-year courses, including 22 weeks' work experience in the final term and summer holiday of the third year: BA in Industrial Design (Textiles): BSc in Clothing, Colour Chemistry, Manufacturing Computing (Textiles), Quality Management, Textiles with Clothing Studies and Textiles with Marketing. There are also BA and BSc Combined Studies degrees.
The first three years of the Colour Chemistry course are spent at the main Heriot-Watt campus just outside Edinburgh.

Assessment: A combination of continuous assessment and exams. Final-year projects form a major part of the degree.

How to Apply: Through UCAS to Heriot-Watt University.
The College welcomes applications from mature students without traditional qualifications, which will be considered on their individual merits. Contact the relevant Course Leader for further advice before submitting a formal application. Relevant

work experience may be taken into account and credit transfer from other courses is possible.

All selected applicants for the Industrial Design course will be invited for interview and expected to present a portfolio of work.

University of Sheffield
Sheffield S10 2TN

Tel: 0742 768555
0742 766222 (Medical School) **Fax:** 0742 728014
Contact: Undergraduate Admissions Officer

Number of Undergraduates: 10,400
Percentage of Mature Students: 17%
Male/Female Ratio: About 4 : 3
Upper Age Limit for Mature Students: None – there is at least one student aged 73.

Learning Facilities: The main library has a million books. There are computer facilities available to all students, and laboratories for all appropriate courses.

Creche Facilities: There is a nursery, a pre-school playgroup and a half-term playscheme for children of primary school age. Fees for students' children are subisidised. Apply early.

Mature Students Adviser: Mrs E.J. Hall, Access Liaison Officer. The University also produces a useful 'Guide for Mature Students'.

Accommodation: Halls of Residence can accommodate over 90% of first-year students. There is a limited number of flats specifically for mature students and a few flats and houses suitable for couples and families. Contact the University's Housing Services Department as soon as possible.

Sheffield is always described as a great place to be a student: whether that is because of the proximity of the Peak District, the friendliness of the people or the famously cheap public transport is difficult to say. Among the University's other attributes are a magnificent international-sized swimming pool and a Careers Advisory Service which a survey of graduates recently voted one of the best in the country. And the Paternoster lift in the Arts Tower is the longest in Europe.

The University is to the west of the city centre, with the Halls of Residence in attractive residential areas a mile or so away.

Degrees Available: BA in the Faculties of Architecture, Arts and Social Science, with a wide choice of subjects; BMus; BEng in a range of subjects, some including a modern language; BA (Law); LLB; BDS; BMedSci; MB, ChB; BSc in a range of subjects and BSc/BEng in Integrated Physical Science.

There are foundation courses in Pure Science and in Engineering, and Access courses are available through the Division of Adult Continuing Education.

Part-time study is possible in Social and Political Studies, History and Humanities.

Assessment: A mixture of exams and continuous assessment, plus practical or clinical work as appropriate to the course.

From 1994, most degrees will be constructed on a credit accumulation basis, so that each unit will be assessed separately.

How to Apply: Through UCAS. You will also be sent a supplementary form which you should return to the Undergraduate Admissions Office. This asks for basic information about yourself, your academic and occupational background and your life experience: it is an additional opportunity for you to provide any relevant information to support your application.

The University will consider every prospective mature student according to individual background and preparation. It welcomes applications from prospective mature students, but stresses that adequate preparation for the particular course you want to follow is vital. Some courses, such as Engineering, Science and Languages, assume a certain amount of prior knowledge.

You are welcome to contact the Access Liaison Officer or the Admission Tutor of your proposed course for an informal discussion before you submit a formal application: they will advise on whether you are likely to be able to follow the course successfully, or suggest an alternative route if necessary.

Sheffield Hallam University
Pond St, Sheffield S1 1WB

Tel: 0742 720911 **Fax:** 0742 532161
Contact: Kate Butler, Admissions Officer

Number of Undergraduates: 16,886
Percentage of Mature Students: 50%
Male/Female Ratio: 6 : 4
Upper Age Limit for Mature Students: None

Learning Facilities: The library has over 500,000 books and subscribes to more than 2000 periodicals. There are computer facilities and labs, and the Learning Resources Centre provides graphics, photography, TV production, off-air recording, desk-top publishing and a supply of audio-visual equipment.

Creche Facilities: A University-subsidised nursery

Mature Students Adviser: No, but the usual welfare services are available to all students.

Accommodation: University-managed accommodation can provide places for 30% of first-year students; the rest are helped to find private accommodation. No special provisions for couples or families.

Sheffield has all the facilities you would expect of one of England's largest cities, including the Crucible Theatre (now the home of world championship snooker) and the recently refurbished Lyceum. The vast Sheffield Arena, built for the International Student Games, attracts top bands previously only seen at Wembley or the NEC.

Sheffield Hallam is in the heart of the city, close to the shopping centre and railway station.

Degrees Available: BA in a range of subjects in Accounting and Financial Services, Applied Social Studies, Art and Design, Business Studies, Critical Studies, Film and Media Studies, Housing, Urban and Planning Studies, Leisure and Food Management, and Public Sector Studies; LLB; BEd leading to a qualification to teach at primary or secondary level; BEng; BSc in Computing, Management Sciences, Professional Training in Health and Social Care, Science and Surveying (Land Management).

There is also a Combined Studies BA or BSc programme allowing a wide range of subject combinations.

Foundation courses are available in all branches of the School of Engineering.

Part-time study is possible and the modular Combined Studies course is particularly suited to this.

Assessment: A combination of exams and continuous assessment; modular degrees are assessed at the end of each unit. Teaching practice is an integral part of BEd degrees.

How to Apply: Through ADAR for Art and Design, otherwise through UCAS for full-time study; direct for part-time. Mature applicants are advised to contact the Admissions Office first for advice on alternative qualifications and application procedures. Credit may be given for previous study, and relevant experience may also be taken into consideration.

Silsoe College
Cranfield University, Silsoe, Bedford MK45 4DT

Tel: 0525 860428 **Fax:** 0525 861994
Contact: Mrs M.J. Merredy, Student Recruitment Executive

Number of Undergraduates: 150, many more post-graduates
Percentage of Mature Students: About 13%
Male/Female Ratio: 4 : 1
Upper Age Limit for Mature Students: None

Learning Facilities: The library has 37,000 books. Laboratory facilities include aerial photographic interpretation, remote sensing and cartography.

Creche Facilities: Normally during holidays.
Mature Students Adviser: No, but welfare services are available to all students.
Accommodation: Halls of Residence and student houses. All first-year students are allocated college accommodation. There are a limited number of flats for couples.

Silsoe was founded in 1960 to provide education for the agricultural engineering industry and became part of Cranfield Institute of Technology (now Cranfield University) in 1975. It is situated in pleasant countryside about halfway between Luton and Bedford.

Degrees Available: BEng; BSc (four-year sandwich), both in subjects related to agriculture and the environment.

Assessment: A combination of exams and continuous assessment of laboratory and course work.

How to Apply: Through UCAS. A wide range of alternative qualifications will be considered. Mature applicants who do not meet the standard entry requirements will be expected to show evidence of their ability to follow the course. You are welcome to discuss your circumstances with the Admissions Tutor before submitting your application.

School of Oriental and African Studies
(SOAS – University of London)
Thornhaugh St, Russell Square, London WC1H 0XG

Tel: 071–637 2388 **Fax:** 071–436 4211
Contact: Admissions Officer

Number of Undergraduates: 1150
Percentage of Mature Students: About 25%
Male/Female Ratio: About 3 : 4
Upper Age Limit for Mature Students: None

Learning Facilities: The library has over 850,000 items and is one of the finest in the world in its field. Students may also use the main University of London library. SOAS courses make extensive use of language labs and audio-visual equipment.

Creche Facilities: No, but the Registry will send details of local childcare facilities on request. Apply early.

Mature Students Adviser: No, but the Student Welfare Officer may be consulted by any student who needs help.

Accommodation: The School has no accommodation of its own, but students are eligible to apply for a place in one of the University of London's Intercollegiate Halls. Contact the University of London Accommodation Office, Senate House, Malet St, London WC1E 7HU, telephone 071–636 2818 for details. The Accommodation Office also keeps a register of other University-owned or rented accommodation and the School sends a booklet, 'Finding Somewhere to Live in London', to all prospective students.

SOAS was founded in 1916 and is a specialist School within the University of London, situated in Bloomsbury, just round the corner from the main University buildings. It offers courses not only in languages and literature: there is the opportunity to study African and Asian politics, history, music, anthropology – every aspect of the cultures of the School's specialist areas.

Degrees Available: BA in a wide range of Arts subjects relating to Asia and Africa, with many degrees specialising in a language from Africa, the Near, Middle or Far East, South Asia or South-East Asia. These include Chinese, Hausa, Hebrew, Japanese, Korean, Kurdish, Sanskrit, Swahili, Tamil, Turkish, Urdu and many more.
There is also an LLB course, recognised by the professional bodies in the UK, which gives students the chance to study the religious, traditional and contemporary legal systems of Africa and Asia.

Assessment: Courses are modular, with units examined at the end of each year. Oral examinations are an important part of language courses.

How to Apply: Through UCAS. SOAS welcomes applications from mature students with non-traditional qualifications and will consider each application on its individual merits. A wide range of qualifications (BTEC awards, Access courses, professional exams, etc) may be recognised as meeting the entry requirements.

School of Slavonic and East European Studies
(SSEES – University of London)
Senate House, Malet St, London WC1E 7HU

Tel: 071–637 4934 x 4040 **Fax:** 071–436 8916
Contact: Registrar

Number of Undergraduates: 364
Percentage of Mature Students: 30%
Male/Female Ratio: 1 : 1
Upper Age Limit for Mature Students: None

Learning Facilities: The library contains about 300,000 items and subscribes to 1100 current periodicals. It is closed at weekends but open till 7 p.m. Monday to Friday during term-time. Students may also use the main University of London library.

Creche Facilities: Available through the University of London Union for a small charge

Mature Students Adviser: Not specifically, but welfare services for all students are available through the School or through the central facilities of the University of London.

Accommodation: The School has no accommodation of its own, but students are eligible to apply for places in the University of London's seven Intercollegiate Halls of Residence. Contact the University of London Accommodation Office, Senate House, Malet St, London WC1E 7HU for details. Applications from prospective students must be received by 31 May, so do not wait until you have exam results or a firm offer of a place. The Accommodation Office can also provide details of accommodation suitable for couples and families. Again, apply early.

SSEES is a specialist School within the University of London. It is one of the few places in the UK offering degrees in Czech or Slovak, Hungarian, Serbian or Croatian or Polish Studies, and the only one where you can specialise in Finnish. Student numbers are low, so there is more personal tuition than is possible in larger institutions. The School is situated in Senate House in Malet St and is therefore conveniently close to all the University facilities.

Degrees Available: BA in East European Languages, Literatures and Regional Studies, either Combined Studies or specialising in a chosen country; also BA in History, Russian or various two-language combinations. Most are four-year courses, involving at least three months, normally a year, abroad.

Assessment: All courses are now modular and assessed at the end of each unit. A combination of written exams, assessed coursework and oral exams in language courses is used.

How to Apply: Through UCAS. The School is happy to consider any qualifications that mature applicants have to offer, but tends to look most favourably on those who have undertaken some form of study since leaving school (such as A levels or a recognised Access course) and thereby proved that they are likely to succeed at degree level.

South Bank University
Borough Rd, London SE1 0AA

Tel: 071–928 8989 **Fax:** 071–815 8155
Contact: Central Registry

Number of Undergraduates: 15,000
Percentage of Mature Students: 74%
Male/Female Ratio: 4 : 3
Upper Age Limit for Mature Students: None

Learning Facilities: Libraries on both sites hold a total of 310,000 books and provide 600 study places. During term-time both are open till nine o'clock Monday to Friday and for part of the weekend. There are computer facilities, laboratories and a language centre.

Creche Facilities: Nursery for children aged six months to five years. Fees are reduced for those on low incomes. There is a long waiting list, so enquire as early as possible.
Mature Students Adviser: There are a number of student counsellors, including one with special responsibility for mature students. The University also produces a helpful Mature Students' Handbook and the Library and Learning Resources

produce a Study Skills Starter Pack aimed at those returning to study after a gap.

Accommodation: Halls of Residence accommodate only about 10% of first-year students. There are no special provisions for couples or families. The Housing Service will help, but local accommodation suitable for families will be expensive.

The South Bank University is on three sites – the main one in Borough Rd, with the Business School a short distance away and the Faculty of the Built Environment a couple of miles across South London. The buildings are modern and better equipped than many for the needs of students with disabilities. The University has recently adopted a no-smoking policy in all its buildings.

Degrees Available: BA mainly in Business-oriented subjects and Modern Languages; BEd leading to a qualification to teach at primary level; BEng; BSc; LLB.

There is no Faculty of Science as such at the South Bank, so a number of common subjects such as Chemistry and Physics are not available. The BSc is awarded by the Faculty of Science, Technology, Health and Society or by the Faculty of the Built Environment, and the emphasis is on such subjects as Construction Management and Quantity Surveying, Food Studies and Nursing, Occupational Health and Radiography.

A Combined BA/BSc Honours course enables you to choose unusual pairings as English Studies and Environmental Science, Health Sciences and Computing, or Modern Languages and Product Design.

Foundation years are available in Chemical, Civil, Electrical, Energy and Mechanical Engineering and in Engineering Systems Design; and in twenty of the Science subjects. The first year of most of these courses is available both at the University and at a nearby franchised college.

Many courses are available part-time – contact the relevant Faculty Office for details.

Assessment: A combination of exams and continuous assessment.

How to Apply: Through UCAS for full-time courses. For part-time courses contact the relevant Faculty Office first.

The University has a very high proportion of mature students and a wide range of non-standard qualifications will be considered. There are both CATS and APEL schemes (see page 12).

University of Southampton
Southampton SO9 5NH

Tel: 0703 595000 **Fax:** 0703 593037
Contact: Assistant Registrar, Admissions

Number of Undergraduates: 7511
Percentage of Mature Students: 12%
Male/Female Ratio: About 4 : 3
Upper Age Limit for Mature Students: 30 for Medicine, otherwise none.

Learning Facilities: The library has over 900,000 books and continues to expand its stock; it provides 1300 study places and is open seven days a week. There are comprehensive computing facilities throughout the University and a Language Centre with computer-assisted learning.

Creche Facilities: For children aged from six months to five years. Apply early as places are always oversubscribed. Telephone the above number, extension 3465, for more information.

Mature Students Adviser: Each faculty has a nominated mature student contact and there is a mature students' conference at the start of each academic year.

Accommodation: 3000 places in Halls of Residence, some catering, some self-catering, accommodate 85% of first-year students. Some bedsit flats are available for married students.

The University of Southampton is on an attractive campus two miles from the town, with all its facilities within easy reach of each other. Still a thriving port, the city also has a 'docklands development' known as Ocean Village, which boasts cafes, bars, cinemas and an arts centre.

Southampton is easy to reach from London and easy to get out of if you wish to visit the Continent, the Channel Islands or, less adventurously, the New Forest.

Degrees Available: BA; BEng; BSc in a range of Science, Maths and Social Science subjects, plus Occupational Therapy, Physiotherapy and Radiography; BM; BMid (Midwifery); BN; LLB.
Combined or Joint Honours degrees offer such interesting combinations as Archaeology and Iberian Studies or Accounting, Computer Science or Economics with a language. Aeronautics and Astronautics, Ship Science, Industrial Applied Mathematics and Marine Sciences are among the more unusual Single Honours subjects available.

Return to Study courses are offered through the Department of Adult and Continuing Education, and part-time study is possible in the Faculties of Arts, Science and Mathematics.

Assessment: Varies from department to department, but most have written exams at the end of the year or semester, plus some continuous assessment of essays, practical work, projects, etc.

How to Apply: Through UCAS. Mature students are not expected to meet the general entrance requirements, but must show commitment through recent study: Access courses, Open University foundation courses, etc.

The University is currently establishing a CATS scheme (see page 12) and a system whereby you may be given credit for previous experience on entry to Nursing courses is under consideration.

Southampton Institute of Higher Education
East Park Terrace, Southampton SO9 4WW

Tel: 0703 229381 **Fax:** 0703 222259
Contact: Registry

Number of Undergraduates: About 7500 full-time, 2000 part-time
Percentage of Mature Students: About 50%
Male/Female Ratio: 3 : 2
Upper Age Limit for Mature Students: None specified

Learning Facilities: The Institute has three new libraries, open 70 hours a week including evenings and weekends and providing 650 study places. There are comprehensive computing facilities, labs, workshops and studios for relevant courses.

Creche Facilities: No
Mature Students Adviser: No, but welfare and counselling services are available to all students. Month-long Gateway courses run during September offer help in study skills, basic maths, etc and there are induction courses aimed specifically at mature students. There is also a Mature Students' Society.
Accommodation: Halls of Residence and other Institute-managed housing can accommodate almost are first-year students. No special provisions for couples or families.

The Institute occupies two sites, one in the centre of Southampton and the other, the Warsash campus, ten miles away on the banks of the River

Hamble. A regular bus service is provided between the two. Smoking is permitted in the Students' Union, but not in the Institute's buildings.

Most of the Institute's degrees are validated by the University of Southampton; those in Art and Design are validated by Nottingham Trent. Some of the latter are taught in part at Salisbury College.

Degrees Available: BA in Arts, Art and Design, Business and Social Science subjects; BSc and BEng in a limited number of subjects; LLB. Some of the more unusual subjects on offer are Corporate Communication, Real Estate Valuation, Maritime Studies and Yacht and Powercraft Design.
Foundation courses are available in almost every case.
Part-time study is possible on some courses.

Assessment: A mixture of exams and continuous assessment, with self- and peer-assessment used on some courses.

How to Apply: Through ADAR for Art and Design, otherwise through UCAS, but mature applicants are welcome to contact Course Leaders or Admissions Tutors direct and may be admitted on the strength of an interview. The Institute operates a CATS scheme (see page 12), so credit may be given for previous study.

Staffordshire University
1 College Rd, Stoke on Trent ST4 2DE

Tel: 0782 744531 **Fax:** 0782 745422

1 Beaconside, Stafford ST18 0AD
Tel: 0785 52331
Contact: Lynne Tolley, Access Unit, Stoke Campus
Number of Undergraduates: 9607 full-time and sandwich, 1603 part-time
Percentage of Mature Students: 32%
Male/Female Ratio: About 3 : 2
Upper Age Limit for Mature Students: None

Learning Facilities: There is a library on each of the three campuses: their collections total 300,000 books and nearly 2000 current periodicals. There are also comprehensive computing facilities and modern language labs.

Creche Facilities: University-subsidised nurseries on both sites are open all year round. The Students' Union Welfare Unit issues a leaflet giving phone numbers, prices and other details.

Mature Students Adviser: Not specifically, but the Access Unit can advise on applications and the Careers Office staff are trained to deal with students of all ages. The University also publishes a brief but useful 'Mature Students' Guide' and a brochure on Access courses.

Accommodation: Over 2500 places are available in self-catering University accommodation. Priority is given to first-year students and about 85% of those who request a place can be allocated one. Two houses are reserved for married students and the Accommodation Service will try to help with off-campus accommodation. The University prides itself on having some of the lowest student rents in the country.

Staffordshire University is divided into three campuses, two close together in the centre of Stoke, the other on a purpose-built site a mile and a half from the centre of Stafford, some 15 miles away. The new computing centre, known as the Octagon, is on the Stafford site. Both sites have their own sports and social facilities. The Business School and the Schools of Sciences, Arts, Design and Ceramics, and Law are in Stoke; the Schools of Engineering and Computing in Stafford.

Both towns are within easy reach of the Peak District, the Staffordshire Dales, Trentham Gardens (landscaped by Capability Brown) and Alton Towers!

Degrees Available: BA in some usual and some unusual Arts and Social Science subjects, including Enterprise in the Public Sector, Film, Television and Radio Studies, and Women in Business; also BA in Fine Art and in Design; LLB; BEng in a wider-than-usual range of specialisms; BSc also in a wide range of subjects including Business Decision Analysis, Computing Science or Software Engineering with a European Language, and Industrial Mathematics, Statistics and Computing. Modular schemes in BA and BSc programmes allow for great flexibility in combining subjects.

There are one-year BSc foundation courses and a BA foundation course in Interactive Systems Design at local franchised colleges; a foundation year can be incorporated into all Engineering courses at the University and is also available in Art and Design. Part-time courses are available, and you are allowed up to eight years to complete a degree.

Assessment: Each module is assessed at the end of the semester in which it is taught, either by exam or on course work or both. Practical work, group presentations or portfolios may all be assessed where applicable.

How to Apply: Through UCAS for all courses except Fine Art and Design, which are through ADAR. You should expect to be interviewed before being offered a place.

Staffordshire has a very positive approach to mature students and will consider a wide range of alternative qualifications and/or experience. The University is a founder member of UCAN, the Universities and Colleges Access Network (Staffordshire and Shropshire): successful completion of an UCAN course will guarantee you an interview.

University of Stirling
Stirling FK9 4LA

Tel: 0786 473171
0786 467044 (Admissions Office)
Contact: Admissions Office

Number of Undergraduates: 3200
Percentage of Mature Students: 15%
Male/Female Ratio: 1 : 1
Upper Age Limit for Mature Students: None

Please see page 2 for general information about Scottish universities and colleges

Learning Facilities: The library has 450,000 volumes, subscribes to 2200 periodicals and provides 650 study places. It is open 75 hours a week, including weekends. There are excellent computing facilities, language laboratories and media services. An optional Information Skills course is available for a small charge to all those wishing to improve their computer literacy.

Creche Facilities: Run by the Students' Association for children aged 18 months to five years; open till six o'clock (later than most).

Mature Students Adviser: Not specifically, but the Department of Continuing Education will advise on applications and there are counsellors available for all students.

Accommodation: 2000 places in Halls and University flats can accommodate all first-years who apply by 1 September. There are a few leased properties suitable for families.

Stirling, situated on the Forth River about halfway between Glasgow and Edinburgh and easy to reach from either, is dominated by the medieval castle which towers above the town: Mary Queen of Scots and her son James (VI of Scotland and I of England) were both crowned here as infants.

The University itself is rather younger, having just celebrated its first 25 years, and occupies what it claims is the prettiest campus in the UK. Certainly few others boast parkland, wooded hillsides and their own private loch. It also has the excellent MacRobert Arts Centre, which includes an art gallery and a theatre said to be one of the finest in Scotland.

Degrees Available: BA in a range of Arts and Social Science subjects and in Accountancy; BSc; BA and BSc with QTS.

Stirling offers a number of interesting subject combinations, including the chance to study French, German, Japanese or Spanish with Business Studies, Computing Science, Film and Media Studies or Marketing.

All courses are modular and organised into semester-units.

Stirling has an arrangement with Inverness College whereby the first two years of courses in Business Studies or Computing may be taken there; students then transfer to Stirling to complete their degree.

Part-time programmes, which may be followed during the day or in the evening, are available for a BA or BSc general degree, or in Community Studies or Education Studies.

Assessment: By exams and continuous assessment, with each unit assessed during and at the end of the semester in which it is taught.

How to Apply: Through UCAS for full-time study, direct to the University for part-time. Stirling is keen to encourage mature students and applicants who are taking an approved Access course are particularly welcome. Relevant experience may be taken into account – contact the Department of Continuing Education for advice.

Stockport College of Further & Higher Education
Wellington Rd South, Stockport SK1 3UQ

Tel: 061–958–3100 **Fax:** 061–480 6636
Contact: For general information, telephone 061–958 3414

Number of Undergraduates: A total student body of about 15,000
Percentage of Mature Students: About 66%

Male/Female Ratio: 1 : 1
Upper Age Limit for Mature Students: None

Learning Facilities: Libraries on both sites provide, in addition to books, over 300 periodicals, a specialist collection of illustrations and information services. Audio-visual and computing facilities may be reserved in the Student Project Room.

Creche Facilities: For children aged two to five.

Mature Students Adviser: Not specifically, but the resources of Student Services are available to all students. The librarians will help with study skills problems and there is a Learning Support Workshop providing confidential help for those who need it.

Accommodation: None owned by the College, but the Accommodation Officer can help find a wide range of types of accommodation.

Stockport College occupies a number of sites, but the main building is in the centre of town, on the A6 and very close to the railway station. Manchester is ten minutes away by train.

In addition to its degree programmes, the College offers a range of courses from GCSE level upwards and caters for the needs of a large section of the local community.

Degrees Available: BA in Professional Studies (Learning Difficulties); BEng in Aeronautical, Civil or Mechanical Engineering; BSc in Architectural Engineering, Biochemistry, Biology or Chemistry.

With the exception of the BA, all courses are designed in association with a university – Leeds, Manchester, Manchester Metropolitan, UMIST or Salford – and involve some study there. Science and Engineering courses last four years and are run on a 2 + 2 basis – two years at Stockport, followed by two years at the relevant university.

The College also offers a 'top up' degree in Education, enabling those who already hold a Certificate in Education to upgrade this to an honours degree.

There are also Access or foundation courses in Art and Design and in Technology.

Assessment: Varies from course to course.

How to Apply: Through UCAS. The leaflet describing full-time courses gives contact names and numbers for each faculty, and you should phone the relevant adviser for an informal discussion before submitting your application.

University College, Stockton on Tees
University Boulevard, Thornsby, Stockton on Tees TS17 6BH

Tel: 0642 335300
Contact: Mrs P.K. Palmer, Admissions Officer

Number of Undergraduates: 450
Percentage of Mature Students: 52%
Male/Female Ratio: 2 : 3
Upper Age Limit for Mature Students: None

Learning Facilities: Modern library, computer facilities and language labs. Students also have access to the resources of the nearby Universities of Durham and Teeside.

Creche Facilities: Not yet, but planned for the future.
Mature Students Adviser: No, but all students may consult the student counsellor in case of need.
Accommodation: A Hall of Residence is due for completion in 1994. First-year students who do not live within reasonable daily travelling distance will be given priority. There is as yet no provision for couples or families.

Stockton is the UK's newest university, created by the Universities of Durham and Teesside and opened by the Queen in May 1993. It is the first new purpose-built university campus in this country for 25 years. Wheelchair access is well catered for throughout. Smoking is not permitted in the teaching building.

The University College has drawn on the established expertise of its two parent universities to develop courses which 'carry Higher Education forward into the next millennium'. Certainly its courses are flexible and it has an accommodating attitude to mature students, as indicated by the high percentage it accepted in its first intake.

Stockton has ambitious plans for the future and its very existence seems to be an exciting step forward.

Degrees Available: BA in European Studies with French or German; BSc in Biomedical Sciences, Environmental Management (including a four-year sandwich course in Environment Technology), Health and Human Sciences. These courses lead to degrees from the Universities of Durham or Teesside.
All courses can be followed part-time.
Foundation courses in Science and Engineering are run at Teesside.

Assessment: A combination of exams, continuous assessment and peer- and self-assessment.

How to Apply: Through UCAS if you are applying to more than one institution; direct to the Admissions Officer if you are applying only to Stockton, or if you wish to study part-time.

It is Stockton's policy to consider all applications individually. Relevant experience and prior learning will be considered, but the College is primarily looking for enthusiastic, motivated students of all ages. The prospectus says, 'Everything you tell us will be of interest and helpful to the selectors.'

University of Strathclyde
Glasgow G1 1XQ

Tel: 041–553 4170/1/2/3 **Fax:** 041–552 0775
Contact: Appropriate Section of Registry

Please see page 2 for general information about Scottish universities and colleges

Number of Undergraduates: About 11,500
Percentage of Mature Students: 20%
Male/Female Ratio: About 7 : 5
Upper Age Limit for Mature Students: None

Learning Facilities: The main library, the Andersonian, is vast and provides 1440 study places. Its stock, added to that of the Jordanhill library and three smaller specialist libraries, totals well over half a million books and subscriptions to 4600 periodicals. Computing and information facilities across the campus provide 465 microcomputers and 125 graphics work stations. There is comprehensive audio-visual back-up for all courses, and labs and technical facilities where appropriate.

Creche Facilities: For children aged three to five, open from 9 a.m. till 4 p.m. only.

Mature Students Adviser: Yes, contact the Adult Information Service. There is also a Mature Students' Society, the largest in Scotland.

Accommodation: In allocating places, priority is given to students who are new to Glasgow. Over 1700 students live on campus in a self-catering student village, and the University has two other residences, one of them catering, and student flats. There are a number of flats suitable for couples and families, but some are 14 miles from the campus and there is a waiting list. The

Accommodation Office will try to help, but you are strongly advised not to bring your family to Glasgow until you are sure you have somewhere suitable to live.

Most of Strathclyde University is on one campus in the centre of Glasgow; a recent merger with the Jordanhill College of Education brought it a second site with its own facilities, a few miles away to the west. Strathclyde became a university in the 1960s, but its origins date back to the Industrial Revolution and allow it to claim David Livingstone and John Logie Baird as former students.

Founded with the aim of providing 'useful learning' to a broader range of students than were catered for by existing universities, Strathclyde has retained this tradition and the merger with Jordanhill (training students for community and social work as well as for teaching) will help carry it on.

Degrees Available: BA in Arts and Business subjects; BEd in Primary Education or Technological Education; BSc in Architecture, Business, Science or Technology subjects, and in Speech Pathology of Prosthetics and Orthotics; LLB (European) or LLB based on Scots law; BEng.

The range of scientific and engineering subjects is impressive and includes Naval Architecture and Offshore or Small Craft Engineering, Forensic and Analytic Chemistry, Horticulture with Horticultural Management, and Laser Physics and Optoelectronics.

All courses are modular. In Arts and Social Studies there is now a part-time programme which enables you to complete your degree over six years, obtaining Continuing Education Certificates along the way.

A foundation course in Arts and Social Studies, taught one evening a week, is offered to mature students wishing to prepare themselves for a degree course in these areas.

Assessment: Usually a combination of exams and continuous assessment, with the balance varying from course to course. Essays, practicals, reports and project work may all be taken into consideration where applicable. Each module is assessed separately, during and at the end of the semester in which it is taught.

How to Apply: Through UCAS. Strathclyde welcomes mature applicants who do not have traditional qualifications, but you are advised to consult the Adult Information Service before submitting your application, in order to find out whether your qualifications and/or experience are likely to be acceptable.

Suffolk College
Rope Walk, Ipswich IP4 1LT

Tel: 0473 255885 **Fax:** 0473 230054
Contact: Assistant Registrar (Admissions)

Number of Undergraduates: 3127 full-time, many more part-time
on various levels of courses.
Percentage of Mature Students: 22%
Male/Female Ratio: About 1 : 1
Upper Age Limit for Mature Students: None

Learning Facilities: The library has 70,000 books and subscribes to
400 periodicals. There are comprehensive computing facilities
with a total of 264 work stations.

Creche Facilities: Yes, for children up to five years old. Students
with financial difficulties may be entitled to help with the fees.
Mature Students Adviser: Not specifically, but there is a counselling service available to all students.
Accommodation: None available through the College at the
moment. The Accommodation Service will help you find
somewhere suitable to live.

*Suffolk College offers a variety of courses from A levels to degrees, and its
intake of students is correspondingly mixed in terms of both age and
interests.*

*The College is only a few minutes' walk from the centre of Ipswich, the
county town of Suffolk. Ipswich is a thriving port with a rich history and
over 600 listed buildings, many dating from medieval times. Within easy
reach of London and Cambridge, it is also close to 'Constable country', to
Aldeburgh, home of the music festival inaugurated by Benjamin Britten,
and to the East Anglian ports of Felixstowe and Harwich, from which
regular ferries sail to five countries on the Continent.*

Degrees Available: BA in the Schools of Art and Design, Business
Studies and Educational and Administrative Studies; BSc in the
Schools of Nursing, Radiography and Science.
All degree courses are modular and may be followed part-time.
The College also offers a flexible Access course, which may be
taken on site or at one of a number of local adult education
centres.

Assessment: Each unit of the modular courses is assessed
separately. Practical and creative work forms an important part
of many courses.

How to Apply: Through ADAR for Art and Design, otherwise through UCAS for full-time courses. If you wish to study part-time, contact the Assistant Registrar (Admissions) first.

The College's admissions policy is to extend access to any student capable of benefiting from a course. Applications from mature students with non-standard qualifications are welcome. The College is implementing an APEL scheme (see page 12), so relevant experience may be taken into account.

University of Sunderland
Langham Tower, Ryhope Rd, Sunderland SR2 7EE

Tel: 091–515 2000 **Fax:** 091–515 2423
Contact: Admissions Officer

Number of Undergraduates: 12,743
Percentage of Mature Students: About 53%
Male/Female Ratio: About 1 : 1
Upper Age Limit for Mature Students: None

Learning Facilities: The library stock totals over 250,000 items, with subscriptions to 1800 periodicals and 650 study places. The main library is open until 10 p.m. Monday to Thursday, until 9 p.m. on Friday and all day Saturday. The Computing Unit is also open long hours. There are comprehensive audio-visual facilities, a Language Learning Unit including computer-aided learning, and a 'state of the art' Science complex opened in 1993.

Creche Facilities: Available for 90 children – one of the biggest nurseries of any University in the UK.

Mature Students Adviser: Advice and support available through Student Services.

Accommodation: About 70% of first-years can be accommodated, usually in catering or self-catering Halls of Residence. Mature students are not usually allocated places in Halls, but can apply for flats or University-managed houses. A very few flats are available for married students or for single parents.

The University occupies two main sites in the city centre with a major new campus, which will be home to the Schools of Business, Computing and Information Systems, due to open in 1994. Sunderland became a city in 1992 and the University has benefited from its expansion and the foreign investment it has attracted.

As well as having close links with local industry, the University offers better than average opportunities to study overseas, with a broadly based

ERASMUS programme (see page 8) and good contacts with US universities.

A unique claim to fame is Radio Wear – Britain's first campus-based commercial radio station.

Degrees Available: BA or BSc in a wide variety of subjects in Art and Design, Arts, Social Science, Health, Science and Technology.

The University runs a foundation course in Engineering. Foundation courses in Business Computing, Engineering and Science are also available at local colleges – contact the Continuing Education Unit (091–515 2925/6) for details. Successful completion of the foundation courses run in association with the University guarantees an offer of a place on an appropriate course.

Part-time study, including some evening courses, is available on a number of courses.

All degree programmes will be modular by the start of the 1994/5 session.

Assessment: A combination of exams and continuous assessment, including assignments and research projects, with each unit assessed separately during and at the end of the semester in which it is taught.

How to Apply: Through ADAR for Art and Design, otherwise through UCAS for full-time courses; for advice on part-time study, contact the Admissions Tutor of the relevant department.

Mature students are encouraged at Sunderland and do not necessarily require formal qualifications. All suitable candidates are interviewed and such factors as previous experience, voluntary work and evidence of commitment to study are taken into account. The University runs a CATS scheme (see page 12) and credit may also be given for prior experience.

University of Surrey
Guildford GU2 5XH

Tel: 0483 300800 (see prospectus for direct lines to individual departments) **Fax:** 0483 300803
Contact: Undergraduate Admissions Officer

Number of Undergraduates: 4000+
Percentage of Mature Students: About 20%

Male/Female Ratio: About 5 : 4
Upper Age Limit for Mature Students: None

Learning Facilities: The library has over 300,000 books and subscribes to 2200 periodicals. Nearly all courses involve computers to some extent and comprehensive campus-wide facilities are available. There is also a well-equipped Language Centre and excellent laboratories for all relevant courses.

Creche Facilities: For children aged three to five, with a half-term play group for older children.

Mature Students Adviser: The University Welfare Officer will try to help with any problems, and there is a Mature Students' Society.

Accommodation: Self-catering University accommodation, either on campus or at Hazel Farm, three miles away, is guaranteed to all first-year students. There are no special provisions for couples or families, but the Accommodation Office will try to help all students find somewhere suitable to live.

The University of Surrey was established in 1966 and was soon at the forefront of technological education and of training which included professional skills. Nowadays, the Faculty of Human Studies (Arts and Social Sciences) is the largest in the University and continues to expand.

The University is ten minutes' walk from the centre of Guildford, the county town of Surrey. In many ways a traditional market town with a cobbled high street, Guildford also offers a wide range of leisure and cultural facilities, notably the Yvonne Arnaud Theatre where many top-class plays run before they transfer to the West End. Fast trains will take you to London in just over half an hour, while gentle Surrey countryside, including the Royal Horitcultural Society's headquarters at Wisley and the lovely Winkworth Arboretum, is on the doorstep.

Degrees Available: BA in Dance in Society (four or five years); BMus; BSc in Science or Social Science subjects, with a number of courses including a foreign language study; BEng in a wide range of specialisms including Chemical and Bioprocess Engineering, Environmental Chemical Engineering and Information Systems Engineering.
Many degrees take four years to complete and include a sandwich year and/or a period of study abroad. Foundation studies are available in Science and Engineering.

Assessment: The University is in the throes of converting to a modular, semester-based system with each unit of a course assessed separately. Assessment is by a combination of exams and course work; most courses include a final-year research project or dissertation.

How to Apply: Through UCAS. The University is committed to the concept of widening access to Higher Education and runs a number of Access courses in association with Guildford College of Further and Higher Education. A wide range of qualifications may be deemed to satisfy the entry requirements – you are welcome to contact the Undergraduate Admissions Office to discuss your individual circumstances before submitting a formal application. The introduction of a CATS scheme (see page 12) is under discussion.

University of Sussex

Sussex House, Falmer, Brighton BN1 9RH

Tel: 0273 678416 **Fax:** 0273 678545
Contact: Undergraduate Admissions Office

Number of Undergraduates: 6277
Percentage of Mature Students: 33%
Male/Female Ratio: 1 : 1
Upper Age Limit for Mature Students: None

Learning Facilities: The library contains over 700,000 volumes and subscribes to 3500 periodicals. There is also a computing centre, language labs and workshops and technical facilities as appropriate to the courses.

Creche Facilities: Yes, with costs graduated according to income. Students pay the lowest rate.

Mature Students Adviser: Yes, in the Undergraduate Admissions Office. The University produces a brochure entitled 'Mature Students: How To Apply' and a video 'Mature Students at Sussex'; it also runs seminars to help prospective mature students in the application process. There is a Mature Students' Society.

Accommodation: A number of self-catering residences both on and off campus. All first-years who accept an offer from the University by October are allocated a place. There are also about a hundred family flats, most of them on campus, but these tend to be small and suitable for a couple with one small child, or to a single parent with one child under ten. The Housing Service produces a useful leaflet and will try to give whatever help and advice students need.

Sussex was the first 'new university' to be founded in the 1960s and prides itself on combining academic challenge with the practical requirements of the modern job market. It has an established record of being receptive to mature students.

The University is on a particularly attractive campus just outside Brighton, close to the sea and to the open spaces of the South Downs.

Degrees Available: BA in a wide range of Arts and Social Science subjects including Geography and Environmental Studies, International Relations, Politics in African and Asian Studies, and Twentieth Century Music Studies; LLB in Law or European Commercial Law, both with a language option; BEng; BSc in a wide range of subjects, including the possibility of combining traditional subjects such as Biology, Chemistry or Maths with European or Japanese Studies.

There are foundation courses in Biological Sciences, Molecular Sciences, Computing Sciences, Physical Sciences and Engineering.

The vast majority of undergraduate courses are full-time, but part-time programmes may be introduced in the near future.

Assessment: A mixture of exams and continuous assessment.

How to Apply: Through UCAS.

Sussex will consider applications from prospective mature students with a wide range of alternative qualifications (BTEC awards, Open University units, professional exams, etc) or none. Credit for prior learning and/or experience is considered on an individual basis. If you are in any doubt about your qualifications, contact the Undergraduate Admissions Office for advice before submitting your application.

Sutton College

Lichfield Rd, Sutton Coldfield, West Midlands B74 2NW

Tel: 021–355 5671 **Fax:** 021–355 0799
Contact: Student Admissions Officer

Number of Undergraduates: 202, out of a total student body of 8842.
Percentage of Mature Students: 53% overall
Male/Female Ratio: About 4 : 5
Upper Age Limit for Mature Students: None

Learning Facilities: The library has 20,000 volumes and the College has computing (including computer-aided engineering) facilities, laboratories, workshops, studios, etc.

Creche Facilities: A playgroup is provided for children aged three to five.

Mature Students Adviser: Not specifically, but every student has a personal tutor and the Student Counselling Service is available to all.

Accommodation: Not available through the College – most students are local, but a list of suitable accommodation is available through student counsellors.

Sutton College is one of the largest Colleges of Further Education in the Midlands, offering A levels, vocational courses such as BTEC and City & Guilds, Access courses and a number of Higher Education programmes. If you are following a full-time Higher Education course you should be eligible for an LEA grant.

The College is in Sutton Coldfield, a pleasant residential area a few miles north of Birmingham and easy to reach from the city centre.

Degrees Available: BA in Three Dimensional Design or Fashion Textiles, validated by De Montfort University.

The College also offers the first (foundation) year of De Montfort's extended BSc course and foundation studies in Engineering, Science and Technology.

Assessment: A combination of exams and practical creative work.

How to Apply: Through ADAR for the BA courses; direct to the College for foundation courses. You should expect to be invited for interview before being offered a place.

University College of Swansea
Singleton Park, Swansea SA2 8PP

Tel: 0792 205678
 0792 295784 (prospectus)
Contact: Central Admissions Office

Number of Undergraduates: About 6000
Percentage of Mature Students: About 17%
Male/Female Ratio: About 1 : 1
Upper Age Limit for Mature Students: None

Learning Facilities: The library, which is open 73 hours a week during term-time, has half a million books and subscribes to 4000 periodicals. There are comprehensive computing facilities, a Media Resources Centre, multi-media language labs and first-class technological facilities for relevant courses. The College also boasts a splendid Arts Centre with a gallery and a theatre-cum-cinema-cum-concert-hall.

Creche Facilities: Run by the Students' Union, with subsidised fees for student parents.

Mature Students Adviser: Not specifically, but the Access Unit will advise on applications and there are counselling and welfare services available to all students.

Accommodation: Six catering Halls of Residence and places for 1700 students in the Student Village and University flats mean that University accommodation is guaranteed to all first-year students who want it, provided they firmly accept an offer of a place at Swansea by 1 September. There is limited accommodation for couples and none for single parents, but the University Accommodation Office will supply a list of suitable accommodation in the private sector.

The University College of Swansea was founded in 1920 and is one of the six colleges which make up the University of Wales. The University buildings occupy a single compact site where students are advised that parking is very limited. The University is close to the seafront, two miles from the centre of Swansea, with the glories of the Gower Peninsula about 15 miles away to the west.

Although studies in the Department of Welsh accommodate both native Welsh- and English-speakers, all other courses are taught through the medium of English.

Swansea is committed to offering access to Higher Education to students with disabilities, and provides facilities for those confined to wheelchairs and support to those with visual or hearing problems or learning difficulties.

Degrees Available: BA in Humanities, including a wide range of European languages (from Catalan to Welsh) which may be taken in conjunction with Business Studies, Computer Studies or Legal Studies; BSc or BSc Econ in the Faculty of Economic and Social Studies; BSc in Business, Management, Maths, Information Technology or Science; BEng; BN; LLB including the option to combine Law with any one of six languages.

In other words, Swansea offers courses in almost every 'usual' subject you can think of, and a few unusual ones too.

Most Engineering, Science, Business, Law and Language courses are four years, including a sandwich element and/or a period of study abroad.

There are foundation years in Science and Engineering for those who do not have Science A levels.

Assessment: Exams are supplemented by projects, essays and dissertations, with satisfactory performance in work placements an integral part of sandwich courses.

How to Apply: Through UCAS. Swansea has a tradition of encouraging mature applicants, and kitemarked Access courses or Open University credits will be deemed to satisfy the entrance requirements. You are welcome to contact the Admissions Officer or the Access Unit in the Department of Continuing Education (which co-ordinates local Access courses) for advice before submitting a formal application.

Swansea Institute of Higher Education
Townhill Rd, Swansea SA2 0UT

Tel: 0792 203482 **Fax:** 0792 208683
Contact: Lesley Gowen, Counsellor

Number of Undergraduates: 3317
Percentage of Mature Students: 84%
Male/Female Ratio: 1 : 1
Upper Age Limit for Mature Students: None

Learning Facilities: The library has 120,000 volumes and over 900 current journals. There is a central Computer Unit and computer facilities in the various faculties.

Creche Facilities: No, but there is some provision via Access funding to help students pay for childcare.

Mature Students Adviser: No, but welfare services are available to all students.

Accommodation: At the moment there are 260 single study-bedrooms on campus, but this is likely to increase by up to 150 in the next two years. About a third of first-year students are allocated places. There are a few flats suitable for couples, but these are normally let to overseas students. Provisions is also being made to accommodate students with a wide range of disabilities in on-campus single study-bedrooms.

The Swansea Institute of Higher Education developed from the Swansea Colleges of Art, Education and Technology, and this background is reflected in the content of its courses and in the fact that it still occupies three main sites slightly north of the city centre.

The city of Swansea has an interesting maritime and industrial history and now boasts a handsomely developed 'dockland'. Within easy reach of excellent walking country, it offers an annual Festival of Music and Arts and first-class rugby and cricket for those who prefer to remain in town.

Degrees Available: BA in the Faculties of Art and Design, Business, Management and Finance, and Tourism, Leisure Management and Health Care; BA/BEd leading to a qualification to teach Business Studies at secondary level or Humanities, Literature and Media Studies or Maths and Science at primary level; BEng in specialisations within the field of Electronic Engineering only; BSc in the Faculties of Art and Design and of Transport, and in Health Care; LLB.
Four-year sandwich courses are available in Business Studies.
There is also a one-year full-time foundation diploma in Art.
Some first degree courses – in Art and Design, Computing, Law (an external degree from the University of London) and Nursing – may be followed part-time.

Assessment: Courses in Art and Design are practical, with the student's creative work playing a major part in assessment. Teaching practice is important in BA/BEd degrees. On other courses, a mixture of exams and continuous assessment is used.

How to Apply: Through ADAR for courses in Art and Design; otherwise through UCAS for full-time study. For part-time courses, contact the Registry for details before making a formal application.
Most courses will consider alternative qualifications and relevant experience; contact the individual Course Director for details. For Art and Design courses you will be expected to produce a portfolio of work.

University of Teesside
Middlesbrough TS1 3BA

Tel: 0642 218121 **Fax:** 0642 342067
Contact: Admissions Officer
Number of Undergraduates: About 4250 full-time, 4250 part-time

Percentage of Mature Students: 45%
Male/Female Ratio: 2 : 1
Upper Age Limit for Mature Students: None specified

Learning Facilities: The library is expanding rapidly and currently holds over 200,000 books, with subscriptions to 1800 periodicals and over 500 study places. Computing facilities have benefited from massive investment in the last few years and the University also has a well-equipped Language Centre and excellent laboratories. Facilities in Civil Engineering and Building, and in Mechanical Engineering are particularly good.

Creche Facilities: For children aged six weeks to five years, open until 6 p.m. Monday to Friday throughout the year.
Mature Students Adviser: The Access Co-Ordinator will advise on applications and professional counsellors may be consulted by all students.
Accommodation: Nearly a thousand places are available in University residences, either Halls, flatlets or purpose-built houses and flats. Priority is given to first-years and overseas students. There are no special provisions for couples or families, but the Accommodation Office will help all students find somewhere suitable to live.

Most of the University of Teesside occupies a single campus near the centre of Middlesbrough. The majority of undergraduates will be based here: part of the Business School is based at Flatts Lane, about five miles out of town, but mainly post-graduate, professional and short courses are taught there.

Middlesbrough and Teesside, undergoing a resurgence thanks to the efforts of the Teesside Development Council, offer excellent opportunities for students to experience the workings of local industries (many of them huge international concerns with household names). Middlesbrough offers good sporting, leisure and cultural facilities for a medium-sized town, with the big-city attractions of Newcastle and the freedom of the North York Moors within easy reach.

Degrees Available: BA in Graphic, Industrial or Interior Design, or in Design Marketing, History of Design, Architecture and the Built Environment or Journalism; BSc in International Business Information Technology, Manufacturing Systems with Business, Media Technology, Physiotherapy or Radiography; BEng in Civil or Chemical Engineering or Instrumentation and Control Engineering; BA, BSc or BEng in a modular scheme in the Schools of Human Studies, Business, Computing and Mathematics or Science and Technology; LLB.

Interesting subjects available within the modular scheme include Applied Science and Forensic Measurement, Food Technology and Nutrition, and Criminology.

Many courses include a year's sandwich placement.

There are foundation studies in Engineering and Science. The University works in conjunction with a number of Associated Colleges, so some teaching, particularly in the first year of study, may be done at local Colleges of Further Education. Most courses are now modular and an increasing number may be followed part-time. A part-time prospectus is available from the Admissions Office.

In conjunction with the University of Durham, Teesside also awards degrees through the University College of Stockton-on-Tees (see separate entry page 336).

Assessment: Each unit of modular courses is assessed separately, during and at the end of the semester in which it is taught. A number of courses have no formal exams and all place strong emphasis on course work – assignments, essays, practical work and projects.

How to Apply: Through ADAR for practical Design courses (you will be asked to submit a portfolio); through UCAS for History of Design, Architecture and the Built Environment and for all other full-time courses.

Teesside actively encourages mature students, operates a CATS scheme and a system for APEL (see page 12) and will welcome applications from those on Access courses or with relevant experience. Contact the individual Course Tutor for guidance on whether or not your qualifications are suitable.

Thames Valley University
St Mary's Rd, Ealing, London W5 5RF

Tel: 081–579 5000 **Fax:** 081–566 1353

Wellington St, Slough SL1 1YG
Tel: 0753 697513 **Fax:** 0753 574264
Contact: Information Centre on the relevant campus

Number of Undergraduates: About 7400 full-time, over 10,000 part-time
Percentage of Mature Students: 40%
Male/Female Ratio: 3 : 4

Upper Age Limit for Mature Students: None

Learning Facilities: Libraries on both main campuses are open six days a week and provide all the necessary materials for TVU students, including books, periodicals, videos, slides and databases. A new Learning Resources Centre at Ealing provides comprehensive computing and audio-visual technology and is open for private study seven days a week during term-time. There are language labs on both Ealing and Slough campuses.

Creche Facilities: A Holiday Club at Ealing at half-term only, for children aged four to twelve. Student Administrative Services have a system of childcare vouchers to help student parents pay nursery fees elsewhere.

Mature Students Adviser: No, but the full range of welfare services is available to all students.

Accommodation: University accommodation is limited. The Ealing campus has an Accommodation Team who will help you find somewhere suitable to live; Student Services at Slough provide a list of addresses. In both areas reasonably priced private rented accommodation is readily available.

Thames Valley University came into being through the merger of four colleges – Thames Valley College, Ealing College London, the London College of Music and Queen Charlotte's College of Health Care – to form the most important source of Higher Education in West London. The two main campuses are about 15 miles apart, linked by British Rail services and the University's free minibus. Central London is half an hour away, and Heathrow even closer.

TVU has pioneered a number of degree courses which respond to the needs of the modern workplace. It has particular expertise in Accountancy, but is continually developing new programmes across all its subject areas. Facilities for the disabled are good and the University is committed to improving them.

Degrees Available: At Ealing: BA in a wide range of Arts and Social Science subjects; BMus; BSc in Health Psychology, Information Management and Psychology in the Community; LLB with the option to include French, German or Spanish law and language.
At Slough: BA in Accounting and Finance; BSc in a limited number of subjects in Business, Technology and Information; LLB in Business Law.
The first year of the BA in Accounting Studies and the LLB in Law may be taken at the Kensington Business School, London SW6, on a franchise basis.

All courses are part of a modular degree scheme and there are wide opportunities for part-time study.

The University offers a foundation year in Accountancy and runs a number of Access courses aimed at mature people wishing to enter Higher Education.

Assessment: Varies from course to course, but almost all include a mix of exams and continous assessment. Some courses have no written exams at all, others include 'seen' exams where you are given the paper in advance. Depending on the subject, assignments, projects, seminar papers, practical work, case studies, essays and dissertations may all be taken into account.

How to Apply: Through UCAS for full-time degree courses, direct to the University for Access and foundation courses or for part-time study. If you live locally and are applying only to TVU, you may also apply direct rather than through UCAS. Application forms are available from the relevant School or from the Information Centres on each campus.

TVU welcomes mature applicants, accepts a wide range of qualifications as satisfying the entry requirements and has an APEL scheme (see page 12) which allows credit to be given for prior learning and/or experience.

Trinity and All Saints
Brownberrie Lane, Horsforth, Leeds LS18 5HD

Tel: 0532 837100 **Fax:** 0532 837200
Contact: Admissions Officer

Number of Undergraduates: 1650
Percentage of Mature Students: 16%
Male/Female Ratio: 1 : 2
Upper Age Limit for Mature Students: None

Learning Facilities: The library has 100,000 volumes and there are computer facilities in the ratio of one work station per nine students. Students also have access to the library at the University of Leeds.

Creche Facilities: Limited, so apply early.
Mature Students Adviser: Not specifically, but there is a wide support system within the College.
Accommodation: Halls of Residence can accommodate most first-years who request a place (about 75%). There is no special

provision for couples or families, but the Students' Union Accommodation Service will help as much as possible.

Trinity and All Saints is a College of the University of Leeds, which awards its degrees, but it retains its independent status. It is situated on the edge of the Yorkshire Dales, about six miles from the centre of Leeds. Large enough to offer a range of courses and facilities, it is still small enough for students to benefit from more individual attention than is always possible elsewhere.

As a Catholic institution it is committed to providing Higher Education for Catholics, and in particular to educating teachers for Catholic schools; it nevertheless welcomes applications from all students who are in sympathy with Christian ideals.

Degrees Available: BA or BSc incorporating a qualification to teach at nursery, primary or secondary level (four years); BA or BSc in Management or Public Media, studied in combination with a small range of Arts and Social Science subjects.
All degree courses are professionally oriented and involve appropriate work experience. From 1994 all courses will be modular, which gives programmes more flexibility and may allow for part-time study in the future.

Assessment: Each unit is assessed separately, usually at the end of the semester in which it is taught. Satisfactory performance on professional attachments is an integral part of all degrees.

How to Apply: Through UCAS.
The College welcomes applications from mature students with non-traditional qualifications and will consider each one on its merits. You are invited to contact the College direct to discuss your individual situation before submitting a formal application. Approach the Admissions Officer (telephone 0532 837123) in the first instance.

———— ————

Trinity College Bristol
Stoke Hill, Bristol BS9 1JP

Tel: 0272 682803 **Fax:** 0272 687470
Contact: Admissions Registrar

Number of Undergraduates: 130
Percentage of Mature Students: About 95%
Male/Female Ratio: Not specified

Upper Age Limit for Mature Students: None specified

Learning Facilities: Trinity has one of the largest theological libraries in the country, with over 50,000 books, a range of pamphlets, audio-visual materials and information services, and subscriptions to 150 periodicals.

Creche Facilities: Yes, and families are encouraged to be part of the College community.

Mature Students Adviser: No, because so many students are mature, but the community life offers support to all who are part of it.

Accommodation: Available for unmarried students in single study-bedrooms at the College and for married students and families in groups of housing units nearby.

Trinity aims to be a caring and stimulating Christian community equipping students and their families for Christian ministry and mission. Worship is an integral part of community life and all members of Trinity are committed Christians. The College courses promote the ability to think maturely and intelligently from a solid theological foundation, while providing flexible and practical pastoral training.

Trinity is housed in a splendid 18th-century mansion on the northern fringes of Bristol. The degree course attracts a mandatory LEA grant, but Trinity does not receive government support, so the grant is unlikely to cover the full cost of the fees. The annual tuition fee for 1993/4 was £3907, and you would probably have had to find over £3000 of that yourself.

Degrees Available: BA in Theological Studies, validated by the University of Bristol. This is a modular course allowing for part-time study.

Assessment: A combination of exams and continuous assessment, including essays, book reviews and targeted communication exercises. Each module is assessed separately, during and at the end of the semester in which it is taught. Placements with a local church and in the community are an integral part of the course.

How to Apply: Direct on a form available from the Admissions Registrar. You have to give the name of two or three referees, one of whom must be the minister of your home church. Mature students who do not meet the standard entry requirements will be considered on the basis of interview and life experience.

Trinity College Carmarthen
Carmarthen SA31 3EP

Tel: 0267 237971/2/3
Contact: Mrs R.M. Williams, Registrar

Number of Undergraduates: 1409
Percentage of Mature Students: About 15%
Male/Female Ratio: 1 : 3
Upper Age Limit for Mature Students: None

Learning Facilities: A new library is currently being built, with phase one completed. The existing collection is about 100,000 books. There are computing facilities, laboratories, workshops, gymnasia, a one-way window classroom in the Education Department, theatre studios and music practice rooms.

Creche Facilities: Arranged by the Students' Union during half-term only.

Mature Students Adviser: Not specifically, but the College has excellent advisers for students of all ages.

Accommodation: First, third and fourth year students are offered College accommodation on a first come, first served basis.

Trinity College Carmarthen was founded in 1848 and its attractive Victorian architecture is now supplemented by modern hostels and teaching accommodation. Carmarthen itself is close to the beautiful coastline of the Gower Peninsula, and the area is full of fascinating old buildings and ruined castles.

Trinity is proud of its Christian heritage and of the Christian values which are an integral part of College life. It is a bilingual College, with the prospectus and official notices, etc printed in both Welsh and English. Degrees are validated by the University of Wales.

Degrees Available: BA in Christian Studies, Humanities, English and Theatre and Media Studies; BSc in Rural Environment only; BEd leading to a qualification to teach at primary level in a range of subjects, and at secondary level in Welsh plus one other subject only. This last course is taught only in Welsh, and the course in Humanities is available through the medium of English or Welsh.

Assessment: Teaching practice is important in the Education degrees, as are field work, practical and creative work in such subjects as Art, History and Rural Environment.

How to Apply: Through UCAS. Mature applicants are not required to have traditional qualifications, although five GCSEs or equivalent, including English Language and Maths, are expected for initial teacher training courses. Credit for prior learning or experience may be given – each case is considered individually.

Trinity College of Music
11–13 Mandeville Place, London W1M 6AQ

Tel: 071–935 5773 **Fax:** 071–224 6278
Contact: Registrar

Number of Undergraduates: About 100
Percentage of Mature Students: Not specified
Male/Female Ratio: About 1 : 2
Upper Age Limit for Mature Students: Not specified

Learning Facilities: The library, which is open 9.30–5.30 Monday to Friday, has a fine specialist collection, including much recorded material. There are high quality listening facilities, a recording studio equipped to professional standard, an electronic music studio, a keyboard laboratory and facilities for students to learn about computerised music-making.

Creche Facilities: No
Mature Students Adviser: No, but members of teaching and non-teaching staff can offer any help that may be required.
Accommodation: None run by the College, but the Registrar can give details about Henry Wood House, a hostel for music students in South London, and about other hostels and rented accommodation.

Trinity is a small and friendly College with the enviable record that three-quarters of its graduates find employment in the music profession. Founded in 1872, it has long been established as one of the finest conservatoires in the UK.

Orchestras, choirs and smaller groups specialising in everything from baroque music to jazz rehearse and perform regularly, giving all students the opportunity to hone their skills in public. The expertise of the resident staff is supplemented by master classes and workshops given by distinguished practising musicians.

The College is in a pleasant part of Central London, close to Oxford St and Regent's Park.

Degrees Available: BMus awarded by the University of London, or BMus Music Plus, a four-year degree awarded by the

University of Westminster. Both pathways demand a very high standard of performance, but the University of London course is geared to those who want to undertake a considerable amount of academic study, while the Westminster course concentrates more on performance, for those who wish to become professional musicians.

Assessment: Exams and performance (or submission of compositions or dissertation if appropriate).

How to Apply: Direct, on an application form available from the Academic Registrar and enclosing the audition fee (currently £30). You have to pass part of the form to your referee, who should return it direct to the College. Entry auditions are held in December and February for courses starting the following September, and applications should be received by early October and early February respectively. If you apply according to the latter timetable, you run the risk that the course will already be full.

The prospectus sets out what is required of you at the audition – there will be a short oral and written exam as well as performance of two contrasting pieces.

University of Ulster
Coleraine, Co. Londonderry BT52 1SA

Tel: 0265 44141 x 4221 **Fax:** 0265 40908
Contact: Registry Office

Number of Undergraduates: 10,615 full-time, about 5500 part-time
Percentage of Mature Students: 23%
Male/Female Ratio: About 4 : 5
Upper Age Limit for Mature Students: None

Learning Facilities: The library has 650,000 books and 1635 study places. There are computing facilities on all campuses, and modern, purpose-built labs, workshops, etc support relevant courses.

Creche Facilities: Three of the four campuses (not Belfast) run creches and playgroups for children aged from four to six weeks to five years. Places are limited, so apply as early as possible.

Phone the above number, extension 4240 for details on the Coleraine campus, 0232 365433 x 2539 for Jordanstown and 0504 265621 x 5218 or 0504 371527 for Magee College.

Mature Students Adviser: No, but the Department of Adult and Continuing Education will advise on applications and qualifications, and help is available to all through Student Services.

Accommodation: There is University-run accommodation on all four campuses, including self-catering Halls of Residence and shared houses and flats. About a quarter of first-year students are accommodated. A few flats are suitable for couples without children. There are a number of suites at Coleraine and Jordanstown that have been specially adapted to suit the needs of wheelchair users. Accommodation is generally cheaper than at many other universities.

The University of Ulster is based on four campuses: at Coleraine, Jordanstown, Belfast and Magee College, Londonderry. Coleraine – close to the magnificent Giant's Causeway – houses the administrative buildings, the Faculties of Education and Humanities, and part of Science and Technology; Jordanstown most of the Science and Technology and Social and Health Sciences departments; Belfast most of the Faculty of Art and Design; Magee College Informatics. Business and Management courses are taught on all four campuses, though the Faculty is based at Jordanstown.

Degrees Available: BA in the Faculties of Art and Design, Business and Management, Education or Humanities – in Education courses last four years if they include either a primary teaching qualification or a sandwich element leading to a Diploma in Industrial Studies; BMus; BEng in the Faculties of Informatics and of Science and Technology – all courses are four-year 'sandwiches'; BSc in the Faculties of Informatics, Science and Technology or Social or Health Sciences – many courses are four years and include a sandwich element; BTech – a four-year sandwich course in Civil Engineering.

There is also a one-year foundation certificate in Art and Design. Foundation courses in Natural Sciences are based at local colleges.

All undergraduate courses are now modular, which allows for part-time study.

Assessment: Each module is assessed separately, at the end of the year or semester in which it is taught. Many courses are largely practical: creative work and performance during industrial placements form an integral part of the degree. Many also require you to produce a dissertation or major project in the final year.

How to Apply: Through ADAR for Art and Design; otherwise through UCAS.

The University has a sympathetic attitude to mature applicants without a traditional academic background, and a wide range of alternative qualifications and experience may be acceptable. The University runs a CATS scheme (see page 12), so credit may be given for prior learning. Applications are considered on their individual merits, the main criterion being that you have a realistic chance of being able to complete the course. You may be asked to take a test to enable the University to assess whether you will be able to cope with the work expected of you.

University of Manchester Institute of Science and Technology (UMIST)
Manchester M60 1QD

Tel: 061–236 3311 **Fax:** 061–228 7040
Contact: Departmental Admissions Tutor

Number of Undergraduates: About 4000, with about 1500 post-graduates
Percentage of Mature Students: About 10%
Male/Female Ratio: About 7 : 3. UMIST is keen to encourage more applications from women
Upper Age Limit for Mature Students: None specified

Learning Facilities: The Joule Library holds 230,000 books and subscribes to 1500 periodicals, providing in-depth coverage of the subjects taught at UMIST. Students may also borrow from the University of Manchester library and use the libraries of Manchester Metropolitan and Salford for reference. There are comprehensive computing facilities with 275 PCs publicly available, and some of the best laboratories and technical resources in the country – the Centre for Electronic Materials and the Manchester Biotechnology Centre have both been declared Centres of Excellence.

Creche Facilities: Yes – contact the Registrar's Department for details.

Mature Students Adviser: Not specifically, but all students have a personal tutor and a full range of counselling and welfare services is available through the Students' Union.

Accommodation: Plentiful: UMIST has Halls of Residence of its own and shares facilities with the University of Manchester. All unmarried first-years who apply by 31 August are guaranteed a place in University-owned accommodation, which includes catering and self-catering Halls and shared flats and houses. There are some flats suitable for married couples – apply to the Accommodation Office, Precinct Centre, Oxford Rd, Manchester M13 9RS for more information.

Strangely for a University devoted to Science and Technology, UMIST's main building is Edwardian art nouveau. The rest of the campus makes up for this aberration, with modern buildings and hi-tech facilities on which millions of pounds have been spent in recent years. Courses are constantly being updated and benefit from the input of the major international research programmes which are carried out at UMIST.

Manchester, with its vast student population (see entries for the University of Manchester, Manchester Metropolitan and the two Salford Universities, pages 234, 236, 314 and 315), is a great place to be a student and UMIST, with its long-established reputation in its specialist fields, is a very prestigious place to study: a recent survey ranked UMIST graduates as the most popular choice for employers in a number of subjects.

The campus is compact and close to the city centre. UMIST has its own Students' Union, but also shares facilities with the University of Manchester.

Degrees Available: BSc or BEng in a range of subjects in Business, Engineering, Science and Technology. Many include a year in industry or a language study with a period spent abroad.
All the Science and Engineering subjects you would expect are offered, plus such unusual specialisms as Clothing Engineering and Management, Paper Science and Textile Design, Science or Technology.

Assessment: The emphasis is on exams, but course work such as lab reports and essays is also assessed and most courses include a major final-year project.

How to Apply: Through UCAS. Mature applicants who are taking or have successfully completed an approved Access course are very welcome. You are invited to contact the Admissions Tutor of the course you wish to follow for informal advice before completing your application form.

———— ❀ ————

United Medical and Dental Schools of Guy's and St Thomas's Hospitals

(UMDS – University of London)
Lambeth Palace Rd, London SE1 7EH

Tel: 071–922 8013
Contact: Admissions Officer

Number of Undergraduates: 1600
Percentage of Mature Students: About 8%
Male/Female Ratio: 3 : 2
Upper Age Limit for Mature Students: None specified, but see general note on page 17

Learning Facilities: There are extensive library and audio-visual resources on each site, with excellent technical and clinical facilities. Both hospitals also have large museums of pathological material.

Creche Facilities: No
Mature Students Adviser: Not specifically, but all students have a personal tutor and the full range of welfare services is available.
Accommodation: 435 students can be accommodated through the School and all first-years are guaranteed a place. Students are also eligible to apply for to the University of London's Intercollegiate Halls. Contact the University of London Accommodation Office, Senate House, Malet St, London WC1E 7HU for details. Applications must be received by 31 May, so do not wait until you have exam results or a firm offer of a place. The Accommodation Office can also provide details of accommodation suitable for couples and families. Again, apply early.

These two historic medical schools have officially been united since 1982, but have links going back to the 18th century, when Guy's School was founded. (St Thomas's is rather older, dating to the 12th century).

Both sites – Guys at its ancient site near London Bridge, St Thomas's at its modern one opposite the Houses of Parliament – enjoy excellent facilities and medical students should expect to spend time at both. Dentistry is taught mainly at Guys.

Degrees Available: MB, BS; BDS. There is also a one-year intercalated BSc degree which students may take between the preclinical and clinical parts of their course.

Assessment: Written and clinical exams.

How to Apply: Through UCAS. While applications from prospective mature students are welcome and considered on their individual merits, you are warned that competition is severe and you are unlikely to be offered a place if you do not have good Science A levels or equivalent.

University College London
(UCL – University of London)
Gower St, London WC1E 3BT

Tel: 071–387 7050 **Fax:** 071–380 7380
Contact: Registrar
Number of Undergraduates: About 11,000
Percentage of Mature Students: 23%
Male/Female Ratio: About 5 : 4
Upper Age Limit for Mature Students: None

Learning Facilities: The College has a total of ten libraries, with one and a quarter million volumes and specialist collections built up over 150 years. There are comprehensive computing facilities, a Language Centre with up-to-date audio and video equipment, open to all students and excellent laboratory and technical facilities for relevant subjects.

Creche Facilities: A day nursery for children up to five years old, open all year round. Student parents with financial difficulties can apply for help with the fees.

Mature Students Adviser: Not specifically, but each student has an academic adviser, and the Dean of Students and the Union Welfare Office can help with personal and financial matters.

Accommodation: College accommodation can house about 3000 students, and a place is guaranteed for all first-years who have accepted an offer from UCL and applied for accommodation by 31 May. Some accommodation is self-catering, some provides meals. A few College flats are reserved for married students.

UCL is the largest and oldest College of the University of London – indeed, apart from Oxford and Cambridge, it is the oldest University College in England. It is rightly proud of its academic reputation and the standard of research and teaching staff in all seven faculties. Because the researchers and the teaching staff are one and the same, the content of courses is absolutely up-to-date. Yet despite its size it aims to give students individual attention, with regular tutorials for groups of as few as four.

UCL's Department of Fine Art is the famous Slade School, which has a worldwide reputation in painting, sculpture and related disciplines.

See also separate entries for the Institute of Archaeology (page 68) and the National Hospital's College of Speech Sciences (page 245).

Degrees Available: BA in a range of Arts subjects and in Law; BSc in the Faculties of the Built Environment, Life Sciences (including four-year courses with State Registration in Physio-therapy and Podiatry), and Mathematical and Physical Sciences; BSc (Econ); BEng, including some four-year sandwich courses; MB BS; LLB.

There is also an intercalated one-year BSc degree which students of Medicine may take between the preclinical and clinical parts of their course.

Some of the less usual subjects available at UCL are Dutch, Scandinavian Studies, History of the Americas, Jewish History, Naval Architecture and Ocean Engineering, Crystallography and Mineral Sciences and Planetary Science.

Part-time study is possible on the modular courses (see below), with students taking up to six years to complete a degree.

Assessment: A combination of exams and continuous assessment of practical work, field work, essays, dissertations or projects as appropriate. Courses in the Faculties of Science and Engineer-ing, and in most Arts subjects, are divided into units, each of which is assessed individually.

How to Apply: Through UCAS. UCL welcomes applications from people who do not have a standard educational background. Before submitting a formal application you are encouraged to write to the relevant Faculty Tutor detailing your experience and qualifications and the course you would like to follow: the tutor will be able to give any advice you might require.

University of Wales

The University of Wales, with its six constituent colleges, is the second largest university in the UK – only the University of London has more students. It is an academic and administrative body: it sets general entrance requirements, validates courses and awards degrees but – given the geographical spread of the colleges – it cannot provide central facilities in the way that the University of London does.

The six colleges, which all have separate entries in this book, are the University Colleges of Aberystwyth, Bangor, Cardiff, St David's Lampeter and Swansea, and the University of Wales College of Medicine in Cardiff. In addition, the University validates the degrees of most other Colleges of Higher Education in Wales.

University of Wales College of Medicine
Heath Park, Cardiff CF4 4XN

Tel: 0222 747747 **Fax:** 0222 742914
Contact: Dr C.B. Turner, Deputy Secretary

Number of Undergraduates: 1605
Percentage of Mature Students: 9%
Male/Female Ratio: 1 : 2
Upper Age Limit for Mature Students: None specified

Learning Facilities: The library has 100,000 volumes and sub-scribes to over a thousand current journals. There are excellent computing facilities and databases covering Medicine, Dentistry and Nursing.

Creche Facilities: Yes, for children aged two to five only.
Mature Students Adviser: Not specifically, but two student counsellors are available to advise all undergraduates.
Accommodation: All first-year students are allocated places in self-catering Halls of Residence run by the University of Wales College of Cardiff. There are some self-contained flatlets for married students.

The College occupies an attractive site in the centre of Cardiff, though it is also possible to study for the Nursing degree in Wrexham.
Students of the College of Medicine join the same Students' Club as those at the University of Wales College of Cardiff, sharing sports and social facilities and mixing with students from all disciplines.

Degrees Available: BDS; BN; MB BCh.
Most students with standard qualifications for Dentistry and Medicine enter the course in the second year; the first year is regarded as a Medical Science Foundation Course for those who do not meet the course entry requirements.

Assessment: Through written and clinical exams.

How to Apply: Through UCAS. For Medicine and Dentistry you are required to meet the standard entry requirements. Mature applicants for Nursing will be considered on an individual basis, but you will be expected to show motivation and evidence of recent relevant study or experience.

Warrington Collegiate Institute
Padgate Campus, Fearnhead, Warrington WA2 0DB

Tel: 0925 814343 **Fax:** 0925 816077
Contact: Central Admissions Office

Number of Undergraduates: A total of 15,000 full- and part-time students on courses at various levels
Percentage of Mature Students: 30%
Male/Female Ratio: About 1 : 1
Upper Age Limit for Mature Students: None specified

Learning Facilities: The library has over 80,000 books, and there are computing facilities, sound, television and photographic studios, a campus theatre, laboratories, gymnasium and outdoor study areas for Sports Science and Environmental Science.

Creche Facilities: Yes
Mature Students Adviser: No, but all students have a personal tutor and the Institute has a team of qualified counsellors.
Accommodation: Available in on-campus Halls of Residence for all first-year and most third-year students who do not live within reasonable commuting distance. No special provisions for couples or families.

The Institute has recently undergone some major restructuring, arranging its courses into faculties and the College of Business Management. With the new image has come a change of name – until recently it was the North Cheshire College. Degrees are awarded by the University of Manchester.

The main Padgate campus is outside Warrington, on an attractively landscaped site. Warrington is a growing industrial town, within easy reach of Manchester and Liverpool.

Degrees Available: BA in Building Maintenance, Environmental Science, Leisure, Media Studies, Performing Arts or Sports Studies, all with Business Management; also BA in Combined

Studies for mature students (students choose modules from the various subject areas, designing their own programme).

Assessment: Courses are modular and each unit is assessed separately. There is an approximately 50 : 50 balance between course work and exams.

How to Apply: Through UCAS, but you are advised to contact the Academic Registrar as early as possible to discuss your circumstances and possibly arrange an informal interview before you submit your application. Mature students without traditional qualifications are welcome, particularly those following a recognised Access course and/or with experience relevant to their proposed course of study.

University of Warwick
Coventry CV4 7AL

Tel: 0203 523523
0203 523723 (Undergraduate Admissions)
Contact: Undergraduate Admissions Office

Number of Undergraduates: 7431
Percentage of Mature Students: about 19%
Male/Female Ratio: 1 : 1
Upper Age Limit for Mature Students: None

Learning Facilities: The library has 750,000 books and subscribes to 5000 periodicals; it is open every day for a total of 75 hours a week during term-time. There is a Computing Services Centre providing computer resources throughout the University and a well-equipped Language Centre offering opportunities to learn a wide range of languages. Labs and technical facilities for scientific subjects are modern and well-equipped.

Creche Facilities: Available for children aged one to five years. The fees are higher than average, but a discretionary hardship fund is available to help student parents.

Mature Students Adviser: Not specifically, but the Senior Tutor's Office and the Careers Advisory Service are available to help mature students. There is also a Mature Students' Society.

Accommodation: A number of self-catering Halls of Residence and campus flats can accommodate half the student population, including all first-years who accept an offer of a place and apply for accommodation by the end of August. There are a number of rooms and a very few flats suitable for married students: in several of the Halls these are reserved for couples who are both enrolled at the University.

Warwick is a self-contained campus university about four miles from the centre of Coventry. Right in the centre of England, it is very easy to get to and offers the local attractions of Stratford-on-Avon, Warwick and Kenilworth castles, the spa town of Leamington and the famous Midlands canal network for quiet walks.

A young and modern university, founded in 1965, Warwick nevertheless has a very high academic reputation and a recent poll placed the quality of its research in the top six in the UK.

Degrees Available: BA in a range of Arts and Social Studies subjects; BA with Qualified Teacher Status – a four-year course leading to a qualification to teach at primary or secondary level; BEng; BSc in the Faculty of Science and in business-oriented subjects in the Faculty of Social Studies; LLB, including a four-year course in European Law with a year abroad.
Part-time study is possible in a few specially designed Arts and Social Studies programmes.
Degree courses are flexible and allow students to choose combinations of subjects that are not always possible elsewhere.

Assessment: A mixture of exams and continuous assessment. Practical work, field work and projects play an important part in many courses.

How to Apply: Through UCAS. Warwick encourages applications from mature students and will consider a wide range of alternative qualifications. You will normally be expected to show evidence of recent relevant study, but the University is also looking for enthusiasm, motivation and ability.

Welsh Agricultural College
Llanbadarn Fawr, Aberystwyth SY23 3AL

Tel: 0970 624471
Contact: Mrs M.D. Frost, Admissions Assistant

Number of Undergraduates: About 80 in a total student body of 400+
Percentage of Mature Students: 3 : 2
Male/Female Ratio: About 20%

Upper Age Limit for Mature Students: None specified

Learning Facilities: The library has over 45,000 books; there are specialist labs, workshops and technical facilities including college farms.

Creche Facilities: Yes

Mature Students Adviser: No, but counselling and welfare services are available to all students.

Accommodation: All first-years can be accommodated in Halls of Residence. No special provisions for couples or families, but a range of privately rented accommodation is available in the area.

The College was established in 1970 and quickly built up a strong reputation in its specialist field. It shares a campus and Students' Union facilities with the University of Aberystwyth, and provides an attractive and remarkably safe environment for study.

Excellent stables nearby supplement studies in Equine Science and Management, as well as providing the opportunities for those who wish to keep their own horse, or to ride one of those provided.

Degrees Available: BSc in Countryside Management, Agriculture and Equine Science and Management.

Assessment: A mixture of exams and practical/project work.

How to Apply: Through UCAS. Mature applicants without formal qualifications are welcome and successful completion of a recognised Access course may be deemed to satisfy the entry requirements. You are welcome to contact the Admissions Administration Assistant to arrange a preliminary visit before submitting your application.

---- ❈ ----

Welsh College of Music and Drama
Castle Grounds, Cathays Park, Cardiff CF1 3ER

Tel: 0222 342854 **Fax:** 0222 237639
Contact: Director of Drama or of Music

Number of Undergraduates: 390
Percentage of Mature Students: 15%
Male/Female Ratio: About 1 : 3
Upper Age Limit for Mature Students: None

Learning Facilities: The library has about 40,000 items including specialist collections of scores and reference works and an audio-visual collection. There is a theatre, sophisticated music studios and recording facilities. The Music Technology Department is available to help students improve their technical skills; there are computer facilities and a language laboratory for singers.

Creche Facilities: No

Mature Students Adviser: No, but Heads of Courses and Heads of Studies are available to help if required.

Accommodation: None provided by the College, but the Students' Union keeps a list of suitable accommodation.

Situated in a lovely park next to the castle in the centre of Cardiff, this is a small college which is able to give individual attention to its students. Both Schools have distinguished full-time and visiting teaching staff and are concerned to prepare their students for successful careers in their chosen professions. Famous names abound in the College prospectus: the late Sir Geraint Evans was a long-time President of the College; its current Vice-Presidents are Dame Gwyneth Jones and Sir Anthony Hopkins; Kenneth Griffith and Siân Phillips are among its fellows.

Degrees Available: BA in Performing Arts (Music); BA in Theatre Studies with options in Acting, Design or Stage Management; BEd in Drama (four years).
Some courses are available in either English or Welsh.
Degrees are validated by the University of Wales.

Assessment: Courses concentrate on performance and practical skills and are assessed accordingly.

How to Apply: Direct to the College on its application form, available from the above address. For Music these should ideally be submitted by March and certainly by May/June at the latest. For Drama, auditions are held in November and March and applications should be received by 31 October and 31 January respectively. You are recommended to contact the College for an initial, pre-audition discussion.
Prospective Music students should normally have achieved Grade VIII in their principal study; they must also show evidence that they can cope with the rigours of an academic degree. This normally means A levels or equivalent in Music and one other subject, but mature students' applications will be considered on individual background and experience.
Admission to the Acting course is by audition, to the other Theatre Studies courses and the BEd course by interview. A levels or equivalent are normally required, but again mature applicants will be considered on their merits and on their ability to meet the demands of the course.

University of the West of England, Bristol
Frenchay Campus, Coldharbour Lane, Bristol BS16 1QY

Tel: 0272 656261 **Fax:** 0272 763804
Contact: Admissions Officer

Number of Undergraduates: About 6000
Percentage of Mature Students: About 35%
Male/Female Ratio: About 1 : 1
Upper Age Limit for Mature Students: None

Learning Facilities: Main libraries on all four sites provide specialist books, periodicals and audio-visual materials for the courses taught there. There are comprehensive computing facilities (all students have access to the personal computer rooms on Frenchay campus, open 24 hours a day, seven days a week), a well-equipped Language Centre and workshops, studios and technical support in appropriate departments.

Creche Facilities: The Halley Nursery at St Matthias campus is run by the Students' Union, the nursery at Frenchay campus by the Staff Association; both cater for children aged two to five. Half-term play schemes for school-age children operate at Frenchay, St Matthias and Redland campuses. Contact the Childcare Co-Ordinator on the above number for details.

Mature Students Adviser: Not specifically, but there are full counselling services available to all students, and the Centre for Student Affairs runs fortnightly meetings for those wishing to improve their study skills.

Accommodation: There are 900 places in self-catering Halls; about a third of first-year students are allocated one. The Accommodation Office will help other students find suitable accommodation. No special provisions for couples or families.

The University of the West of England occupies four sites within easy reach of each other and of the centre of Bristol. The Faculties of Humanities and of Health and Community Studies are at St Matthias campus, which is housed in a listed seventeenth-century mansion. All the other facilities are purpose-built: Art, Media and Design is at the Bower Ashton campus, Education at the Redland campus and everything else, including administration and the main Students' Union facilities, at the Frenchay campus about four miles north of the city centre.

The University has a particularly thriving Centre for the Performing Arts: students can have individual music lessons, participate in creative writing workshops or contribute to a major musical production.

Degrees Available: BA in the Faculty of Art and Design and in a range of Arts and Social Science subjects; BEd, either two years for those who already have appropriate post-A level experience, or four years (the two-year course is for teaching at secondary level only, the four-year for primary or secondary); BEng; BSc in a range of subjects in the Faculties of Applied Sciences, Built Environment, Computer Studies and Mathematics and Health and Community Studies, including Nursing; LLB.

Among the more unusual subjects on offer are Modern Languages and Information Systems; Science, Society and the Media; Aerospace Manufacturing Engineering; and Valuation and Estate Management. Foundation years are available in Accountancy, Art and Design, Computing, Science and various Engineering specialisms. Some include a sandwich element.

Many part-time courses are available with day and/or evening teaching – contact the Admissions Officer for details.

The first or foundation year of some courses may be taught under a franchise arrangement at Bridgwater College, Chippenham Technical College, City of Bath College, Gloucester College of Arts and Technology, Soundwell College, Avon and Gloucestershire College of Health or Swansea Institue of Higher Education.

Assessment: A combination of exams and continuous assessment, including presentations, projects, dissertations, etc. Satisfactory completion of teaching practice or an industrial placement is an integral part of Education or sandwich courses and in the latter case a written report will count towards your final mark.

Most courses are modular and each unit is assessed separately, during and at the end of the year in which it is taught.

How to Apply: Through ADAR for Art and Design, otherwise through UCAS for full-time study. For part-time study or for the foundation courses, apply direct to the University on a form obtainable from the Admissions Officer.

The University welcomes applications from prospective mature students who can show, normally through evidence of recent study, that they can cope with the demands of the course. A wide range of alternative qualifications, including Access or Open University courses and GNVQs, may be acceptable, and credit may be given for prior learning and/or experience.

West Herts College
Hempstead Rd, Watford WD1 3EZ

Tel: 0923 257565
Contact: Campus Co-Ordinator

Number of Undergraduates: About 100 on degree courses, but a total student body of 35,000, full- and part-time
Percentage of Mature Students: About 10%
Male/Female Ratio: About 10 : 1
Upper Age Limit for Mature Students: None

Learning Facilities: The libraries hold a total of 45,000 books, including a specialist publishing and printing collection. Computing and technical faciities are available to support study and teaching.

Creche Facilities: There is a playgroup for children aged 3-5; the possibility of opening a creche for younger children is under discussion.
Mature Students Adviser: No, but counselling services are available to all students.
Accommodation: None available through the College, but Student Services will help if necessary.

West Herts is a multi-sited college offering a wide range of courses, mainly to locally based students, at every level from GCSE to degree. Degree courses are mostly taught at the main Watford campus.

The College is an Associate College of the University of Hertfordshire, which validates its degrees, and has a long-established reputation in the teaching of practical and vocational courses relating to the printing industry.

Degrees Available: BA in Business Administration, Imagemaking and Design or Media Production Management; BSc in Graphic Media Studies (four-year sandwich).
There are also foundation courses in Art and Design and Computer Techology.

Assessment: Exams and assessment of practical/creative work.

How to Apply: Through ADAR for Imagemaking and Design or Media Production Management; otherwise through UCAS. Successful completion of an approved Access course may be deemed to satisfy the entry requirements; relevant experience will be taken into consideration. For Imagemaking and Design you will be asked to submit a portfolio of work.

West London Institute of Higher Education

Gordon House Campus, 300 St Margarets Rd, Twickenham
TW1 1PT

Tel: 081–891 0121 **Fax:** 081–891 0487

Lancaster House Campus, Borough Rd, Isleworth TW7 5DU
Tel: 081–568 8741 **Fax:** 081–569 9198
Contact: Academic Registry (at Twickenham), which will refer you
to relevant Admissions Tutors

Number of Undergraduates: 3730
Percentage of Mature Students: 75%
Male/Female Ratio: 2 : 3
Upper Age Limit for Mature Students: None

Learning Facilities: There are two campus libraries with a total of
186,000 items and subscriptions to 1100 periodicals. The
Computer Centre provides computer back-up throughout the
Institute; IT and CD-Rom facilities are available for student use.
Relevant subjects have well-equipped labs and workshops.
Creche Facilities: No
Mature Students Adviser: Not specifically, but personal tutors and
qualified counsellors are available to help.
Accommodation: 344 places are available in on-campus residences.
Priority is given to first-year and overseas students and about
30% of first-years can be accommodated. There are no special
provisions for couples or families.

*The Institute is an amalgam of a number of colleges, including the oldest
teacher training school in the Commonwealth, and is best known for its
outstanding record in Physical Education and sporting activities. The
Twickenham campus is beside the River Thames in south-west London,
the Isleworth campus about a mile and a half away. Both are attractive
green sites in pleasant residential areas.*

*Sporting enthusiasts are drawn to the area because of the proximity of
the famous rugby ground, with Wimbledon and Wembley both within
easy reach; Kew Gardens, Hampton Court Palace, Richmond Park and
Osterley Park are all nearby, and central London is twenty minutes away
by train.*

Degrees Available: BA and BSc in an integrated degree scheme:
there are only 13 major subjects, but unusual combinations such
as Geography and Environmental Issues with Leisure Management or Music with Business Studies are available; BEd leading
to a qualification to teach at nursery, primary or secondary level:
Physical Education or Geography and Environmental Issues are

the main subjects studied in the secondary course; BSc in Occupational Therapy or Physiotherapy.

Degrees are validated by the University of Brunel.

The Institute runs a two-year Music Foundation Course and an Associate Student Scheme. Modular degree courses may be followed part-time.

Assessment: Most undergraduate degrees are modular and each unit is assessed separately. Assessment is by exams, continuous assessment, project work and practicals where appropriate.

How to Apply: Normally through UCAS for full-time study, but mature applicants should contact the Academic Registry to discuss their qualifications first. Apply direct to the Academic Registry for part-time study.

A wide range of alternative qualifications may be considered. The Institute runs a CATS and an APEL scheme (see page 12), so prior learning and/or experience may be taken into account. If you do not have formal qualifications you should expect to be invited for a special entry interview.

------ ❊ ------

West Surrey College of Art and Design
Falkner Rd, Farnham, Surrey GU9 7DS

Tel: 0252 732232/237
Contact: Registry

Number of Undergraduates: 1650
Percentage of Mature Students: About 42%
Male/Female Ratio: 47 : 53
Upper Age Limit for Mature Students: None

Learning Facilities: The library has 50,000 books, plus collections of slides, audio-visual material and videotapes. There are sophisticated computer facilities, an IT resource specialising in electronic imaging and computer-aided design, and well-equipped studios and workshops.

Creche Facilities: No
Mature Students Adviser: Not specifically, but the Registry Staff, Careers Officer and Welfare Officer are all available to give advice, depending on the nature of the problem.
Accommodation: The College runs self-catering Halls of Residence and houses and can accommodate about 75% of first-year students. Mature students are given priority in the allocation of flats and single rooms.

The College is part of the Surrey Institute of Art and Design, which validates its degree courses. Teaching is done by qualified academics, with regular visiting staff who are actively engaged in the relevant professions. The College's James Hockey Gallery is one of the largest in the South East and attracts important exhibitions of contemporary art.

The College is close to the centre of Farnham, a historic market town in rural Surrey, easily accessible from London and from Heathrow or Gatwick.

Degrees Available: BA in the Departments of Design and of Fine Art and Audio-Visual Studies. Subjects available include Animation, Twentieth Century Design History, Film and Video, Woven and Printed Textiles, and Three-Dimensional Design.
The College offers BTEC Diplomas in Foundation Studies and in Design, which are considered suitable preparation for the degree courses.
The BA in Fine Art may be followed part-time.

Assessment: Courses are practical, with emphasis on the student's creative work. For some courses you will be required to produce a dissertation in your final year.

How to Apply: Through UCAS or ADAR – see prospectus for details.
The College welcomes applications from mature students who do not have traditional qualifications, but you must be able to provide evidence of ability to follow your chosen course.

West Sussex Institute of Higher Education
The Dome, Upper Bognor Rd, Bognor Regis, West Sussex
PO21 1HR

Tel: 0243 865581 **Fax:** 0243 828351

Bishop Otter College, College Lane, Chichester PO19 4PE
Tel: 0243 878911
Contact: Admissions Office (at Bognor)

Number of Undergraduates: About 1700
Percentage of Mature Students: About 50%
Male/Female Ratio: About 1 : 3
Upper Age Limit for Mature Students: None

Learning Facilities: The libraries hold a total of 170,000 volumes and subscribe to 750 periodicals. During term-time they are open until 9 p.m. Monday to Thursday, and on Saturday mornings. Each site also has a Media Resources Centre and comprehensive computing and IT facilities. Workshops and studios, laboratories and gymnasia support appropriate courses. The Mitre Gallery at Bishop Otter College displays a fine collection of 20th-century art, including works by Henry Moore, Graham Sutherland and David Hockney.

Creche Facilities: At Bognor campus, for children aged nought to five and open from 8 a.m. to 6 p.m. Monday to Friday all year round.

Mature Students Adviser: Not specifically, but all students have a personal tutor and can also seek help and advice from the Co-Ordinator of Student Services.

Accommodation: Catering Halls of Residence on campus can accommodate most first-year students; the Institute also has purpose-built hostels and converted houses. There are no special provisions for couples or families, but the Colleges keep lists of accommodation for rent in the private sector.

West Sussex Institute was created in 1977 from the merger of three older colleges, Bognor Regis College, Bishop Otter College in Chichester, and West Sussex College of Nursing and Midwifery, which is based partly at Bishop Otter and partly in Shoreham. The Institute is now an Accredited College of the University of Southampton, which validates its degrees.

The two main sites are about eight miles apart, with free transport provided between them. Both are in pleasant locations, Bognor in a terrace of 18th-century mansions built for the Prince Regent and his cronies, Bishop Otter in extensive grounds adjacent to Chichester's Festival Theatre. Broadly speaking, Education, Maths, Geography and History are based at Bognor, everything else except Health at Chichester, but this is not a clear-cut distinction and many students will find they spend time at both sites.

Degrees Available: BA in a range of Arts subjects, including Art, Dance, Media Studies, Related Arts or Social Work Studies; BA with QTS for teaching at upper or lower primary level in a choice of nine subjects, or at secondary level in Maths or Physical Education only; BSc in Health Studies or Sports Studies.

Education courses normally last four years, but students with suitable post-A level qualifications or experience may complete the BEd in Secondary Maths in two years. The Institute also offers what is known as the 'Crawley Route' – a BEd with specialisation in English only, leading to a qualification to teach at primary level, and based at Crawley College. This course is aimed at mature students with non-traditional qualifications, who wish to undertake teacher training close to their homes. All courses are modular and all except teacher training may be followed part-time.

Assessment: A combination of exams and continuous assessment, with the balance varying from course to course. Essays, practical work, projects, reports and teaching practice will all be taken into consideration where relevant.

How to Apply: Through ADAR for Art and Related Arts, direct to the Institute for Health Studies or Social Work Studies; otherwise through UCAS for full-time study. For part-time, contact the Admissions Office direct. West Sussex IHE is committed to the concept of wider access to Higher Education, as will be seen from its high percentage of mature students. Those without traditional qualifications but with some evidence of recent study such as an Access course and/or relevant experience are very welcome. The Institute runs a CATS and an APEL scheme (see page 12), so credit can be given for prior learning and/or experience. For details of the Special Entry Procedure, contact the Admissions Office.

If you are applying for an Education course you should expect to be invited for interview before being offered a place.

West Yorkshire College of Health Studies
Lea House, Stanley Royd Hospital, Aberford Rd, Wakefield WF1 4DG

Tel: 0924 201688 x 3712 **Fax:** 0924 200947
Contact: Registry

Number of Undergraduates: About 1300
Percentage of Mature Students: About 33%
Male/Female Ratio: About 1 : 2
Upper Age Limit for Mature Students: None

Learning Facilities: There are libraries on all the College's five sites. There are two computer laboratories at the College, and students may also have access to the facilities of Leeds or Huddersfield University or Bretton Hall, depending on their course.

Creche Facilities: No
Mature Students Adviser: No, but students may use the counselling services in the Health Authority or universities.

Accommodation: About 95% of first-year students can be accommodated, normally in nurses' homes attached to the hospitals with which the College is associated. There are no special provisions for couples or families.

The College was formed through the amalgamation of the teaching facilities of a number of local hospitals and now has bases at Wakefield and Pontefract, Dewsbury, Halifax and Huddersfield. The big-city facilities of Leeds and Bradford are near at hand, as are the Yorkshire moors and Brontë country.

Degree courses are offered in association with the University of Leeds.

Degrees Available: BHSc in Midwifery (four years) or Physiotherapy.

Assessment: Written and clinical exams.

How to Apply: Through UCAS. The College has a higher than average percentage of mature students on its undergraduate courses and welcomes applications from those without a conventional academic background. Successful completion of a kitemarked Access course is recognised as an acceptable entry qualification, and relevant prior learning and/or experience may be taken into account.

———— ❋ ————

Westhill College, Birmingham
– see Newman and Westhill Colleges, page 252

———— ❋ ————

University of Westminster
309 Regent St, London W1R 8AL

Watford Rd, Northwick Park, Harrow HA1 3TP
Tel: 071–911 5000
Contact: Central Student Administration at Regent St

Number of Undergraduates: 8000 full-time, many more part-time
Percentage of Mature Students: About 20%
Male/Female Ratio: About 5 : 4
Upper Age Limit for Mature Students: None

Learning Facilities: There are eight main libraries, each providing coverage of the subjects taught at its site and open seven days a week during term-time. They house over 250,000 books and subscribe to 2500 periodicals. Specialist collections include maps, government publications and slides. Comprehensive computing and audio-visual services are available on all campuses; relevant courses benefit from well-equipped laboratories, studios and technical facilities, with those for Art and Design and for Electronics and Manufacturing Systems Engineering being of a particularly high standard. The University believes that all students should have the opportunity to learn a second language and offers courses in 25 of them.

Creche Facilities: In the West End and at Harrow, for children aged two to five years. The West End nursery is open 50 weeks a year, the Harrow one during term-time only.

Mature Students Adviser: Not specifically, but advice is available through the Counselling and Advisory Service, which also runs regular workshops on Life as a Mature Student, Study Skills and Exam Anxiety.

Accommodation: The University has 800 places in self-catering Halls of Residence and hopes to have 500 more for the 1994/5 session. Two Halls are in the West End, the rest up to 50 minutes away. Priority is given to first-year students whose homes are more than 35 miles from Central London. There are no special provisions for couples or families, but the University Housing Service keeps lists of accommodation for rent in the private sector and will try to help you find somewhere suitable to live.

The ancestor of the University of Westminster, the Royal Polytechnic Institution, was founded in 1838 and established a studio for the fledging process of photography just three years later. It was also one of the first institutions to teach Architecture or Management. Having been refounded by the philanthropist Quintin Hogg in 1881, it continued to expand and became the Polytechnic of Central London in 1970. In 1990 it merged with the Harrow College of Higher Education to become one of the largest Universities in the UK.

The University has a total of 16 sites. Most of the main teaching sites are in the West End, within easy reach of each other, the Students' Union in Bolsover St and the administrative building in Regent St. The Harrow campus, half an hour away by tube and in a comparatively peaceful green setting, is the home of the Schools of Design and Media, Business and Management, and Computing and Engineering.

Degrees Available: BA in a wide range of Art and Design, Arts, Built Enviroment, Business, Social Science subjects; BEng; BSc in a range of subjects covering Biological and Health Sciences, Built Environment, Communication and Computer Science; LLB.

A number of unusual subjects are on offer, among them Commercial Music, Contemporary Media Practice, European Land Management and French or German, Cognitive Science and Photographic and Electronic Imaging Sciences. Law is available with one of four European languages and there is a wide choice of Modern Languages, including Arabic and Russian.

All degree courses are modular and may be followed part-time. For information about part-time day and/or evening studies, contact the Centre for Access and Continuing Education at 35 Marylebone Rd, London NW1 5LS, telephone 071–911 5000, extensions 3206 and 3182, or at the Harrow site, Watford Rd, Northwick Park, Harrow HA1 3TP, same phone number, extensions 4083 and 4155.

Foundation studies are available in Accounting, Art and Design, Modern Computing and Modern Science.

Assessment: A lot of modules place the emphasis on continuous assessment of course work, essays, practical work, projects, etc. Many but not all supplement this with formal exams. Each unit is assessed separately, during and at the end of the semester in which it is taught.

How to Apply: Through ADAR for Art and Design, otherwise through UCAS for full-time study; for part-time contact one of the Centres for Access and Continuing Education (see above).

The University welcomes applications from prospective mature students who do not have traditional qualifications. It operates a CATS and an APEL scheme (see page 12), so will give credit for prior learning and/or experience. Successful completion of a kitemarked Access course may be deemed to satsify the entry requirements.

You are likely to be invited for an interview – and possibly asked to do a short test – before being offered a place. For Art and Design you should provide evidence of some grounding in the subject, such as a foundation course, or produce samples of work that would justify your admission in the 'outstanding student' category.

Westminster College Oxford
Oxford OX2 9AT

Tel: 0865 247644 **Fax:** 0865 251847
Contact: Registrar

Number of Undergraduates: About 1400 full-time, many more part-time

Percentage of Mature Students: About 25%
Male/Female Ratio: 8 : 1
Upper Age Limit for Mature Students: None

Learning Facilities: The library has 100,000 volumes, about 450 subscriptions to current periodicals, audio-visual material and CD-Rom facilities. It has a specialist collection of children's books and has recently become the home of the archives of the Wesley Historical Society, making it an important centre for the study of Methodism in particular and theology in general. The College also has information technology teaching rooms and a well-equipped television studio.

Creche Facilities: During half-term only.

Mature Students Adviser: Alison Heynes in the Department of Continuing Education. The College also has a number of 'Mature Student Advice Cards' and sends out the UCAS booklet 'Stepping Up: A Mature Student's Guide to Higher Education'.

Accommodation: The College lets rooms in 38 purpose-built houses to over 500 students and can help other students find suitable lodgings.

Westminster College was established in London by the Methodist Church in 1851; it moved to Oxford in 1959 and remains a Christian institution, committed to providing its students with an excellent intellectual, pastoral and physical environment. Situated on a pleasant campus overlooking Oxford, the College is nevertheless well aware of the multicultural nature of modern society and has strong links with inner-city schools in a predominantly Muslim area of Birmingham.

Westiminster's first degrees are validated by the University of Oxford, with which it has close ties. In addition to having their own Students' Union, students at Westminster are entitled to join the Oxford Union and use its facilities.

Degrees Available: BEd with Qualified Teacher Status leading to a qualification to teach at lower primary or upper primary/middle level (four years); BTh.
There are opportunities for part-time study and for open learning.

Assessment: A combination of exams and continuous assessment, with teaching practice important in the BEd degrees.

How to Apply: Through UCAS, but at the same time you should complete a yellow Mature Student Application Form (obtainable from the Department of Continuing Education at the above address and telephone number, extension 3293) and return it direct to the College. This is another opportunity for you to explain what relevant qualifications or experience you have and why you want to undertake the course for which you are applying.

The College welcomes applications from mature students and will give you sympathetic consideration. You are welcome to contact the Department of Continuing Education for advice and information; they also run informal briefing sessions for prospective mature students.

Wimbledon School of Art

Merton Hall Rd, London SW19 3QA

Tel: 081–540 0231 **Fax:** 081–543 1750
Contact: Sue Lang, Academic Registrar

Number of Undergraduates: 544
Percentage of Mature Students: 22%
Male/Female Ratio: 2 : 3
Upper Age Limit for Mature Students: None

Learning Facilities: The library has 27,000 volumes. There are computing facilities, a slide library, photographic and printmaking facilities and well-equipped theatre workshops and studios.

Creche Facilities: No
Mature Students Adviser: No, but the Student Counsellor may be consulted by appointment by all students.
Accommodation: The School has no accommodation at present, but is negotiating the acquisition of a local Hall of Residence. A list of local lodgings is sent to all prospective students in July.

Wimbledon School of Art was founded in 1890 and has a long-standing reputation for excellence in its field. All its teaching staff are working professionals who bring up-to-the-minute practical knowledge to their classes.

The School is in a pleasant residential part of South London: even outside the tennis season Wimbledon has plenty to offer, including a thriving local theatre, and the centre of the capital is within easy reach.

Degrees Available: BA in Fine Art or in Theatre Design, validated by the University of Surrey.
A one-year Diploma in Foundation Studies in Art and Design is also available.

Assessment: Courses are practical and involve students in a succession of projects; you are expected to complete each one satisfactorily before progressing to the next.

How to Apply: Through ADAR. You will normally be expected to have completed a one-year foundation course or equivalent, to attend an interview and to submit a varied portfolio of work. Applications for the foundation course should be submitted to the School by 30 June on forms available from the Academic Registrar.

Winchester School of Art
Park Avenue, Winchester SO23 8DL

Tel: 0962 842500 **Fax:** 0962 842496
Contact: Academic Registrar

Number of Undergraduates: 550
Percentage of Mature Students: 25% of total student body
Male/Female Ratio: 1 : 3
Upper Age Limit for Mature Students: None

Learning Facilities: The library has 22,000 volumes, 90,000 slides, 3000 videos and 150 current journals. It is closed at weekends, but open until 8.30 pm, Monday to Thursday. The School also has specialist facilities such as computer-aided design and manufacturing, workshops and technician support in each department.

Creche Facilities: At nearby King Alfred's College
Mature Students Adviser: No, but prospective mature students are invited to an interview with an Admissions Tutor to discuss a suitable course; there are also full counselling services available to all students.
Accommodation: A building programme is underway to provide the School with more accommodation, and it is hoped that this will be complete for the 1995/6 session. In the meantime, only 15% of first-year students can be given a hostel place and there is no provision for couples or families. The Accommodation Officer will help you find private rented accommodation.

Founded more than a hundred years ago, Winchester School of Art offers first-class specialist training and is particularly keen to prepare its students for the possibility of working in Europe. It has its own studios in Barcelona and all courses include study visits to major European art centres. Teachers at Winchester are all practising professionals in their fields. The School is now an accredited institution of the University of Southampton, but retains its independence.

Winchester itself, the capital of the ancient kingdom of Wessex, is a lovely little city whose 900-year-old cathedral is famous for its choral music. London, Southampton and through it the Continent are within easy reach.

Degrees Available: BA in Fine Art, Design and related subjects. Courses in Art and Design and in History of Art may be followed part-time.

There is a foundation course in Art and Design, and drawing courses for mature students.

Assessment: There are no formal exams. All courses concentrate on practical work and the presentation of a final-year portfolio or exhibition; many also include a dissertation.

How to Apply: Normally through ADAR or UCAS, but mature students may apply direct: contact the Admissions Adviser for advice and an application form. The deadline is 31 May, though earlier application is strongly recommended.

Formal qualifications are not essential. For studio courses, high-quality recent work in Art and Design is the most important requirement. You must also be able to satisfy the Admissions Tutors that you will be able to cope with the demands of the course. CATS credits (see page 12) may be transferred to the History of Art course.

Wirral Metropolitan College

Borough Rd, Birkenhead L42 9QD
Tel: 051–653 3555 **Fax:** 051–653 4261

Carlett Park, Eastham L62 0AY
Tel: 051–327 4331 **Fax:** 051–327 6271

Withens Lane, Wallasey L45 7LT
Tel: 051–639 8371 **Fax:** 051–638 4188
Contact: College Advisers at any site

Number of Undergraduates: Nearly 200, out of about 1750 on Higher Education courses and a total student body of 22,000
Percentage of Mature Students: Not specified

Male/Female Ratio: About 2 : 3
Upper Age Limit for Mature Students: None

Learning Facilities: Well-stocked libraries on all three sites provide videos and access to databases as well as books. There are 500 linked computing over the three sites.

Creche Facilities: On all three sites – contact the individual site's Child Care Officer for information.
Mature Students Adviser: No, but all students have a personal tutor and there is a confidential counselling service.
Accommodation: No, most students are local.

Wirral Metropolitan College provides courses at every level from Community Education to degree courses, and is very much part of the community it serves. In addition to its three main sites it runs courses in over a hundred community venues in the region and is the local Open University centre.

Degrees Available: BA in Combined Studies, Fine Art, Media Studies or Professional Studies; BSc in Applied Chemistry (full- or part-time) or Life Sciences. Degrees are in collaboration with or set by the Universities of Liverpool, Manchester or Sheffield. There are also a number of Access and foundation courses, and it is possible to take the first year of Liverpool John Moores degrees in Accounting and Finance, and Business Information Systems at the Wirral.

Assessment: Some exams, but the emphasis tends to be on continuous assessment.

How to Apply: Through ADAR for Combined Studies, Fine Art or Media Studies; otherwise contact the College Advisers for information and an application form. If you do not have standard qualifications you may be asked to do a Mature Matriculation exam.

University of Wolverhampton
Wulfruna St, Wolverhampton WV1 1SB

Tel: 0902 321000 **Fax:** 0902 322528
Contact: For general information and advice, the Higher Education Shop (telephone 0902 321032)

Number of Undergraduates: 12,650

Percentage of Mature Students: 45%
Male/Female Ratio: 1 : 1
Upper Age Limit for Mature Students: None

Learning Facilities: There are six main libraries, two in Wolverhampton itself and one on each of the other campuses. They hold
a total of nearly 375,000 books, subscribe to 3500 periodicals and
provide 1405 study places. There is a Computer Centre
providing a wide range of facilities throughout the University,
and a Learning Development Unit with audio-visual and other
media equipment. The School of Languages and European
Studies has well-equipped language labs with facilities for
computer-aided learning, and there is an impressive array of
modern laboratories in the Faculty of Science and Technology.

Creche Facilities: For children aged from two to five on the
Wolverhampton, Dudley and Walsall campuses. University-
subsidised places are available in a creche near the Shropshire
campus. In all cases, you should apply as soon as you have the
offer of a place at the University.

Mature Students Adviser: The Higher Education Shop gives
advice about the University, courses and HE in general, and
aims to be particularly welcoming to mature students; the
Counselling and Guidance Unit and the Students' Union Advice
Unit will help with financial and personal problems respectively.

Accommodation: Over the five campuses, the University can
accommodate 1700 students in Halls of Residence, some part-
board, some self-catering. Priority is given to first-year students
who live more than 70 miles away, and about 25–30% of first
years are allocated places. There is very limited University
accommodation for families, but the Residential Services
Department keeps lists of suitable accommodation which can be
rented privately. As Wolverhampton is the only University in
the area, competition for cheap accommodation is not as fierce as
it often is in university towns, and rents are comparatively low.

*The University of Wolverhampton prides itself on the welcome it extends
to mature students and on the fact that its courses offer them considerable
flexibility. The University occupies five campuses and students are
sometimes required to travel between them – free coaches and shuttles are
provided. The main campus is in Wolverhampton itself; the others are at
Compton Park, three miles from the centre of Wolverhampton; in
Dudley, Walsall and on a new campus in Telford (known as the
Shropshire campus). The Schools of Art and Design, Languages and
European Studies, Legal Studies, Applied Sciences, Computing and
Information Technology, Construction, Engineering and Technology,*

and Health Studies are based in Wolverhampton, the Business School at Compton Park, Humanities and Social Science at Dudley, Education at Walsall.

Given that it lies at the heart of what used to be called the Black Country, the University's pleasant, green environment often surprises first-time visitors. In addition to the facilities Wolverhampton and the other University towns have to offer, Birmingham's big-city attractions are near at hand and access to the largely undiscovered countryside of Shropshire and the Welsh Borders is easy.

Degrees Available: BA or BSc: modular degrees in the Faculty of Art, Design and Social Studies and the Faculty of Science and Technology offer a wide choice of subjects from Glass Design to British Sign Language Interpreting and including Ceramics, Church Studies, Russian and East European Studies and Tourism and Hospitality Management, as well as many more frequently found subjects; specialist degrees in many Arts, Business, Science and Social Science subjects are also available. BEd leading to a qualification to teach at primary or secondary level, including a two-year accelerated version of the course; BEng or BSc Honours Engineering in Manufacturing only; LLB including an option with French.

There is a four-year Applied Science course aimed at mature students without traditional qualifications: the first (foundation) year is taught at one of a number of local colleges, with students transferring to Wolverhampton for years two to four.

A course in Design for Floorcoverings and Interior Textiles is taught mainly at Kidderminster College, which has excellent specialist facilities to support this programme.

The modular structure allows for part-time study on most courses.

Assessment: Each module is assessed separately, during and at the end of the semester in which it is taught. A combination of exams and continuous assessment is used – this may include essays, dissertations, practical or field work, presentations or seminar papers, depending on the subject.

How to Apply: Through ADAR for courses in the School of Art and Design, otherwise through UCAS for full-time study; direct to the University for part-time.

Wolverhampton is committed to extending access to Higher Education to those who have not traditionally benefited from it, and it welcomes applications from mature students who do not have formal qualifications but who can show motivation and commitment to study.

A wide range of alternative qualifications are considered. The University operates a CATS and an APEL scheme (see page 12), so credit may be given for prior learning and/or experience. You are encouraged to contact the Higher Education Shop for advice before submitting your application.

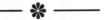

Worcester College of Higher Education
Henwick Grove, Worcester WR2 6AJ

Tel: 0905 748080
Contact: Mr R.B. Coveney, Registrar

Number of Undergraduates: 2300
Percentage of Mature Students: 20%
Male/Female Ratio: 2 : 3
Upper Age Limit for Mature Students: None

Learning Facilities: The Peirson Library holds an extensive collection of books and other materials. There are comprehensive computing facilities and all students have the opportunity to acquire or improve their computing skills. The Media Services Unit provides audio-visual back-up, desk-top publishing facilities, photographic services, etc.

Creche Facilities: For children aged three months to five years; open all year except Bank Holidays. Places are limited, so apply to the Supervisor, The Creche, at the above address as soon as possible.

Mature Students Adviser: Not specifically, but there is a Welfare and Counselling Service for all students. A booklet entitled 'Mature Students: A Brief Guide to Higher Education' is available from the Academic Registry.

Accommodation: There is accommodation for nearly 600 students on campus, with priority given to first-years. No special provision for couples or families at present.

The College occupies a single site about two miles from the centre of historic Worcester. It is a small and friendly place with an established reputation in the field of teacher training.

Built on the River Severn, the city's attractions include a magnificent cathedral and easy access to the Malvern Hills, the Vale of Evesham and the Cotswolds.

Degrees Available: BA and BSc in a limited number of subjects; BEd leading to a qualification to teach at primary or secondary level (four years).

All courses are modular and part-time study is possible for BA and BSc degrees.

Assessment: Some subjects have traditional exams, some have dispensed with them altogether. All courses use some continuous assessment – of essays, dissertations, project and practical work, problem solving and presentations as appropriate. Teaching practice is a major part of the BEd course.

How to Apply: Through UCAS for full-time study; if you wish to study part-time, contact the Academic Registry for details. Worcester will consider a wide range of alternative qualifications and give credit for prior learning and/or experience. There is also an internal entry route which involves writing an exploratory essay. You are advised to contact the College for details about this route and to discuss your individual circumstances before submitting a formal application.

Writtle College
Chelmsford CM1 3RR

Tel: 0245 420705 **Fax:** 0245 420456
Contact: Mrs Pam Wright, Academic Registrar

Number of Undergraduates: About 380
Percentage of Mature Students: About 53%
Male/Female Ratio: 2 : 1
Upper Age Limit for Mature Students: None

Learning Facilities: There is a large library, with one of the best collections in the UK in its field; it is open most evenings and Saturday mornings. Writtle also has computing facilities, a new hi-tech Design Centre, laboratories and extensive practical facilities relevant to the courses.

Creche Facilities: No
Mature Students Adviser: Not specifically, but trained counsellors are available for consultation by all students.
Accommodation: Halls of Residence can accommodate about 70% of first-year students. There are no special provisions for couples or families.

Writtle was once the most important settlement in Essex; now it is an attractive village a few miles from Chelmsford. The College is the largest in the country specialising in preparing students for employment in the countryside and amenity industries. It is a Regional College of Anglia Polytechnic University, which validates most of its degrees (the degree in Horticulture is offered in association with the University of Hertfordshire).

Degrees Available: BA/BSc in Leisure Management; BSc in Agriculture and related subjects including Equine Science and Management, Horticulture and Sports Turf Management.
Many courses contain a sandwich element and some may be studied part-time.

Assessment: Some exams, but also continuous assessment of projects, practical work, work experience, essays and dissertations where relevant.

How to Apply: Through UCAS for full-time study, direct to the College for part-time.
Writtle will consider a variety of alternative qualifications and give credit for prior learning and/or experience. Individual applications are considered on their merits and the aim is to admit anyone who seems likely to benefit from a course.

Wye College (University of London)
Wye, Ashford TN25 5AH

Tel: 0233 812401 **Fax:** 0233 813320
Contact: Academic Registrar

Number of Undergraduates: 800
Percentage of Mature Students: About 13%
Male/Female Ratio: 3 : 2
Upper Age Limit for Mature Students: None

Learning Facilities: The library, which is open long hours during term-time, has 35,000 books and specialised databases. Students are also entitled to use the main University of London library. Comprehensive computing facilities at Wye include courses for students with all levels of computing experience. The College also has a number of related enterprises such as a Countryside Management Centre and a Farm Business Service which provide valuable specialist support for teaching and research.

Creche Facilities: No, but the Families Association may be able to help.

Mature Students Adviser: No, but you will have a personal Director of Studies, and advice is also available from Careers Officers or the College Counselling Service. The College publishes a brief but practical leaflet giving advice to mature students.

Accommodation: The main College building and a new Hall of Residence can accommodate all single first-years who require a place. There is very limited family accommodation.

Although Wye has been a College of the University of London since 1900, it is about 60 miles from the capital, in a small town overlooking the North Downs in rural Kent. There has been a College at Wye since the 15th century and some of the original buildings remain. Wye itself has a population of only about 2000, but the larger towns of Ashford, Canterbury and Dover are within easy reach.

Wye is a specialist college with an international reputation in the science and management of agriculture, horticulture, the environment and the food industry. It is small enough to be particularly friendly and to give individual attention to students' needs.

Degrees Available: BSc in Agriculture and related subjects.

Assessment: A combination of exams, continuous assessment and practical work. Some courses involve a major project in the final year.

How to Apply: Normally through UCAS, but you are advised to write to the Registrar, giving personal details and asking for information, before submitting a formal application.
Access courses, BTEC diplomas or professional qualifications may be accepted as alternatives to the standard entry requirements, provided they meet the University of London regulations. You should expect to be invited for an interview.

University of York
Heslington, York YO1 5DD

Tel: 0904 430000 **Fax:** 0904 433433
Contact: Silvana Hine, Undergraduate Admissions

Number of Undergraduates: 3900
Percentage of Mature Students: About 13%

Male/Female Ratio: About 6 : 5

Upper Age Limit for Mature Students: None

Learning Facilities: The central library contains about 465,000 books, government publications, microform and audio-visual materials; it has subscriptions to about 2700 current periodicals and can accommodate 725 readers. The University has comprehensive computing facilities and offers short courses; there is also a Language Teaching Centre open to all students and laboratories for all Science and Engineering courses.

Creche Facilities: Run jointly by the University and the Students' Union. Student parents pay a reduced fee.

Mature Students Adviser: No, but all students have personal tutors, and professional counsellors are available. There is a Mature Students' Association.

Accommodation: The University has enough accommodation to house all first-year undergraduates and a substantial proportion of its other students – self-catering Halls of Residence are comparatively cheap. There is a limited number of one-, two- and three-bedroomed flats suitable for students with partners and/or children.

York is one of the prettiest cities in England, overflowing with history (and tourists) and boasting not only the glorious Minster but some of the best museums in the country. It is also on the main London-Edinburgh railway line, so easily accessible from just about anywhere.

The University is small, friendly and compact, situated on a single campus about two miles from the city centre.

Degrees Available: BA in all the usual Arts and Social Science subjects (though York is one of the few places where you can study Hindi) and in the School of Computer Science; BA or BSc in the School of Mathematical Sciences; BSc in a range of Science subjects (including a number of four-year sandwich courses); BSc or BEng in Computer Science and BEng in Electronic Engineering with various options (including four-year sandwich courses); BA or BEng in Music Technology.

A part-time degree in Social Policy and Administration may be completed in six years. There are also part-time certificates in Social Studies and in Local History; successful completion of the former may exempt students from the first year of relevant full-time degree courses.

Assessment: Varies from course to course, but most use a combination of exams and continuous assessment.

How to Apply: Through UCAS. The University will accept a range of alternative qualifications and give credit for prior learning. All applications are considered on individual merit.

Before submitting a formal applicaiton, you are welcome to contact the Admissions Tutor of the appropriate department, giving a brief description of your experience and educational and/or occupational background: the Tutor will be able to advise you on the admissions policy of his/her department.

...Pick out a main course...

Alphabet Soup
57000 Varieties
Pick 'n' mix

—MarcV-J

Which Subject Where?

The following is a simplified list of the subjects available either as single honours or as part of a joint honours degree in the institutions listed in this book. A place name without qualification refers either to the university (e.g. Dundee) or to the only college included from that place (e.g. Bolton). Where two institutitions in the same city are listed, the other's name is qualified (e.g. Dundee IT).

An * after the name of an institution indicates that the subject may also be taken in conjunction with Education, leading to a degree with Qualified Teacher Status.

Accountancy/Accounting – Aberdeen, Aberystwyth, Bangor, Bolton, Bournemouth, Cardiff, Central England, Central Lancs, City U, Coventry, De Montfort, Derby, Dundee, Dundee IT, East Anglia, East London, Essex, European Business School, Exeter, Glasgow Caledonian, Hertfordshire, Holborn, Huddersfield, Hull, Kent, Lancaster, Leeds, Liverpool, Luton, Middlesex, Napier, Newcastle, Northumbria, Paisley, Portsmouth, Queen's,

Reading, Salford, Sheffield Hallam, South Bank,
Southampton, Southampton IHE, Staffordshire, Stirling,
Strathclyde, Sunderland, Swansea IHE, Ulster,
Wolverhampton

Accountancy, Computerised – East Anglia

Accounting and Finance/Financial Analysis/Management –
Bangor, Brighton, Buckingham, Essex, Glamorgan,
Greenwich, Gwent, Heriot-Watt, Humberside, Kingston,
Lancaster, Leeds, Leeds Metropolitan, Liverpool John
Moores, London Guildhall, LSE, Loughborough,
Manchester, Manchester Metropolitan, Middlesex, Nene,
Newcastle, North London, Nottingham Trent, Oxford
Brookes, Plymouth, Robert Gordon, Salford, Sheffield,
South Bank, Staffordshire, Teesside, Thames Valley,
Warwick, West of England, Wolverhampton

Accounting and Finance, International – Brighton, Central
England

Accounting and Law – Brighton, Gwent, Kingston,
Manchester, Newcastle

Accounting Studies Europe – Thames Valley

Acoustics, Engineering, and Vibration – Southampton. *See
also* Electroacoustics

Acoustics with Oceanography – Southampton. *See also*
Oceanography

Acting – ALRA, Central School, Middlesex. *See also* entries
under Drama; Performance Arts; Visual Performance

Actuarial Science/Studies – City U, Heriot-Watt, Kent, LSE,
Swansea

Administration – Bangor, Humberside, Strathclyde. *See also*
Business Administration; entries under Management;
Organisation and Management Studies

Advertising, Creative – Bournemouth

Advertising, Media and Marketing – Bournemouth,
Lancaster

Aeronautical Systems – Salford

Aeronautics and Astronautics – Southampton

Aerospace Materials Technology – Queen Mary & Westfield

African and Asian Studies – Edge Hill, Sussex

African and Caribbean Studies – Kent

African Studies – Birmingham, SOAS

Afro-Portuguese, Brazilian and Religious Studies – King's

Agricultural Business Management – Newcastle, Royal
Agricultural College, Scottish Agricultural College, Wye.

See also Farm Business Management; Food Production and Land Use

Agricultural Economics and Management – Queen's

Agricultural and Environmental Science – Newcastle

Agricultural and Equine Business Management, International – Royal Agricultural College

Agricultural, Food and Environmental Chemistry – Glasgow

Agricultural and Food Marketing – Aberystwyth, Newcastle

Agricultural Science – Aberystwyth, Edinburgh, Queen's

Agricultural Technology and Management – Silsoe

Agriculture/and Countryside/Land Management/the Environment – Aberdeen, Aberystwyth, Bangor, Edinburgh, Harper Adams, Newcastle, Nottingham, Plymouth, Queen's, Reading, Royal Agricutural College, Welsh Agricultural College, Writtle, Wye.
See also Environmental Science in Agriculture

Agriculture, Forestry and Rural Economy – Edinburgh

Agriculture and Retailing – Bournemouth

Agri-Food Marketing and Business Studies – Harper Adams

Agroforestry – Bangor

Agronomy – Newcastle

Airframe Structures – Humberside

Akkadian – Cambridge, Liverpool

American and Latin-American Studies – Manchester

American Studies – Aberystwyth, Birmingham, Canterbury, Central Lancs, Crewe & Alsager, Derby, Dundee, Edinburgh, Essex, Greenwich, Hull, Keele, Kent, King Alfred's, Lancaster, Leicester, Liverpool IHE, Manchester, Middlesex, Nene, Nottingham, Reading, Ripon & York, Sheffield, Staffordshire, Sunderland, Sussex, Swansea, Thames Valley, Warwick, West London, Wolverhampton

Amharic Studies – SOAS

Analytical Science – Birmingham, Greenwich

Anatomy/Anatomical Science – Bristol, Cambridge, Cardiff, Dundee, Glasgow, Liverpool, Manchester, Queen's, Sheffield, UCL

Ancient World Studies – UCL. *See also* Archaeology; Classics; History, Ancient; entries under Egyptian

Anglo-Saxon, Norse and Celtic – Cambridge

Animal Management – Bangor

Animal Production Science – Newcastle

Animal Science *see also* **Biology, Animal**

Animation – West Surrey. *See also* Illustration and Animation

Anthropology – Durham*, East London, Goldsmiths, LSE, Oxford Brookes, UCL

Anthropology, Social – Brunel, East London, Edinburgh, Hull, Kent, LSE, Manchester, Queen's, St Andrews, SOAS, Sussex, Swansea, UCL

Applied Studies – Derby

Aquaculture – Scottish Agricultural College, Stirling

Aquatic Biology – Aberystwyth, Buckingham, Hull, King's. *See also* Marine Biology

Aquatic Bioscience – Glasgow

Arabic – Durham, Edinburgh, Exeter, Leeds, Oxford, Salford, St Andrews, SOAS, Westminster

Arabic/and Islamic Studies – Exeter, SOAS. *See also* Islamic Studies

Aramaic – Cambridge

Arboriculture and Amenity Forestry – Aberdeen

Archaeological Conservation – Cardiff, UCL

Archaeology/Archaeological Sciences – Institute of Archaeology, Birmingham, Bournemouth, Bradford, Bristol, Cardiff, Durham*, Edinburgh, Exeter, Glasgow, King Alfred's, King's, Lampeter, Leicester, Liverpool, Manchester, Newcastle, Nottingham, Queen's, Reading, Sheffield, Southampton, Trinity Carmarthen, Warwick, York. *See also* Ancient World Studies

Archaeology and Anthropology – Cambridge, Oxford

Archaeology, Environmental – Edinburgh

Architectural Design/Technology – Brighton, Luton, Middlesex, Ulster

Architectural History – Edinburgh

Architecture/Architectural Studies – Architectural Association, Bath, Cardiff, Central England, De Montfort, Duncan of Jordanstone, East London, Edinburgh, Edinburgh College of Art, Glasgow School of Art, Greenwich, Huddersfield, Humberside, Kent I, Kingston, Leeds Metropolitan, Liverpool, Liverpool John Moores, Manchester, Manchester Metropolitan, Newcastle, North London, Nottingham, Oxford Brookes, Plymouth, Portsmouth, Queen's, Sheffield, South Bank, Strathclyde, UCL, Westminster

Architecture, Interior – Brighton, Robert Gordon. *See also* Design, Interior

Area Studies – Aberystwyth

Art – Aberystwyth, Anglia*, Bath CHE*, Bedford*, Bishop Grosseteste*, Bretton Hall*, Canterbury*, Cardiff IHE*,

Chester*, Exeter*, Glamorgan, Goldsmiths*, Gwent*, Homerton*, Leeds Metropolitan*, Liverpool IHE*, London Guildhall, Manchester Metropolitan*, Middlesex*, Reading*, Ripon & York*, UC Salford, Sheffield Hallam, West of England*, West Sussex*, Worcester*. *See also* entries under Design; Drawing; Fine Art; Graphic Art

Art, History of – Aberdeen, Aberystwyth, Anglia, Birkbeck, Birmingham, Bristol, Cambridge, Courtauld, Edinburgh, Glasgow, Goldsmiths, Kent, King Alfred's, Leeds, Leicester, Manchester, Manchester Metropolitan, Nottingham, Open U, Oxford Brookes, Plymouth, Reading, St Andrews, Southampton IHE, Sussex, Thames Valley, UCL, Warwick, York

Art, History of, and Heritage – Buckingham

Art and Archaeology – SOAS

Art and Archaeology, History of – SOAS

Art and Architecture, History of – East Anglia, Liverpool, Reading

Art in a Community Context/for Society – Roehampton*, West of England, Wolverhampton

Art, Craft and Design – Edge Hill*, Trinity Carmarthen*

Art and Design – Bangor*, Bedford, Bishop Grosseteste*, Bradford & Ilkley, Bretton Hall, Camberwell, Derby*, Harrogate, Hertfordshire*, King Alfred's*, LSU*, Nene*, Newman & Westhill*, North East Wales, Plymouth*, Portsmouth, St Mark & St John*, S. Martin's*, Suffolk, Warwick*, Wolverhampton*, Worcester

Art, Design/and Film/Photography, History/Theory of – Bolton, Camberwell, Cardiff IHE, De Montfort, Derby, East London, Essex, Leeds Metropolitan, Middlesex, Northumbria, Portsmouth, Sheffield Hallam, Staffordshire, Wolverhampton

Art and Design, Spatial – Swansea IHE

Art, Design and Technology – Liverpool John Moores*

Art Education Studies – Cardiff IHE

Art and Literature, History of – East Anglia. *See also* Literature

Art and Media Studies – Swansea IHE. *See also* Cultural Studies; Media Studies

Art Practice, Contemporary – Northumbria

Artificial Intelligence – Aberdeen, Birmingham, Edinburgh, Leeds, Manchester, Middlesex, Nottingham, Sussex, Westminster. *See also* Computing

Arts, American and Commonwealth – Exeter

Arts, Applied – Derby
Arts, Integrated/Interactive/Related – Crewe & Alsager,
    Gwent, Manchester Metropolitan, West Sussex
Arts in Healing and Learning – Derby
Arts Management/Studies – Central England*, De Montfort,
    Thames Valley
Arts Practice in the Community – Middlesex
Arts Therapies – Derby
Asian Studies, Contemporary – De Montfort
Asian Studies, East – Portsmouth, Sheffield
Asian Studies, South – North London, SOAS
Asian Studies, South-East – Hull, SOAS
Astronomy – Central Lancs, Glasgow, Hertfordshire,
    Newcastle, Plymouth, Queen Mary & Westfield, St
    Andrews, Sheffield, UCL
Astronomy, Observational, and Instrumentation – Central
    Lancs
Astrophysics – Birmingham, Cardiff, Central Lancs,
    Edinburgh, Hertfordshire, Keele, King's, Liverpool John
    Moores, Newcastle, Queen Mary & Westfield, St
    Andrews, UCL
Audiotechnology – Salford
Audio-Visual Media Studies – Central Lancs
Audio-Visual Production, European – Humberside
Automotive Engineering Design/Manufacture – Coventry,
    Sunderland
Avionics/Avionic Systems – Bristol, Glasgow, Humberside,
    Queen Mary & Westfield

Baking Technology and Process Management – South Bank
Band Musicianship – UC Salford. *See also* Jazz and Popular
    Music; entries under Music
Banking – Bangor
Banking and Finance – Cardiff, City U, Loughborough,
    Ulster
Banking and Insurance – Bangor
Behavioural Biology/Science – Dundee IT, Glamorgan,
    Huddersfield, Nottingham, Paisley, St Andrews
Bengali Studies – SOAS
Biblical Studies – Aberdeen, Bangor, Glasgow, Heythrop,
    King's, Manchester, Queen's, St Andrews, Sheffield
Bioanalytical Science – Kingston

Biochemistry/Biochemical Sciences – Aberdeen, Aberystwyth, Bangor, Bath, Birmingham, Bristol, Cambridge, Cardiff, Central Lancs, Coventry, Dundee, Durham, East Anglia, East London, Edinburgh, Essex, Glasgow, Greenwich, Heriot-Watt, Imperial, Keele, Kent, King's, Kingston, Lancaster, Leeds, Leicester, Liverpool, Manchester, Newcastle, North East Surrey, North East Wales, North London, Nottingham, Oxford, Queen Mary & Westfield, Queen's, Reading, Royal Holloway, St Andrews, Salford, Sheffield, Southampton, Staffordshire, Stirling*, Stockport, Strathclyde, Surrey, Sussex, Swansea, UMIST, UCL, Warwick, Westminster, Wolverhampton, Wye, York

Biochemistry, Agricultural – Newcastle, Nottingham

Biochemistry, Applied – Brunel , Central Lancs, Liverpool John Moores, Paisley, Ulster

Biochemistry, Cellular – West of England

Biochemistry, Clinical/Medical – Birmingham, Brunel, East London, Glasgow, King's, Leicester, Royal Holloway, Sheffield, Surrey, West of England

Biochemistry, Environmental – Aberystwyth

Biochemistry, Microbial, and Genetics – West of England

Biochemistry, Nutritional – Nottingham

Biochemistry, Physiological – Buckingham

Biochemistry, Toxicology – Surrey. *See also* Toxicology and Pharmacology

Biodiversity – King's

Biogeochemistry, Environmental – Glasgow

Biological Imaging – Derby, North East Surrey

Biological Sciences – Anglia, Birkbeck, Birmingham, Buckingham, Derby*, Durham*, East Anglia, Edge Hill*, Edinburgh, Essex, Exeter, Glamorgan, Glasgow Caledonian, Heriot-Watt, Homerton*, Kent, King Alfred's*, King's, Lancaster, Leicester, LSU*, Napier, Newcastle, Newman & Westhill*, North East Surrey, North East Wales, North London, Oxford, Plymouth, Queen Mary & Westfield, Queen's, Reading, Scarborough*, Roehampton, S. Martin's*, Salford, Sheffield, Sussex, Swansea, Ulster, Warwick, West of England*, Wolverhampton, Worcester*

Biological Sciences, Applied – Manchester Metropolitan, Suffolk, West of England

Biological Sciences of Agriculture – Aberdeen. *See also* entries under Agriculture

Biology – Aberdeen, Aberystwyth, Aston, Bangor, Bath, Bolton, Brighton, Bristol, Cardiff, Chester*, Coventry, Crewe & Alsager*, De Montfort, Derby, Dundee, Exeter*, Glamorgan, Greenwich, Gwent*, Hull*, Imperial, Keele*, Leeds, LSU, Luton, Manchester, Manchester Metropolitan, North East Wales, Nottingham, Nottingham Trent, Open U, Oxford Brookes*, Paisley, Plymouth, Portsmouth, Queen Mary & Westfield, Ripon & York*, Royal Holloway, St Andrews, St Mary's*, Southampton, Staffordshire, Stirling*, Stockport, Sunderland, Sussex, Swansea, UCL, Warwick*, Wolverhampton, Wye, York

Biology, Animal – Aberdeen, Bangor, Birmingham, East London, Leeds, Newcastle, Nottingham, Reading, St Andrews, Wye

Biology, Applied – Aston, Bangor, Bath, Brunel, Cardiff, Central Lancs, Coventry, De Montfort, East London, Hertfordshire, Imperial, King's, Kingston, Leeds, Liverpool, Liverpool John Moores, Newcastle, Nottingham Trent, Portsmouth, Salford, South Bank, Southampton, Sunderland, Thames Valley

Biology, Applied Animal – Bangor

Biology, Applied Cell – Manchester

Biology, Applied Environmental – Manchester, York

Biology, Applied Plant – Aberystwyth, Nottingham

Biology, Cell/Molecular – Anglia, Bath, Birkbeck, Birmingham, Dundee, Durham, East Anglia, Edinburgh, Essex, Glasgow, Huddersfield, Hull, King's, Kingston, Leicester, Liverpool, Manchester, Newcastle, Nottingham, Oxford Brookes, Plymouth, Portsmouth, Queen Mary & Westfield, Queen's, Reading, Royal Holloway, St Andrews, Sheffield, Southampton, Stirling, Surrey, UCL, West of England, York

Biology, Cell and Immuno – Aberystwyth

Biology, Developmental – Glasgow

Biology, Environmental – Aberystwyth, Anglia, Bangor, Bath CHE*, Birmingham, City C, Dundee, Essex, Greenwich, Hull, Liverpool, Manchester, Nene, Newcastle, Nottingham, Oxford Brookes*, Plymouth, Queen's, Reading, Royal Holloway, St Andrews, South Bank, Staffordshire, Sunderland, Swansea, West of England

Biology, Field, and Habitat Management – Edge Hill. *See also* Environmental Studies

Biology, Human – Aberdeen, Aston, City C, East London, Hertfordshire, King's, Leeds, Leeds Metropolitan,

Loughborough, Nene, Oxford, Oxford Brookes, Plymouth, Stockton, Suffolk, Sussex, UCL, Wolverhampton
Biology, Human and Applied – Liverpool IHE*
Biology, Mathematical – Strathclyde
Biology, Medical – Brunel
Biology, Molecular – *see* Biology, Cell/Molecular
Biology, Molecular Plant – Leeds
Biology, Plant – Bangor, Birmingham, East Anglia, Leeds, Newcastle, Royal Holloway, St Andrews. *See also* Botany
Biology, Plant and Animal – Newcastle, Scottish Agricultural College, Sheffield
Biomarketing and Management – East London
Biomaterials – Birmingham
Biomedical Marketing – Wolverhampton
Biomedical Materials Science – UMIST
Biomedical Sciences – Aberdeen, Anglia, Bradford, Brighton, Cardiff IHE, Central Lancs, De Montfort, East London, Keele, King's, Kingston, Liverpool John Moores, North East Surrey, Portsmouth, Queen's, Sheffield, Sheffield Hallam, Stockton, Sunderland, Ulster, West of England, Westminster, Wolverhampton
Biometry – Aberystwyth
Biomolecular Science – Bath, King's
Biophysics/Biophysical Science – East London, Kingston, Leeds, Liverpool John Moores
Biophysics, Medical – East London
Biophysics, Cell/Molecular – East Anglia, King's, Leeds
Bioprocessing – Loughborough
Bioscience, Environmental – Strathclyde
Biosciences – Sheffield Hallam, Strathclyde
Biosciences, Applied – Glasgow Caledonian, Robert Gordon
Biotechnology – Aberdeen, Birmingham, Cardiff, Central Lancs, De Montfort, Dundee IT, East London, Glamorgan, Greenwich, Hull, Imperial, King's, Leeds, Liverpool John Moores, Luton, North East Surrey, Plymouth, Reading, Royal Holloway, Sheffield, Strathclyde, Sunderland, Surrey, UCL, West of England, Westminster, Wolverhampton
Biotechnology, Agricultural – Aberdeen, Nottingham
Biotechnology, Applied – Silsoe
Biotechnology, Medical – East London
Biotechnology, Microbial – Liverpool
Biotechnology, Plant – Leicester
Biotechnology, Process – Swansea, Teesside

Botany – Aberystwyth, Bangor, Bristol, Dundee, Edinburgh, Glasgow, Reading, Royal Holloway, Southampton, Swansea. *See also* Biology, Plant

Botany, Agricultural – Bangor, Glasgow

Broadcast Engineering – Liverpool John Moores

Broadcast Journalism – Nottingham Trent. *See also* entries under Journalism

Broadcasting Studies – Falmouth, Leeds

Brewing and Distilling – Heriot-Watt

Building Conservation Technology – Bournemouth

Building/Building Studies/Construction/Engineering/ Management/Technology – Anglia, Brighton, Bucks CHE, Central Lancs, Coventry, Dundee IT, Glamorgan, Glasgow College of Building, Greenwich, Heriot-Watt, Kingston, Liverpool John Moores, Napier, NESCOT, North East Wales, Northumbria, Nottingham Trent, Oxford Brookes, Reading, Robert Gordon, UC Salford, South Bank, Ulster, West of England, Warrington, Wolverhampton. *See also* entries under Construction; Project Management for Construction

Building Economics and Quantity Surveying – Heriot- Watt

Building Environmental Engineering – Bath

Building Surveying – Anglia, Bolton, Brighton, Central England, Central Lancs, De Montfort, Glamorgan, Glasgow College of Building, Greenwich, Heriot-Watt, Leeds Metropolitan, Liverpool John Moores, Luton, Northumbria, Reading, Robert Gordon, Salford, Sheffield Hallam, South Bank, West of England, Westminster, Wolverhampton. *See also* Surveying

Built Environment Studies – Coventry, Middlesex, Nene

Bulgarian Studies *see* European Languages, Literatures and Regional Studies

Burmese Studies – SOAS

Business/Business Studies – Anglia, Bedford, Birmingham, Bolton, Bournemouth, Brighton*, Buckingham, Bucks CHE, Canterbury, Central England, Central Lancs, Cheltenham, City U, Coventry, Crewe & Alsager*, De Montfort, Derby, Doncaster, Dundee IT, East London, Edge Hill*, Edinburgh, European Business School, Glamorgan, Glasgow Caledonian, Greenwich*, Gwent, Hertfordshire, Huddersfield*, Hull, Humberside, King Alfred's, Kingston, Leeds Metropolitan, Liverpool John Moores, London Guildhall, Luton, Manchester Metropolitan, Middlesex, Napier, Nene, NESCOT, North

East Wales, North London, Northumbria, Nottingham
Trent, Oxford Brookes, Plymouth, Portsmouth, Robert
Gordon, Roehampton, Salford, UC Salford, Sheffield,
Sheffield Hallam, South Bank, Southampton IHE,
Staffordshire, Stirling, Suffolk, Sunderland*, Swansea,
Swansea IHE*, Teesside, Thames Valley, Ulster, West of
England*, West London, Westminster, Wolverhampton*,
Wye

Business, American – Swansea

Business, European – Bucks CHE, Coventry, Glasgow
Caledonian, Hertfordshire, Humberside, London
Guildhall, Loughborough, Manchester Metropolitan,
Nene, Nottingham Trent, Oxford Brookes, Portsmouth,
Sunderland, Swansea, Ulster, Wolverhampton

Business, International – Aston, Brighton, Bucks CHE,
Central Lancs, Greenwich, Heriot-Watt, Humberside,
Lancaster, Liverpool John Moores, Luton, North London,
Northumbria, Plymouth, Sheffield Hallam, South Bank,
Staffordshire, Strathclyde, Teesside, Thames Valley,
Warwick, Staffordshire, West of England, Westminster

Business, Maritime – Plymouth

**Business Administration/Control/Management/Operation/
Organisation/Policy** – Aberystwyth, Anglia, Askham
Bryan, Aston, Bath, Birmingham, Bolton, Bournemouth,
Bradford & Ilkley, Bucks CHE, Cardiff, Central England,
Coventry, De Montfort, Derby, Doncaster, Dundee IT,
Farnborough, Greenwich, Heriot-Watt, Keele, King's,
Kingston, Leeds Metropolitan, Liverpool John Moores,
London Guildhall, Luton, Middlesex, Nene, Newcastle,
North East Wales, Nottingham Trent, Oxford Brookes,
Paisley, Queen's, Trinity & All Saints, Robert Gordon,
S. Martin's, Salford, Southampton IHE, Staffordshire,
Stirling*, Suffolk, Sunderland, Thames Valley, West of
England, West Herts, Worcester. *See also* Administration;
entries under Management; Organisation and
Management Studies

Business Administration/Management, European – Anglia,
Buckingham, Central Lancs, Dundee IT, European
Business School, Glamorgan, Middlesex, Newcastle,
Robert Gordon, Wolverhampton

Business Analysis – North London, Wolverhampton

Business Communication/Systems – Southampton IHE,
Teesside

Business Communication, International – Ulster

Business Computing/Systems – Canterbury, Central Lancs, Cheltenham, City U, Coventry, Greenwich, London Guildhall, Luton, North London, Sunderland

Business Decision Analysis – Liverpool John Moores, Staffordshire, West of England

Business Enterprise – Staffordshire

Business and Environmental Technology – Staffordshire

Business Information Management/Studies/Systems/ Technology – Anglia, Bournemouth, Bucks CHE, Cardiff IHE, Central England, Central Lancs, Cheltenham, Coventry, De Montfort, East Anglia, East London, Glamorgan, Gwent, Humberside, Kingston, Leeds Metropolitan, Liverpool John Moores, London Guildhall, Luton, Manchester Metropolitan, Middlesex, Napier, North East Wales*, North London, Northumbria, Nottingham Trent, Plymouth, Portsmouth, Salford, Sheffield Hallam, Southampton IHE, Staffordshire, Suffolk, Teesside, Thames Valley, West of England, Westminster, Wolverhampton

Business Information Systems, Applied – De Montfort

Business Information Systems/Technology, European – Brighton, Coventry, London Guildhall

Business Information Systems/Technology, International – Sheffield Hallam, Northumbria, Teesside

Business and Innovation – Staffordshire

Business Management and the Environment – Silsoe

Business Management, International – Newcastle

Business and Manufacturing Systems – Wolverhampton. *See also* entries under Manufacturing

Business and Media Communications – Greenwich

Business Operation and Control – Salford

Business Organisation – Heriot-Watt

Business Policy – Middlesex

Business and Quality Management – Nottingham Trent

Business and Retail Services – Greenwich

Business in Science – West of England

Business and Software Development – Strathclyde

Business Studies *see* Business

Business Systems Modelling – Greenwich

Byzantine Studies – Queen's

Catalan – Cambridge, Swansea

Caribbean Studies – North London

Cartography – Oxford Brookes. *See also* Mapping Science

Catering and Accommodation – Central England

Catering Management/and Food Studies – Cardiff IHE, Cheltenham, Colchester, Huddersfield. *See also* entries under Food; Hospitality Management; Hotel Management

Catering Systems – Sheffield Hallam

Cell Science, Applied – Liverpool

Celtic/Celtic Civilisation/Studies – Aberdeen, Aberystwyth, Edinburgh, Glasgow, Queen's. *See also* entries under Irish, Scottish, Welsh

Ceramics Design – Bucks CHE, Camberwell, Central St Martins, Duncan of Jordanstone, Falmouth, Loughborough College of Art, Middlesex, West of England, Westminster, Wolverhampton. *See also* entries under Craft; Design

Ceramics Engineering/Science/Technology – Leeds, Sheffield, Staffordshire

Chemical and Pharmaceutical Science – Sunderland

Chemical Science – Glamorgan, King's, Lancaster, Leeds, Liverpool, Manchester Metropolitan, North East Wales, Salford, UC Salford

Chemistry – Aberdeen, Anglia, Aston, Bangor, Bath, Birkbeck, Birmingham, Brighton, Bristol, Cambridge, Cardiff, Central Lancs, Coventry, Crewe & Alsager*, De Montfort, Derby, Dundee, East Anglia, Edinburgh, Essex, Exeter*, Glasgow, Glasgow Caledonian, Greenwich, Heriot-Watt, Hertfordshire, Huddersfield, Hull*, Imperial, Keele*, Kent, King's, Kingston, Lancaster, Leeds, Leicester, Liverpool, Loughborough, Manchester, Manchester Metropolitan*, Newcastle, North East Wales, North London, Nottingham, Nottingham Trent, Open U, Oxford, Paisley, Portsmouth, Queen Mary & Westfield, Queen's, Reading, Robert Gordon, St Andrews, St Mary's*, Salford, Sheffield, Sheffield Hallam*, Southampton, Staffordshire, Stirling*, Stockport, Strathclyde, Sunderland, Surrey, Sussex, Swansea, Teesside, Thames Valley, UMIST, UCL, Warwick, Wolverhampton, York

Chemistry, Analytical – Birkbeck, Plymouth, Swansea, UMIST

Chemistry, Applied – Aston, Brunel, Cardiff, Central Lancs, Colchester, De Montfort, Derby*, Dundee IT, Durham*, Greenwich, Kingston, Leeds Metropolitan, Liverpool John Moores, Manchester Metropolitan, Napier, Northumbria,

Nottingham Trent, Plymouth, Portsmouth, Salford, UC Salford, Sheffield Hallam, Strathclyde, Wolverhampton, Wirral

Chemistry, Applied and Analytical – Staffordshire

Chemistry, Biological – Central Lancs, Dundee, Essex, Keele, Kent, Leicester, North London

Chemistry, Biomedical – East Anglia, Sheffield Hallam

Chemistry, Biomolecular and Biomedical – Swansea

Chemistry, Computer-Aided – Surrey, UMIST

Chemistry, Environmental – Bangor, Birmingham, Coventry, East Anglia, Essex, Edinburgh, Glasgow, Greenwich, Hertfordshire, Lancaster, Luton, North London, Plymouth, Queen Mary & Westfield, Queen's, Staffordshire, UMIST

Chemistry, Forensic and Analytical – Strathclyde

Chemistry, Industrial – Cardiff, Essex, Paisley, UMIST

Chemistry, Manufacturing – Teesside

Chemistry, Materials – Nottingham

Chemistry, Medicinal – Brunel, Dundee, Essex, Exeter, Glasgow, Keele, Kingston, Loughborough, Newcastle, Sussex, UMIST, UCL

Chemistry, Pharmaceutical – Coventry, Kent

Chemistry, Theoretical and Computational – King's

Chemistry and Chemical Technology – Bradford, Exeter

Chemistry, Drug Design and Toxicology – Hull

Chemistry for Europe – Surrey

Chemistry, Industrial Economics and Technology – York

Chemistry, Life Systems and Pharmaceuticals – York

Chemistry and Physics of Polymers – Lancaster. *See also* entries under Polymer

Chemistry, Resources and the Environment – York

Childhood Studies – Bath CHE*, Bristol, Manchester Metropolitan, Suffolk

Chinese/Chinese Studies – Cambridge, Durham, Edinburgh, Leeds, Oxford, SOAS, Westminster

Chiropractic – Glasgow Caledonian

Christian Ministry – S. Martin's. *See also* Religious Studies, Theology

Christian Studies – Trinity Carmarthen. *See also* Religious Studies, Theology

Church History/Studies – Aberdeen, Glasgow, Lampeter, Wolverhampton. *See also* Religious Studies; Theology

City and Regional Planning – Cardiff

Civilisations of the Mediterranean and Middle East, Ancient
– Edinburgh

Classical and Byzantine Studies – King's

Classics/Classical Studies/Civilisation – Birkbeck,
Birmingham, Bristol, Cambridge, Durham, Edinburgh,
Essex, Glasgow, Keele, Kent, King's, Lampeter, Leeds,
Liverpool, Manchester, Newcastle, North London,
Nottingham, Open U, Oxford, Queen's, Reading, Royal
Holloway, St Andrews, St Mary's, Swansea, UCL,
Warwick. *See also* Ancient World Studies; Greek; Greek
and Roman Studies; History, Ancient; Latin; Roman
Civilisation

Clinical Sciences – King's

Clothing Engineering and Management – UMIST. *See also*
entries under Textiles

Clothing Studies – London College of Fashion, Manchester
Metropolitan, Nottingham Trent. *See also* Fashion

Coaching Science – Liverpool John Moores

Cognitive Science – Bangor, Birkbeck, Exeter, Hertfordshire,
Leeds, Sheffield, Sussex, Westminster

Colour Chemistry – Heriot-Watt, Leeds, Scottish College of
Textiles

Colour and Polymer Chemistry – Leeds

Combined Studies (Arts, Humanities, Social Sciences) –
Anglia, Aston, Bath CHE, Birkbeck, Birmingham, Bolton,
Bradford & Ilkley, Central England, City C, Crewe &
Alsager, De Montfort, Dundee, Durham, East London,
Essex, Glasgow Caledonian, Gwent, Hull, Humberside,
Kent, King Alfred's, Leicester, Liverpool, Liverpool John
Moores, London Guildhall, Loughborough, Manchester,
Manchester Metropolitan, Middlesex, Napier, Nene,
Newcastle, North East Wales, North London, Nottingham
Trent*, Paisley, Queen Margaret, Queen's, Reading,
Roehampton*, St Andrews, St Mary's, Scarborough,
Sunderland, Sussex, Ulster, Warrington, Wirral

Combined Studies (Education) – Manchester*

Combined Studies (Engineering) – Liverpool John Moores

Combined Studies (Law) – Central England

Combined Studies (Science, Technology) – Anglia, Aston,
Bath CHE, Birkbeck, Bolton, De Montfort, Derby, Dundee
IT, East Anglia, Essex, Glasgow Caledonian, Heriot-Watt,
Hertfordshire, Lancaster, Leicester, Liverpool, Liverpool
John Moores, London Guildhall, Middlesex, Napier, Nene,
North East Wales, North London, Nottingham Trent,

Paisley, Queen Margaret, Queen Mary & Westfield, Queen's, Roehampton, St Mary's, Sunderland

Command and Control, Communications and Information Systems – Shrivenham

Commerce/Commercial Management – Birmingham, Dundee IT, Glasgow Caledonian, Loughborough, Napier, Robert Gordon, UMIST

Communication/Communications Analysis/Science/Studies/ Systems – Anglia, Bangor*, Brunel, Cardiff, Central School, City U, City C, Coventry, Edge Hill, Glamorgan, Glasgow Caledonian, Goldsmiths, Humberside, Lancaster, Leeds, Liverpool, London Guildhall, Middlesex, Napier, Northumbria, Nottingham Trent, Queen Margaret, Robert Gordon, Sheffield Hallam, Staffordshire, Sunderland. *See also* Inquiry and Communication; Language and Communication; entries under Speech

Communication, Applied Human/Clinical – Central School, Manchester Metropolitan, Queen Margaret, Sheffield, Westminster

Communication, Advertising and Marketing – Ulster

Communication Arts/Media – Huddersfield, Kent IHE, London College of Printing, Loughborough

Communication and Control Technology – Derby, Staffordshire

Communication and Cultural Studies – North London, Trinity & All Saints

Communication and Image Studies – Kent

Communications, Electronic – Middlesex

Communications, International – Staffordshire

Communications Systems – Anglia, Humberside, Sunderland

Communications and Society – Leicester

Community Health Studies – Bradford & Ilkley, Dundee IT, Reading. *See also* Health Studies

Community and Race Relations – Edge Hill

Community Sport/Dance – Liverpool John Moores

Community Studies, Applied – Liverpool John Moores, Manchester Metropolitan

Community Studies, European – South Bank

Community/and Youth Studies – Bolton, Bradford & Ilkley, Cardiff IHE, Derby, Durham, Luton, Newman & Westhill, Reading, St Mark & St John, S. Martin's, Sunderland, Ulster

Computation/Computational Sciences – Glamorgan, Greenwich, Liverpool, Oxford, St Andrews, UMIST

Computer Aided Design/and Manufacture – Bucks CHE, Cardiff IHE, East London, Wolverhampton

Computer Communications – Greenwich, Nene

Computer Education and Maths/Science/Technology – Middlesex*

Computer Electronics/and Robotics – Liverpool, Strathclyde

Computer Illustration – Portsmouth. *See also* Illustration

Computer and Microelectronic Systems – Liverpool

Computer Modelling for Business – Lancaster

Computer Studies – *see* Computing

Computer Systems, Microelectronic – Manchester

Computer Visualisation and Animation – Bournemouth

Computers, Management and Electronics – Salford

Computing/Computer Science/Systems/Studies – Aberdeen, Aberystwyth, Anglia, Aston, Bangor, Bath, Birmingham, Bolton, Bradford, Brighton, Bristol, Brunel, Buckingham, Cambridge, Cardiff, Central Lancs, Cheltenham, Chester, City U, Coventry, De Montfort, Derby, Dundee, Dundee IT, Durham*, East Anglia, Edinburgh, Essex, Exeter, Farnborough, Glamorgan, Glasgow, Glasgow Caledonian, Goldsmiths, Greenwich, Heriot-Watt, Hertfordshire, Huddersfield, Hull, Imperial, Keele, Kent, King Alfred's, King's, Kingston, Lancaster, Leeds, Leeds Metropolitan, Leicester, Liverpool, Liverpool John Moores, London Guildhall, Loughborough, LSU, Luton, Manchester, Manchester Metropolitan, Napier, Newcastle, NESCOT, North East Wales, North London, Northumbria, Nottingham, Nottingham Trent, Open U, Oxford Brookes, Paisley, Portsmouth, Queen Mary & Westfield, Queen's, Reading, Robert Gordon, Royal Holloway, Salford, UC Salford, Sheffield, Sheffield Hallam, South Bank, Southampton, Southampton IHE, Staffordshire, Stirling*, Strathclyde, Sunderland, Surrey, Sussex, Swansea, Teesside, Ulster, UCL, Warwick, West of England, West London, Westminster, Wolverhampton, York. *See also* Artificial Intelligence; entries under Information

Computing, Applied – De Montfort, East Anglia, Middlesex, Roehampton, Ulster. *See also* Information Systems

Computing, European – Hertfordshire, Northumbria, Wolverhampton

Computing, Manufacturing – Loughborough, Scottish College of Textiles

Computing, Scientific – Brunel, South Bank

Computing in Business/Industry – Aberdeen, Brunel, Dundee IT, North East Wales, Northumbria, Robert Gordon, Stirling, Teesside

Computing with Human Factors – London Guildhall

Computing and Informatics/Information Systems – Bradford, Brighton, Central England, London Guildhall, Manchester, Plymouth, Swansea IHE, Ulster

Computing for Real Time Systems – West of England

Conservation/Conservation Management – Camberwell, Stirling

Conservation, Environmental – Birkbeck

Conservation and Rehabilitation/Restoration – De Montfort, Lincolnshire, London Guildhall, South Bank

Construction/Construction Engineering/and Management – Anglia, Bolton, De Montfort, Derby, Hertfordshire, Leeds Metropolitan, Loughborough, Luton, Middlesex, Paisley, Robert Gordon, Salford, Sheffield Hallam, South Bank, Southampton IHE, Thames Valley, UMIST, West of England, Westminster, Wolverhampton. *See also* entries under Building; Project Management for Construction

Consumer and Food Safety – Greenwich

Consumer Electronics and Retail Management – Liverpool John Moores

Consumer Product Design/Management – Coventry, Robert Gordon, South Bank. *See also* Engineering, Product Design; Product Design

Consumer Protection/and Trading Standards – Glasgow Caledonian, Manchester Metropolitan

Consumer Science/Studies/Technology – Glasgow Caledonian, Liverpool John Moores, North London, Roehampton

Consumer Science/Studies, Applied – Manchester Metropolitan, Northumbria, Queen Margaret, UC Salford

Consumer Services Management – Leeds Metropolitan

Contemporary Studies – Hertfordshire

Control Systems – Anglia

Coptic – Cambridge

Corporate Communication – Queen Margaret, Southampton IHE

Corporate Environmental Management – Liverpool John Moores

Countryside/and Environmental Management – Aberdeen, Humberside, Liverpool John Moores, Newcastle, Welsh Agricultural College, Wye. *See also* entries under Environment(al); Rural Countryside Planning – Cheltenham

Crafts – Manchester Metropolitan. *See also* entries under Design

Craft, Design and Technology – Liverpool John Moores*

Craft, 3D – Portsmouth. *See also* Design, 3D

Craft Technology, Small – Newcastle. *See also* entries under Naval; Yacht and Powercraft Design

Creative Arts/Media – Bath CHE, Bradford & Ilkley*, Crewe & Alsager, Glamorgan, Lancaster, Manchester Metropolitan, Nottingham Trent, Sunderland, West London*

Creative Studies in English – Bath CHE*, Portsmouth. *See also* entries under English; Experience of Writing; Writing

Criminal Justice/Criminology – Bucks CHE, Central England, Coventry, Glamorgan, Keele, Liverpool John Moores, Middlesex, Nottingham Trent, Teesside, Thames Valley

Crop Production Ecology and Management – Royal Agricultural College

Crop Protection – Newcastle, Reading

Crop Science – Aberdeen, Reading

Crop Sciences, Applied – Liverpool John Moores

Crop and Soil Sciences – Aberdeen, Bangor

Crystallography and Mineral Sciences – UCL

Cultural and Community Studies – Sussex

Cultural/and Critical/Media Studies – Cheltenham, Crewe & Alsager, East London, Greenwich, Gwent, Middlesex, Norfolk, Portsmouth, Staffordshire, West of England. *See also* Art and Media Studies; entries under Media; Popular Culture

Culture and Communication – Lancaster

Cultural and Social Studies, European – Bolton, Edge Hill, Wolverhampton

Cybernetics, Human – Reading

Cybernetics and Control Engineering – Reading

Czech – Glasgow. *See also* European Languages, Literatures and Regional Studies

Czech with Slovak – Cambridge, Oxford

Dance – Bretton Hall, Crewe & Alsager, Derby, Liverpool John Moores*, London Contemporary Dance, Middlesex, Roehampton*, West Sussex*, Wolverhampton

Dance in Society – Surrey

Dance Theatre – Laban

Dance, South Asian – De Montfort

Dance and Drama – Bedford, Birmingham

Dance Education – Middlesex

Dance Performance – Middlesex

Dance, Physical Theatre and Media – UC Salford

Danish – East Anglia, Edinburgh

Data Analysis for Scientists – Derby

Deaf Studies – Central Lancs, Wolverhampton

Decision Sciences – Hertfordshire

Dental Technology – Greenwich, Manchester Metropolitan, Sheffield

Dentistry – Birmingham, Bristol, Dundee, Glasgow School of Art, King's, Leeds, Liverpool, London Hospital Medical College, Manchester, Newcastle, Queen Mary & Westfield, Queen's, Sheffield, UMDS, University of Wales College of Medicine

Design/Design Arts/Crafts/Studies – Blackpool, Central Lancs, Chelsea, Colchester, Cumbria, Duncan of Jordanstone, East London, Goldsmiths, Gwent, London Guildhall, Nottingham Trent, Open U, Plymouth, UC Salford, Sheffield Hallam, Staffordshire, Ulster, Winchester. *See also* entries under Craft; Graphic Design

Design, Environmental – Bucks CHE, Portsmouth

Design, History/Theory of – Brighton, Central Lancs, Gwent, Manchester Metropolitan

Design, History of 20th Century – West Surrey

Design, Interior – Bournemouth, Duncan of Jordanstone, Humberside, London Guildhall, Middlesex, Napier, North London, Nottingham Trent, Southampton IHE, Teesside, West Surrey. *See also* Architecture, Interior

Design, Spatial – UC Salford

Design, 3D – Bath CHE, Bucks CHE, Cardiff IHE, Central England, Central Lancs, De Montfort, Goldsmiths, Kent IHE, Kingston, Leeds Metropolitan, Loughborough College of Art, Manchester Metropolitan, Northumbria, Plymouth, Ravensbourne, UC Salford, Sheffield Hallam, Sunderland, Sutton, West Surrey, Wimbledon. *See also* Ceramics; entries under Craft; Glass; Sculpture; entries under Wood

Design, Total – Goldsmiths

Design, 2D – Hertfordshire

Design, Architecture and the Built Environment, History of – Teesside

Design Development and Management, European – Winchester

Design Management – De Montfort, London Guildhall, West Surrey

Design Marketing – Teesside

Design and Media Arts/Management – Thames Valley, Westminster

Design Practice – UC Salford

Design Representation – Hertfordshire

Design for Society – Wolverhampton

Design Studies, European – Winchester

Design and Technology – Bath CHE*, Brighton*, Crewe & Alsager*, Edge Hill*, Goldsmiths*, Greenwich*, Gwent*, Huddersfield*, King Alfred's, Leeds Metropolitan*, Liverpool John Moores*, Middlesex*, Nottingham Trent*, Ripon & York*, St Mark & St John*, Sheffield Hallam*, West of England*, Wolverhampton*

Design and Technology, Electronic – East Anglia

Design Technology and Business/Management Studies – Edge Hill, Plymouth

Design Visualisation – Bournemouth

Development Studies – Central Lancs, Derby, East Anglia, Exeter, Kent, Leeds, SOAS, Staffordshire, Swansea

Diagnostic Imaging see Radiography and Diagnostic Imaging Dietetics – Leeds Metropolitan, Queen Margaret. *See also* entries under Nutrition

Distributed Information Systems – East London Divinity see Theology

Documentary Communication – Humberside

Drama/Dramatic Arts/Studies/and Theatre Arts/Studies – Aberystwyth, Bangor*, Birmingham, Bishop Grosseteste*, Bretton Hall, Bristol, Cardiff IHE*, Central School, Chester*, Crewe & Alsager, Derby, East Anglia, Exeter*, Goldsmiths, Homerton*, Hull, Kent, King Alfred's*, Kingston*, Liverpool IHE*, Liverpool John Moores, Loughborough, Manchester, Manchester Metropolitan*, Middlesex, Nene, Plymouth*, Queen Margaret, Queen Mary & Westfield, Reading*, Roehampton*, Royal Holloway, Royal Scottish Academy, S. Martin's, St Mary's*, Scarborough*, Trinity Carmarthen*, Warwick*,

Welsh College of Music and Drama*, West London. *See also* Acting, Performance Arts; entries under Theatre Drama, Society and Education – Central School
Drama and Television – Ripon & York
Drama, Theatre and Television Studies – King Alfred's
Drawing – Derby, Winchester. *See also* Art; Fine Art
Dutch – Cambridge, Hull, UCL

Earth and Environment – Middlesex
Earth Science/Studies – Aberystwyth, Anglia, Kingston, Liverpool John Moores, Nene, Open U, Oxford, Plymouth, Southampton, West London
Earth Science, Applied – Middlesex
Earth Science, Environmental – Greenwich, Royal Holloway
Earth's Resources – Cheltenham
Ecology/Ecological Science – Aberdeen, East Anglia, Edinburgh, Greenwich, Imperial, King's, Lancaster, Leeds, Leicester, North London, Queen Mary & Westfield, Sheffield, Stirling, UCL, Wolverhampton
Ecology, Applied – East London, Liverpool John Moores
Ecology, Human – Huddersfield
Ecology, Terrestrial – Newcastle
Ecology and Conservation/Environment – Cardiff, Sussex, York
Ecology and Ecotechnology – Middlesex
Econometrics – Essex, Liverpool, LSE, Manchester
Economic Analysis – Kent
Economic History – Aberdeen, Birmingham, Bristol, Edinburgh, Exeter, Glasgow, Hull, LSE, Manchester, Portsmouth, Southampton, Sussex, Swansea, Warwick
Economic and Management Sciences – St Andrews
Economic and Social History – Aberystwyth, Birmingham, Bristol, East Anglia, Exeter, Hull, Kent, Leeds, Leicester, Liverpool, Manchester, Queen's, St Andrews, Strathclyde, York
Economic/and Social Policy – Birkbeck, Stirling
Economics/Economic Science/Studies – Aberdeen, Aberystwyth, Bangor, Bath, Birmingham, Bradford, Bristol, Brunel, Buckingham, Bucks CHE, Cambridge, Cardiff, Central England, Central Lancs, City U, Coventry, De Montfort, Derby, Dundee, Durham, East Anglia, East London, Edinburgh, Essex, European Business School, Exeter, Glasgow Caledonian, Greenwich, Heriot- Watt,

Hertfordshire, Holborn, Huddersfield, Hull, Keele, Kent, Kingston, Lancaster, Leeds, Leeds Metropolitan, Leicester, Liverpool, Liverpool John Moores, London Guildhall, LSE, Loughborough, Luton, Manchester, Manchester Metropolitan, Middlesex, NEC, Nene, Newcastle, Northumbria, Nottingham, Nottingham Trent, Open U, Oxford, Oxford Brookes, Portsmouth, Queen Mary & Westfield, Queen's, Reading, Royal Holloway, St Andrews, Salford, Sheffield, SOAS, Southampton, Staffordshire, Stirling*, Strathclyde, Sunderland, Surrey, Sussex, Swansea, Thames Valley, UCL, Warwick, West of England, Westminster, Wolverhampton, Wolverhampton, York

Economics, Agricultural – Aberdeen, Aberystwyth, Edinburgh, Glasgow, Manchester, Newcastle, Nottingham, Reading

Economics, Applied – Dundee IT, East London, Hertfordshire, Plymouth, Ulster

Economics, Business/Financial/Industrial/Management – Birkbeck, Brunel, Buckingham, Cardiff, Coventry, Dundee, Durham, East Anglia, East London, Exeter, Glasgow Caledonian, Kingston, Leicester, Liverpool, London Guildhall, Middlesex, Newcastle, North London, Nottingham, Nottingham Trent, Paisley, Queen Mary & Westfield, Reading, Salford, Southampton, Staffordshire, Surrey, Teesside, Thames Valley, Warwick, Westminster, Wolverhampton

Economics, European – Kent, Middlesex, Nottingham Trent, Paisley, Staffordshire, Thames Valley

Economics, European Business – Anglia

Economics, International – Hull, Manchester Metropolitan

Economics, Land – Paisley

Economics, Mathematical – Birmingham, LSE

Economics, Public Sector – East London

Economics, Quantitative – Southampton

Economics, Technological – Stirling

Economics of Agriculture, Food and Natural Resources – Exeter

Economics and Econometrics – Nottingham, York

Ecotoxicology, Freshwater – Luton

Education/Educational Studies – Aberystwyth, Bangor, Bath, Bretton Hall, Brighton, Cambridge, Canterbury, Cardiff, Cardiff IHE, Central England, Central Lancs, Cheltenham, De Montfort, Derby, Exeter, Goldsmiths, Greenwich,

Homerton, Hull, Keele, King's, Lancaster, Middlesex, Newman & Westhill, North London, Oxford Brookes, Roehampton, S. Martin's, Sheffield Hallam, Stirling, Warwick, West Sussex, Wolverhampton, York

Education, Community/Informal – Canterbury, East London, Moray House, Strathclyde

Education, Nursery – Bretton Hall, Brighton, Canterbury, Charlotte Mason, Cheltenham, Crewe & Alsager, Greenwich, Homerton, Kingston, Liverpool IHE, Nene, Newman & Westhill, North East Wales, Plymouth, Reading, Ripon & York, Roehampton, St Mark & St John, S. Martin's, Scarborough, Sunderland, Swansea IHE, Trinity & All Saints, Westminster College

Education, Primary – Anglia, Bretton Hall, Brighton, Canterbury, Cardiff IHE, Central England, Charlotte Mason, Cheltenham, Crewe & Alsager, Exeter, Goldsmiths, Greenwich, Homerton, King Alfred's, Kingston, Leeds Metropolitan, Liverpool John Moores, Middlesex, Moray House, Nene, Newman & Westhill, North East Wales, North London, Northumbria, Nottingham Trent, Plymouth, Reading, Ripon & York, Roehampton, St Mark & St John, S. Martin's, St Mary's, Scarborough, Sheffield Hallam, South Bank, Strathclyde, Sunderland, Swansea IHE, Trinity & All Saints, Trinity Carmarthen, Ulster, Warwick, West London, Westminster College, West Sussex, Wolverhampton, Worcester

Education, Psychology of – Open U

Education, Secondary – Anglia, Crewe & Alsager, Exeter, Goldsmiths, Greenwich, Huddersfield, Leeds Metropolitan, Liverpool John Moores, Middlesex, Moray House, North East Wales, North London, Nottingham Trent, Portsmouth, Ripon & York, St Mark & St John, S. Martin's, St Mary's, Sheffield Hallam, Swansea IHE, Trinity & All Saints, Trinity Carmarthen, Warwick, West London, Wolverhampton, Worcester

Education and Society – Open U

Education Studies, Special – Crewe & Alsager

Educational Curriculum and Management – Open U

Egyptian, Ancient – Cambridge

Egyptian and Semitic Studies, Ancient – UCL

Egyptology – Liverpool, Oxford. *See also* Ancient World Studies; History, Ancient

Electrical and Information Sciences – Cambridge

Electroacoustics – Salford. *See also* entries under Acoustics

Electronic Imaging/and Media Communications – Bradford, NESCOT

Electronic Materials, Science of – Dundee

Electronic Media – Wolverhampton

Electronic Systems/Design/Manufacture/Management – Bournemouth, Cardiff IHE, Dundee IT, East London, Gwent, Loughborough, Middlesex, Paisley, Ulster

Electronics – Cardiff, Cardiff IHE, Central Lancs, East Anglia, Edinburgh, Glamorgan, Greenwich, Heriot-Watt, Hertfordshire, Keele, King's, Kingston, Liverpool, Middlesex, Napier, North London, Nottingham Trent, Open U, Oxford Brookes, Reading, Royal Holloway, St Andrews, Sheffield, Southampton IHE, Staffordshire, Swansea, Ulster, Wolverhampton

Electronics, Applied – Bath, Royal Holloway

Electronics, Computer/Digital – Kent, North London

Electronics, Ecological/Environmental – Glasgow, Hull

Electronics, Instrumentation – Anglia

Electronics, Physical – Portsmouth, Warwick

Electronics Business Management – Plymouth, Thames Valley

Electronics, Music and Media Technology – Leeds Metropolitan. *See also* Music Technology

Embroidery – Manchester Metropolitan

Employment/and Urban Studies – Gwent, North London. *See also* Urban Studies

Energy Management/Studies/Systems/Technology – Brighton, Coventry, De Montfort, Glamorgan, Middlesex, Nene, Southampton IHE, Sunderland

Engineering – Aberdeen, Aston, Bolton, Central England, Dundee IT, Edinburgh, Exeter, Glasgow Caledonian, Hertfordshire, Lancaster, Leicester, Liverpool John Moores, Oxford Brookes, Paisley, Portsmouth, Queen Mary & Westfield, Southampton IHE, Strathclyde, Sussex, Warwick

Engineering, Aeromechanical Systems – Shrivenham

Engineering, Aeronautical – Bath, Cambridge, City U, De Montfort, Glasgow, Loughborough, North East Wales, Queen Mary & Westfield, Queen's, Salford, Stockport

Engineering, Aerospace/Manufacturing/Systems – Coventry, Farnborough, Hertfordshire, Kingston, Liverpool, Manchester, North East Wales, Southampton, UMIST, West of England

Engineering, Agricultural – De Montfort, Harper Adams, Newcastle, Silsoe, Writtle

Engineering, Air Transport – City U

Engineering, Architectural – Cardiff, Manchester Metropolitan, Queen's, Stockport, Westminster

Engineering, Automobile/Automotive/Automotive Electronic Systems – Bolton, Kingston, Loughborough, Swansea IHE

Engineering, Biochemical – Birmingham, Swansea, UCL

Engineering, Biomedical and Bioelectronic – Salford

Engineering, Building Design/Production/Services – Central Lancs, Coventry, Heriot-Watt, Hertfordshire, Liverpool, Loughborough, Northumbria, Reading, South Bank, Strathclyde, Ulster, UMIST

Engineering, Chemical – Aston, Bath, Birmingham, Bradford, Cambridge, Edinburgh, Exeter, Glamorgan, Heriot-Watt, Leeds, Loughborough, Newcastle, Nottingham, Paisley, Queen's, Sheffield, South Bank, Strathclyde, Surrey, Swansea, Teesside, UMIST, UCL

Engineering, Civil – Aston, Birmingham, Bolton , Brighton, Cambridge, Cardiff, City U, Coventry, Dundee, Dundee IT, East London, Edinburgh, Exeter, Glamorgan, Glasgow, Glasgow Caledonian, Greenwich, Heriot-Watt, Hertfordshire, Humberside, Kingston, Leeds, Leeds Metropolitan, Liverpool, Liverpool John Moores, Loughborough, Manchester, Middlesex, Napier, Newcastle, North East Wales, Nottingham, Nottingham Trent, Oxford Brookes, Paisley, Plymouth, Portsmouth, Queen Mary & Westfield, Queen's, Salford, Sheffield Hallam, Shrivenham, South Bank, Southampton, Stockport, Strathclyde, Sunderland, Surrey, Swansea, Teesside, Ulster, UMIST, UCL, Warwick, Westminster

Engineering, Civil and Environmental – Heriot-Watt, Leeds, Newcastle, UCL

Engineering, Civil Offshore – Glasgow

Engineering, Civil and Structural – Aberdeen, Bath, Bradford, Coventry, Dundee, Humberside, Sheffield, UMIST, UCL Engineering, Civil and Transportation – Napier

Engineering, Clinical, and Materials Science – Liverpool

Engineering, Communications – Bath, Coventry, Edinburgh, Kent, King's, North London, Plymouth, Staffordshire, Sunderland, UMIST

Engineering, Composite Materials – Plymouth

Engineering, Computer/and Control/Information/Systems –
Bangor, Bucks CHE, City U, Coventry, East Anglia, East
London, Kent, Lancaster, Manchester, Middlesex, Queen
Mary & Westfield, Queen's, Sheffield, South Bank,
Sussex, Swansea IHE, Teesside, UMIST, Warwick,
Westminster

Engineering, Computer-Aided – Glasgow Caledonian,
Greenwich, Huddersfield, Hull, Liverpool John Moores,
Middlesex, Sheffield Hallam, South Bank, Staffordshire

Engineering, Concurrent – Bournemouth

Engineering, Cost – Robert Gordon

Engineering, Digital Systems – Sunderland, West of England

Engineering, Electrical – Bangor, Bath, De Montfort,
Doncaster, Glasgow, Greenwich, Humberside, Liverpool,
North East Wales, Queen Mary & Westfield, Sheffield,
Sheffield Hallam, Southampton, Staffordshire, Teesside,
Warwick

Engineering, Electrical and Electronic – Aberdeen, Anglia,
Bath, Bradford, Brighton, Bristol, Brunel, Cardiff, City U,
Dundee, Dundee IT, East London, Exeter, Glamorgan,
Glasgow, Greenwich, Heriot-Watt, Hertfordshire,
Huddersfield, Imperial, King's, Leeds, Leicester, Liverpool
John Moores, Loughborough, Manchester, Manchester
Metropolitan, Napier, Newcastle, North East Wales,
Nottingham, Nottingham Trent, Paisley, Plymouth,
Portsmouth, Queen's, Robert Gordon, Salford, South
Bank, Strathclyde, Sunderland, Surrey, Sussex, Swansea,
Ulster, UMIST, UCL

Engineering, Electromechanical – Aston, Edinburgh,
Loughborough, Manchester, Southampton, Strathclyde,
Sussex, UMIST

Engineering, Electronic – Bangor, Birmingham, Bolton,
Bradford, Brighton, Bristol, Central England, Central
Lancs, De Montfort, Dundee, Dundee IT, East Anglia,
Glamorgan, Glasgow, Glasgow Caledonian, Greenwich,
Huddersfield, Kent, King's, Lancaster, Leeds,
Loughborough, Manchester, Middlesex, Newcastle, North
East Wales, Nottingham, Oxford Brookes, Paisley,
Plymouth, Queen Mary & Westfield, Reading, Salford,
Sheffield, Southampton, Staffordshire, Sussex, Swansea
IHE, Teesside, UMIST, UCL, Warwick, West of England,
Westminster, York

**Engineering, Electronic and Computer/Communications/
Control Systems –** Aston, Birmingham, Bolton, Bradford,

Brighton, Bristol, East London, Essex, Glamorgan,
Glasgow, Huddersfield, Hull, Humberside, Leeds
Metropolitan, Leicester, Liverpool, Liverpool John Moores,
Loughborough, Manchester, Napier, North London,
Northumbria, Portsmouth, Queens, Salford, Sheffield,
Sheffield Hallam, Shrivenham, Ulster, UMIST
Engineering, Energy Resource – Heriot-Watt, Napier, South
Bank
Engineering, Environmental – Brighton, Cardiff, Cardiff IHE,
Coventry, Derby, Lancaster, Leeds, Middlesex, Newcastle,
NESCOT, Nottingham, Portsmouth, Sheffield Hallam,
Silsoe, Southampton, Strathclyde, Sunderland, Surrey
Engineering, European – Hull, UC Salford, South Bank,
Swansea
Engineering, European Manufacturing and Mechanical –
Sheffield Hallam
Engineering, Export – Central England
Engineering, Fire – Leeds
Engineering, Food – Newcastle
Engineering, Fuel and Energy – Leeds
Engineering, Geological – Queen Mary & Westfield
Engineering, Information/Systems – Coventry, Greenwich,
Heriot-Watt, Imperial, King's, Shrivenham, Surrey,
UMIST, Westminster, York
Engineering, Instrumentation and Control – Teesside
Engineering, Integrated/and Manufacture – Aberdeen,
Cardiff, Dundee IT, Greenwich, Luton, Nottingham Trent,
Portsmouth, Queen's, Reading, Sheffield Hallam,
Staffordshire, Sunderland, UMIST
Engineering, Manufacturing – Aston, Birmingham, Brunel,
Cambridge, Cardiff, De Montfort, Dundee, East London,
Hull, Loughborough, Middlesex, North East Wales,
Nottingham, Nottingham Trent, Queen's, Salford,
UC Salford, Sheffield Hallam, Staffordshire, Strathclyde,
Sunderland, Ulster, Wolverhampton
Engineering, Manufacturing Systems – Aberdeen, Bolton,
Cardiff, Coventry, East London, Glamorgan, Glasgow
Caledonian, Greenwich, Hertfordshire, King's, Kingston,
Leeds, Leeds Metropolitan, Liverpool John Moores,
Manchester Metropolitan, Middlesex, North East Wales,
Northumbria, Plymouth, Portsmouth, Staffordshire,
Strathclyde, UMIST, Warwick, West of England,
Westminster
Engineering, Marine – Newcastle

Engineering, Materials – Birmingham, Coventry, Dundee IT, East London, Greenwich, Hull, Imperial, Newcastle, Nottingham, Sheffield Hallam, Strathclyde, Sunderland, Surrey, Swansea. *See also* entries under Materials

Engineering, Mathematical – Leeds, Loughborough

Engineering, Mathematical Chemical – Leeds

Engineering, Mechanical – Aberdeen, Aston, Bath, Birmingham, Bolton, Bournemouth, Brighton, Brunel, Cambridge, Cardiff, Central England, Central Lancs, City U, Coventry, De Montfort, Doncaster, Dundee, Dundee IT, Edinburgh, Exeter, Glamorgan, Glasgow, Greenwich, Heriot-Watt, Hertfordshire, Huddersfield, Hull, Humberside, Imperial, Kingston, Lancaster, Leeds, Leicester, Liverpool, Liverpool John Moores, Loughborough, Manchester, Manchester Metropolitan, Middlesex, Newcastle, North East Wales, Northumbria, Nottingham, Nottingham Trent, Oxford Brookes, Paisley, Plymouth, Portsmouth, Queen Mary & Westfield, Queen's, Reading, Robert Gordon, Salford, Sheffield, Sheffield Hallam, Shrivenham, Southampton, Staffordshire, Stockport, Strathclyde, Sunderland, Surrey, Sussex, Swansea, Teesside, Ulster, UMIST, UCL, Warwick, West of England, Westminster

Engineering, Mechanical Computer Integration/Design/ Systems – Glasgow, Sheffield, Westminster

Engineering, Mechanical with Food – Queen's

Engineering, Mechanical and Manufacturing – Sheffield Hallam

Engineering, Mechanical and Marine – Liverpool John Moores

Engineering, Mechanical and Materials – Loughborough, UMIST

Engineering, Mechanical and Optical – Loughborough

Engineering, Medical – Staffordshire

Engineering, Microelectronic/and Software/VLSI Systems – Hull, Newcastle, Northumbria, UC Salford, Staffordshire, UMIST

Engineering, Minerals – Birmingham, Camborne, Leeds, Nottingham

Engineering, Mining – Camborne, Doncaster, Imperial, Leeds, Nottingham

Engineering, Nuclear – Manchester

Engineering, Offshore – Heriot-Watt, Newcastle

Engineering, Operations – Exeter

Engineering, Optoelectronic – Hull, UMIST

Engineering, Polymer – North London

Engineering, Power – Staffordshire

Engineering, Product Design – Central England, Glasgow
School of Art, South Bank, Westminster, Wolverhampton.
See also Consumer Product Design; Product Design

Engineering, Quarry and Road Surfacing – Doncaster

Engineering, Robotic and Electronic – Salford

Engineering, Software *see* Software Engineering

Engineering, Special Environment – Brunel

Engineering, Structural – Heriot-Watt, Manchester,
Newcastle, South Bank, UCL

Engineering, Telecommunications – East London

Engineering, Very Large Scale Integrated Circuit – Hull,
Kent

Engineering Business Development – Bournemouth

Engineering Design/and Manufacture/Materials – Central
Lancs, City U, Hull, Middlesex, Open U, Portsmouth,
Staffordshire, Teesside, Warwick

Engineering Geology/and Geotechnics – Greenwich,
Portsmouth

Engineering Management – Coventry, City U, Edinburgh,
Hertfordshire, Greenwich, Napier, Wolverhampton

Engineering Management, European – Wolverhampton

Engineering Marketing – Ulster

Engineering Mechanics – Open U

Engineering Science/Technology – Brunel, De Montfort,
Hull, Liverpool, Loughborough, Queen Mary & Westfield,
Swansea

Engineering Surveying – Nottingham Trent, Wolverhampton

Engineering Systems – Bath, Huddersfield, Manchester
Metropolitan, Napier, Plymouth, Portsmouth, South Bank,
Wolverhampton

Engineering Technology, Civil – UCL

English/English Language/Literature/Studies – Aberdeen,
Aberystwyth, Anglia*, Bangor, Bath CHE*, Birkbeck,
Birmingham, Bishop Grosseteste*, Bretton Hall*, Bristol,
Buckingham, Cambridge, Canterbury*, Cardiff, Cardiff
IHE*, Central England, Central Lancs, Charlotte Mason*,
Cheltenham*, Chester*, Crewe & Alsager*, De Montfort,
Derby*, Dundee, Durham*, East Anglia, Edge Hill*,
Edinburgh, Essex, Exeter*, Glamorgan, Glasgow,
Goldsmiths*, Gwent*, Hertfordshire*, Homerton*,
Huddersfield*, Hull, Keele*, Kent, King Alfred's*, King's,

Kingston*, Lampeter, Lancaster, Leeds, Leeds
Metropolitan*, Leicester, Liverpool, Liverpool John
Moores*, Loughborough, LSU*, Luton, Manchester,
Manchester Metropolitan*, Middlesex*, NEC, Nene,
Newcastle, Newman & Westhill*, North East Wales*,
North London, Northumbria, Nottingham, Nottingham
Trent*, Oxford, Oxford Brookes*, Plymouth*, Queen Mary
& Westfield, Queen's, Reading*, Ripon & York*,
Roehampton*, Royal Holloway, St Andrews, St Mark & St
John*, S. Martin's*, St Mary's*, Salford, Scarborough*,
Sheffield, Sheffield Hallam*, South Bank, Southampton,
Stirling*, Strathclyde, Sunderland, Sussex, Swansea,
Teesside, Trinity & All Saints*, Thames Valley*, Trinity
Carmarthen*, Ulster, UCL, Warwick*, West of England*,
West London, Westminster, Westminster College*, West
Sussex*, Wolverhampton*, Worcester*, York. *See also*
Creative Studies in English; entries under Language;
Literature; Writing

English, Contemporary Writing in – Luton
English, International – Hull
English, Medieval – Cardiff
English and American Literature/Studies – Kent, King
  Alfred's, Warwick
English and European Literature – Warwick
English for International Business – Central Lancs
English and Latin Literature – Warwick
English Literature in History – Lampeter
English and Media Studies – Swansea IHE
English and Scottish Literature – Aberdeen
English and Spanish-American Literature – Warwick
English Text and Theory – Lampeter
Enterprise and Innovation, International – Staffordshire
Enterprise and Operations – Middlesex
Enterprise in the Public Sector – Staffordshire
Entomology – Imperial
Environment and Business Management – Middlesex
Environment and Development/Planning – LSE, Stockton
Environment and Social Values/Society – Glamorgan,
  Middlesex
Environment Studies, Rural – Trinity Carmarthen, Wye
Environmental Analysis – Huddersfield
Environmental Biology see Biology, Environmental
Environmental Chemistry – see Chemistry, Environmental
Environmental Control – Greenwich

Environmental Geoscience – Edinburgh, Sheffield, UCL

Environmental Health – Cardiff IHE, Greenwich, King's, Leeds Metropolitan, Manchester Metropolitan, Nottingham Trent, Strathclyde, Ulster, West of England

Environmental Management/Planning – Bangor, Bath, Birmingham, Bradford, Central England, Central Lancs, Cheltenham, Doncaster, Duncan of Jordanstone, Hull, Keele, Lancaster, Leeds, Leeds Metropolitan, London Guildhall, Luton, Manchester Metropolitan, Middlesex, NESCOT, North East Wales, Nottingham Trent, Queen's, Sheffield Hallam, Silsoe, Southampton IHE, South Bank, Stockton, West of England, Worcester, York. *See also* entries under Countryside; Rural

Environmental Modelling – Greenwich

Environmental Monitoring/Protection – Bournemouth, Colchester, Derby, East London, Farnborough, Glamorgan. *See also* Resources and the Environment

Environmental Pollution Science – Glamorgan

Environmental Protection, Rural – Harper Adams

Environmental Risk Management – Cardiff IHE

Environmental Science/Studies/Systems/Technology – Aberdeen, Aberystwyth, Bangor*, Bedford, Birkbeck, Birmingham, Bolton, Bradford, Bretton Hall*, Brighton, Canterbury, Central England*, Charlotte Mason*, Coventry, Crewe & Alsager*, Derby, Dundee, Dundee IT, Durham*, East Anglia, East London, Edge Hill*, Greenwich, Gwent*, Hertfordshire, Humberside, Kingston, Lancaster*, Leeds, Liverpool, Liverpool IHE*, Luton, Manchester Metropolitan, Middlesex, Nene, North East Wales, North London, Northumbria, Nottingham Trent*, Open U, Oxford Brookes, Paisley, Plymouth, Queen Mary & Westfield, Reading, Ripon & York*, Robert Gordon, Roehampton, St Mary's, Salford, UC Salford, Scarborough, Sheffield, Sheffield Hallam*, South Bank, Southampton, Staffordshire, Stirling, Stockton, Sunderland, Sussex, Ulster, Warrington, West of England, West London*, Westminster, Wolverhampton, Worcester, Wye

Environmental Science, Applied – King's, Middlesex, Portsmouth, Suffolk

Environmental Science, Human – King's

Environmental Science in Agriculture – Nottingham. *See also* entries under Agriculture

Environmental Toxicology – Anglia, Glasgow Caledonian

Equine Management/Science/Studies – Coventry, Humberside, Welsh Agricultural College, Writtle
Ergonomics – Loughborough
Estate Management/Surveying – Central England, Greenwich, Heriot-Watt, Luton, North East Wales, Northumbria, Nottingham Trent, Oxford Brookes, South Bank, Ulster
Ethics, Social – S. Martin's
Ethnomusicology – Queen's
European Administration – Cardiff, Humberside
European Area Studies – Bournemouth
European Arts – Kent
European Community/and Integration Studies – Aberystwyth, Cardiff, Edinburgh, Queen's
European Integration Studies – St Andrews
European Languages, Literatures and Regional Studies, East – SSEES
European Policy – Southampton IHE
European Regional Development Studies – Luton
European and Social Studies – East Anglia
European Society and Policy – Plymouth
European Studies – Aberdeen, Aberystwyth, Anglia, Bedford, Bradford, Brunel, Central England, Central Lancs, Derby, Dundee, East Anglia, East London, Essex, Greenwich, Gwent, Hertfordshire, Hull, Humberside, Keele, Kent, King's, Leeds, Leicester, Liverpool IHE, Liverpool John Moores, LSE, Loughborough, LSU, Manchester, Manchester Metropolitan, Middlesex, North London, Northumbria, Nottingham, Nottingham Trent, Open U, Plymouth, Portsmouth, Queen Mary & Westfield, Reading, Royal Holloway, St Mary's, Salford, Southampton, Staffordshire, Stirling, Stockton, Strathclyde, Sunderland, Surrey, Sussex, Thames Valley, Ulster, UCL, Wolverhampton
European Studies, Contemporary East – Sheffield, SSEES. *See also* Slavonic and East European Studies
Eurotechnology – Central Lancs
Evolution, Human – Liverpool
Exercise and Health – Staffordshire. *See also* Fitness and Health; Physical Education
Exercise Science – Brighton. *See also* Physical Education
Experience of Writing – Derby. *See also* Creative Studies in English; entries under Writing
Exploration and Mining Geology – Cardiff

Export Studies and Languages – Napier

Facilities Management – NESCOT, West of England
Family Studies – Wolverhampton
Farm Business Management – Newcastle. *See also* entries
　　under Agriculture
Fashion – Bretton Hall, Central England, Central Lancs,
　　Central St Martins, Cheltenham, De Montfort, Derby, East
　　London, Epsom, Glasgow Caledonian, Kent I, Kingston,
　　Lincolnshire, London College of Fashion, Manchester
　　Metropolitan, Northumbria, Nottingham Trent,
　　Ravensbourne, UC Salford, Southampton IHE, West of
　　England, West Surrey, Westminster,Winchester. *See also*
　　Clothing; Textiles
Feminist and Gender Studies – Staffordshire. *See also*
　　Women's Studies
Film and Drama/Photography/Television/Video/Visual
　　Media Studies – Derby, East Anglia, Glasgow, Gwent,
　　Kent, Manchester Metropolitan, Middlesex, North
　　London, Portsmouth, Reading, Sheffield Hallam,
　　Southampton IHE, Stirling*, Westminster, West Surrey.
　　See also entries under Photography; Media, Professional;
　　Televsion; Visual Cultures
Film and Literature – Warwick
Finance/Financial Management/Services/Studies –
　　Bournemouth, Central England, Central Lancs,
　　Cheltenham, European Business School, Glasgow
　　Caledonian, Humberside, Liverpool John Moores, London
　　Guildhall, Manchester, Manchester Metropolitan, Napier,
　　North London, Nottingham Trent, Paisley, Portsmouth,
　　Queen's, Sheffield Hallam, South Bank, Stirling*,
　　Strathclyde, West of England, Wolverhampton
Finance and Trade, International – Portsmouth
Finances and Accounting, European – Leeds Metropolitan
Financial Management, European – Bangor
Financial Studies, International – Sheffield Hallam
Fine Art – Bath CHE, Bretton Hall, Brighton, Cardiff IHE,
　　Central England, Central Lancs, Central St Martins,
　　Chelsea, Cheltenham, Coventry, Cumbria, Duncan of
　　Jordanstone, East London, Edinburgh, Exeter, Falmouth,
　　Glasgow School of Art, Goldsmiths, Hertfordshire,
　　Humberside, Kent I, Kingston, Leeds, Leeds Metropolitan,
　　Liverpool John Moores, London Guildhall, Loughborough

College of Art, Mancheser Metropolitan, Middlesex, Newcastle, Norfolk, Northumbria, Nottingham Trent, Oxford, Oxford Brookes, Plymouth, Sheffield Hallam, Southampton IHE, Staffordshire, Sunderland, Ulster, UCL, West of England, West Surrey, Wimbledon, Winchester, Wirral. *See also* entries under Art; Drawing

Fine and Applied Art – Nene

Fine Art and Textile Design – Scarborough*

Fine Arts Valuation – Southampton IHE

Fine Craft Design – Ulster

Finnish *see* European Languages, Literatures and Regional Studies

Fisheries Science/Studies – Plymouth

Fitness and Health – East London. *See also* entries under Exercise; Health Studies, Physical Education

Floorcovering Design – Wolverhampton

Food and Agriculture – Plymouth

Food and Environmental Management – Humberside

Food and Catering Industry/Management – Bath CHE, Bournemouth, Humberside, UC Salford. *See also* Hospitality Management; Hotel Management

Food Industry Marketing and Management, European – Humberside

Food Manufacturing Management – Manchester Metropolitan, Queen Margaret

Food Marketing Economics – Reading

Food Marketing Management – Sheffield Hallam. *See also* Marketing and Food Management

Food Product Development – Glasgow Caledonian

Food Production and Land Use – Scottish Agricultural College. *See also* entries under Agriculture

Food Production, Management and Marketing – Reading, Scottish Agricultural College

Food Quality – Bournemouth, Humberside

Food Quality and Production – Newcastle, Plymouth

Food Science/Studies/Food and Nutrition – Cardiff IHE, Huddersfield, Humberside, Leeds, Liverpool John Moores, Newcastle, North East Wales, North London, Nottingham, Oxford Brookes, Queen Margaret, Queen's, Reading, Robert Gordon, South Bank, Strathclyde, Surrey. *See also* Dietetics, entries under Nutrition

Food Studies, European – Humberside

Food Systems Management – Plymouth

Food Technology/Manufacture – Humberside, Manchester
    Metropolitan, Queen's, Reading, Teesside, Ulster,
    Wolverhampton
Food and Welfare Studies – Duncan of Jordanstone
Footwear and Accessories, Design and Product
    Development in – Cordwainers. *See also* Leather
Forest Management – Aberdeen
Forest Products Technology – Bucks CHE, Dundee IT
Forestry – Bangor, Central Lancs
Forestry and Forestry Products – Bangor
French/French Studies – Aberdeen, Aberystwyth, Anglia*,
    Aston, Bangor, Bath, Birkbeck, Birmingham, Bradford,
    Bristol, Cambridge, Cardiff, Central England, Central
    Lancs, Chester, Coventry, Crewe & Alsager*, De Montfort,
    Derby, Durham, East Anglia, East London, Edinburgh,
    Essex, Exeter, Glamorgan, Glasgow, Goldsmiths, Heriot-
    Watt, Hull, Keele*, Kent, King Alfred's, King's, Kingston,
    Lampeter, Lancaster, Leeds, Leicester, Liverpool,
    Liverpool IHE, Liverpool John Moores, London Guildhall,
    LSU*, Luton, Manchester, Manchester Metropolitan,
    Middlesex, NEC, Newcastle, North London,
    Northumbria*, Nottingham, Nottingham Trent, Oxford,
    Oxford Brookes, Portsmouth, Queen Mary & Westfield,
    Queen's, Reading, Ripon & York*, Roehampton, Royal
    Holloway, St Andrews, Salford, Sheffield, SOAS,
    Southampton, SSEES, Staffordshire, Stirling*, Stockton,
    Strathclyde, Sunderland*, Surrey, Sussex, Swansea,
    Trinity & All Saints, Trinity Carmarthen*, Thames Valley,
    Ulster, UCL, Warwick, West of England, Westminster,
    Westminster College*, Wolverhampton*, York
French, Applied – UMIST
French, Business – Central Lancs
Freshwater Biology – Liverpool. *See also* Aquatic Biology;
    Marine Biology
Fuel and Combustion Science – Leeds
Furnishings, Design and Manufacture – London Guildhall
Furniture Design/Craftsmanship/Production/Restoration –
    Bournemouth, Bucks CHE, London Guildhall,
    Loughborough College of Art, Middlesex, Nottingham
    Trent

Gaelic Studies – Aberdeen
Garden Design – Greenwich, Middlesex

Gender Studies – Hull, Sunderland

Gender and Women's Studies *see* Feminist and Gender Studies; Women's Studies.

General Studies *see* Combined Studies

Genetics – Aberdeen, Aberystwyth, Birmingham, Cambridge, Cardiff, Edinburgh, Glasgow, Leeds, Leicester, Liverpool, Manchester, Nottingham, Queen Mary & Westfield, Queen's, St Andrews, Sheffield, Swansea, UCL, York

Genetics, Molecular – Dundee, King's, Sussex

Geochemistry – Leicester, Manchester, Reading, St Andrews

Geochemistry, Applied – Greenwich

Geochemistry, Environmental – Royal Holloway

Geographical Information Systems – Kingston

Geographical and Land Information Management – East London

Geography – Aberdeen , Aberystwyth, Anglia, Bath CHE*, Bedford*, Birkbeck, Birmingham, Bishop Grosseteste*, Bradford & Ilkley*, Brighton, Bristol, Cambridge, Canterbury*, Cardiff IHE*, Central Lancs, Charlotte Mason*, Chester*, Coventry, Crewe & Alsager*, Derby*, Dundee, Durham*, Edge Hill*, Edinburgh, Exeter, Glamorgan, Glasgow, Glasgow Caledonian, Greenwich, Gwent*, Hertfordshire*, Homerton*, Huddersfield, Hull, Keele, King Alfred's*, King's, Kingston*, Lampeter, Lancaster, Leeds, Leeds Metropolitan*, Leicester, Liverpool, Liverpool IHE*, Liverpool John Moores, London Guildhall, LSE, Loughborough, LSU*, Luton, Manchester, Manchester Metropolitan*, Middlesex*, NEC, Nene, Newcastle, Newman & Westhill*, North East Wales*, North London, Northumbria, Nottingham, Nottingham Trent, Open U, Oxford, Oxford Brookes*, Plymouth*, Portsmouth, Queen Mary & Westfield, Queen's, Reading*, Ripon & York*, Roehampton*, Royal Holloway, St Andrews, St Mark & St John*, S. Martin's*, St Mary's*, Salford, Scarborough*, Sheffield, SOAS (with particular reference to Asia and Africa), Southampton, Staffordshire, Strathclyde, Sunderland, Sussex, Swansea, Thames Valley, Trinity and All Saints*, Trinity Carmarthen*, Ulster, UCL, Warwick*, West of England*, West London, Westminster, Westminster College*, West Sussex*, Wolverhampton*, Worcester*

Geography, Environmental – Queen Mary & Westfield, UCL

Geography, Human – Aberdeen, Cheltenham*, Lampeter, Lancaster, Liverpool John Moores, Loughborough, Queen Mary & Westfield, Queen's, Reading, South Bank

Geography, Physical – Aberdeen, Birkbeck, Cheltenham*, Lampeter, Luton, Queen Mary & Westfield, Reading

Geography and Environmental Issues/Management – West of England, West London*

Geography and Planning – Strathclyde

Geology/Geological Sciences – Aberdeen, Aberystwyth, Anglia, Birkbeck, Birmingham, Bristol, Cambridge, Cardiff, Cheltenham, Derby, Durham, Edinburgh, Glamorgan, Glasgow, Greenwich, Imperial, Keele, Kingston, Leeds, Leicester, Liverpool, Luton, Manchester, Oxford Brookes, Portsmouth, Queen's, Royal Holloway, St Andrews, Southampton, Staffordshire, Sunderland, UCL, West London

Geology, Applied – Birmingham, Hertfordshire, Oxford Brookes, Plymouth, Queen Mary & Westfield, Staffordshire, Sunderland

Geology, Environmental/and Resource – Birmingham, Hertfordshire, Manchester, Plymouth, Portsmouth, Royal Holloway, Sheffield, Sunderland

Geology, Industrial – Camborne

Geology, Mining – Imperial. *See also* Engineering, Minerals; Engineering, Mining; entries under Minerals

Geology, Physical, and Geomorphology – Liverpool

Geophysics/Geophysical Sciences – East Anglia, Edinburgh, Lancaster, Leeds, Leicester, Liverpool, Southampton, UCL

Geophysics, Exploration – UCL

Geophysics and Planetary Physics – Newcastle

Georgian Studies – SOAS

Geoscience – Exeter, St Andrews

Geoscience, Marine – Southampton. *See also* entries under Marine

Geotechnics – Oxford Brookes

German or German Studies – Aberdeen, Aberystwyth, Anglia, Aston, Bangor, Bath, Birkbeck, Birmingham, Bradford, Bristol, Cambridge, Cardiff, Central England, Central Lancs, Chester, Coventry, De Montfort, Derby, Durham, East Anglia, East London, Edinburgh, Essex, Exeter, Glamorgan, Glasgow, Goldsmiths, Heriot-Watt, Hull, Keele, Kent, King's, Kingston, Lampeter, Lancaster, Leeds, Leicester, Liverpool, Liverpool John Moores, London Guildhall, LSU, Luton, Manchester, Manchester

Metropolitan, Middlesex, NEC, Newcastle, North London, Northumbria*, Nottingham Trent, Oxford, Oxford Brookes, Portsmouth, Queen Mary & Westfield, Queen's, Reading, Royal Holloway, St Andrews, Salford, Sheffield, Southampton, SSEES, Staffordshire, Stirling*, Stockton, Strathclyde, Sunderland*, Surrey, Sussex, Swansea, Thames Valley, Ulster, UCL, Warwick, West of England, Westminster, Wolverhampton*, York

German, Applied – UMIST

German, Business – Central Lancs

Glass Design/Science – Middlesex, Sheffield, Wolverhampton. *See also* Design, 3D

Global Relationships – Bath CHE*

Government – Central England, Central Lancs, Kent, LSE, Ulster

Government and European Community Studies – Newcastle

Government and European/Foreign Policy – Aberystwyth, Teesside

Government and Politics – Manchester, Open U

Government and Public Policy – Northumbria, Nottingham Trent

Graphic Arts – Anglia. *See also* entries under Art

Graphic Arts and Design – Leeds Metropolitan

Graphic Communications Management – Napier

Graphic Design – Bath CHE, Brighton, Camberwell, Central Lancs, Central St Martins, Coventry, Cumbria, Derby, Duncan of Jordanstone, Humberside, Luton, Kingston, Liverpool John Moores, Norfolk, Nottingham Trent, Northumbria, Portsmouth, Plymouth, UC Salford, Southampton IHE, Teesside, West of England, Wolverhampton. *See also* entries under Design

Graphic Design and Advertising – Bucks CHE

Graphic Design and Illustration – Lincolnshire. *See also* Illustration

Graphic Information Design – Falmouth, Westminster

Graphic and Media Design – London College of Printing

Graphic Media Studies – West Herts

Greek, Ancient – Birmingham, Cambridge, Durham*, Edinburgh, Glasgow, Kent, King's, Lampeter, Leeds, Manchester, Newcastle, Nottingham, Queen's, Reading, Royal Holloway, St Andrews, Swansea, UCL. *See also* Classics: Greek and Roman Civilisation/Studies: Hellenic Studies; Latin.

Greek, Modern – Birmingham, Cambridge, Edinburgh, King's, Oxford
Greek and Roman Civilisation/Studies – Birmingham, Durham, Exeter*, Lampeter, Swansea. *See also* Ancient World Studies; Classics; Greek, Ancient; History, Ancient; Latin
Green Studies – Glamorgan
Gujarati Studies – SOAS

Haematology – West of England
Hausa Studies – SOAS
Health/and Community/Human Studies – Bath CHE, Bournemouth, Cardiff IHE, Central England, Central Lancs, Chester, Crewe & Alsager, De Montfort, East London, Essex, Glasgow Caledonian, Leeds Metropolitan, Liverpool John Moores, Luton, Manchester Metropolitan, North London, Roehampton, Sheffield Hallam, Stockton, Sunderland, West Sussex, Wolverhampton, Worcester
Health Administration/Policy/Studies – S. Martin's, Sheffield Hallam
Health Care – Swansea IHE
Health Care Information Systems/Technology – Cardiff IHE, City U, Derby
Health Education – Glasgow Caledonian
Health and Exercise Systems – Oxford Brookes
Health Promotion – Bangor, S. Martin's
Health Science – Aberdeen, Greenwich, Leeds Metropolitan, Luton, Queen Margaret, UC Salford, South Bank, Teesside
Health Science, European – Northumbria
Health and Social Care – Gwent
Health and Society – Derby
Health, Welfare and Social Policy – Anglia
Hebrew, Biblical/Classical – Cambridge, Glasgow, Liverpool, Oxford, St Andrews, SOAS, UCL
Hebrew, Modern – Cambridge, SOAS
Hebrew Studies – SOAS
Hellenic Studies – King's. *See also* entries under Greek.
Heritage Conservation – Bournemouth
Heritage and History – Derby
Heritage Management/Studies – Bucks CHE, S. Martin's
Hindi/Hindi Studies – Cambridge, SOAS, York
Hispanic Studies – Aberdeen, Birkbeck, Birmingham, Bristol, Cardiff, Glasgow, King's, Liverpool, Manchester,

Nottingham, Portsmouth, Queen Mary & Westfield,
Salford, Sheffield, Stirling, UCL. *See also* Catalan; Ibero-
American Studies; Latin American Studies; Portuguese;
Spanish

Historical and Geographical Studies – Liverpool John
Moores*

Historical and Political Studies – Huddersfield

History/Historical Studies – Aberdeen, Aberystwyth,
Anglia*, Bangor*, Bedford*, Birkbeck, Birmingham, Bishop
Grosseteste*, Bolton, Bradford, Bradford & Ilkley*, Bristol,
Cambridge, Canterbury*, Cardiff, Cardiff IHE* , Central
Lancs Charlotte Mason*, Cheltenham*, Chester*, Crewe &
Alsager*, De Montfort, Derby*, Durham, East Anglia,
Edge Hill*, Edinburgh, Essex, Exeter, Glamorgan,
Glasgow, Glasgow Caledonian, Goldsmiths*, Greenwich,
Gwent, Hertfordshire*, Homerton*, Hull, Keele*, Kent,
King Alfred's*, King's, Kingston*, Lampeter, Lancaster,
Leeds, Leeds Metropolitan*, Leicester, Liverpool,
Liverpool John Moores*, London Guildhall, LSE, LSU*,
Manchester, Manchester Metropolitan*, Middlesex*,
Nene, Newcastle, Newman & Westhill*, North East
Wales*, North London, Northumbria, Nottingham,
Nottingham Trent, Oxford Brookes*, Plymouth*,
Portsmouth, Queen Mary & Westfield, Reading*, Ripon &
York*, Roehampton*, St Andrews, St Mark & St John*,
S. Martin's*, St Mary's*, Salford, Scarborough, Sheffield,
Sheffield Hallam, SOAS, Southampton, SSEES,
Staffordshire, Stirling*, Sunderland, Sussex, Swansea,
Teesside, Thames Valley, Trinity and All Saints*, Trinity
Carmarthen*, Ulster, UCL, Warwick*, West of England*,
West London, Westminster, Westminster College*, West
Sussex*, Wolverhampton*, Worcester, York

History, American – East Anglia, UCL

History, Ancient – Birmingham, Bristol, Cardiff, Durham*,
Edinburgh, Exeter, Keele, King's, Lampeter, Leicester,
Liverpool, Manchester, Newcastle, Nottingham, Queen's,
Royal Holloway, St Andrews, Swansea, UCL, Warwick.
See also Ancient World Studies; Classics; entries under
Egypt; Greek and Roman Civilisation

History, Ancient and Medieval – Royal Holloway, Swansea

History, Ancient and Modern – Oxford

History, Cultural – Aberdeen

History, East Mediterranean – Birmingham

History, English – East Anglia

History, European – East Anglia, Edinburgh, Swansea

History, European Cultural – Middlesex

History, Intellectual – Sussex. *See also* Ideas, History of; Philosophy

History, International – Keele, Leeds, LSE

History, Maritime – Plymouth

History, Medieval – Birmingham, Cardiff, Glasgow, Hull, Queen Mary & Westfield, St Andrews, Sheffield. *See also* Medieval Studies

History, Medieval and Modern – Royal Holloway

History, Modern/Contemporary – Bath CHE*, Birmingham, Buckingham, Dundee, Edinburgh, Glasgow, Hull, Liverpool, London Guildhall, Luton, Manchester, Oxford, Plymouth, Queen Mary & Westfield, Queen's, Reading, St Andrews, Salford, Sheffield, Southampton, Strathclyde, Sussex, Ulster

History, Modern and Economic – Royal Holloway

History, Political – Sussex

History, Social – Lancaster, Sheffield

History, Social, and Heritage Studies – Kent

History and Society – Exeter, Worcester

History and Society, American – Manchester

History of Art *see* Art, History of

Home and Community Studies – Bradford & Ilkley

Home Economics – Bath CHE, Cardiff, Leeds Metropolitan*, Liverpool John Moores*, Sheffield Hallam, Trinity and All Saints, Worcester*

Home Economics and Resource Management – South Bank

Horticulture – Central Lancs, Greenwich, Hertfordshire, Nottingham, Reading, Scottish Agricultural College, Writtle, Wye

Horticultural Technology – Myerscough, Nottingham

Horticulture Business Management – Wye

Horticulture and Retailing – Bournemouth

Hospitality Management/Studies – Blackpool, Bournemouth, Bucks CHE, Central England, Central Lancs, City C, Glasgow Caledonian, Leeds Metropolitan, Napier, North London, Plymouth, Queen Margaret, Robert Gordon, UC Salford, Strathclyde, Thames Valley, Ulster. *See also* entries under Food; Hotel Management; Leisure; Recreation; Tourism

Hospitality Management, International – Brighton, Nottingham Trent, Surrey

**Hotel/and Catering/Institutional/Licensed Retail/
   Restaurant/Tourism Management** – Blackpool, Cardiff,
   Cardiff IHE, Cheltenham, Duncan of Jordanstone,
   Huddersfield, Manchester Metropolitan, Middlesex,
   Napier, North London, Oxford Brookes, Portsmouth,
   Sheffield Hallam, South Bank, Strathclyde, Surrey, Ulster,
   Wolverhampton. *See also* entries under Food; Hospitality
   Management; Leisure; Recreation; Tourism
Hotel Management, International – Buckingham,
   Manchester Metropolitan, North London
Housing/Housing Development/Management/Studies –
   Anglia, Cardiff IHE, Central England, Edinburgh,
   Edinburgh College of Art, Sheffield Hallam, South Bank,
   Ulster, West of England, Westminster
Human/Computer Interface Design – Middlesex
Human Factors in Computing – Luton
Human Organisation/Resource Management – Glamorgan,
   Glasgow Caledonian, Huddersfield, Keele, Liverpool John
   Moores, LSE, Middlesex, Northumbria, Paisley, Stirling,
   Teesside, Wolverhampton
Human Sciences *see* Biology, Human
Human Studies, Interdisciplinary – Bradford
Human Technology Systems – Southampton IHE
Humanities – Brighton, Central England*, Colchester,
   Exeter*, Glamorgan, Greenwich, Hertfordshire, Hull,
   Kent, Luton, Manchester Metropolitan, Nene*,
   Nottingham Trent, Roehampton, Scarborough, Swansea
   IHE*, Teesside, Thames Valley, Ulster
Humanities, Science and Society – Greenwich
Hungarian – Cambridge. *See also* European Languages,
   Literatures and Regional Studies
Hydrography – Plymouth

Ibero-American Studies – Leeds, Southampton, UCL. *See also*
   American Studies, Hispanic Studies, Spanish.
Ideas, History of – Cardiff, Middlesex, Teesside. *See also*
   History, Intellectual; Philosophy
Illustration – Anglia, Duncan of Jordanstone, Kingston,
   Loughborough College of Art, Portsmouth, West of
   England, Westminster, Wolverhampton. *See also* Graphic
   Design and Illustration; Printmaking
Illustration and Animation – Manchester Metropolitan. *See
   also* Animation

Imaging – Manchester Metropolitan

Immunology – Aberdeen, East London, Edinburgh, Glasgow, King's, NESCOT, Strathclyde, UCL, West of England

Individual and Society, The – Nottingham Trent

Indonesian Studies – SOAS

Industrial and Business Studies/Systems – De Montfort, Heriot-Watt, Westminster

Industrial Design – Brunel, Central Lancs, Coventry, Hertfordshire, Luton, Napier, Northumbria, Robert Gordon, Scottish College of Textiles, Teesside

Industrial Design Engineering/Technology – Brunel*, Loughborough*

Industrial Information Technology – Central England, Central Lancs

Industrial Management – Nottingham Trent

Industrial Relations – Cardiff, Kent, LSE, Strathclyde

Industrial Studies – East London, Leeds, Nene, Sheffield Hallam

Infectious Diseases – East London

Informatics *see* Information Technology

Information and Communication Technology – Queen's

Information and Library Management/Studies – Aberystwyth, Brighton, Central England, Liverpool John Moores, Loughborough, Manchester Metropolitan, Northumbria, Robert Gordon

Information Management/Science/Studies – Aberystwyth, Dundee IT, Essex, Lampeter, Leeds Metropolitan, Liverpool, North London, Queen Margaret, Queen's, Sheffield, Strathclyde, Thames Valley, Westminster, Wolverhampton

Information and Publishing – Loughborough

Information Systems/Technology – Anglia*, Birkbeck, Bournemouth, Bucks CHE, Canterbury, De Montfort, Derby, East London, Edinburgh, Essex, European Business School, Glamorgan, Glasgow Caledonian, Huddersfield, Kent, Kingston, Lampeter, Leeds, Leeds Metropolitan, Liverpool John Moores*, Loughborough, Luton, Manchester Metropolitan, Middlesex, Napier, Nene, North East Wales, North London, Nottingham Trent, Paisley, Portsmouth, Queen Margaret, Queen's, St Mark & St John, S. Martin's, Salford, Sheffield Hallam, Shrivenham, Staffordshire, Sunderland, Surrey, Swansea IHE, Teesside, Thames Valley, West of England,

Wolverhampton, York. *See also* entries under Computer/
Computing

Information Technology, Business/Management – Paisley,
Swansea

Information Technology, European – Sheffield Hallam

Information Technology and Human Factors/in Society –
Loughborough, Manchester Metropolitan, Portsmouth

Inquiry and Communication – Crewe & Alsager. *See also*
entries under Communication(s)

Instrumental Chemistry and Marketing – De Montfort

Instrumentation and Control/Measurement – Glasgow
Caledonian, Middlesex, Sheffield Hallam

Insurance/Insurance Studies – Bangor, Central England,
London Guildhall

Insurance and Investment – City U

Intelligent Systems – Oxford Brookes

International Relations – Keele, Kent, Lancaster, LSE,
Nottingham Trent, Plymouth, Reading, St Andrews,
Staffordshire, Sussex

International Studies – Birmingham, Leeds, Southampton,
South Bank

Interpreting and Translating – Heriot-Watt

Investment – Central England

Irish/Irish Studies – Aberystwyth, Liverpool, North London,
St Mary's, Ulster. *See also* Celtic

Islamic and Medieval History – St Andrews

Islamic Studies – Durham*, Lampeter, Oxford. *See also*
entries under Arabic

Italian/Italian Studies – Aberystwyth, Anglia, Bath,
Birmingham, Bristol, Cambridge, Cardiff, East London,
Edinburgh, Exeter, Glasgow, Hull, Kent, Lancaster, Leeds,
Leicester, Luton, Manchester, NEC, Oxford, Oxford
Brookes, Portsmouth, Queen's, Reading, Royal Holloway,
Salford, SSEES, Strathclyde, Sussex, Swansea, UCL,
Warwick, Westminster

Jain Studies – De Montfort

Japanese/Japanese Studies – Cambridge, Cardiff, Durham,
Edinburgh, King Alfred's, Lancaster, Leeds, Liverpool
John Moores, Oxford, Sheffield, SOAS, Stirling,
Wolverhampton Jazz and Popular Music – Middlesex. *See
also* Band Musicianship; entries under Music

Jewellery/and Metalwork Design – Central St Martins,
     Duncan of Jordanstone, Middlesex. *See also* entries under
     Metal; Silversmithing
Jewish History – UCL
Jewish Studies – Jews' College
Journalism – Central Lancs, City U, Napier, Sheffield,
     Southampton IHE, Teesside, West Surrey. *See also*
     Broadcast Journalism
Journalism, Multimedia – Bournemouth
Journalism, Film and Broadcasting – Cardiff. *See also* entries
     under Film; Media; Radio; Television
Journalism, TV and Broadcast – De Montfort
Jurisprudence – Aberdeen

Knitwear Design/and Production – Hinckley, Nottingham
     Trent
Korean Studies – Sheffield, SOAS
Kurdish Studies – SOAS

Labour Studies – Warwick
Land Economy – Aberdeen, Cambridge
Land Management/Technology – Askham Bryan, De
     Montfort, East London, Portsmouth, Reading, Sheffield
     Hallam
Land Management, European – East London, Westminster
Land Resources Management – Askham Bryan
Landscape Architecture/Design – Central England,
     Cheltenham, Edinburgh College of Art, Greenwich,
     Kingston, Leeds Metropolitan, Manchester Metropolitan,
     Sheffield, Writtle
Landscape and Design Heritage – Plymouth
Landscape Management – Reading
Language Arts – Nene*
Language and Communication – Cardiff, Hertfordshire*. *See
     also* entries under Communication(s)
Language and International Trade – Portsmouth
Language and Literature – Bedford*, Bradford & Ilkley*,
     Derby, Manchester. *See also* entries under English; entries
     under Literature
Language Sciences, Clinical – Leeds Metropolitan. *See also*
     Speech and Language Therapy

Language Studies – Cardiff, Essex, Ripon & York*, St Mark & St John, York. *See also* individual languages

Languages, Applied – Bournemouth, Brighton, Leeds Metropolitan*, Portsmouth, Ulster

Languages, European/Modern – Aberystwyth, Aston, Bangor, Bath, Bolton, Central England, Central Lancs, De Montfort, Durham, East Anglia, European Business School, Exeter, Glasgow Caledonian, Huddersfield, King's, Lampeter, Lancaster, Leeds Metropolitan, Leicester, Liverpool, Liverpool John Moores, London Guildhall, LSU, Manchester Metropolitan, Northumbria*, Nottingham, Oxford, St Andrews, Salford, Sheffield*, Sheffield Hallam, South Bank, Staffordshire, Stirling, Strathclyde, Sunderland, West of England*, Wolverhampton. *See also* individual languages

Languages, Middle Eastern – Manchester

Languages for Business – Oxford Brookes, Wolverhampton. *See also* individual languages

Latin – Birmingham, Cambridge, Durham*, Exeter, Glasgow, Keele, Kent, King's, Lampeter, Leeds, Manchester, Newcastle, Nottingham, Queen's, Reading, Royal Holloway, St Andrews, Swansea, UCL. *See also* Classics; Greek and Roman Studies; Roman Civilisation

Latin American Development – Portsmouth

Latin American Studies – Aberdeen, Essex, Liverpool, Middlesex, Newcastle, Portsmouth. *See also* Hispanic Studies; Ibero-American Studies; Portuguese; Spanish

Law – Aberdeen, Aberystwyth, Anglia, Birkbeck, Birmingham, Bristol, Brunel, Buckingham, Buckland, Cambridge, Central England, Central Lancs, Coventry, De Montfort, Derby, Dundee, Durham, East Anglia, East London, Edinburgh, Essex, Exeter, Glamorgan, Glasgow Caledonian, Greenwich, Hertfordshire, Holborn, Huddersfield, Hull, Keele, Kent, King's, Kingston, Lancaster, Leeds, Leeds Metropolitan, Leicester, Liverpool, Liverpool John Moores, London Guildhall, LSE, Luton, Manchester, Manchester Metropolitan, Middlesex, NEC, Nene, Newcastle, North London, Northumbria, Nottingham, Nottingham Trent, Oxford, Oxford Brookes, Plymouth, Queen Mary & Westfield, Queen's, Rapid Results, Reading, Sheffield, Sheffield Hallam, SOAS, South Bank, Southampton, Southampton IHE, Staffordshire, Strathclyde, Surrey, Sussex, Swansea,

Swansea IHE, Teesside, Thames Valley, Ulster, UCL, Warwick, West of England, Westminster, Wolverhampton

Law, American – East Anglia

Law, Biology and the Environment – Buckingham

Law, Business – Bournemouth, Brunel, City U, Liverpool John Moores, London Guildhall, North London, Stirling, Strathclyde, Thames Valley, Wolverhampton

Law, Common and Civil – Queen's

Law, English and European – Buckingham, Essex, Queen Mary & Westfield, Reading

Law, English, European and International – Kingston

Law, English and French – Essex, Kent, King's, LSE, Manchester, Reading, Thames Valley, UCL

Law, English and German – Kent, King's, LSE, Thames Valley, UCL

Law, English and Italian – Kent, UCL

Law, English and Spanish – Kent, Thames Valley

Law, Environmental – Greenwich

Law, European – Aberdeen, Birmingham, East Anglia, Exeter, Nottingham Trent, Strathclyde, Thames Valley, Warwick, West of England, Wolverhampton

Law, European Business – Coventry, Dundee IT, Sussex

Law, Scottish – Glasgow, Strathclyde

Law and Society – Exeter

Leather Technology – Nene. *See also* Footwear and Accessories

Legal and Administrative Studies – Robert Gordon

Legal and Economic Studies – London Guildhall

Legal Studies – Coventry, Dundee IT, Glamorgan, Glasgow Caledonian, London Guildhall, Napier, Staffordshire, Swansea

Legal Studies, European – Kent, King's, Lancaster

Leisure/Leisure and Tourism Administration/Management/ Studies – Bedford, Bolton, Brighton, Bucks CHE, Cheltenham, Coventry, Farnborough, Glasgow Caledonian, Leeds Metropolitan, Luton, Manchester*, North London, UC Salford, Scottish Agricultural College, Southampton IHE, Staffordshire, Swansea IHE, Thames Valley, Warrington, West London, Worcester, Writtle

Leisure Marketing – Bournemouth

Life Sciences – Aberystwyth, East London, Liverpool, Manchester, Middlesex, South Bank, Westminster, Wirral

Life Sciences, Environmental – Nottingham

Life Sciences, Human see Biology, Human

Life Sciences, Plant – Nottingham. *See also* Plant Sciences

Library and Information Studies see Information and Library Management

Lighting Design – Rose Bruford. *See also* Theatre Design

Linguistics – Bangor, Cambridge, Central Lancs, East Anglia, East London, Edinburgh, Essex, Glamorgan, Hertfordshire, Kent, Lancaster, Leeds, Luton, Manchester, Newcastle, Reading, Sheffield, SOAS, Sussex, UCL, Westminster, Wolverhampton, York

Linguistics, Applied – Birkbeck

Linguistics, Computational – Essex, UMIST

Literary and Historical Studies – Humberside, Staffordshire

Literature/Literary Studies – Bangor*, Bolton, Essex, Greenwich, Kent, Open U, Portsmouth, Staffordshire. *See also* Art and Literature, History of; entries under English; individual languages

Literature, American – Essex

Literature, American and English – East Anglia, Kent, Manchester. *See also* American Studies; entries under English

Literature, Comparative – East Anglia, Sunderland

Literature, English (Medieval and Renaissance) – Cardiff. *See also* English

Literature, English and European – Essex. *See also* individual languages

Literature, English, and Theatre Studies – Leeds. *See also* entries under Drama; Theatre

Literature, Foreign – Luton. *See also* individual languages

Literature and Communication Studies – Liverpool John Moores*

Literature and History of Wales – Aberystwyth

Literature and Media Studies – Swansea IHE*

Literature, Life and Thought – Liverpool John Moores

Literature and Philosophy – Middlesex

Logic and Metaphysics – St Andrews

Logic and Philosophy of Science – St Andrews

Logistics Systems – Bournemouth

Management/Management Studies/Science – Aberdeen, Aston, Birkbeck, Brunel, Bucks CHE, Cambridge, Central England, Central Lancs, De Montfort, Dundee, European Business School, Exeter, Glasgow, Holborn, Huddersfield, Hull, Keele, Kent, King's, Lancaster, Leeds, LSE,

Loughborough, Luton, Nottingham, Open U, Paisley, Queen Margaret, Reading, Royal Holloway, St Andrews, Sheffield, South Bank, Southampton, Stirling, Strathclyde, Sunderland, Swansea, Trinity & All Saints, UMIST, Warwick. *See also* Administration; Business Administration; Organisation/and Management Studies

Management Support Systems – Westminster

Management, American – Swansea

Management, European – Kent, Middlesex, Swansea

Management, Industrial – Queen's

Management, International – Bath, Bradford, Hull, Liverpool John Moores, Reading, UMIST

Management, Operational Research and Statistics – Dundee

Management and Systems/Technology – Brunel, City U

Management Decision Making – De Montfort

Manufacturing Computing – Scottish College of Textiles

Manufacturing and Computing – Loughborough

Manufacturing and the Environment – Glamorgan

Manufacturing Management/Studies/Systems/Technology – Anglia, Bath, Bolton, Bradford, Cardiff, Cardiff IHE, Central Lancs, Hertfordshire, Humberside, Leeds Metropolitan, Manchester Metropolitan, Middlesex, North East Wales, Paisley, Salford, UC Salford, Sunderland, Teesside, Ulster, Wolverhampton. *See also* Business and Manufacturing Systems

Manufacturing Management International – Middlesex

Mapping Science – Luton, Newcastle. *See also* Cartography

Marine Biology, Applied – Heriot-Watt

Marine Chemistry – Bangor

Marine and Environmental Biology – St Andrews

Marine/and Freshwater Biology – Aberdeen, Bangor, Liverpool, Newcastle, Queen Mary & Westfield, Stirling, Swansea. *See also* Aquatic Biology

Marine Geography – Cardiff

Marine Navigation – Plymouth

Marine Resource Management – Aberdeen

Marine Sciences – Southampton

Maritime Studies/Technology – Cardiff, Liverpool John Moores, Plymouth, Southampton IHE

Marketing/Marketing Management/Studies – Central England, Central Lancs, Coventry, De Montfort, Derby, European Business School, Glamorgan, Glasgow Caledonian, Huddersfield, Lancaster, Liverpool John Moores, London Guildhall, Luton, Middlesex, North

London, Oxford Brookes, Paisley, Plymouth, Roehampton, Salford, Staffordshire, Stirling, Strathclyde, Teesside, Wolverhampton

Marketing, European – Humberside, Leeds Metropolitan

Marketing, International – Bournemouth, Greenwich

Marketing and Consumer Studies – Queen Margaret

Marketing Design – Southampton IHE

Marketing and Food Management – Silsoe. *See also* entries under Food

Marketing Retailing and Distribution – Huddersfield

Materials/Materials Science/Technology – Aston, Bath, Birmingham, Brunel, Cambridge, Coventry, Imperial, Leeds, Liverpool, Loughborough, Manchester, Manchester Metropolitan, North East Wales, Open U, Oxford, Queen Mary & Westfield, Sheffield, Shrivenham, Strathclyde, Surrey, UMIST, Wolverhampton. *See also* entries under Polymer

Materials, Physics/Chemistry of – Durham

Materials Design and Processing – Nottingham

Materials Science, Biomedical – Manchester, Queen Mary & Westfield

Mathematical and Management Studies – Brunel

Mathematical Methods for Information Technology – Nottingham Trent

Mathematical Modelling – North London

Mathematical Sciences – Bath, City U, De Montfort, Liverpool, Middlesex, Newcastle, North London, Oxford Brookes, Paisley, Portsmouth, Robert Gordon, Strathclyde, Teesside, Westminster

Mathematics – Aberdeen, Aberystwyth, Anglia, Aston, Bangor, Bath, Bedford*, Birmingham, Bishop Grosseteste*, Bolton, Bradford & Ilkley*, Brighton, Bristol, Brunel, Canterbury*, Cardiff, Cardiff IHE*, Central Lancs, Charlotte Mason*, Cheltenham*, Chester*, Coventry, Crewe & Alsager*, De Montfort, Derby*, Dundee, Durham*, East Anglia, East London, Edge Hill*, Edinburgh, Essex, Exeter*, Glamorgan, Glasgow, Glasgow Caledonian, Goldsmiths*, Greenwich*, Gwent*, Heriot-Watt, Hertfordshire, Homerton*, Huddersfield*, Hull*, Imperial, Keele*, Kent, King Alfred's*, King's, Kingston, Lancaster, Leeds, Leeds Metropolitan*, Leicester, Liverpool, Liverpool IHE*, London Guildhall, LSE, Loughborough*, LSU*, Manchester, Manchester Metropolitan*, Middlesex*, Napier, Nene*, Newcastle,

Newman & Westhill*, North East Wales*, North London*,
Northumbria*, Nottingham, Nottingham Trent*, Oxford,
Oxford Brookes*, Plymouth*, Queen Mary & Westfield,
Queen's, Reading*, Ripon & York*, Roehampton*, Royal
Holloway, St Andrews, St Mark & St John*, S. Martin's*,
St Mary's*, Salford, Scarborough*, Sheffield, Sheffield
Hallam*, Southampton, Stirling*, Strathclyde,
Sunderland*, Surrey, Sussex, Swansea, Swansea IHE*,
Trinity & All Saints*, Trinity Carmarthen*, UMIST, UCL,
Warwick*, West of England*, Westminster College*, West
Sussex*, Wolverhampton*, Worcester, York

Mathematics, Applicable – Bath CHE*, Cardiff, Derby,
Hertfordshire, King Alfred's, Manchester Metropolitan,
Paisley, Portsmouth, Queen Mary & Westfield,
Shrivenham, Stirling*, Swansea

Mathematics, Applied – Aberystwyth, Bangor, Cambridge,
Dundee, Exeter, Open U, Queen Mary & Westfield,
Queen's, Reading, St Andrews, Swansea, Warwick

Mathematics, Business/Industrial – Aberystwyth, Brunel ,
Glasgow Caledonian, Kent, LSE, Loughborough,
Middlesex, Queen Mary & Westfield, Staffordshire

Mathematics, Computational/Computing – Glamorgan,
Liverpool, Loughborough, Oxford, Oxford Brookes,
Portsmouth, Queen's, Sheffield Hallam, Swansea,
Westminster

Mathematics, Engineering – Queen Mary & Westfield,
Swansea

Mathematics, Environmental – Lancaster

Mathematics, European – Kent

Mathematics, Industrial Applied – Southampton

Mathematics, Pure – Aberystwyth, Bangor, Cambridge,
Cardiff, Exeter, Hull, Liverpool, Open U, Queen Mary &
Westfield, Queen's, Reading, St Andrews, Sheffield,
Swansea, UMIST

**Mathematics, Statistics and Computing/Operational
Research** – Birkbeck, East London, Greenwich, Liverpool
John Moores, Ulster, UMIST, Warwick, West of England

Mathematics for Management – Brighton, Brunel, King's,
Portsmouth, South Bank

Measurement and Instrumentation Science – Glamorgan,
Manchester Metropolitan

Mechanical Design, Materials and Manufacture –
Nottingham

Mechanical Systems and Design Engineering – Liverpool

Mechatronics – Coventry, De Montfort, Dundee IT, Hull, King's, Lancaster, Leeds, Middlesex, Swansea IHE

Media/Media Arts/and Cultural Studies – Birmingham, Cumbria, De Montfort, East Anglia, East London, Falmouth, Glamorgan, Gwent, Liverpool John Moores, Middlesex, Luton, North East Wales, Nottingham Trent, Plymouth, Queen Margaret, Royal Holloway, St Mark & St John, UC Salford, Sheffield Hallam, South Bank, Southampton IHE, Staffordshire, Suffolk, Sunderland, Sussex, Thames Valley, Ulster, Warrington, West Herts, Westminster, West Surrey, West Sussex, Wirral. *See also* Art and Media Studies; Cultural Studies; Popular Culture

Media, Professional (Graphics, Photography, Video) – Cheltenham. *See also* entries under Graphic; Photography; Visual Arts

Media and Communication – Central England, Cheltenham, Greenwich, King Alfred's, Wolverhampton

Media and Consumer Technology – Staffordshire

Media and Information Studies – Brighton

Media, Language and Business – UC Salford

Media and Performance – UC Salford

Media and Popular Music – UC Salford

Media Practice, Contemporary – Westminster

Media Production – Bournemouth, Farnborough, Humberside, Northumbria

Media Technology – Central Lancs, Luton, Swansea IHE, Teesside

MediaLab Arts – Plymouth

Medical Electronics/Instrumentation – Coventry, Hertfordshire, Liverpool

Medical Informatics – Manchester

Medical Science – Birmingham, Leeds, Queen Mary & Westfield

Medicine – Aberdeen, Birmingham, Bristol, Cambridge, Charing Cross, Dundee, Edinburgh, Glasgow, King's, Leeds, Leicester, Liverpool, London Hospital Medical College, Manchester, Newcastle, Nottingham, Oxford, Queen Mary & Westfield, Queen's, Royal Free, St Andrews, St Bart's, St George's, St Mary's Hospital, Sheffield, Southampton, UCL, UMDS, University of Wales College of Medicine

Medieval Studies – Birmingham, Durham, Lancaster, Manchester, Swansea. *See also* History, Medieval

Mediterranean Studies, Ancient – Bristol

Metallurgy – Birmingham, Brunel, Cambridge, Greenwich, Leeds, Liverpool, Manchester, Oxford, Surrey, UMIST

Metals Design – Middlesex

Metals Science – Sheffield, Surrey

Metalwork and Jewellery – Bucks CHE. *See also* entries under Jewellery; Silversmithing

Meteorology – Reading

Microbiology – Aberdeen, Aberystwyth, Anglia, Birmingham, Bristol, Cardiff, Dundee, East Anglia, East London, Edinburgh, Glasgow, Heriot-Watt, Imperial, Kent, King's, Leeds, Leicester, Liverpool, Manchester, Newcastle, NESCOT, North London, Plymouth, Queen Mary & Westfield, Queen's, Reading, Sheffield, Staffordshire, Strathclyde, Sunderland, Surrey, Swansea, UCL, Warwick, Westminster, Wolverhampton

Microbiology, Applied – Liverpool John Moores, Manchester, Nottingham

Microbiology, Environmental – Aberdeen, Aberystwyth, Surrey

Microbiology, Medical – Edinburgh, Leeds, Newcastle, Surrey, UCL, West of England

Microbiology, Nutritional – Nottingham

Microelectronics/Microelectronic Systems/Design – Aberdeen, Anglia, Bournemouth, Brunel, Derby, Edinburgh, Northumbria, Oxford Brookes

Middle Eastern Studies – Manchester, St Andrews

Midwifery – Avon & Gloucester, Bournemouth, Bradford, Central Lancs, De Montfort, King's, Liverpool John Moores, Newcastle, Northumbria, Oxford Brookes, S. Martin's, Southampton, West Yorks

Minerals Estate Management – Sheffield Hallam

Minerals Surveying and Resource Management – Camborne

Minerals Surveying Science – Glamorgan. *See also* Engineering, Minerals; Engineering, Mining; Geology, Mining

Molecular Sciences – Sussex

Money, Banking and Finance – Birmingham, Middlesex

Movement Science/Studies – Greenwich*, King Alfred's*, Leeds Metropolitan, Liverpool, Nene*

Museum and Exhibition Design – Humberside

Music/Music Studies – Anglia*, Bangor*, Bath CHE*, Birmingham Conservatoire, Bishop Grosseteste*, Bretton Hall*, Bristol, Cambridge, Canterbury*, Cardiff, Cardiff IHE*, Charlotte Mason*, Central England*, Colchester,

Crewe & Alsager*, Dartington, Derby*, Durham, East
Anglia, Edge Hill*, Edinburgh, Essex, Exeter*, Glasgow,
Goldsmiths, Gwent*, Homerton*, Huddersfield*, Hull,
Keele*, King Alfred's*, King's, Kingston*, Lancaster,
Leeds, Liverpool, Liverpool IHE*, Manchester,
Manchester Metropolitan*, Middlesex*, Nene*, Newcastle,
Newman & Westhill, Nottingham, Open U, Oxford,
Oxford Brookes*, Plymouth*, Queen's, Reading*, Ripon &
York*, Roehampton*, Royal Academy of Music, Royal
College of Music, Royal Holloway, Royal Northern
College, Royal Scottish Academy*, S. Martin's*,
Scarborough*, Sheffield, SOAS, Southampton,
Sunderland*, Sussex, Thames Valley, Trinity Carmarthen*,
Trinity College of Music, Ulster, Warwick*, West London,
West Sussex*, Wolverhampton*, Worcester*, York

Music, Academic and Practical Applications of – Surrey

Music, Commercial – Westminster

Music, Electronic – Hertfordshire, Keele. *See also* Electronics,
Music and Media Technology

Music, World – King Alfred's

Music Acoustics and Recording – UC Salford

Music and Sound Recording – Surrey

Music Studies, Applied – Strathclyde

Music Studies, Popular – Bretton Hall, Liverpool, UC
Salford. *See also* Band Musicianship; Jazz and Popular
Music

Music Studies, Twentieth Century – Sussex

Music Technology – Edinburgh, London Guildhall,
Middlesex, Rose Bruford, York

Musical Theatre – ALRA

Musician Performers Course – Thames Valley

Musicianship – Thames Valley

Musicology – Lancaster

Natural Resources – Newcastle

Natural Sciences – Brunel, King's

Natural Sciences, Applied – Sunderland

Nautical Studies – Bath, Plymouth

Naval Architecture – Newcastle

Naval Architecture, Warship – UCL

**Naval Architecture and Ocean/Offshore/Small Craft
Engineering** – Glasgow, Strathclyde, UCL. *See also* Craft
Technology, Small; Yacht and Powercraft Design

Near Eastern Studies, Ancient – SOAS
Nepali Studies – SOAS
Neurology – Cardiff
Neuroscience – Aberdeen, Central Lancs, Edinburgh,
 Glasgow, Manchester, Nottingham, St Andrews, Sussex,
 UCL
Neuroscience, Applied – Manchester
Norwegian – East Anglia
Numerical Analysis and Computer Science – Dundee
Nursing/Nursing Studies – Anglia, Birmingham,
 Bournemouth, Bucks CHE, Central England, City U, De
 Montfort, Dundee IT, Edinburgh, Essex, Glasgow,
 Glasgow Caledonian, Hertfordshire, Hull, King's, Leeds
 Metropolitan, Liverpool, Liverpool John Moores,
 Manchester, Middlesex, North East Wales, Northumbria,
 Nottingham, Oxford Brookes, Queen Margaret, Robert
 Gordon, S. Martin's, Sheffield Hallam, South Bank,
 Southampton, Sunderland, Surrey, Swansea, Ulster,
 University of Wales College of Medicine, West of England
Nursing, Community – King's
Nursing Studies, European – Brighton
Nutrition, Applied – Greenwich, Leeds Metropolitan
Nutrition/Nutrition Studies, Human – Cardiff IHE, Glasgow
 Caledonian, Humberside, King's, North London,
 Nottingham, Oxford Brookes, Queen Margaret, Robert
 Gordon, Southampton, Surrey, Teesside, Ulster. *See also*
 Dietetics, Food and Nutrition, Food Technology
Nutrition and Physiology, Animal – Leeds

Occitan – Cambridge
Occupational Safety and Health – Greenwich, Leeds
 Metropolitan, Nottingham Trent, South Bank, Sunderland
Occupational Therapy – Canterbury, Coventry, Derby, East
 Anglia, Glasgow Caledonian, Institute of Health Care
 Studies, Liverpool, Nene, Northumbria, Oxford Brookes,
 Queen Margaret, Ripon & York, Robert Gordon, St Loye's,
 S. Martin's, UC Salford, Sheffield Hallam, Southampton,
 Ulster, West London
Ocean Science – Bangor, Plymouth
Oceanography – Bangor, Liverpool, Southampton. *See also*
 Acoustics with Oceanography
Oceanography, Geological – Bangor
Office Management, International – Bucks CHE

Operational Management/Research – Central England, Essex, Exeter, Hertfordshire, Lancaster, Leeds, Staffordshire, Swansea

Ophthalmic Optics – Aston

Optical Management – Anglia

Optoelectronics and Laser Engineering – Heriot-Watt, Hull, Northumbria, Swansea IHE. *See also* Physics, Laser, and Optoelectronics

Optometry – Cardiff, City U, Glasgow Caledonian, UMIST

Organisation/and Management Studies – Bradford & Ilkley, Central Lancs, Edge Hill, Lancaster, Queen Margaret, Swansea IHE. *See also* entries under Management

Organisational Behaviour – Glasgow Caledonian, Luton

Oriental Studies – Cambridge, Liverpool, Oxford. *See also* individual languages.

Orthoptics – Glasgow Caledonian, Liverpool, Sheffield

Osteopathy – British School of Osteopathy

Outdoor/and Science Education – Liverpool John Moores*, Stockton

Painting – Loughborough College of Art, Wimbledon, Wolverhampton. *See also* Art; Drawing; Fine Art

Palaeoecology – Queen's

Paper Science – UMIST

Parasitology – Glasgow, Imperial, King's

Pathobiology – Reading

Pathology – Bristol, Cambridge, West of England

Pathology, Experimental – Glasgow

Peace and War Studies – Bolton, Ulster. *See also* War Studies

Peace Studies – Bradford

Performance Arts/Studies – Cheltenham*, De Montfort, King's, Middlesex*, Nene, North East Wales*, Northern School, Northumbria, S. Martin's, Warrington, Welsh College of Music and Drama. *See also* Acting; entries under Drama, Music, Theatre; Visual Performance

Performance Writings – Dartington

Perfumery, Business of – Plymouth

Persian/Persian Studies – Cambridge, Edinburgh, Oxford, SOAS

Personnel/Personnel Management – Central England, Plymouth

Pharmaceutical and Cosmetic Sciences – De Montfort

Pharmaceutical Sciences – Greenwich

Pharmacology – Aberdeen, Bath, Bristol, Cambridge, Cardiff, Central Lancs, Dundee, East London, Edinburgh, Glasgow, King's, Leeds, Liverpool, Manchester, NESCOT, Portsmouth, Sheffield, Southampton, Sunderland, UCL, West of England

Pharmacy – Aston, Bath, Bradford, Brighton, Cardiff, De Montfort, King's, Liverpool John Moores, Manchester, Nottingham, Portsmouth, Queen's, School of Pharmacy, Robert Gordon, Strathclyde, Sunderland

Philosophy – Aberdeen, Birkbeck, Birmingham, Bolton, Bristol, Cambridge, Cardiff, City U, Crewe & Alsager, Dundee, Durham, East Anglia, Edinburgh, Essex, Glamorgan, Glasgow, Greenwich, Hertfordshire, Heythrop, Hull, Keele, Kent, King's, Lampeter, Lancaster, Leeds, Liverpool, Liverpool John Moores, LSE, Manchester, Middlesex, NEC, North London, Nottingham, Open U, Oxford, Queen's, Reading, St Andrews, St Mark & St John, Sheffield, Southampton, Staffordshire, Stirling, Sunderland, Sussex, Swansea, Ulster, UCL, Warwick, Wolverhampton, York. *See also* History, Intellectual; Ideas, History of

Philosophy, Politics and Economics – Keele, Oxford, York

Philosophy, Mental – Aberdeen, Edinburgh

Philosophy, Moral – St Andrews

Philosophy, Scholastic – Queen's

Philosophy, Social – Swansea

Photographic and Electronic Imaging Sciences – Westminster

Photography/and Audio-Visual Media/Film/Television – Blackpool, Derby, Central Lancs, Napier, Nottingham Trent, Portsmouth, Westminster, West Surrey, Wolverhampton. *See also* entries under Film; Media; Television; Visual Arts

Photography, Editorial – Brighton

Photography, History and Theory of – Gwent

Physical and Adventure Education – Bangor*

Physical Education – Bangor, Bedford*, Brighton*, Cardiff IHE*, Charlotte Mason*, Cheltenham*, Chester*, Crewe & Alsager*, Durham*, Edge Hill*, Exeter*, Goldsmiths*, Gwent*, Leeds Metropolitan*, Liverpool IHE*, Liverpool John Moores*, Moray House*, North East Wales*, Nottingham Trent*, Plymouth*, Reading*, Ripon & York*, St Mark & St John*, S. Martin's, St Mary's*, Sheffield Hallam*, Trinity & All Saints*, Trinity Carmarthen*,

Warwick*, West London*, West Sussex*,
Wolverhampton*, Worcester*. *See also* entries under
Exercise; Fitness and Health; Sports Science

Physical Education and Sports Science – Loughborough,
Newman & Westhill*

Physical Science – Crewe & Alsager*, Greenwich*,
Nottingham Trent*, Oxford Brookes, S. Martin's*,
Sheffield, Sussex, UCL

Physical Science for Microelectronics – Paisley

Physical Sciences, Environmental – Liverpool

Physics – Aberdeen, Aberystwyth, Bath, Birkbeck,
Birmingham, Brighton, Bristol, Brunel, Cambridge,
Cardiff, Coventry, Crewe & Alsager*, De Montfort, Derby,
Dundee, Durham*, Edinburgh, Essex, Exeter*, Glasgow,
Glasgow Caledonian, Greenwich, Heriot-Watt, Hull,
Imperial, Keele*, Kent, King's, Kingston, Lancaster, Leeds,
Leicester, Liverpool, Liverpool John Moores,
Loughborough, Manchester, Manchester Metropolitan*,
Newcastle, North East Wales, North London,
Northumbria*, Nottingham, Open U, Oxford, Oxford
Brookes, Paisley, Portsmouth, Queen Mary & Westfield,
Queen's, Reading, Royal Holloway, St Andrews, Salford,
Sheffield, Sheffield Hallam*, Southampton, Staffordshire,
Strathclyde, Surrey, Sussex, Swansea, UMIST, UCL,
Warwick, Wolverhampton, York

Physics of Information Technology – King's

Physics, Applied – Anglia, Bangor, Bath, Central Lancs,
Coventry, Dundee IT, Durham, East Anglia, Essex, Heriot-
Watt, Hertfordshire, Hull, Kingston, Lancaster, Liverpool
John Moores, Manchester Metropolitan, Napier,
Northumbria, Oxford Brookes, Portsmouth, Queen's,
Reading, Robert Gordon, Royal Holloway, Salford,
Shrivenham, Staffordshire, Strathclyde, UCL

Physics, Applied, for Europe – Central Lancs

Physics, Chemical – Bristol, East Anglia, Edinburgh,
Glasgow, Kent, Liverpool, Manchester, Queen Mary &
Westfield, Sheffield, Sussex, UMIST, UCL

Physics, Computational – UMIST, York

Physics, Computer-Aided – Lancaster

Physics, Engineering – Coventry, Lancaster, Loughborough,
Manchester Metropolitan, Sheffield Hallam

Physics, Interdisciplinary – East Anglia

Physics, Laser, and Optoelectronics – St Andrews, Strathclyde. *See also* Optoelectronics and Laser Engineering

Physics, Mathematical – Edinburgh, King's, Liverpool, Nottingham, Sussex, UMIST

Physics, Medical – Newcastle, Sheffield

Physics, Pure and Applied – Nottingham

Physics, Radiation, and Environmental Science – Liverpool

Physics, Technological – Essex, Glasgow

Physics, Theoretical – Birmingham, Essex, Exeter, Kent, Lancaster, Newcastle, Queen Mary & Westfield, Queen's, Royal Holloway, St Andrews, Sheffield, York

Physics, Theoretical and Computational – Cardiff

Physics and Optical Science – Reading

Physiology/Physiological Sciences – Aberdeen, Bristol, Cambridge, Cardiff, Central Lancs, Dundee, East London, Edinburgh, Glasgow, Greenwich, King's, Liverpool, Manchester, Newcastle, Oxford, Queen's, Reading, St Andrews, Salford, Sheffield, Southampton, Staffordshire, Sunderland, UCL, Westminster

Physiology, Animal – Leicester, Wolverhampton, York

Physiology, Applied – Sunderland

Physiology, Applied Human – NESCOT

Physiology, Human – East London, Wolverhampton

Physiology, Mammalian – West of England

Physiology and Sports Science – Glasgow. *See also* Sports Science

Physiotherapy – Avon & Gloucester, Bath, Birmingham, Bradford, Brighton, Coventry, East Anglia, East London, Glasgow Caledonian, Hertfordshire, Institute of Health Care Studies, Keele, King's, Leeds Metropolitan, Liverpool, Manchester, Northumbria, Nottingham, Queen Margaret, Robert Gordon, UC Salford, Sheffield Hallam, Southampton, Teesside, Ulster, West London, West Yorks, Wolverhampton

Planetary Science – UCL

Planning/Planning Studies/Planning and Development – Anglia, Birmingham, Coventry, Liverpool John Moores, North East Wales, Oxford Brookes, Sheffield Hallam, Strathclyde. *See also* entries under Town; Urban

Planning, European – Westminster

Plant and Crop Science – Nottingham, Wolverhampton

Plant Pathology and Microbiology – West of England

Plant Physiology – Aberystwyth

Plant Physiology and Biotechnology – West of England

Plant Science, Applied – Manchester, Plymouth, Queen's

Plant Science, Environmental – Reading

Plant Sciences – Aberdeen, Cambridge, Imperial, King's, Leicester, Liverpool, Manchester, Newcastle, Queen's, Sheffield, Wye

Plant and Soil Sciences – Aberdeen

Podiatry – Brighton, Cardiff IHE, Glasgow Caledonian, Huddersfield, LSU, Matthew Boulton, Nene, New College, Plymouth, Queen Margaret, Queen's, UC Salford, Sunderland, UCL, Westminster

Policy and Administration, International – Staffordshire

Policy Studies – Kent, North London, Staffordshire

Polish – Cambridge, Glasgow, SSEES. *See also* European Languages, Literatures and Regional Studies

Political Economy – East London, Glasgow, Hertfordshire, Kent, Staffordshire

Politics/Political Science/Studies – Aberdeen, Aberystwyth, Anglia, Bath, Birkbeck, Birmingham, Bradford, Bristol, Buckingham, Bucks CHE, Cardiff, Central Lancs, De Montfort, Dundee, Durham, East Anglia, East London, Edinburgh, Essex, Exeter, Glasgow, Glasgow Caledonian, Goldsmiths, Greenwich, Hull, Keele, Kent, Lancaster, Leeds, Leicester, Liverpool, Liverpool John Moores, London Guildhall, Loughborough, LSU, Manchester, Middlesex, Newcastle, North London, Nottingham, Nottingham Trent, Oxford Brookes, Plymouth, Portsmouth, Queen Mary & Westfield, Queen's, Reading, Salford, Sheffield, SOAS, South Bank, Southampton, Staffordshire, Stirling, Strathclyde, Sunderland, Sussex, Swansea, Teesside, Warwick, West of England, Westminster, Wolverhampton, York

Politics, European – Buckingham, Humberside, Hull, Swansea

Politics, International – Aberystwyth, Keele, Leeds, Southampton

Politics and East Asian Studies – Newcastle

Politics and International Relations – Hull

Polymer Science/Technology – Birmingham, Coventry, Lancaster, Manchester Metropolitan, Napier, North London, Sheffield, UMIST. *See also* Chemistry and Physics of Polymers

Polymeric Materials – Manchester, Queen Mary & Westfield, UMIST. *See also* entries under Materials

Popular Culture/and the Media – East London, King Alfred's. *See also* entries under Cultural; Media

Population Studies – LSE, Southampton

Portuguese – Birmingham, Cambridge, Cardiff, King's, Leeds, Manchester, Oxford, Southampton. *See also* Hispanic Studies.

Prakrit – Cambridge

Printing Management – London College of Printing, Manchester Metropolitan, Nottingham Trent

Printing/and Packaging/Photographic Technology – Manchester Metropolitan, West Herts

Printmaking – Derby, Loughborough College of Art, Wolverhampton

Probability and Statistics – Sheffield

Process Technology and Management Studies – South Bank

Product Design/Development/Engineering/Manufacture – Anglia, Bournemouth, Brunel, Bucks CHE, Cardiff IHE, Central England, Central Lancs, Central St Martins, De Montfort, Derby, East London, Huddersfield, Liverpool John Moores, Loughborough, Middlesex, Roehampton, UC Salford, South Bank, Southampton IHE, Suffolk, Sunderland, Swansea IHE, Thames Valley, Westminster. *See also* Consumer Product Design; Engineering, Product Design

Production and Operations Management – Nottingham

Professional Studies (Learning Difficulties) – Stockport, Wirral. *See also* Social and Professional Studies

Project Management – Anglia, Leeds Metropolitan

Project Management for Construction – UCL. *See also* entries under Builidng, Construction

Property Development and Asset Management – Salford

Property Management – Anglia, Sheffield Hallam

Property Valuation and Finance – City U

Prosthetics and Orthotics – UC Salford, Strathclyde

Psycholinguistics – Essex

Psychology – Aberdeen, Aston, Bangor, Bath, Birkbeck, Birmingham, Bolton, Bristol, Brunel , Buckingham, Bucks CHE, Cambridge, Cardiff, Cardiff IHE, Central Lancs, Chester, City U, Crewe & Alsager, De Montfort, Derby, Dundee, Durham, East London, Edinburgh, Essex, Exeter, Glamorgan, Glasgow, Glasgow Caledonian, Goldsmiths, Greenwich, Hertfordshire, Hull, Humberside, Keele*, Kent, King Alfred's, Lancaster, Leeds, Leicester, Liverpool, Liverpool IHE, London Guildhall, LSE,

Loughborough, Luton, Manchester, Manchester
Metropolitan, Middlesex, Nene, Newcastle, Northumbria,
Nottingham, Open U, Oxford, Oxford Brookes, Plymouth,
Portsmouth, Queen Margaret, Queen's, Reading, Royal
Holloway, St Andrews, S. Martin's, Sheffield, Sheffield
Hallam, South Bank, Southampton, Staffordshire, Stirling,
Strathclyde, Sunderland, Surrey, Sussex, Swansea,
Teesside, Thames Valley, Trinity & All Saints, UCL,
Warwick, West of England, Westminster, Wolverhampton,
Worcester, York

Psychology, Applied – Bournemouth, Cardiff, Central Lancs,
Goldsmiths, Liverpool John Moores, Surrey, Sussex,
Ulster

Psychology, Applied Social – Kent

Psychology, Business – Derby

Psychology, Developmental – Sussex

Psychology, European Social – Kent

Psychology, Experimental – Oxford

Psychology, Health – Thames Valley

Psychology, Human – Aston, De Montfort

Psychology, Occupational – Ulster

Psychology, Social – Bradford, Kent, LSE, Loughborough,
Sussex, Ulster. *See also* Psychosocial Studies

Psychology in the Community – Thames Valley

Psychology and Counselling – Roehampton

Psychosocial Studies – East London. *See also* Psychology,
Sociology

Public Administration/Management/Policy – Aston,
Birmingham, Brighton, Central England, De Montfort,
European Business School, Glamorgan, Glasgow
Caledonian, Goldsmiths, Hertfordshire, Kent, Luton,
Manchester Metropolitan, Newcastle, Nottingham Trent,
Open U, Robert Gordon, Sheffield Hallam, Southampton,
Southampton IHE, Teesside

Public Media – Trinity & All Saints

Public Policy, European – Portsmouth

Public Relations – Bournemouth, Central Lancs, Leeds
Metropolitan, St Mark & St John

Public Sector Management – Sheffield Hallam

Public Services Management – Liverpool John Moores

Publishing – Napier, Oxford Brookes, Robert Gordon, West
Herts. *See also* Writing and Publishing

Quality Management/Technology – Paisley, UC Salford,
Scottish College of Textiles

Quantitative Methods – Luton, Teesside

Quantity Surveying – Anglia, Bath. Bolton, Central England,
Central Lancs, Dundee IT , Glamorgan, Glasgow College
of Building, Greenwich, Kingston, Leeds Metropolitan,
Liverpool John Moores, Luton, Napier, North East Wales,
Northumbria, Nottingham Trent, Portsmouth, Reading,
Robert Gordon, Salford, Sheffield Hallam, South Bank,
Staffordshire, Ulster, West of England, Westminster,
Wolverhampton

Race and Ethnic Studies – Central Lancs. *See also*
Community and Race Relations, Urban Policy Studies

Radio, Film and Television Studies – Canterbury. *See also*
entries under Broadcasting; Film; Journalism; Television

Radiography – Bradford, Glasgow Caledonian, King's,
Portsmouth, Robert Gordon, S. Martin's, South Bank,
Teesside

Radiography, Diagnostic – Anglia, Avon & Gloucester,
Canterbury, Central England, Derby, Hertfordshire,
Institute of Health Care Studies, Keele, Kingston,
Liverpool, Queen Margaret, UC Salford, Sheffield Hallam,
Shrivenham, Southampton, Suffolk, Ulster

Radiography, Therapeutic – Anglia, Avon & Gloucester,
Derby, Hertfordshire, Keele, Kingston, Liverpool, Queen
Margaret, Sheffield Hallam, Shrivenham, Southampton,
Suffolk, Ulster

Radiography and Diagnostic Imaging – Bangor

Real Estate Management/Valuation – Southampton IHE,
West of England

Recreation Management/Studies – Cardiff IHE, Cheltenham,
Coventry, Loughborough, St Mark & St John, Sheffield
Hallam. *See also* Leisure; Tourism

Recreation/and Sports Science – Birmingham, Moray
House*. *See also* Sports Science

Recreation and Tourism – Staffordshire. *See also* Leisure;
Tourism

Regional Development, European – Ulster

Regional Development Studies – Luton

Regional Science – Reading

Religion, Comparative – Manchester, SOAS

Religion, Ethics and Western Society – Lampeter

Religious and Ethical/Moral Studies – North East Wales*, Plymouth*

Religious Studies – Bangor, Bath CHE*, Bishop Grosseteste*, Bradford & Ilkley*, Bristol, Cambridge, Canterbury*, Cardiff, Cardiff IHE*, Charlotte Mason,* Cheltenham*, Chester*, Crewe & Alsager*, Derby*, Edge Hill*, Edinburgh, Glamorgan, Gwent*, Hertfordshire*, Homerton*, King Alfred's*, King's, Lampeter, Lancaster, Leeds, LSU*, Manchester, Manchester Metropolitan*, Middlesex*, Newcastle, Open U, Ripon & York*, St Mark & St John*, S. Martin's*, Scarborough*, SOAS, Stirling*, Sunderland, Trinity Carmarthen*, Warwick*, West London, Westminster College*, West Sussex*, Wolverhampton*, Worcester. *See also* Biblical Studies; Christian Ministry; Christian Studies; Church History/Studies; Theological and Religious Studies; Theology

Resources and the Environment – Kingston. *See also* entries under Environment(al)

Restoration and Conservation *see* Conservation

Retail/and Distribution Business/Management – Bournemouth, Dundee IT, Glasgow Caledonian, London College of Printing, Oxford Brookes, Queen Margaret, Surrey, Ulster

Retail Marketing – Manchester Metropolitan. *See also* Marketing

Risk Management – Glasgow Caledonian

Robotics and Automated Manufacture/Systems – Plymouth, Sussex

Roman Civilisation – Leeds. *See also* Classics, Latin

Romanian – SSEES. *See also* European Languages, Literatures and Regional Studies

Rural Resources Development/Management/Science – Aberystwyth, Anglia, Bangor Harper Adams, Newcastle, Plymouth, Royal Agricultural College, Scottish Agricultural College, Writtle. *See also* entries under Countryside; Estate Management

Rural Technology with Business Studies – Harper Adams

Russian/Russian Studies – Bangor, Bath, Birmingham, Bradford, Bristol, Cambridge, Durham, Edinburgh, Essex, Exeter, Glasgow, Heriot-Watt, Keele, Leeds, Liverpool John Moores, Manchester, Middlesex, Northumbria, Nottingham, Oxford, Queen Mary & Westfield, Queen's, St Andrews, Sheffield, SSEES, Strathclyde, Surrey, Swansea, Thames Valley, Westminster, Wolverhampton

Russian and East European Studies – Strathclyde, Sussex, Wolverhampton. *See also* Soviet and East European Studies

Russian and Soviet Studies – Manchester, Portsmouth. *See also* Soviet and East European Studies

Sanskrit/Sanskrit Studies – Cambridge, Edinburgh, Oxford, SOAS

Scandinavian Studies – East Anglia, Edinburgh, Hull, Lampeter, UCL. *See also* individual languages

Science – Aberdeen, Anglia*, Bangor*, Bedford, Bishop Grosseteste*, Bradford & Ilkley*, Canterbury*, Charlotte Mason*, Cheltenham*, Dundee IT, Exeter*, Glasgow, Hertfordshire*, Huddersfield*, Kingston*, Leeds Metropolitan*, Manchester Metropolitan*, Middlesex*, Napier, Newcastle, Newman & Westhill, North East Wales*, Nottingham Trent*, Oxford Brookes, Paisley, Plymouth*, Portsmouth*, Reading*, Roehampton*, St Mark & St John*, Sheffield Hallam*, Strathclyde, Sunderland*, Swansea IHE*, Ulster, West Sussex*, Wolverhampton*

Science, Applied – Teesside, Wolverhampton

Science, Clinical – Bournemouth

Science, History of – Kent

Science, History and Philosophy of – Cambridge, Leeds, Queen's

Science and Design Technology – Edge Hill*

Science and the Environment – De Montfort, Liverpool John Moores*, Trinity Carmarthen*, Westminster College*

Science, Society and the Media – West of England

Science and Technology – Gwent*, Manchester, Nene*, Trinity & All Saints*

Science and Technology Policy – Middlesex

Science, Technology and Society – Middlesex

Sciences, Combined – West of England

Scientific Cultures – Derby

Scottish Ethnology – Edinburgh

Scottish Literature and Scottish History – Edinburgh

Scottish Literature/Studies – Glasgow, St Andrews, Stirling, Strathclyde. *See also* Celtic

Scriptwriting for Film and Television – Bournemouth

Sculpture – Loughborough College of Art, Wimbledon, Wolverhampton. *See also* Art; Design, 3D

Secretarial Studies – Glasgow Caledonian, Northumbria

Semitic Studies – SOAS

Serbo-Croat – Nottingham. *See also* European Languages, Literatures and Regional Studies

Service Sector Management – Brighton, Glasgow Caledonian

Ship Science – Southampton

Sign Language Interpreting, British – Wolverhampton

Silversmithing and Jewellery/Metalwork – Camberwell, London Guildhall, Loughborough College of Art. *See also* Jewellery; entries under Metal

Sinhalese Studies – SOAS

Slavonic and East European Studies – Glasgow. *See also* European Studies, Contemporary East

Slovak *see* European Languages, Literatures and Regional Studies

Social Administration – Paisley, Roehampton

Social Behaviour – Kent, Nene

Social and Behavioural Sciences, Combined – Ulster

Social Biology – Roehampton

Social and Computer Sciences – Brunel

Social, Cultural and Policy Studies – Derby

Social and Cultural Studies – Bucks CHE , Nottingham

Social, Economic and Political Studies – King Alfred's

Social and Educational Studies – Canterbury

Social and Management Sciences – Napier

Social Philosophy and Applied Ethics – Cardiff

Social and Political Sciences/Studies – Cambridge, Sheffield

Social and Professional Studies (Learning Disabilities) – King Alfred's. *See also* Professional Studies

Social Policy – Anglia, Bangor, Birmingham, Cardiff, Central Lancs, Dundee, Durham, Edinburgh, Glasgow, Goldsmiths, Hull, Humberside, Kent, Leeds, LSE, Manchester, Middlesex, Newcastle, Plymouth, Royal Holloway, Sheffield, Sheffield Hallam, Southampton, Stirling, Teesside, Wolverhampton, York

Social Policy and Administration/Management/Planning – Bath, Brighton, Bristol, Durham, Kent, Leeds Metropolitan, London Guildhall, LSE, Loughborough, Nottingham, Portsmouth, Southampton, Sussex, Ulster

Social Policy, European – Anglia

Social Policy Research – East London

Social Research – Aberdeen, Middlesex, North London

Social Science/Studies – Aston, Bath CHE, Bretton Hall,

City U, Coventry, Crewe & Alsager, Derby, East London, Glasgow, Glasgow Caledonian, Greenwich, Hertfordshire, Leeds Metropolitan, Luton, Manchester Metropolitan, Newcastle, Newman & Westhill, Nottingham Trent, Queen Margaret, Sheffield Hallam, South Bank, Southampton IHE, Sunderland, Thames Valley, West of England, Westminster, Worcester

Social Science/Studies, Applied – Bradford, Central Lancs, Coventry, Crewe & Alsager, Edge Hill, Keele, Kingston, Lancaster, Open U, Paisley, Ripon & York, Robert Gordon, Scarborough, Sheffield Hallam, Staffordshire, Sunderland

Social Studies, European – West of England

Social Studies in Technology – Manchester Metropolitan

Social Work/and Social Policy/and Community Studies – Anglia, Bath, Bucks CHE, Central Lancs, Coventry. Dundee, Dundee IT, East London, Glasgow, Hertfordshire, Lancaster, Middlesex, Moray House, North London, Northumbria, Oxford Brookes, Paisley, Plymouth, Reading, UC Salford, South Bank, Stirling, Strathclyde, Ulster. *See also* entries under Community; Youth Studies

Society, Economy and Social Policy – Exeter

Sociology – Aberdeen, Anglia, Bangor, Bath, Bath CHE*, Bedford, Birmingham, Bradford, Bristol, Brunel, Bucks CHE, Cardiff, Central England, Central Lancs, Cheltenham, City U, Crewe & Alsager, Durham, East Anglia, East London, Edinburgh, Essex, Exeter, Glamorgan, Glasgow, Glasgow Caledonian, Goldsmiths, Greenwich, Hull, Keele*, Kent, Kingston, Lancaster, Leeds, Leicester, Liverpool, Liverpool IHE, Liverpool John Moores, London Guildhall, LSE, Loughborough, LSU, Manchester, Middlesex, Nene, Northumbria, Nottingham, Open U, Oxford Brookes, Plymouth, Portsmouth, Queen Margaret, Queen's, Reading, Royal Holloway, St Mark & St John, St Mary's, Salford, Sheffield, Sheffield Hallam, Southampton, Staffordshire, Stirling, Strathclyde, Sunderland, Surrey, Sussex, Swansea, Teesside, Trinity & All Saints, Ulster, Warwick, West of England, Westminster, Wolverhampton, York. *See also* Psychosocial Studies

Sociology, Applied – Surrey

Software Engineering/Technology – Aberystwyth, Anglia, Bath, Birmingham, Central Lancs, City U, Coventry, De Montfort, Derby, Glamorgan, Glasgow, Greenwich, Hull,

Kingston, Leicester, Liverpool John Moores, Manchester Metropolitan, Napier, Newcastle, Paisley, Queen's, Sheffield, Sheffield Hallam, South Bank, Staffordshire, Stirling, Teesside, Ulster, UMIST, Westminster, Wolverhampton

Software Engineering, Applied – Central England

Software Engineering, International – Sheffield Hallam

Software Engineering Management – Bournemouth

Software Systems – Humberside

Soil and Forest Science – Bangor

Soil Science – Aberdeen, Bangor, Newcastle, Reading

Soils and the Environment – Reading

Soviet and East European Studies – Nottingham. *See also* European Studies, Contemporary East; Russian and Soviet Studies; Slavonic and East European Studies

Spanish/Spanish Studies – Aberystwyth, Anglia, Bradford, Bristol, Cambridge, Cardiff, Central England, Central Lancs, Coventry, Derby, Durham, East London, Edinburgh, Essex, Exeter, Glamorgan, Heriot-Watt, Hull, Kingston, Leeds, Liverpool John Moores, London Guildhall, Luton, Manchester, Middlesex, Newcastle, Northumbria*, Oxford, Portsmouth, Queen's, St Andrews, Salford, Sheffield, Southampton, Staffordshire, Stirling*, Strathclyde, Sunderland, Swansea, Thames Valley, Trinity & All Saints, Ulster, UCL, Westminster, Wolverhampton*. *See also* Hispanic Studies

Spanish and Latin American Studies – Goldsmiths, NEC, Newcastle, North London, Swansea. *See also* Ibero-American Studies

Spanish, Business – Central Lancs

Speech/Speech Communication/Science – National Hospital, Newcastle, Sheffield. *See also* entries under Communication; Language and Communication

Speech and Language Pathology/Therapy – Cardiff IHE Central England, Manchester*, Manchester Metropolitan, Queen Margaret, Strathclyde, Ulster. *See also* Language Sciences, Clinical

Sport in the Community – Strathclyde

Sport and Leisure/Recreation Studies – Birmingham, Bucks CHE, Staffordshire, Ulster. *See also* entries under Exercise; Fitness and Health; Physical Education; Leisure; entries under Recreation

Sports Science /Studies – Bangor, Bedford, Birmingham, Brighton, Canterbury*, Cardiff IHE, Chester*, Crewe &

Alsager, Greenwich, King Alfred's, Leeds, Liverpool John Moores, LSU, Newman & Westhill, North London, Northumbria, Nottingham Trent, Portsmouth, Roehampton*, S. Martin's, St Mary's, South Bank, Staffordshire, Suffolk, Sunderland, Teesside, Warrington, West London, West Sussex, Wolverhampton, Worcester. *See also* Physical Education

Sports Therapy – St Mary's

Sports Turf Management – Writtle

Statistics/Statistical Science – Aberdeen, Aberystwyth, Bath, Brighton, Brunel, Cardiff, Central Lancs, City U, Coventry, Dundee, East London, Exeter, Glasgow, Glasgow Caledonian, Goldsmiths, Heriot-Watt, Hertfordshire, Keele, Kent, Lancaster, Leeds, Liverpool, London Guildhall, LSE, Middlesex, Newcastle, Open U, Queen Mary & Westfield, Reading, St Andrews, Sheffield, Sheffield Hallam, Southampton, Strathclyde, Surrey, Swansea, UCL

Statistics, Applied – Central Lancs, Greenwich, Liverpool John Moores, North London, Oxford Brookes, Plymouth, Reading, Sheffield Hallam, Staffordshire, West of England

Statistics, Applied International – Sheffield Hallam

Statistics, Managerial – Exeter

Statistics, Mathematical – Exeter, Hull, Liverpool

Statistics and Operational Research – Queen's, UCL

Strategic Systems Management – Bournemouth

Sumerian – Cambridge

Surface Pattern – Huddersfield

Surveying – Anglia, Glamorgan. *See also* Building Surveying

Surveying and Mapping Science – East London, Newcastle

Surveying for Resource Development – Glamorgan

Swahili Studies – SOAS

Swedish – East Anglia, Lampeter. *See also* Scandinavian Studies

Systems – Open U

Systems Accounting and Decision Management – De Montfort

Systems Analysis – West of England

Systems Design, Digital – Luton

Systems Design, Interactive – Staffordshire

Systems Integration – Manchester

Systems Modelling – Anglia, Sheffield Hallam

Systems Modelling, International – Sheffield Hallam

Systems Science/Technology – Anglia, Westminster

Tamil Studies – SOAS

Taxation and Revenue Law – Bournemouth

Technical Communication – Coventry

Technical Education – Glasgow

Technologies, Combined – Anglia, East London

Technology – Bangor*, Bedford, Central England*, Central Lancs, Charlotte Mason*, Derby, Huddersfield*, Middlesex*, Moray House*, Northumbria*, Reading*, Sheffield Hallam*, South Bank, Strathclyde*, Sunderland*, Trinity & All Saints*, Trinity Carmarthen*, Wolverhampton*, Worcester*

Technology and Business Studies/Systems – Glamorgan, Middlesex, Robert Gordon

Technology Management – Bradford, Cardiff IHE, Humberside, Liverpool John Moores, Oxford Brookes, Paisley, South Bank, Southampton IHE, Staffordshire, Stirling, Sunderland, Swansea IHE

Technology, Multimedia – Leeds Metropolitan

Technology, New – East London

Technology and Society – Paisley

Telecommunications – Anglia, Queen Mary & Westfield

Television Production and Design – Manchester Metropolitan

Television and Radio – UC Salford. *See also* entries under Broadcasting; Film; Media; Radio

Textiles/Textile Arts/Design/Management/Manufacture/ Materials/Studies/Technology – Bangor*, Bath CHE, Bolton, Bradford & Ilkley, Bretton Hall, Brighton, Bucks CHE, Central St Martins, De Montfort, Derby, Duncan of Jordanstone, East London, Goldsmiths, Huddersfield, Leeds, Liverpool John Moores, Loughborough College of Art, Manchester Metropolitan, Nottingham Trent, Scottish College of Textiles, UMIST, West of England, West Surrey, Sutton, Ulster, Winchester. *See also* Clothing; Fashion

Thai Studies – SOAS

Theatre/Theatre Arts/Studies – Bretton Hall, Central School, Dartington, Glamorgan, Glasgow, Lancaster, Liverpool John Moores, Manchester Metropolitan, North East Wales, North London, Plymouth, Rose Bruford, Southampton IHE, Ulster, Warwick, Welsh College of Music and Drama, Wolverhampton. *See also* Acting; entries under Drama; Performance Arts; Visual Performance

Theatre Design/and Technology – Bretton Hall, Central Lancs, Central St Martins, Middlesex, Nottingham Trent,

Rose Bruford, Welsh College of Music & Drama, Wimbledon. *See also* Lighting Design

Theatre and Media Drama – Glamorgan

Theatre and Media Studies – Bolton, Trinity Carmarthen

Theological and Pastoral Studies – Oak Hill

Theological and Religious Studies – Roehampton*

Theological Studies, Applied – Newman & Westhill

Theology – Aberdeen, Aberystwyth, Bangor, Birmingham, Bristol, Cambridge, Cardiff, Chester, Durham, Edinburgh, Exeter, Glasgow, Greenwich, Heythrop, Hull, Kent, King's, Lampeter, Leeds, Liverpool IHE*, London Bible College, LSU, Manchester, NEC, Newman & Westhill*, Nottingham, Oxford, Queen's, Ripon & York*, St Andrews, St Mark & St John, St Mary's*, Trinity & All Saints*, Trinity Bristol, Westminster College. *See also* Biblical Studies; Christian Ministry; Christian Studies; Church History/Studies; Religious Studies

Theology, Systematic – Edinburgh

Third World Studies – Coventry, East London, Greenwich, Liverpool, Middlesex

Thought and Literature, European – Anglia. *See also* individual languages; entries under Literature; Philosophy

Time-Based Media – West of England

Topographic Science – Glasgow, Swansea

Tourism/Tourism Studies/Management – Bangor, Birmingham, Bolton, Bournemouth, Brighton, Bucks CHE, Canterbury, Cardiff IHE, Central England, Cheltenham, Derby, Glasgow Caledonian, Humberside, Leeds Metropolitan, Napier, Oxford Brookes, Plymouth, Queen Margaret, Sheffield Hallam, South Bank, Surrey, Westminster, Wolverhampton. *See also* Hospitality Management; Leisure; Recreation Management; Travel and Tourism Development

Town Planning – Edinburgh College of Art, Newcastle, Sheffield Hallam, South Bank, Westminster. *See also* Planning; entries under Urban

Town and Country /Regional Planning – Duncan of Jordanstone, Liverpool, Manchester, UCL, West of England

Toxicology and Pharmacology – School of Pharmacy. *See also* Biochemistry Toxicology; Pharmacology

Transport – Plymouth, Ulster, Westminster

Transport Design – Coventry

Transport and Distribution – Huddersfield

Transport, International – Cardiff

Transport Management – Aston, Loughborough, Swansea IHE

Travel and Tourism – Glasgow Caledonian, Hertfordshire, Luton, Northumbria. *See also* Tourism

Travel and Tourism Development – Dundee IT. *See also* Tourism

Tropical Environmental Science – Aberdeen

Turkish/Turkish Studies – Cambridge, Oxford, SOAS

Typography – Portsmouth

Typography and Graphic Communication – Reading

Underwater Studies – Plymouth. *See also* entries under Marine

United States and Latin-American Studies – King's

United States Studies *see* American Studies

Urban Estate Management – Glamorgan, Kingston, Liverpool John Moores, Westminster

Urban/and Community Development – Leeds Metropolitan, Middlesex, West of England

Urban Planning and Management – Nottingham. *See also* Planning; entries under Town

Urban Policy/Studies – Bolton, East London, Edge Hill, Greenwich, Humberside, Kent, Liverpool, Liverpool John Moores, North London, Sheffield, Sheffield Hallam, Westminster. *See also* Employment and Urban Studies

Urdu Studies/Urdu and Pakistan Studies – SOAS

Valuation Surveying – Staffordshire

Veterinary Medicine/Science – Bristol, Cambridge, Edinburgh, Glasgow, Liverpool, RVC

Victorian Studies – Lampeter

Video Imaging and Communications – UC Salford

Vietnamese Studies – SOAS

Visual Arts/Culture/Studies – Bolton, Central Lancs, Charlotte Mason*, Cheltenham*, Crewe & Alsager*, De Montfort, Derby, Falmouth, Lancaster, Lincolnshire, Liverpool John Moores, Nene, Norfolk, North East Wales*, Oxford Brookes*, Portsmouth, UC Salford, Staffordshire, Swansea IHE, West Surrey. *See also* entries under Art; Design; Film; Media; Photography; Television

Visual Communication Design – Falmouth, Middlesex, Ravensbourne
Visual Communications – Central England, Derby, East London, Ulster
Visual Performance – Brighton, Dartington, Kent. *See also* Acting; Performance Arts; Theatre

War Studies – King's, Wolverhampton. *See also* Peace and War Studies
Water Resources – Bangor
Welfare – Kent
Welsh/Welsh Studies – Aberystwyth, Bangor, Cardiff, Cardiff IHE*, Glamorgan, Gwent*, Lampeter, North East Wales*, Swansea, Trinity Carmarthen*. *See also* Celtic
Welsh and Literature of the Media – Bangor
Welsh History – Aberystwyth, Bangor, Cardiff
Welsh and Welsh Drama – Trinity Carmarthen*
Wildlife Conservation – East London
Women in Business – Staffordshire
Women and New Technology – East London
Women's Health – Luton
Women's Studies – Anglia, Bolton, Central Lancs, Cheltenham, Coventry, Derby, East London, Edge Hill, Glamorgan, Lancaster, Leeds, Liverpool, Liverpool John Moores, Luton, Middlesex, North London, Queen's, Ripon & York, Roehampton, Sheffield Hallam, Staffordshire, West of England, Wolverhampton. *See also* Feminist and Gender Studies
Wood Engineering/Preservation/Science – Bangor, Bucks CHE
Wood, Metal, Ceramics, Plastics – Brighton
Wood, Metals and Plastics (3D Design) – Wolverhampton. *See also* Design, 3D
Writing – Crewe & Alsager*. *See also* Experience of Writing
Writing, Studies in Contemporary – Middlesex. *See also* Creative Studies in English; entries under English; Literature
Writing and Publishing – Middlesex

Yacht and Powercraft Design – Southampton IHE
Youth Studies/Youth and Community Education/Studies/ Work – Crewe & Alsager, Manchester Metropolitan,

North East Wales, St Mark & St John. *See also* entries under Community

Zoology – Aberdeen, Aberystwyth, Bangor, Bristol, Cambridge, Cardiff, Dundee, East Anglia, Edinburgh, Glasgow, Imperial, King's, Leeds, Leicester, Liverpool, Manchester, Newcastle, Nottingham, Queen Mary & Westfield, Reading, Royal Holloway, Sheffield, Southampton, Swansea, UCL
Zoology, Agricultural – Newcastle, Queen's
Zoology, Applied – Bangor, Leeds, Reading

— 7 —

*Hell... I've **still** not begun preparing my seminar on "Time Management" for tomorrow*

TIME, please

—marcvj

Doing the Work: Teaching Methods, Study Techniques and Assessment

TEACHING METHODS

One of the many baffling things you will come across in your first weeks in Higher Education is the variety of teaching methods employed on the course – and the possibly unfamiliar terms used to describe them. Depending on what you are studying, you may be called upon to attend lectures, seminars, tutorials, practical or clinical sessions and field courses, and you'll feel less intimidated by the whole thing if you understand what is required of you in each case.

Lectures

These are the most formal of teaching sessions and many courses still largely depend on them. Typically you could find yourself expected to attend three lectures a week in each subject or unit you are taking. A lecture normally takes place in a lecture theatre, where the students sit in formal rows and the lecturer speaks from a dais. It lasts about fifty to fifty-five minutes and covers a specific topic or aspect of a topic: as a rule of thumb, you might expect to be able to answer one essay-type question in an exam on the basis of a lecture and the back-up work associated with it.

A lecture may be addressed to as few as twenty or as many as several hundred students: if the theme of the lecture is a compulsory aspect of a popular subject such as English, everyone who is studying that subject at the same level as you should be present.

Many lecturers will give hand-outs covering the main points of the material they are covering, but it is still worth taking your own notes on points that strike you as important. If nothing else, this concentrates the mind: by no means all lecturers are interesting speakers and it is all too easy to let thoughts wander if you know you are not going to be asked embarrassing questions about what has just been said.

Some lecturers welcome questions during lectures; most do not, in which case you either have to waylay the lecturer after the class and ask your question in haste while you are both on your way to your next commitments, or wait until a seminar or tutorial to sort out your problem.

Seminars and Tutorials

These are smaller and less formal sessions than lectures; they are likely to take place in a modestly proportioned classroom or in the tutor's study, with everyone sitting round in a group to facilitate discussion. The terms seminar and tutorial are not interchangeable, but different institutions use them in slightly different ways and it is often difficult to tell exactly where a seminar ends and a tutorial begins. Seminars may have as many as twenty-five students; in small colleges a tutorial may be one-to-one, but will typically consist of about six students. Individual tutorials, unless they are to discuss a specific piece of work (see below) are not necessarily a good thing: it is far more difficult to have a stimulating exchange of views with just you and your tutor than if there are a number of other students contributing to the discussion.

The object of a seminar or tutorial is to discuss an aspect of a subject, specified in advance, in more depth than is possible in the formal surroundings of a lecture theatre. The seminar will normally take place after the lecture, so even if you haven't done any extra work you should have a certain background knowledge of the subject.

It is quite common for one student to be asked (with a week or more's notice) to begin the discussion by presenting a paper. Don't panic about this. A seminar paper is really just an essay that is read aloud. Everybody will do it sooner or later, and you are not expected to be the world expert on the causes of the Second World War or the role of Charles Babbage in the development of Computing Mathematics. What you *are* expected to do is give some thought to the subject and summarise what you consider to be the most important points, raising any points for debate that occur to you.

In other words, list the facts so that the rest of the group (who will not have prepared for the session anything like as thoroughly as you have) know what they are supposed to be talking about, and ask a few questions to set the discussion going. Don't feel that you need to be able to answer all the questions you raise – that's what the others are there for.

If you're not doing the presentation, try to contribute to the discussion anyway. The more people do that, the more interesting and worthwhile the session is likely to be. And don't worry if you haven't got anything earth-shattering to say – asking a relevant question or restating a basic point in a clearer way are equally valid contributions.

Seminar papers may be 'marked' and counted as part of your assessment; even if they are not your tutor should give you some sort of feedback. If they don't, catch them on their own and ask how you're getting on. At best, this is reassuring, at worst it can alert you to problems at an early stage and help put you back on the right track.

In addition to group seminars or tutorials, you may occasionally have individual tutorials to discuss a particular piece of work which the tutor has just marked. In these circumstances your tutor will obviously be able to give you individual attention and address any problems that have arisen about your work, so don't be nervous about raising any worries you may have.

Practical and Clinical Work

If you are studying a Science subject you will spend a substantial proportion of study time in a laboratory; if you're doing Medicine, after the first two years the vast majority of formal teaching will be done in a hospital; in Education you will be shown into a classroom and sooner or later expected to teach; in Art, Design, Music or the Performing Arts you may be in the studio or the workshop for several hours every day.

In all these cases, you will be doing two vital things: you will be watching a practical demonstration of the theory you have been taught on other parts of the course, whether it's performing surgery or designing a textile; and you will be practising that theory yourself, gaining hands-on experience of the subject in which one day soon you may be earning a living.

Practicals are done under supervision, at least in the early stages of a course: somebody will soon stop you if you seem likely to pull a muscle or blow the place up. Later, when you are experienced and confident, you will be left more to yourself and in your final year you will probably have to develop your own project or pursue your own line of research (see below).

Field Work

This is a form of practical work that normally takes place away from the university or college, and may last for anything from half a day to a number of weeks. If you are studying Archaeology or Geography, for example, you may be expected to spend a substantial part of a holiday on field work, helping to excavate Roman remains, mapping land-scape types or studying population settlement patterns. Again, this is practical experience which will give you a better understanding – and enjoyment – of the theory you are taught in the classroom. You will almost certainly have to write a report on any field work you do and this may count towards your degree (see below).

You will probably have to pay something towards the cost of a field trip – and if the Roman remains being dug up happen to be in Rome, this can be quite expensive. Try to find out about this at your interview or an early stage so that you can budget for it.

STUDY TECHNIQUES

Taking Notes

It is impossible to lay down hard and fast rules about how to take notes during lectures – much depends on the lecturer's style, the nature of any hand-outs and the balance you can achieve between listening, understanding and writing. With practice you will find out what works best, though if you do not feel confident it is worth considering a Study Skills course before you start your studies proper (these are often run by the Department of Continuing Education in the summer holidays or in the early part of the first term).

The ideal set-up is for the lecturer to be an interesting speaker who hands out useful material. Then you can listen and think about what is being said, secure in the knowledge that there will be a sensible written record to take away with you. This will not always be the case, and you may find it easier and more soothing to scribble away as fast as possible, in the hope that you will provide the sensible written record yourself and be able to reflect on it later.

Whatever you do, don't try to write the lecture down verbatim. That way lies madness and writer's cramp. If the lecturer is any good at all, they will begin by giving an outline of what the lecture is to be about, stressing major points that will be developed in the course of the next hour. Make a careful note of these, and you will be better able to assess what is important and what is not in the verbiage that follows. Then, with a bit of luck, the lecturer will end by summarising the main points again and you will have a second chance to ensure that at least the structure is right.

Remember that you are likely to have a seminar or tutorial on the same subject, probably within a week or so: this is an opportunity to bring up anything you don't understand or to clarify points of detail. Remember also that you are not going to be spoon-fed on this type of course – you are expected to go down to the library and read around the subject for yourself. You will probably be given a list of relevant books and learned articles as background to a subject – if not, ask for one.

It is good discipline to go over the day's lecture notes *every evening* to make sure that they are both legible and comprehensible. If you've written down something that is complete gibberish – and that's easy to do when you're writing quickly – you are more likely to be able to sort it out while the lecture is still fresh in your mind. If you leave it till revision at the end of term, you'll have forgotten what it was all about.

Private Study and Research

If you are taking an Arts, Humanities or Social Science course, you are likely to find there are far fewer hours of time-tabled classes than you did at school. This does *not* mean you are in for an easy time – it simply means that you have to take more responsibility for your own study, doing background reading and producing essays. The balance between formal classes and private study is different on Science and Engineering courses, where you may find there is quite a full timetable, with lectures every morning and lab work every afternoon. If you are studying something like Music or Dance there may be fewer classes but you will be expected to take any opportunity for practice that presents itself.

Private study allows you to read or write at your own pace, and gives you more time to stop and think than is possible in lectures. This is important, particularly in the period between a lecture and a seminar or tutorial – you need time to think about a subject in order to deepen your understanding of it. And, as we will see when we come to talk about exams, understanding is vital. The more you understand, the less need there is to rely on memory and the less likely you are to be stumped by unexpected questions.

When you are doing background reading, it is a good idea to take notes, particularly if you come across anything that seems important but which wasn't mentioned in the lecture. After all, you are supposed to be developing your own critical powers, not just slavishly reproducing what it says in the books. If you can produce a new angle on a subject or justify a new line of thought, that should be all to the good.

Again, when taking notes, don't copy word for word. Weigh up and sift what is said. If it's your own book and you have no moral objection to defacing it, use highlighter pens or notes in the margin to draw attention to something you might want to come back to. (If it's a library book or one you acquired second-hand, you'll probably find someone has done this already, saving you a lot of trouble.) Alternatively, make a note on your pad of the page or chapter number so that precious time isn't wasted searching for the same reference later.

Don't worry about the style of what you are writing down. Nobody but you is going to read your notes, so there are no marks for literary merit. Get the gist of an article, chapter or whatever down on paper in a way that makes sense to you – that is all that matters. As long as you understand what you are reading and writing, you will be able to develop these notes into an essay or an exam answer at a later stage.

The techniques of reading round a subject, sifting out what is important and forming your own opinions will become all the more crucial later on in the course when you have to do a dissertation or project (see next sections). Both these require independent research into a specialist area of study, and you will be expected to come up with your own conclusions. So, from the very beginning of the course, you should cultivate the habit of thoughtful reading: you don't have to agree with what you read, but if you disagree you have to be able to say why.

Essays, Reports and Dissertations

Whatever your subject, you are likely to have to produce one
or other of these at some stage of your student career. Two
cliches will help you develop a workable technique. One is
the King of Hearts' instruction to Alice: 'Begin at the
beginning and go on till you come to the end; then stop'; the
other is the stock advice given to after-dinner speakers: 'Tell
them what you're going to say, say it, then tell them you've
said it.'

In other words, organisation of thought is the key. With
reports – on practical laboratory work, for example – it is
absolutely crucial, as clear and meticulous presentation of
facts is more important than writing like Trollope. If you are
writing up an experiment, the report should cover the aim of
the experiment; what you did; what happened; and why
you think it happened. In that order. It is obviously illogical
to present the information any other way.

The same applies in more literary essays, but here it is up
to you to impose the logical order. Your essay subject may
take the form of a question, or you may be asked to 'discuss',
'compare and contrast', 'assess the significance of' – all
approaches which call for coherent thinking. And this
applies whether you are answering an exam question in
forty minutes and 350 words, or spending the majority of
your final year working towards a 20,000-word dissertation
(which is only a long essay, when all is said and done).

The first and last paragraphs are the linchpins of your
essay. Here, summarise your answer in a few succinct
sentences, sketching the points you are going to make or
underlining the fact that you have made them (much the
same technique as that used by the ideal lecturer mentioned
above). This is not the place to develop theories or to go into
detail – that comes in the middle of the essay.

Plan in rough form what you are going to say. You can
obviously do this more fully when writing an essay in your
own time than when you are under the pressure of exam
conditions, but even then it is important to sort out your
ideas before writing them up. You may think of a dozen
points to cover, but some of them will be more important
than others, and some will stand on their own while others

grow out of one another. Put them in a sensible order before you start. This is a good technique in exams, as if you run out of time and don't finish an essay answer properly, the examiner will see the points you *intended* to make and give you some credit for them.

Whatever you are writing, stick to the point. It is easy to let one train of thought lead to another that may or may not be relevant, but no matter how interesting your essay is, you won't get good marks if you don't answer the question. Read a chunk at random from the middle of the essay to check that it is relevant to the first and last paragraphs – if it isn't, cross it out, ruthlessly.

Projects

If you are studying something other than an Arts or Social Science subject, you may be asked to produce a final-year project rather than a dissertation, either individually or as part of a group.

A project is likely to be more practical than a dissertation, involving experiments or case studies as well as in-depth reading, but it offers the same opportunities to research in depth a specific area of your subject, or, if you are working in a creative field such as Art and Design or Fashion, to produce a number of pieces of work in a chosen medium or style. You will probably be allowed to choose your specialist area yourself (subject to the approval of tutors), so you can pick something that really interests you and pose questions to which you would like to find out the answers.

Your tutor will help you decide on the aims and parameters of the project. It is very important that these are defined from the word go. There is no point in embarking on extensive research of any kind without knowing where you want it to lead. It is a common mistake to be over-ambitious in your aims: try to be realistic about what you set yourself to do, and listen to your tutor's advice.

Once the guidelines are established, the work itself can be divided into three basic phases: collecting information, analysing it and writing up results. Whether you are on your own or part of a team, the first step should be to draft a timetable. You may have all year to do this thing, but a few hours devoted to dividing the project into stages, calculating how long each stage is likely to take and by what date it should be completed will be time well spent. Remember the basic rule of planning: everything will take longer than you expect it to, and again, try not to overstretch yourself. If you are working in a team, try to allocate tasks and areas of responsibility so that you are not all running around chasing the same piece of information.

You may be asked to submit drafts of progress at various stages, and this will help you to keep to a timetable – and to stick to the point. If you are working on a subject that fascinates you, it is all too easy to go off at a tangent and lose the momentum of your research. Interim reports to your tutor will help to keep work under control.

Managing your Time

One of the most difficult things which students going straight from school to university have to cope with is the responsibility for planning their own work. If you only have fifteen hours of timetabled classes a week (and that's quite likely in the Arts and Social Sciences), it is very tempting to loll about in bed, play a lot of tennis or go to the pub for hours on end.

As a prospective mature student, you have probably had some experience of organising your own life – fitting shopping and housework round work commitments; reading a report for tomorrow's meeting rather than watching *Prime Suspect*; bestirring yourself to go to an evening class on a cold night; that sort of thing. It's this self-discipline that must now be brought in to play. You're taking on this course voluntarily, and you're probably going to be broke for the next three years, so you might as well do the work and get the most you can out of your studies.

If you have taken on a full-time course, treat it like a full-time job: under normal circumstances expect it to occupy you for thirty to forty hours a week. So, if you only have fifteen hours of classes, you should plan to spend at least fifteen hours on 'homework' or private study. The modular structure of many degrees makes this easy to calculate – you will be told that completion of a unit will involve roughly fifty hours of study (or eighty hours, or one hundred, depending on its credit rating and the academic rigour of the course), so you can deduct the number of hours spent in lectures and tutorials and arrive at a ballpark figure of how much work you are supposed to do on your own.

This private study will not be completely unstructured. You will be set exercises, problems, passages for translation, book reviews, essays and so forth, and given a deadline for handing them in. That deadline may be the same time next week, or the end of term, or the end of the year, depending on the nature of the work involved. Sometimes – probably once per term or semester for each unit you are studying – you will have a seminar paper to prepare (see above), so in the week when this happens you should plan for your workload to be higher than usual.

Don't work solidly for hours on end. Few people can concentrate on the same thing for more than about an hour, or two at the most. At the end of that time, you are entitled to a cup of coffee, or a change of subject. Try to spend studying time constructively – set yourself mini-targets to achieve in a session (these two chapters, this page of problems, or whatever) and make a distinction between having a break and giving up because you are bored or in difficulties. Something that was posing problems before you went to put the kettle on is not magically going to get easier when you come back.

Study Conditions

In addition to knowing what is expected of you and allocating the time for it, there are two other fundamental points which you should take into consideration when planning your studies. You must be comfortable when working and you must be able to concentrate in peace and quiet, without interruptions. If you are living in student accommodation, this shouldn't be too much of a problem – Halls of Residence were designed with this in mind, and if you are sharing a house or flat with fellow students, they should at least understand your needs. The following paragraphs, therefore, are really aimed at students working from their family home.

If you possibly can, provide yourself with a study. This may mean tidying out the box room, or setting up a desk in your bedroom (and persuading your partner not to interrupt while you are working), or clearing a shelf and a space on the kitchen table. Always working in the same place and keeping all your books, files and equipment there saves mountains of time which would otherwise be spent searching for bits and pieces.

For advice on studying at home, and persuading your family to let you work in peace, see Chapter 8.

ASSESSMENT

Most courses covered in this book are still assessed in part by traditional, 'unseen' exams, done under strictly supervised conditions in draughty gyms, but it is very rare to find a course that takes no account at all of work done during the year. 'Continuous assessment' is a blanket term used to describe more or less any form of assessment that takes place outside the examination room. Depending on the subject, this could include essays, practical work, seminar presentations, multiple-choice tests, writing up of lab results – anything that forms a normal part of your course work. In a modular system, your final-year project or dissertation may count for an entire unit (say thirty or forty credits).

You will always be told if a particular piece of work is going to be 'assessed', and this will happen increasingly as the course progresses. First year work and exams (or Level 1 modules) do not usually count towards the class of degree: you merely have to complete them satisfactorily before you are allowed to progress to the next stage. However, throughout your second and third years (or levels) you will be producing work whose marks do count towards your degree.

If your course is not modularised, it is quite common for as much as 30–40 per cent of your final mark to be based on course work. In the modular system you accumulate the requisite number of credits simply by passing, but you will also be given marks or grades that indicate in more detail how well you are doing. Assessment of each unit is completed by the end of the semester (or term or year, depending on how the course is organised), so at the end of the final year you will already have been examined in one way or another on all the second year units and probably half the third year ones as well. All this helps to take pressure off the dreaded final exams.

Self- and Peer-assessment

This is a comparatively new concept which is becoming more widespread, particularly in the 'new' universities. Broadly speaking, the idea of self-assessment is that at the start of a project you and your tutor (or mentor, as this person is sometimes called) establish the target towards which you are working, as outlined under *Projects*, above. You then do the work, either alone or in a group, and at the end, with the help of your tutor, assess whether or not you have achieved the aims.

Peer assessment is comparable, but involves others in the group assessing how well you have achieved your aims. In order to do this they may be given guidelines or they may work out a system of assessment for themselves.

The theory is that under this system you (and your peers) take much more responsibility for your studies than if you were merely trying to satisfy an examiner. You have to analyse not only what you did well, but what you failed to do, or did superficially. It is easy to submit an essay that 'will do', in order to get it in on time or to scrape a pass with a minimum of effort. If you set your own standards as well as your own aims, the hope is that you will rise to the challenge and try to produce something that is better than adequate.

Exams and Revision

Whatever other forms of assessment are used, exams are still important, though they may take a number of different forms. You will have to take oral exams to test your proficiency in a foreign language; clinical exams in Medicine and related subjects will also be oral, requiring a diagnosis on the spot. Some courses use 'open book' exams, in which reference books are allowed into the exam with you; others let you see the paper in advance so that you prepare the answers to known questions. But through it all the old-fashioned 'unseen' predominates. And whatever form your exams take, you still have to prepare for them and sit them in conditions that make many people nervous.

It is easy to say that being nervous about exams is a complete waste of time and will not help you do justice to yourself. But there are ways of making exams less terrifying, and they can be summed up in two words: 'proper preparation'.

The best way to prepare for exams is to study sensibly throughout the year, rather than trying to cram everything into two or three frantic weeks. Self-discipline again. The semester system which means you are examined on things you have studied in the last six months makes this much easier – in the old days, and in some more 'traditional' institutions even now, you might be being examined on something you studied nearly three years earlier.

Mention has been made elsewhere of the importance of going through notes as soon as possible after the lecture, and of the absolute necessity of making sure you understand the bare bones of each subject. University-level study is all about understanding – once you have grasped the concept, you can embellish and discuss without committing every detail to memory.

Don't be afraid to ask questions. It is not a sign of stupidity not to grasp everything first-time round. Far from losing face, you'll probably find one of your younger colleagues coming up to you afterwards and saying, 'I'm so glad you asked that – I didn't have the nerve.'

If you miss out on work, whether through illness or any other reason, make sure you catch up. Borrow notes from friends or ask the tutor to give you a bit of extra time. This is particularly important in scientific and technical subjects where one bit of the course builds on another and assumes that you have mastered what has gone before.

Understanding is the key to revising, too. If you find something in your notes or in a text book that doesn't make sense, ask your tutor. If your tutor is not available or not approachable, discuss the problem with a colleague (but be sure you are happy with the answer – there's no guarantee they will be any less confused than you are). If this doesn't help, find other books or articles in the library on the same subject: somebody may have tackled it from a fresh angle and provided an insight that makes all the difference to you.

Looking for a fresh angle can also help if you find a subject boring (and there are bound to be compulsory elements of the course that you find less riveting than the bits you chose for yourself). Academics and educationalists are fond of saying that no subject is intrinsically boring, that what is wrong is the approach, and that tackling a subject from a different perspective should shed blinding new light on it. This may sound a bit pie in the sky, but there is an element of truth in it: if one of your fellow students is very keen on something you find dull, don't hesitate to pick their brains to see if the enthusiasm rubs off.

Looking up past exam papers and working through some of the questions that have been asked in recent years is useful preparation, but it isn't safe to assume that the paper will take exactly the same form every time. It is also a waste of time trying to predict what questions will come up. Important aspects of the subject will crop up time after time, and it is certainly not safe to limit revision to five topics on the basis that there are only five questions to answer: this year there may be a compulsory question on an area you've skipped.

You can reduce exam nerves by taking a few simple practical precautions, too. It is *not* essential to study till two in the morning before an exam. Much better to give up early, go for a gentle stroll or a quiet pint, then get a decent night's sleep. Relaxation exercises, even something as simple as controlled deep breathing, can be an enormous help. Last-minute cramming can seriously overtax a tired brain and do no good at all.

It may sound silly, but make sure you know where the exam is due to be held, and at what time. There is no excuse for turning up late or at the wrong venue. Check that you have all the pens, pencils and equipment you need, that you are not going to run out of ink and that your calculator batteries are not going to give out. Allow plenty of time to get to the examination hall: if you spend half an hour in an unexpected traffic jam and arrive in a panic just as the papers are being handed out, you are not giving yourself your best chance.

Once in the exam room, *read the paper*. Twice. If not three times. More people fail through not doing what they are supposed to do than for any other reason. Read the instructions. If you are asked to answer Question 1, then any two questions from Section B and two from Section C, do it. Even if you answer a third question from Section B brilliantly, you will get no marks for it at all.

And answer the question that's written on the paper, not the question you expected to be asked.

Plan your time sensibly. Five essay questions in three hours equals half an hour each, with a quarter of an hour at either end for reading the paper, deciding which questions to tackle, and checking. If all five questions are equally weighted (i.e. each carries 20 per cent of the marks), you are not going to get more than twenty marks for your first answer even if you spend all three hours over it. Much better to do a sketchy answer to the fifth question, which could earn you five or even ten marks, than polish and polish in the hope of getting eighteen out of twenty on the first one.

Finally, bear in mind one other important point. The examiner is not the enemy. Nobody is out to trap you; nobody is going to dance in the streets if you fail. Nor is anyone looking for perfection. The purpose of any exam is to assess whether you have reached a *satisfactory level of competence* in the subject. If you make a tiny slip and lose a couple of marks through nervousness, it doesn't matter, provided you demonstrate a reasonable grasp of the subject.

If you have done the work sensibly and steadily, and been resolute about asking for clarification whenever you came across anything you didn't understand, you should have very little to worry about.

— 8 —

Personal Matters

by Philippa Gregory

IT SEEMED LIKE A GOOD IDEA . . .

Of the many challenging personal decisions which will confront you over the next few years, the first one is probably the hardest: do you really want to do this?

For some people the answer is simple. They missed out on college or university education first time around and there has been a yawning gulf in their lives ever since. Too sensitive to prop up the bar and declaim 'The university of life was good enough for me . . .' they have lived with a sense of an opportunity missed and – given the chance for education as an adult – they dive right in.

But for most of us it's a more complicated process. On the one hand are a set of hopes and fantasies about academic life, which includes a bit of Hollywood, a bit of *Brideshead*

Revisited and a bit of genuine expectation. On the other is a lifetime which has been lived perfectly well without adult education and will, no doubt, proceed equally well in the future.

Do bear in mind that a degree will not necessarily get you a better job, or indeed any job at all. Graduate unemployment in 1994 stood at 50 per cent – so there is no meal-ticket with the degree certificate.

You may see graduates zooming past you on the fast track in your company but that *may* be for all sorts of reasons other than their degree. They may have skills or qualities which you could learn in other ways. Maybe they're more assertive than you? Maybe they're better at sales? Maybe they speak another language or use computers? These skills can be learned on other courses. You don't need a degree. So if your main goal is promotion, or a new job: do your research. Check with your company or with career advisors that the degree is what they want – and not some other qualification or quality.

For women this is particularly difficult. If you are a highly skilled secretary without a degree and all the management are graduate men then it may not be the degree which has made the difference but their gender. You won't solve that by being able to put a BA after your name. You will have to challenge the sexism directly.

Having a BA won't turn you into a man – and nor will it give you the elegant colour-supplement lifestyle of the upper middle classes. Our society is so full of snobbery and university so long been the preserve of the middle classes that we manage to confuse the two. If you want the social cachet of a degree then you can buy one in the post from so-called American Universities, put up the framed certificate on the wall of your hall, and rearrange your furniture in the sitting room in the attempt to look more Conran and less *Coronation Street*. Don't waste three years of your life just to put a couple of letters after your name, or to cock a snook at your stuck-up neighbours, or to prove something to your partner or parents.

The best reason for doing a degree course is *not* for the prize at the end, but for the work in the middle. If the reading list is as appetising as a menu, if you look at the library and think 'let me at that!', if you long to understand your subject in depth and if your lack of reading and knowledge drives you crazy then you should apply for a place and you should be given one. In many ways my life did not begin until I started my degree at Sussex when I was twenty-one. Thereafter everything made more and more sense. It was a cosmic enlightening and I would recommend it to anyone who suffers from the sense of groping around in the dark.

Mixed motives are fine – but your primary reason for attending university or college must be the desire to be there for three years, reading and writing and discussing.

THE EDUCATING RITA SYNDROME

The film *Educating Rita* could serve as a health warning for mature students embarking on education. Rita is a bright, uneducated hairdresser who discovers literature, and automatically discards her loving but thick husband, toys with the affections of her brilliant but cynical supervisor and settles in the end for the joys of a Life of the Mind. It is a superbly observed film but probably not a good model for anyone wanting a half-satisfactory life.

The main problem is finding *yourself* when some bits (like your brain) are growing like Topsy, and other bits (like your love for your partner, child and dog) are staying the same. To add to this stimulating brew is the fact that all of your fellow-students are undergoing the same process of dramatic change and growth. It's an explosive and heady mixture – but it ain't real life. After a short three years you will be returned to the real world again with leisure to contemplate the gaining of a BA and the related costs.

IN THE SWIM BUT NOT DROWNING

Some universities and colleges have a high proportion of mature students and here your experience may well be less disruptive. Your student colleagues will also have homes, families and other obligations. In these circumstances you can keep your major growth and changes in perspective. You are all becoming better-educated and wider-read and you can share your feelings about your new view of the world.

Even among mature students there will be people who have come to university or college to change themselves and don't want to stay in the same relationship/marriage/job/ gender any more. The key to survival here is endurance. I know an extremely wise psychotherapist whose clients agree not to make any major life changes until six months after therapy. A similar health warning could be posted on the portals of institutes of learning. Until you have completed your BA and returned to work and the routine of your life you may not know for sure what permanent changes you want to see. Stay very calm and keep life-shattering decisions to a minimum. Do not decide *anything* during your finals exams. The stress of putting three years of your life on the line is often enough to send very rational people completely barking.

When the results are out and the adrenaline levels are back to normal you may well find that your partner/home/ job do indeed lack intellectual stimulation. Or you may find that they are ten times more interesting now that you can bring more skills and ideas to them. Wait and see.

Institutions which take mainly young students may throw you a bit. The temptation is to fling yourself heart and soul into the whole experience and the danger is to come out rather confused. Most 40+ year olds will not enjoy the Tequila benefit night at the student bar which is an orgy of alcohol abuse and sickness, and there is no reason why you should attempt it. Your young colleagues will not despise you for refusing to drink yourself into oblivion and be sick all the next day, actually they won't remember whether you were there or not. They won't thank you for sounding off like their parents either.

There is a middle course to tread and it is a tricky one. You must treat your young colleagues as your intellectual equals – as they undoubtedly are – and keep your more worldly wisdom to yourself unless invited to advise. Never ever speak the words 'When I was your age . . .' After all, do *you*

think that people a few years older than you are automatically wiser?

The exception to this rule is excessive use or trading of
drugs. A lot of young students occasionally use drugs and
you may think that they are old enough to make their own
decisions. However, if you know of a student trading in
drugs then he or she should be reported to the police at once.
They will accept anonymous information and it might lead
them to the arrest of a major supplier.

It is very difficult if the carefree young student life looks
far more attractive than going home to the laundry and
cooking the dinner. No mature student has escaped the
feeling that they are doing a double-shift and being envied
for it as well. But the solution of Throwing It All Up, and
joining the student commune is rarely as successful as it
may at first appear.

The easiest way to think of the whole powerful emotional
mix of student life is to treat it as a job. If in your previous
career you did not regularly take drugs, offer chance sexual
encounters, and work 5 per cent of the day, then there is no
reason to behave like this at university – whatever anyone
else is doing. Also, do not be fooled by the mad abandon of
campus life as perceived by the person who trudges off to
the bus at 5 p.m. You may think that your younger
colleagues are doing no work at all and that, come the end of
the year, you will triumphantly scoop a First while they are
still struggling with the spelling of their name. But you may
have it horridly wrong. Because you do not see them in the
library from 9–5 does not mean that they are not working,
and their proclamations of laziness and stupidity may be a
myth which you discover only after you have been lulled
into three years of idleness. As someone who has been
trained to work regularly every day, every week, you have
the advantage of a work ethic – keep it! It is one of your
greatest assets.

And don't mourn for the campus life too much. For every
raver there is a thoroughly lonely person weeping into their
thin pillow and wishing they had your cosy little home and
doting family.

THE COSY LITTLE HOME

Working from home is universally regarded as an ideal existence. This is a wickedly misleading myth. Working from home is a knack which depends on various structural and emotional changes in order to happen at all. Without them, it is totally impossible.

Structural changes

It may sound obvious but you have to have somewhere to work. However tiny your hutch there must be a corner set aside for your specialised needs. You will need a desk with adequate lighting, a shelf for your books and papers, adequate heating and ventilation. Too many mature students crouch over the coffee table in the sitting room, with the central heating turned off during the day to save money, and bundle their essays and books into a confusing heap when everyone else comes home in the evening. Sooner or later something will crack, and it may be the bones of your cricked neck.

Make sure there is adequate light, heat and ventilation. Don't sit in a dark room with just an angle-poise lamp shining on your work – it is very bad for the eyes. Have a decent light in the centre of the ceiling and supplement this with lamps if necessary.

Obviously unpleasant extremes of temperature are not conducive to productive study, but it is easy to overlook the importance of adequate ventilation. In this day and age you are unlikely to poison yourself unawares by a faulty gas fire – though if you are in cheap rented accommodation where the landlord couldn't care less, this can still happen – but you can still make yourself surprisingly sleepy or induce unnecessary headaches working in a stuffy room.

Get a comfortable chair with adequate support for your back. Bending over books or a keyboard for hours at a sretch can send you screaming to an osteopath.

The kitchen table is not a bad place to work if the house is empty from 8–5, and if you can have a shelf exclusively for storing your books and files. The chances are that the kitchen will be warmer than other rooms. The great disadvantage is that anyone passing by will see you doing 'nothing' – sitting around reading a book in the middle of the day – and will be tempted to interrupt you. Also it is far too easy to be seduced by housework and clean down the work tops rather than write that essay. Only when you are faced by the question of the symbolism of machinery in Dickens' *Hard Times* will you discover what high standards of hygiene and tidiness you have.

If your house is filled with people, your working from home becomes even more difficult. Don't waste valuable study time caring for them, unless they are ill and can show a doctor's certificate to prove it. Unemployed daughters and dozy adolescent sons can get themselves out of bed or stay in it all day rather than you interrupting your work schedule to nanny or harass them.

Under these circumstances the kitchen table is obviously out as a study base since they will drift through and chat interminably. You have to find somewhere else.

Best of all is a room of your own, even if it is the dining room or the spare bedroom. Invest a little time and trouble in getting it set up for you to work. Pens, paper, lights and heaters are inevitable costs but A4 files for old essays and notes fit wonderfully into cut-out cereal packets, an old chest of drawers makes a perfect filing system, and bookshelves can be made out of two housebricks and a plank. You can always clear it all away if you decide to give a dinner party or if an overnight guest comes to stay.

If there are no free rooms at all in your house then you will have to find a little roost where you can generally perch. This is the counsel for desperation, and only to be taken as a last resort.

A fold-out writing table or a little writing case in which you can keep your current reading book, your notes, and your current essay can move with you around the house. If half a dozen sons come into the kitchen you can pick yourself up and transfer to the sitting room. If a brace of teenage daughters come in and watch TV you can move to an upstairs room. Provided you don't move more frequently than every two hours you can use the move as an opportunity to take a little break and a stretch. The writing-case arrangement is ideal with smaller children who need company while they watch TV or do their homework, but don't require your full attention. It should always go with you in the car when you wait outside the school gates, or loiter in the park. It is amazing how much work you can get done while taxi-ing children around.

This is how you cope at home – but there will be days when you desperately need to have a clear stretch of time ahead of you without continual interruptions. Either bribe or order your family out of the house, or simply out of one room, or investigate other possibilities altogether. A woman barrister left her baby and childminder in her house, and worked in the house next door loaned by her neighbour who was out at work all day and at a safe distance from the tantalising giggles or heartbreaking shrieks of her new baby. See if you can organise house swaps or house shares with fellow students. See if you can set up a study party in which you use your house only once a week, but go to others for the other days.

The safest place for you to be is the university or college library. If you can train yourself to be there at 9 a.m. and work a good four or five hours, then other reading can be done at home in the evening.

Equally good, and probably closer and more convenient, is your local library. If you've never been inside the door; now is the time to check it out. Most libraries have a reference section with a silence rule and desks and chairs. This is your natural habitat. Bag a table near the window for the benefit of natural light, and get going. You may be surprised how well stocked the library is with books, and almost anything can be ordered from other libraries in the county. Learn to use the index cards or microfiche – a librarian will always show you, they are amazingly helpful. Leave plenty of time (sometimes up to eight weeks) for books to be ordered from other libraries for you, and you may find that you can do a lot of your research and reading in the library near your home.

DON'T forget to eat just because there is no canteen to feed you, nor family to remind you it is lunch time. Studying is hard work and you will get hungry and tired.

DON'T forget to take breaks. You should never work for more than two hours without a little break – 15 minutes is fine. Get up, make yourself a hot drink, have a little potter round the house, stretching those weary neck muscles and blinking those foggy eyes. Studying is hard labour, you are using muscles from your brain to your backside which have been dormant for too long.

And **DO** give yourself little treats. Set a target – like reading and taking notes from a book, and when you have finished reward yourself with ten minutes with the newspaper, a quarter of an hour on the telephone, or ten minutes in the garden. Unlike work with colleagues nobody tells the home-worker that they have done well. You have to reward yourself and motivate yourself. Be a good boss – give yourself an occasional hurrah.

Emotional changes

First: *The door*. This must remain shut.

Most people find the easiest method is to shut themselves firmly inside for an agreed period of time, such as two hours, and ban interruptions from the family for that period. When the time is up you have to come out smiling and be thoroughly helpful with whatever crises broke out during your absence. Coming out every ten minutes to monitor an ominous silence, or dashing out to referee fights between partner and children merely emphasises everyone's belief (and yours) that they cannot get on without you. They can, truly they can. But they will never know this if you emerge like the fairy godmother every five minutes. Shut the door and get on with your work and let them get on with theirs.

Secondly: *The telephone*. Let it ring.

If it is really important they will call back. If you cannot bear to leave it, then answer with an assumed voice, and say you are out. Best of all get an answerphone so you can talk on the telephone when it suits you, and not when it suits the caller. At the very least learn the courage to say, politely and pleasantly, 'I AM VERY SORRY BUT I AM WORKING NOW AND CANNOT TALK. WILL YOU RING ME BACK IN TWO HOURS TIME?'

Thirdly: *The doorbell.* An upstairs room comes into its own with the doorbell. Don't go downstairs. Open the window and call down. If it is a friend you can cheerfully wave as if you are Rapunzel, imprisoned in her tower. Yell that you will take a break in an hour and will they come back then for fifteen minutes as your reward. If it is a tradesman you can shout helpful instructions. If it is the Mormons you can quietly shut the window and creep away.

If you are working in a downstairs room peep around the curtains – don't answer the door unless it is the fire brigade come to douse your burning bedrooms. Do everything you can to avoid interruptions. Nobody, but nobody, takes the idea of academic work seriously. They all think that you can stop and start again with no damage to your concentration and mental flow. This is not true. Too many interruptions and your brain will fuse and melt down. This is a neuro-logical fact. (It isn't really, I made it up.) Guard your work time, no one else will.

And now the hard ones . . .

Your partner

It is almost impossible to do a degree without the consent and support of your partner. He or she will have to take on some of the tasks you have usually done, they will certainly miss your inert body on the sofa watching TV, they will certainly notice that the bedside light stays on for longer while you read and read and read. If they were initially supportive then the theory has to be converted into effective practice. Whatever domestic share they took they will have to do a little more. They will have to accept your absence from home when you are at college, or from the sitting room or bed when you are working in your study. Make agreements as to when and for how long you shall be left undisturbed and keep them. Don't over-run even when you are about to split the atom – it just isn't fair on them. Don't encourage popping in, which isn't fair on you.

If they were not initially supportive you will either have to study by stealth, which makes the whole difficult thing a bit more difficult, or you will have to talk them round or confront them. This is a really tricky one. Previously pleasant husbands get threatened and aggressive, previously nice wives get bitter and feel inferior. Do your best to explain how important this is to you, discuss personal growth without implying that you are a soaraway sunflower and they are a little chickweed, and never never flirt with your university colleagues. If you have persuaded your partner that you are there for the life of the mind they will be rightly offended if you spend all day in the student bar draped over the sociology lecturer.

Emotionally this is often a difficult time. Your partner who always seemed perfectly pleasant may suddenly appear woefully thick. After all, you now know so much, don't you? You've read all these books, written all these essays! You have these brilliant friends who have read what you are reading! And here you are, yoked for life to this fool who knows nothing!

This is something of a tragic illusion. You are on the heady swoop of an upward learning curve and good luck to you. Your partner is probably as nice as he or she ever was, and does not deserve to endure every day at breakfast secret, concealed IQ tests in which you discover that they know nothing.

In all relationships there are a variety of roles to play. Perhaps you are becoming the intellectual of the partnership, the clever one. Your partnership will still need a practical one, a sensible one, a witty one, a wise one, and your partner may be any one of these without ever opening a book.

If you are indeed as clever as all this, you will defer all decisions about the relationship until you have completed your degree and the dust has settled a bit. You may well find then that you have changed and grown so much that a previously secure relationship has become too limiting. Or you may find that you have both grown and changed and your relationship is stronger and more interesting than ever. Given half a chance and the supply of ideas and conversation from you and your new friends and your partner will learn by osmosis and grow with you.

Your parents

If your parents always thought you were a genius they may see this time as you coming into your own and be wonderfully supportive. Thank them graciously and accept any help they offer. This is not a good time to rebuke them for failing you the first time around. If they did such a rotten job of bringing you up in the first place then you wouldn't be seeking an education now. They must have done *something* right to produce you, you little marvel.

On the other hand if they always thought you were a bit thick they can be dramatically undermining at this stage. If you are struggling with your work you don't need them nodding wisely to each other and mouthing 'two short planks' over your head. Avoid this kind of parent completely at the start of every new subject. This is the time when it looks absolutely mysterious and you think you will never understand anything. Everybody feels like this, not just you. Wait until you start to get exciting glimmerings of what the whole thing is about and then you can talk with enthusiasm about your insights, rather than weep with despair about your fear of being stupid. The learning curve will lift you up, I promise. That's the time to drop into the conversation that you are working on particle physics, enjoy their amazement and ignore their criticism.

Your children

Of all of the members of the family your children are often the most helpful. They are enduring a very similar process and they understand about homework and avoiding trouble with your teacher. They will hate not having you at their beck and call if that is how it has always been before, but they may well understand if you show them your books and the notes you have taken and the essay you are writing.

Don't miss out on the opportunity to ask their advice. They are professional students while you are just beginning. They may well know some dodges that have never occurred to you. And do look at their study guides and apparently easy-peasy school books. On my shelf at the moment is *Look and Remember History Book III* – a useful, visual, stimulating book. I wouldn't quote from it in an academic essay for fear of looking silly, but I do use it for light reading or to look at easy diagrams of industrial processes.

Your friends

If you have been one of the lads at the pub, or one of the girls at coffee mornings you may find that your perspectives on life change so radically that you don't fit in any more. This is not the fault of your friends who are no doubt pleasingly consistent and have been good enough for you up to now. It's very tempting to be evangelical about your amazing new life and try to persuade them all that they should go to university or college. You may find some takers but you are probably in grave danger of being an Ad Ed Bore. Enjoy them for what they are, and if you drift gently away then so be it. There is no need to grind their faces into the fact that you are now Too Clever for Tupperware.

SINGLE PARENTS

Being a single parent can combine amazingly well with studying especially with school age children. Your holiday time will generally overlap and your working day is also similar. The usual school crises, when the boiler bursts and they all arrive home, is as bad for you as for any working parent. You need backup for emergencies and for the one day when you can't get to the school gates on time. University and college authorities should be understanding about you taking time off for childhood illnesses, and many campuses are quite child-friendly with open spaces and car-free areas where older children can wait while you change your library books.

Smaller children and babies can sometimes be booked into the college or university crèche where available. These always have a waiting list so you need to reserve a place when you apply to attend university. Other arrangements for child care can often be combined successfully with studying for a degree, especially if your baby sleeps during the day – when you can work; or at night. There may well be other parents on your course who would welcome the chance to share a child-minder with you or to swap child-care days. You have their pre-school children for one day, and then they have yours. Provided the children get on reasonably well, and as long as you and your colleague agree policy on things like sweets, safety and smacking, this can often work well.

As a single parent you will get the following supplements to your grant for a dependent child. The age is counted from the start of your academic year.

Under 11 years	£370
11–15	£735
16–17	£970
18 or over	£1400

Your own Local Education Authority has more information about extra help for single parents.

MONEY

You should be eligible for a grant – see Chapter 3 – but if you have been working before you took the decision to attend college or university the sudden disappearance of an income will be a shock to both you and your partner.

Firstly remember that all students are broke, and so their fashion styles and eating and drinking habits reflect this. You will have no difficulty in keeping your end up at the university or college of your choice with only a grant to spend. Only the exceptional spoilt brats have more.

You will undoubtedly have to reduce your lifestyle for the three years you are at university and your partner's and family's consent to these changes will make them less painful for you all. But this is the time to take up free hobbies like walking, or taking holidays with your relations.

Making family budgets and keeping to them is notoriously difficult and everyone gets in a muddle at some time. If IBM with all their computers and accountants and advisors can overdraw by millions then you with your pocket calculator can be forgiven for getting things wrong now and then.

The easiest way to look at it is to calculate your pre-college income which has now gone. That's the amount you have to save from your usual annual expenditure. If your earnings were the second income in the household, or if they were only pocket money, the slack is quite easily taken up. If you were the main breadwinner then you will have to consider other serious options such as moving to a smaller house and using the profit to finance your study years, asking your partner to work longer hours or to take a job, borrowing money, or drastically reducing expenses. You will certainly want to work for money in the vacations and perhaps also take an evening job. Many students do this to supplement their grants and it will not disadvantage you in your academic studies provided you do not work all hours and collapse with exhaustion.

Some jobs lend themselves to running in parallel with studying. I treasured the weeks I worked as a temp secretary for an ego-ridden executive when I was an undergraduate. He had no work for me to do at all, I was there to demonstrate his managerial secretary-owning status. For the handsome sum of £5 an hour I sat at a comfortable desk and studied and typed my essay on a state of the art electric typewriter. Many jobs include a bit of slack time when you can read or take notes and be paid to do so. Think of it as sponsorship.

These are decisions of such magnitude that they will concentrate your mind splendidly on whether you really want to study or not. They must be shared with your partner who is going to have to support you in financial terms as well as emotionally. If your three years of joyful academic explorations means three years of overtime and hard grind for him or her then you must both be sure that it is a thoroughly Good Thing for you *both*.

CONCLUSION

It's a huge plunge: to leave a comfortable routine at home or a good job at work to start at the bottom of a career which will only last three years. It's virtually unpaid, it is not respected in our society, it is difficult to do, and at the end of it you may not have improved your career prospects, you may even be unemployed.

But you will have adjusted the vital mistake you made in your youth when you did not give yourself a chance to study. You will have broadened your horizons in remarkable and unforseeable ways. You will have learned things which will change the way you see the world, you will have learned habits of study and self-discipline which will make you more effective in any work you do in the future. You will have destroyed for ever the undermining fear that you are not clever, that you cannot understand things, and that libraries and books are for other, more able, people. You will have claimed your heritage as a thinking person in our society and our culture will be always open to you.

And Afterwards . . .

There will come a moment, probably in late June at the end of your third year, when a member of staff in your department pins a list of names on the noticeboard, including yours, and you realise you've got your degree. After all that hard work, you've achieved what you set out to do. It's a wonderful feeling and one that you will always cherish.

But what happens next?

The answer depends largely on why you wanted a degree in the first place. If you've been sponsored, you may have a job to walk into, with greater responsibility and more money than ever before. If not, but you took the course to improve employment prospects, you will have to start looking for a job, and you will be in competition with all the other recent graduates, young and not so young.

Most universities and colleges run careers advisory services, which provide information, directories of job opportunities and contacts. They may run recruitment fairs during the year, inviting employers from different industries to come down and meet their final-year students. They should also provide advice or courses on presenting your CV, interview techniques and so on. But they will not find you a job.

You should take every possible advantage of the information and support careers advisers offer – that's what they're there for, after all – but you are really on your own now. It is up to you to get out there, to apply for jobs and go for interviews, just as it was before you took your degree.

Ageism is a problem you should be prepared to face. Employers tend to have preconceived notions of the age group their applicants should be. As we have seen, many vocational courses will not accept applicants over the age of about forty or even less, because it is assumed that graduates should have a reasonable working life ahead of them. There are also some jobs – in 'young' professions like advertising, say – for which you might be considered 'too old' at thirty-five. Employers may assume that you will expect to be paid more because you are older; they may be concerned that the people with whom you would be working are ten years younger than you; they may think you can't possibly be a dynamic ideas person if you're forty plus.

It is up to you to convince a prospective employer that you can deal not only with the demands of the job but with your colleagues as well. Be realistic about this – if you don't fancy yourself as the office mum (or dad), it can be very uncomfortable being the only oldie around; it can be even more difficult being junior to someone half your age. If you have been used to earning good money but took a degree in order to change career, starting at the bottom of a new ladder will almost certainly have undesirable financial implications too.

So it is not going to be easy, but it wasn't easy before you had a degree: now you have a indication of your achievements to show to a prospective employer.

That degree certificate says more about you than you might imagine: it announces that you have attained a certain level of knowledge in a subject and allows people to assume that you are reasonably bright, but it is also proof that you have application, time-management skills, self-discipline and maturity – all qualities that will be useful in the outside world. It makes you a more attractive job candidate overall.

If you are not concerned with employment prospects, but took your course for more personal reasons – whether you call it expanding your horizons, bettering yourself intellectually or giving yourself an excuse to get out of the house – you may find you are hooked on education. If so, and you obtained a good enough degree (usually first or upper second class honours), you can apply for post-graduate study.

This normally means carrying out in-depth research into an aspect of a subject covered at degree level. Arrangements vary enormously, but there will probably be a lot of choice about how you study. With the approval of your tutor, you choose what you wish to research. You can elect to work full-

or part-time, to follow a programme which requires submission of a dissertation or one where you take exams. You can work towards a Masters degree or, if you feel your research is going to make a significant contribution to knowledge, you can apply for a PhD programme.

Whatever happens, there will be new opportunities. In the course of studying for a degree, you have acquired knowledge and made friends. But you have also learned more about how to think, how to sift important information from waffle, how to take responsibility for your own tasks and achievements. It can only give you more openings in life, and more confidence in your ability to succeed.

Bibliography

The indispensable sources of information for any prospective mature student are the UCAS and ADAR handbooks and the individual university and college prospectuses.

Other useful publications include:

Stepping Up: A Mature Students' Guide to Higher Education (published by UCAS with support from the Employment Department)

University and College Entrance: the Official Guide (published by UCAS; the 1994 edition is in association with the *Independent* and Letts Study Guides)

Boehm, Klaus, and Lees-Spalding, Jenny, eds., *The Student Book* (revised annually, published by Papermac)

The Potter Guide to Higher Education (revised annually, published by Dalebank Books)

Student Grants and Loans: A Brief Guide (for students in England and Wales, published annually by the Department for Education)

Grants and Loans to Students (for students in Northern Ireland, published annually by the Education and Library Boards and the Department of Education for Northern Ireland)

Student Grants in Scotland (published annually by the Scottish Office Education Department)

Northedge, Andrew, *The Good Study Guide* (Open University, 1990, the best overall handbook of study skills that I have found)

Duncalf, Brian, *How to Pass Any Exam* (Kyle Cathie, 1994, a friendly and encouraging guide to exam technique)

I have also drawn on information from the following papers:

Abramson, Michael, *Five Years of Franchising Summary Report* (University of Central Lancashire, 1993)
— *Travelling Further and Higher: Good (and Bad) Practice in FHE Franchising and Partnership* (1993)
— *Rationales for Academic Franchising: A Critical Appraisal* (1994)

Bird, John, et al., *Franchising and Access to Higher Education: A Study of HE/FE Collaboration* (University of the West of England/Employment Department, 1993)

Brown, Sally, and Dove, Peter, eds., *Self and Peer Assessment* (SCED, 1991)

Jones, Philip, ed., *Register of Recognised Access Courses to Higher Education* (CNAA, 1992)

An Overview of Recent Developments in Higher Education in the UK (HEFCE, 1994)

Research Assessment Exercise 1992: The Outcome (Universities Funding Council)

Useful Addresses

ADAR, Art and Design Admissions Registry, Penn House, 9 Broad St, Hereford HR4 9AP, telephone 0432 266653

BTEC, the Business and Technology Education Council, Central House, Upper Woburn Place, London WC1H 0HH, telephone 071-413 8400

City and Guilds of London Institute, 76 Portland Place, London W1N 4AA, telephone 071-278 2468

ECCTIS 2000, Fulton House, Jessop Ave, Cheltenham GL50 3SH, telephone 0242 225914

ERASMUS, the European Community Action Scheme for the Mobility of University Students, c/o the UK ERASMUS Students' Grants Council, University of Kent, Canterbury CT2 7PD, telephone 0227 762712

National Open College Network, telephone 051-709 9090

NCVQ, the National Council for Vocational Qualifications, 22 Euston Rd, London NW1 2BZ, telephone 071-387 9898

Open Learning Foundation Group, 24 Angel Gate, City Rd, London EC1V 2ES, telephone 071-833 3757

SCOTVEC, the Scottish Vocational Education Council, Hanover House, 24 Douglas St, Glasgow G2 7NQ, telephone 041-248 7900

SKILL, the National Bureau for Students with Disabilities, 336 Brixton Rd, London SW9 7AA, telephone 071-274 0565

SOED, The Scottish Office Education Department, Student Awards Branch, Room 107, Gyleview House, 3 Redheughs Rigg, Edinburgh EH12 9HH, telephone 031-244 5823

The Student Loans Company Ltd, 100 Bothwell St, Glasgow G2 7JD, telephone 0345 300 900

UCAS, the Universities and Colleges Admissions Service, Fulton House, Jessop Ave, Cheltenham GL50 3SH, telephone 0242 222444

Abbreviations Used in this Book

SKILL	National Bureau for Students with Disabilities
SWAP	Scottish Wider Access Programme
TEC	Training and Enterprise Council
TEMPUS	Trans-European Mobility Scheme for University Students
UCAS	Universities and Colleges Admissions Scheme
UCCA	Universities Central Council on Admissions (now merged with PCAS to form UCAS)

Degrees

BA	Bachelor of Arts
BAcc or BAccg	Bachelor of Accountancy
BAgr	Bachelor of Agriculture
BArch	Bachelor of Architecture
BBA	Bachelor of Business Administration
BChD	Bachelor of Dental Surgery
BCom	Bachelor of Commerce
BD	Bachelor of Divinity
BDS	Bachelor of Dental Surgery
BEcon	Bachelor of Economics
BEconSc	Bachelor of Economic Science
BEd	Bachelor of Education
BEng	Bachelor of Engineering
BFA	Bachelor of Fine Art
BHSc	Bachelor of Health Science
BHum	Bachelor of Humanities
BM	Bachelor of Medicine
BM BCh or BM BS	Bachelor of Medicine and Surgery
BMedSc or BMedSci	Bachelor of Medical Science
BMid	Bachelor of Midwifery
BMus	Bachelor of Music
BN or BNurs	Bachelor of Nursing
BPharm	Bachelor of Pharmacy
BPhys	Bachelor of Physiotherapy
BSc	Bachelor of Science
BScEcon	Bachelor of Science in Economics
BScEng	Bachelor of Science in Engineering
BSocSci or BSSC	Bachelor of Social Science
BTech or BTechnol	Bachelor of Technology

BTechEd	Bachelor of Technical Education
BTh	Bachelor of Theology
BVetMed	Bachelor of Veterinary Medicine
BVMS	Bachelor of Veterinary Medicine and Surgery
LLB	Bachelor of Laws
MA	Master of Arts (often a first degree in Scotland)
MB Bch, MB BS or MB ChB	Bachelor of Medicine and Surgery
MB BCh BAO	Bachelor of Medicine, Surgery and Obstetrics
MusB	Bachelor of Music

Index